W9-BNX-978

READINGS ON EQUAL EDUCATION
(formerly *Educating the Disadvantaged*)

ADVISORY PANEL

Michael Apple, University of Wisconsin-Madison
Terry Astuto, Columbia University
William Boyd, Pennsylvania State University
James P. Comer, Yale University
Sharon C. Conley, University of Arizona
Robert Donmoyer, Ohio State University
Walter Feinberg, University of Illinois
Michelle Fine, University of Pennsylvania
Michelle Foster, University of Pennsylvania
Norris Haynes, Yale University
David Kirp, University of California-Berkeley
Peter Kuriloff, University of Pennsylvania
Marvin Lazerson, University of Pennsylvania
Henry Levin, Stanford University
Martha McCarthy, Indiana University
Catherine Marshall, Vanderbilt University
Mary Anne Raywid, Hofstra University
Michael Sedlak, Michigan State University
Jeffrey Shultz, Beaver College
Jonas Soltas, Columbia University
Allan Tom, Washington University
Henry Trueba, University of California-Santa Barbara
Mark Yudof, University of Texas
Perry Zirkel, Lehigh University

READINGS
ON EQUAL
EDUCATION

Volume 10

CRITICAL ISSUES FOR A NEW

ADMINISTRATION AND CONGRESS

Edited by

Steven S. Goldberg

BISHOP MUELLER LIBRARY
Briar Cliff College
SIOUX CITY, IA 51104

AMS PRESS, INC.
NEW YORK

Copyright © 1990 by AMS Press, Inc.
All rights reserved.

Library of Congress Catalogue Number: 77-83137
International Standard Book Number: Set 0-404-10100-3
International Standard Book Number: Vol. 10 0-404-10110-0
International Standard Series Number: 0270-1448

MANUFACTURED IN THE UNITED STATES OF AMERICA

All AMS Books are printed on acid-free paper that meets the
guidelines for performance and durability of the Committee
on Production Guidelines for Book Longevity of the Council on
Library Resources.

Copyright © 1990 by AMS Press, Inc.
All rights reserved.

AMS Press, Inc.
56 East 13th Street
New York, N.Y. 10003

LC
4091
.E3
v. 10
1990

TABLE OF CONTENTS

21729796

IV. Bilingual Education

V. Desegregation

VI. Examining the Consequences of Inequality

VII. Future Research on Inequality

PREFACE

In the past eight years, the Reagan Administration was successful in implementing its call for less federal involvement in education. Indeed, this Administration convinced the American public that its social program budget should be reduced and that regulations be eliminated. Policy formulation and implementation were to be left with local officials who were better able, in the Reagan view, to deal with their own concerns. In fact, the budget was effectively reduced and the Department of Education staff cut. Over two hundred programs are still under review. Yet, contrary to President Reagan's campaign pledges, the Department of Education was not eliminated (Cohen and Astuto, 1986).

During this period, the states had been encouraged to develop their own agendas for educational reform. But reform, as defined by Republican policymakers, has changed the nation's priorities (Timar and Kirp, 1989). Now, emphasis is placed on "excellence"—requiring teachers, students, and schools to meet predetermined curriculum and graduation standards—rather than on "equity." Since the United States Supreme Court held in 1954 that black students must be given equal access to educational programs, federal policy has been concentrated on efforts to bring into the mainstream those who were previously denied equal opportunity based on race, gender, or handicap. With the President's emphasis on the report issued by his National Commission on Educational Excellence, "A Nation at Risk" (1983), the concept of equal education based on equal access to programs—developed over four decades—has been abandoned.

The nation's governors followed this course. In their 1986 document, "A Time for Results," they called for year-round schooling, increased use of technology, assessment of student learning, and pay for teachers based on the results they achieve. Other interest groups, including a consortium of large education colleges which referred to itself as the Holmes Group, called for similar changes. Although all of this activity created a media focus on education, the Presidential panel's original assumption—that education was undergoing "a rising tide of mediocrity"—was not supported by adequate data. Implicit in the call for an emphasis on a new agenda was the belief that previous programs based on equal access had failed to raise the educational level of many students.

There is now a new administration and President Bush has asserted that he will be the "Education President." For him to reach this goal for all students, the President must examine the current status of minorities whose needs may not have been met by the new type of educational reform that we have seen during the 1980s. In an effort to document their most compelling educational concerns, this volume presents the latest literature in the field of equal education.

The essays included here address these questions:

—What children are "at-risk" and how are they served?

—How do we measure the special needs of minority students?

—What are the needs and critical problems facing handicapped students?

—How can we serve the unmet and rapidly increasing population of children whose primary language is not English?

—Is desegregation of urban schools still possible?

—What research issues need to be addressed in the future?

These are the critical issues that a new administration and Congress must face in the next four years. It is not enough for standards to be raised in an attempt to meet a goal of excellence if minority students and teachers are precluded from obtaining the opportunity they require to reach those standards.

References

Clark, D. & Astuto, T. (1986). The significance and permanence of changes in federal education policy. Educational Researcher, October, 4–13.

National Commission on Excellence in Education. (1983). A nation at risk. Washington, D.C.: Author.

National Governors' Association. (1986). A time for results. Washington, D.C.: Author.

Timar, T. & Kirp, D. (1989). Education reform in the 1980s: Lessons from the states. Phi Delta Kappan, March, 504–511.

I.
"AT-RISK" STUDENTS

A RESEARCH AGENDA ON EFFECTIVE SCHOOLING FOR DISADVANTAGED STUDENTS

John Ralph

In January 1989, the U.S. Department of Education funded for the first time a research and development center dedicated solely to the examination of effective schooling for disadvantaged youth—the Center on Effective Schooling for Disadvantaged Students. Until then there had been no comprehensive research effort by the federal government to study the education problems of disadvantaged youth. The purpose of the center is to synthesize what researchers know about effective instructional practices, effective classroom management, effective parent involvement strategies, effective discipline techniques—in a word, what researchers know about effective schooling—and bring that knowledge to bear on the special problems and specific needs of disadvantaged students.

This paper in its original form served as the planning paper (inside the Office of Research) to develop a research agenda for the Center on Effective Schooling for Disadvantaged Students. At a minimum, a research agenda requires (1) a delineation of the problem, (2) an inventory of what is already known, and (3) a compelling argument as to which questions are most urgent. This paper dwells mostly on requirement 2, building a framework to synthesize the current and past research. The value of such a framework is that it may stimulate better arguments about what's to be done. I hope, too, it encourages a more comprehensive approach to the many vexing problems which plague at-risk youth.

The first section gives some background and offers a working definition of the educationally disadvantaged student. In recent years the terms "at risk" and "disadvantaged" have become so muddled that researchers and policymakers don't always know whom to help (Ralph, 1989). I propose a definition, for the purposes of this research review, which identifies the educationally disadvantaged youth by the level of his academic knowledge and basic skills.

The second section surveys the research on four factors which contribute to a child becoming educationally disadvantaged: classroom or instructional factors, school factors, home or family factors, and community factors. For framing a research agenda, these four factors are not equally important. Scholars can more readily investigate some research issues than others, and some research may have greater implications for policy than others. Similarly, some research questions invite a long-term plan for data collection and analysis whereas some questions can be answered by synthesizing the existing work.

A truly comprehensive research agenda attempts to maximize what scientists may learn across all four factors. It should speak to the concerns of policy-makers, yield to the current methodologies of social science research, and strike a balance between long-term interests in significant questions and the topical interests for which short-term investigations are adequate.

SOME BACKGROUND

In October of 1986, the Office of Research invited a group of educational researchers to consider research issues related to schools with high concentrations of low-income students. This seminar was based on a finding in the First Interim Report of the congressionally mandated study of Chapter 1 (1986) that indicated lower achievement levels for children from both poor and nonpoor families in schools with high concentrations of poor families. Several themes emerged from that seminar meeting.

First, there are few systematic data on the problems of schools with high concentrations of low-income families. Even the descriptive literature is based on case-study evidence that extrapolates from a few sites to all urban schools or all schools in poor neighborhoods. Second, the seminar participants suggested (a) the problems encountered by high-poverty schools and classrooms, while by no means insurmountable, are qualitatively different from the problems faced by predominately middle-class schools and classrooms and (b) school ethos and the influence of peers on values and learning are critical challenges facing schools with high concentrations of low-income students.

The discussion of seminar participants suggested a need for research that advances our knowledge of (a) instructional strategies that do the most to improve the achievement of students in schools with high levels of low-income students and (b) how school staffs can forge a school ethos based on a positive peer culture that contributes to student achievement. The following sections of this paper expand considerably on the issues raised in the seminar to include four factors that contribute generally to being educationally disadvantaged.

DEFINITION

Many studies have found that effective schools are most important for minority and disadvantaged youngsters, who are especially sensitive to the quality and details of their school experiences (Alexander, Entwisle, & Thompson, 1987; Heyns, 1978; St. John, 1971). For the purposes of this research overview the term "educationally disadvantaged" will be used to identify the target population of students. We are defining this population to include students who are likely to leave school (at whatever level or age) with an inadequate level of basic skills (Slavin, 1988). This definition carries three implications.

First, completing high school reduces the likelihood of failing to acquire basic literacy and numeracy skills, but dropping out of school, while often a symptom of failing to learn, is not coincident with being educationally disadvantaged. As the Young Adult Literacy Study has shown, 5 percent of the white dropout population demonstrate literacy skills higher than those of the average college graduate (Pendleton, 1987). Conversely, high school graduates who have inadequate reading and writing skills are, according to this definition, educationally disadvantaged.

Second, the population eligible for compensatory education programs is not synonymous with the population of disadvantaged children and youth. There is much to be learned from evaluation studies of Chapter 1, Head Start, and Follow-Through, but the complicated formulas that drive these programs and their implementation have tended to diffuse their impact and minimize their utility for research.

Third, by focusing on educational outcomes—that is, failure to acquire basic skills—many theoretical issues are left open as to the origin and causes of this condition. We are most concerned with the population that suffers from the cumulative disadvantages of independent at-risk factors—growing up in poverty, in a single-parent family, or in an inner-city neighborhood—any one of which may be weakly correlated with school failure but which together form a qualitatively more potent set of obstacles for academic success. This group has been identified as America's urban underclass, or the "truly disadvantaged" (Wilson, 1987).

WHAT FACTORS CONTRIBUTE TO BEING EDUCATIONALLY DISADVANTAGED?

There are four categories of factors that contribute to being at risk of failure to learn: Students without sufficient educational support and experience in either the classroom, the school, the home, or the community may be educationally disadvantaged (Natriello, Pallas, & McDill, 1987). Ideally, a comprehensive research effort will address research issues within each area. But since these four areas vary widely in what is already known, the sophistication of past work, and the extent to which the important questions are researchable (because appropriate methods of analysis or tools of measurement may be unavailable) the greater challenge may lie in tying these four diverse research areas into a unified program.

THE EFFECTIVENESS OF THE CLASSROOM

How can teachers and curriculum approaches be most effective for disadvantaged students?

This category includes research that is directed at improving instructional effectiveness at raising student achievement. In some ways it is the most controversial research. Even though it is the most refined methodologically, its overall potential for effecting significant school change is still widely debated among social scientists, not to mention teachers and principals.

Two strands of work are relevant for improving education for the disadvantaged population and cultivating excellence for every child. One is based on work which identifies those instructional approaches or strategies which are effective for all children. The other is based on examining the relevant interaction effects—that is, the effects of instructional strategies which may work differently or more (or less) powerfully for low ability or low socioeconomic status (SES) children versus high ability or high SES children.

Hawley and Rosenholtz (1984) find, in broad terms, that effective teachers:

(a) optimize academic learning time,
(b) reward achievement in appropriate ways,
(c) utilize "interactive" teaching practices,
(d) hold and communicate high expectations for student performance, and
(e) select the appropriate unit of instruction. (p. 52)

Within this list, some variables have a differential impact for high- and low-ability students. For example, process-product research has shown that the "appropriate unit of instruction" varies according to the student's ability level; low-ability students are more successful wth material that allows for a higher percentage of correct answers (Brophy & Good, 1986). Another example lies in the use of teacher praise: for high-ability students, praise should be less frequent, less effusive, and based on the relative complexity of the task. For low-ability students, praise should be more generous and tied more closely to the performance of individual tasks. Conversely, negative reinforcement or negative affect tends to slow the progress of low-SES children more than that of high-SES pupils (Brophy, 1981).

Brophy and Good (1986) conclude the following about the relationships between socioeconomic status and teaching effects:

> [L]ow-SES-low-achieving students need more control and structuring from their teachers: more active instruction and feedback, more redundancy, and smaller steps with higher success rates. This will mean more review, drill, and practice, and thus more lower-level questions. Across the school year, it will mean exposure to less material, but with emphasis on mastery of the material that is taught and on moving students through the curriculum as briskly as they are able to progress. (p. 365)

But Brophy and Good also stress the importance of tailoring instruction to the classroom context:

> [E]ffective instruction involves selecting... and orchestrating those teaching behaviors that are appropriate to the context and to the teacher's goals, rather than mastering and consistently applying a few "generic" teaching skills. (p. 360)

Having met the particular demands of the classroom context, this body of research then reveals what kinds of approaches tend to be most effective: "The most consistently replicated findings link achievement to the quantity and pacing of instruction." The amount of instruction can be further analyzed by its practical dimensions: (a) opportunity to learn or amount of content covered; (b) proportion of time and overall academic emphasis in classroom activities; (c) efficiency in monitoring, pacing, and engaging students in academic work; (d) difficulty level of the materials (for maximizing learning rate); and (e) degree of active involvement with the teacher. Other studies have focused on the quality of teachers' lessons, but in general the findings on quantity of instruction are "stronger and more consistent than the findings on quality." It remains unclear whether the lackluster impact currently attributed to qualitative aspects of teaching is a function of the state of theory, the state of methodology, or a "true fact" about the teaching process itself.

These findings are especially significant for disadvantaged youth in urban schools. Greenwood, Whorton, and Delquadri (1984) found that urban youth on average were engaged in significantly less academic interaction with teachers or peers than their counterparts in suburban schools. Suburban schools were estimated to provide an additional one and a half months of academic-related activity compared to the average urban school. Similar findings have been reported on suburban teachers' willingness to spend after-school time with students (Rosenbaum, Rubinowitz, & Kulieke, forthcoming). Furthermore, in schools with higher rates of poverty, less time is spent on regular reading instruction (Final Report from the National Assessment of Chapter 1, 1987).

Aside from quantity of instruction, the instructional issues most critically in need of further research have been summarized by Stein, Leinhardt, and Bickel (1988):

> (1) in direct instruction: a need to examine new forms which it might take in order to teach adequately higher-order cognitive skills; (2) in the process-product findings: the need to unpack generic variables in order to get at more fine-grained guides for practice; and (3) in cognitive strategies research: the need to address knowledge components of effective strategy use and the implementation requirements of various instructional approaches to strategy training. (p. 181)

The common element shared by all three concerns is the "need to address the content of instruction." For example, we have little particular knowledge about the application of specific teaching strategies to instruction in the basic academic areas of mathematics, literature, science, and history. The next step may lie in the integration of the cognitive strategies of disadvantaged students with effective instructional strategies in the basic academic areas.

Of the critical research areas discussed by Stein, et al., the impact of direct instruction on thinking skills lies at the center of an important ongoing debate. Recent trends show improvements in "lower-order abilities" that are not correlated with similar gains in higher-order, problem-solving cognitive skills (National Assessment of Educational Progress, 1988). Some researchers suggest there may be a trade-off between "direct instruction," which seems most effective at raising basic skills, and the less scripted approach necessary to foster problem-solving and more analytical mental skills (Doyle, 1983). Stein, et al. (1988), argue that direct instruction has thus far only been applied to developing lower-level skills; with more knowledge of "what comprises expertise in these more complex domains," direct instruction might also teach students how to write an interpretative essay.

There are three further areas of classroom-level research that are particularly relevant for the educationally disadvantaged: (a) research on language skills and student achievement; (b) recent research in the area of teacher background characteristics and student achievement; and (c) research in the area of coursetaking differences and academic tracks.

Language Skills. Many researchers have explored the link between home or "first language" skills and gains in both English language learning and school achievement. Much of the research on language differences among disadvantaged youth has built on programmatic evaluations of bilingual education in its various forms (e.g., TBE versus immersion). The more general approach treats language ability as a general skill—one that affects all disadvantaged youth and one that clearly shapes the general context for effective instruction (Fillmore, 1986; Willig, 1985).

It is of paramount importance for all children to become literate in standard English. Veltman (1983) and others have shown the importance of exploring effective instructional practices for language minority youth who lack language skills both in English and in their primary language. Analyses of language skills and their bearing on school achievement should investigate the effects of confounded socioeconomic factors that contribute to both language learning and school achievement (Baratz-Snowden & Duran, 1987). While the debate about programmatic effectiveness continues, more basic research is needed on the factors that contribute to language learning and language competence for all disadvantaged youngsters.

Teacher Characteristics. In the past, researchers primarily investigated classroom effects by examining the effects of teacher background characteristics on student achievement. While pointing to the shrinking pool of qualified minority teachers, recent policy reports (such as the Holmes Group report, 1986, and the Carnegie Forum on Education and the Economy report, 1986) have brought new attention to the issue of teachers' backgrounds.

Past research generally failed to find substantial relationships between teacher traits and teacher competence, but some studies found a positive relationship between the verbal test scores of low-income minority students and teachers' verbal ability (Summers & Wolfe, 1977; Hanushek, 1977; Bruno & Doscher, 1981). Alexander, Entwisle, and Thompson (1987) have found that teachers with a background of high socioeconomic status experience special difficulties relating to minority youngsters: what matters is status differences between the student and the teacher, rather than racial differences. The impact of teachers with high socioeconomic status—who form negative expectations and attitudes—is greatest on the school performance of low-SES black youngsters. Finally, some recent research results show teacher-related effects on children in the first grade that have a greater impact on learning than the child's background and family variables (Pallas, Entwisle, Alexander, & Cadigan, 1987). In the end, it is most important for researchers to revisit the effort to specify the effects of what teachers do and what they know than to further estimate the gross effects of teacher backgrounds or teacher traits. In other words, future research should focus on what it is about teachers' actions, knowledge, and beliefs that may make teachers more or less effective. For example, teachers, principals, and researchers have noted that we need to advance our knowledge of the more subtle, yet powerful, cues that teachers give, and students interpret, regarding expectations that teachers have for educationally disadvantaged students. Earlier research failed to attribute any significant effect to teachers themselves because measures of teachers' abilities, knowledge and skills were too crude. More recent findings point to the need for specifying, not who it is, but what it is that makes some teachers more effective than others for disadvantaged students.

Curriculum Differences. Differences in the content of instruction, especially between the instruction of low-achieving and high-achieving youth, remain a lively and difficult problem. At the secondary level, early research on tracking, without adequate controls for preexisting differences among students, overestimated its effect on student learning. There is still much debate over the measurement of ability, but the effect of the college track now appears to give only a slight advantage over noncollege-track classes (Jencks & Brown, 1975; Alexander & Cook, 1982).

Gamoran (1987), however, has found that the differences in student achievement between college-bound and noncollege-bound tracks is greater than the differences in achievement between dropouts and nondropouts. While a dramatic comparison, this contrast may reflect the surprisingly high level of achievement among a portion of high-school dropouts. Gamoran also finds that differences in tracking or course-taking do not explain either racial or ethnic differences in achievement:

> [T]he gap between blacks and whites in the same programs of study is larger than the overall gap between blacks and whites. The Hispanic deficit shows indications of this pattern, but the fluctuations are much smaller. (p. 149)

The effect of track assignment is clearest on aspirations and college entry (which seems quite powerful, Alexander and McDill, 1976), but this general area of research is clouded by how little we know about the actual content of classes within curriculum tracks (Oakes, 1985). Even less is known about the integrity of course labels and whether the effects of curriculum are masked by terminology differences across districts (cf. Garet and DeLaney, 1988; Lee and Bryk, 1988).

Appraising course content and its impact are likely to be increasingly important policy issues as a growing consensus urges more curriculum uniformity both over time and across classrooms. Past reforms, in the name of serving all youngsters, adapted new curricula for individual needs. A more fruitful strategy may be to meet individual needs with a common curriculum while adapting pedagogical techniques to engage the hard-to-reach student (Bennett, 1988; Graham, 1987).

In summary, we need to know which variables within models of effective instruction are especially critical for high educational attainment among low socioeconomic or low ability youth. Some of the important issues include differences between classrooms in the quantity of instructional strategy; hypothesized differences between effective instruction in higher-order thinking and effective instruction in basic skills; effective strategies for learning English-language skills; hypotheses that link what teachers do to the effects teachers have; and the effects of coursetaking, course content, and academic tracking.

THE INFLUENCE OF THE SCHOOL

How can school principals and the administrative decisions that principals make—such as how to allocate resources, how to assume or delegate the authority for setting instructional goals, how to maintain academic purpose and order throughout the school—affect the learning of the educationally disadvantaged?

Traditionally, educational researchers thought of school-level processes as management issues only. Thus, a well-run school may "shape" the academic work of classrooms but classrooms were still where students learned. The effective schools research gave new life to an old idea—that schools have an ethos, a climate based on decisions about a school's overall academic emphasis and its skillful maintenance of order and purpose. Researchers now share the view that whole schools can be run effectively or ineffectively, and that school-level variables can have a direct impact on the educational experiences of students (Stedman, 1987).

The issue of school effectiveness is especially pertinent to the study of disadvantaged youth for three reasons. First, renewed interest in the effectiveness of whole schools began as researchers sought ways to improve inner-city schools. Their studies have focused on schools serving disadvantaged youth. Second, the findings of the National Assessment of Chapter 1 study (1986) show that students who attend high-poverty schools achieve less, independent of the individual effects of family and background. Third, when the "whole school" holds high expectations for disadvantaged youth—which are then translated into rigorous academic programs—there is evidence that school achievements rise and dropout rates fall (Bryk & Thum, 1989).

Yet, despite the enduring intellectual appeal behind the concept of effective schools for disadvantaged youth, the research to date has yielded surprisingly little information (beyond anecdotal and small-sample studies) about what schools look like in areas of concentrated poverty, how administrators make decisions, what effects different administrative choices may have, or a host of other descriptive data. Some recent work has begun to systematically describe what school principals generally do, based on self-reports (Gottfredson & Hybl, 1987; Dwyer, Barnett, & Less, 1987). There are no "process data"—for example, equivalent to the data gathered on teacher behavior and effects—that indicate how links occur between administrative actions and teacher behavior or that indicate how the actions of principals may directly influence the behavior of students.

What might a fine-grained analysis of principals' behavior reveal? The teacher and classroom effectiveness research clearly shows how much effective instruction depends on contextual factors; it follows that the behavior of the principal can be a crucial factor in an effective school (Persell, 1982). Principals can influence teachers' expectations of their students and encourage them to alter their standards, help teachers choose the most effective instructional approaches, guide the formulation of reasonable and appropriate instructional objectives. Not least, principals can recruit capable teachers, work to retain the best, and ensure adequate preservice and inservice teacher education.

Conventional wisdom has it that the environment in which principals work varies greatly across schools and districts. Certainly the organizational environment for urban public school principals differs sharply from the organizational environment for private and parochial schools, but we know little about what that means. What are the effects of administrative autonomy or the effects of different forms of accountability on the implementation and maintenance of effective school programs (cf. Chubb, 1988)? In private and public schools alike, principals and superintendents must have accountability mechanisms to ensure that high expectations and well designed initiatives amount to more than well-laid plans. Last, given that many schools with high concentrations of disadvantaged students are located in urban districts with large and intricate bureaucracies, some attention should be given to the organizations context within which school leadership occurs.

In addition to theoretical issues, there are many concrete problems, relevant to the concerns of principals and school leaders, that researchers should address. For example, aggressive leadership by high school principals may be critically important in the reduction of dropout rates, but there is little systematic information about effective programs or strategies. A report by the General Accounting Office (1986) concluded:

> It is not generally known "what works" in terms of specific programs that prevent students from dropping out of school or encouraging actual dropouts to reenter school and achieve a high school diploma. (p. 29)

Some evidence indicates that dropouts have little contact with counselors, teachers, or school officials of any sort prior to leaving school even though the General Accounting Office also reported that administrators believe "a caring and committed staff" to be among the most important factors for reducing dropout rates (Finn, 1987; GAO, 1986, 1987).

The overarching problem for school leaders is that they need meaningful, concrete descriptions, definitions, and measures of school-level variables that bear upon educational excellence for disadvantaged students. In *Dealing with Dropouts*, the OERI Urban Superintendents Network listed numerous everyday concerns of school administrators on which researchers could shed some light (OERI Urban Superintendents, 1987). Some analytical studies attempt to formulate context variables that describe the plight of high-poverty schools (Natriello, 1986; Cusick, 1986; Metz, 1986) but new work is also needed: (a) to look at specific administrative practices and how they vary in relation to the needs and achievements of disadvantaged students (in place of the current work based on self-reported goals and global assessments of the school's workings); (b) to specify the effect of administrative practices on classroom behaviors and school achievements of disadvantaged youngsters; and (c) to employ research designs that carefully distinguish schools with high concentrations of disadvantaged students that positively influence student progress from those that have less impact (cf. Good & Brophy, 1986).

Amid the many reforms underway in urban school districts (Oakes, 1987), we have examples of high-performing schools in disadvantaged neighborhoods thriving alongside truly "bankrupt" schools. To be scientifically useful, we need systematic descriptions and measures of effective and ineffective schools, with special attention to the subset of effective and ineffective schools in very poor neighborhoods. From these data, researchers can test for the most effective approaches to school organization and school leadership for educationally disadvantaged children.

THE INFLUENCE OF THE HOME

In what ways can schools assist disadvantaged families to ensure that their children receive the greatest benefits from school opportunities?

The term "disadvantaged," as first used in the 1960s, tended to focus attention on the effects of family poverty on children's social and cognitive development. The earliest debates about whether disadvantaged children suffered from cultural deficits or cultural differences overlooked how little we really knew about the impact of home environments on school performance. To date, we have very little work that clarifies the links between socioeconomic status, family life, and children's learning.

Some recent work has focused on teachers training parents to become educators. Bloom (1980) has argued that home-related variables, that is, the variables that describe the real-life processes by which parents help, encourage, and monitor their children's learning, are both powerful and alterable factors for predicting academic success. Clark's (1983) observations on the educational environments of poor black children allow us a glimpse at the dynamics of family relationships, but little is known about the optimal strategies, available to schools, for empowering parents to help their children—much less the conditions under which parents not only can but *do* become better teachers. Epstein (1984) has observed that single parents are as responsive to teacher initiatives as two-parent families, but are also more dependent on teachers to show them what to do.

Other interesting avenues of work include research that explores efforts to "bind" the school more closely to the family. The appeal of Bronfenbrenner's (1979) work lies in the potential for schools to enhance community bonds among isolated families. Similarly, the parent-contract approach of Henry Levin (in his accelerated learning model for disadvantaged children, 1987) may point to fruitful strategies for parent involvement in their child's education. Principals can encourage contact with teachers and staff by simply scheduling opportunities for direct parent involvement in their children's schooling, but there are also many innovative approaches to effectively involving parents that researchers should examine. For example, some schools have implemented home-based school contact programs while others have experimented with ways to keep parents closely informed when their child is truant. Also, the dynamics of magnet school opportunities have sharply altered the kind and level of parent involvement in school systems like Prince Georges County, Maryland.

From the perspective of teachers and principals, implementation studies are needed to identify effective methods for encouraging parental involvement—studies, that is, that indicate the concrete circumstances, procedures, and results that are associated with different approaches to parent involvement. In addition to synthesizing what the literature already shows, new work is needed to develop and examine innovative approaches for effectively involving parents in their children's education.

THE INFLUENCE OF THE COMMUNITY

In what ways do communities and peer groups affect the education of disadvantaged youngsters?

Previous empirical work in this area is relatively sparse for researchers who want to analyze the effect of community variables on effective schooling; thus, even the conceptual framework is still obscure. Coleman and Hoffer have emphasized the importance of "communities of families" or links between parents, teachers, and pupils (the more combinations the better) within a neighborhood and its school, but the parameters of community support are unexplored (cf. Cower, 1985) Can the educational successes of certain immigrant groups be explained by their "social capital"—that is, their community-wide emphasis on academic work and achievement? How important is the neighborhood setting—for example, if it is socially or economically isolated—to fostering a "community of parents" that reinforces mutual educational purposes and values. In sum, many school districts have made efforts to increase school-community collaborations in working with educationally disadvantaged youth and across districts we see interesting variations in community-school relations. Yet, we have little evidence regarding the effects on student achievement, or the effects on intermediate variables such as attendance, effort, or academic course enrollment. More information is needed on differences between specific collaborative efforts and what effects those differences have.

While not traditionally labelled a community variable, the study of peer environments represents another aspect of the local forces that impinge on the school and sanction students' behaviors. The academic effect of peer environment works in two directions. First, when there are examples of academic achievement to serve as role models, the aspirations of all students tend to rise, and higher achievements tend to follow. Conversely, a climate in which few students are high achievers tends to lower aspirations for all students and invites peer pressure for conformity to lower standards. However, when students attend schools with many high-achieving classmates, they sometimes lose self-esteem and motivation because they cannot measure up to their competitors. Overall, the impact of "student composition effects" is greater on aspirations than is the impact of achievement.

More recent data have vividly portrayed the open hostility of peer cultures in inner cities to academic work and learning (Fordham & Ogbu, 1987). The anti-school mindset can be especially potent when cultural differences lead to group alliances, and, from there, norms of peer solidarity evolve into a culture resistant to school authority and influence. Metz (1986) has observed a pattern in which young American Indian children approach school eager to learn, but over time become sullen, uncooperative, and isolated within their peer group.

Sociologists have long noted the influence of adolescent culture on students' motivation to learn (Coleman, 1961), but we have not learned very much about the makeup and origins of "oppositional cultures"—peer group values that actively oppose outward signs of achievement efforts—which would in turn point the way toward counteracting them. Are anti-school values more prevalent among disadvantaged youth than others? Found more in urban schools than in rural schools? Why do some disadvantaged youngsters develop positive values when their friends develop "oppositional" values? New work is needed to first identify the variables and forces that are at work in these oppositional cultures and second to formulate the strategies to successfully alter peer group values that impede learning.

In general, future research needs to examine how effective schools tailor their approaches to local communities. Given the many differences among neighborhoods and among communities, researchers need to advance our knowledge regarding how community involvement strategies may vary given the type of community in which a school is embedded.

SUMMARY

Many researchers conclude that most successful innovations in classroom practices or school organization have positive effects on low- as well as average- and high-achieving students. Slavin (1988), for example, observes that research "tends to find that teacher behaviors which are successful with low achievers tend to be very similar to those successful with all students." Research focused on education for the disadvantaged, however, should always be alert for differences in treatment effects (a) between low-ability or low-SES and high-ability or high-SES youth; (b) between children who speak English as their first language and language minority children—or children whose language development lags behind their peers; (c) between children reared in the cultural mainstream and children from other backgrounds.

Future research should also focus on the positive effects that home, community, and school variables have on academic success. The point of studying all these issues is to uncover what makes a difference in the education of disadvantaged children and then to translate the findings into usable tools for school improvement. A research agenda on effective schooling for disadvantaged students should point the way for future intervention strategies which will raise academic achievement for disadvantaged students. As the research now stands, some home, some community, and some school variables appear to be more manipulable than others, but even for those variables too little is known about their potential for successfully raising academic achievement. The research base in the areas of home, community, and school factors is sparse and only a vague outline of a rather complex picture has emerged.

In addition to these general themes, we need more specific and definitive information on:

1. What teaching and instructional factors explain differences in academic achievement among disdvantaged youngsters? What teaching and instructional strategies are most effective for raising the academic achievements of disadvantaged students?

2. What factors identify and explain how school principals or school organizations can be most effective in raising the academic achievements of disadvantaged students? What strategies may principals pursue to most effectively raise the academic achievements of disadvantaged students?

3. What factors distinguish between schools and teachers which effectively involve parents in the education of their children and those which achieve little parental support? What strategies can principals and teachers employ to involve parents as partners in actively educating their children?

4. What factors matter most for effectively engaging the whole community—parents, neighbors, ministers, and businessmen, in addition to the peer groups within each school—in support of

academic excellence? What strategies can schools employ to ensure the active and consistent support of the community for a school's academic goals?

CONCLUSION:

The central research question is what makes some schools and educational strategies successful in raising achievement levels of those students having the greatest difficulty in terms of learning and motivation. What classroom and school-level strategies—within well-specified contexts such as grade-level or content area—will enable teachers to meet the varying needs of educationally disadvantaged students who, as a group, have wide differences in background, academic preparation, and learning ability. This suggests a research program that:

○ is sensitive to interaction effects—those classroom processes and instructional strategies that work differently or less well (or more powerfully) for the disadvantaged.

○ is cross-disciplinary in approach. The best approach for pursuing work of lasting consequence (and of the widest credibility) is to draw from across disciplines for the methodological tools and theoretical frameworks that suit the research questions.

○ is grounded in working classrooms—that is, school-based research perhaps done in conjunction with several school districts—to test for the practical significance of theoretical perspectives and to provide ready insight into implementation issues.

○ is sensitive to context such as achievement level, students' age, and content of instruction. The learning problems of disadvantaged elementary-aged children are very different from the problems of poorly educated adolescents—which in turn are unlike the problems of poorly educated young adults. A full research agenda should be mindful of the arguments that weigh the merits of early identification and early intervention (in the elementary grades) against programs that focus on specific problems for middle and high school youth.

○ provides some grade or age level focus in the research plan. For example, research in reading suggests that intervention as early as grade four may be most effective for preventing reading achievement fall-off in later years (Chall and Snow, 1982). Others argue that the impact of intensive instruction may be greatest in secondary school since this is a "last chance" for teenage youth without basic skills. Practitioner and policy maker concerns with school transitions could be addressed with a focus on children between the ages of ten and fifteen.

○ is based on data of sufficient rigor and scope that the general research conclusions will have application for disadvantaged youth across the country—in poor rural schools, in large city schools, and in private, parochial, and public schools.

REFERENCES

Alexander, K. L., and McDill, E. 1976. Selection and allocation within schools. *American Sociological Review* 41:963–80.

Alexander, K. L., and Cook, M. A. 1982. Curricula and coursework: A surprising ending to a familiar story. *American Sociological Review* 47:636.

Alexander, K. L.; Entwisle, D. R.; and Thompson, M. S. 1987. School performance and status relations. *American Sociological Review* 52:665–82.

Baratz-Snowden, J. C., and Duran, R. 1987. The educational progress of language minority students: Findings from the 1983-84 NAEP reading survey. Princeton, N.J.: National Assessment of Educational Progress, Educational Testing Service.

Bennett, W. J. *American Education: Making It Work.* 1988. Washington, D.C.: U.S. Government Printing Office.

Bloom, B. S. 1980. The new direction in educational research: Alterable variables. *Phi Delta Kappan* 61:382–85.

Bronfenbrenner, U. 1979. Who needs parent education? In *Families and Communities as Educators,* ed. Hope Jensen Leichter. New York: Teachers College Press.

Brophy, J. E. 1981. Teacher praise: A functional analysis. *Review of Education Research* 51:5–32.

Brophy, J. E., and Good, T. L. 1986. Teacher behavior and student achievement. In *Handbook of Research on Teaching,* ed. Merlin C. Wittrock. New York: Macmillan.

Bruno, J. E., and Doscher, M. L. 1981. Contributing to the harms of social isolation: Analysis of requests for teacher transfer in a large urban school district. *Education Administration Quarterly* 17:93–108.

Bryk, A. S., and Thum, Y. M. 1989. The effects of high school organization on dropping out: an exploratory investigation. Madison, Wis.: Center for Policy Research in Education.

Carnegie Forum on Education and the Economy. 1986. *A nation prepared: Teachers for the 21st century.* New York.

Chall, J. S. and Snow, C. E. 1982. "Families and Literacy: The Contribution of Out-of-School Experiences to Children's Acquisition of Literacy." Final Report to the National Institute of Education, U.S. Department of Education.

Chubb, J.E. 1988. Why the current wave of school reform will fail. *The Public Interest* 90:28–49.

Clark, R. 1983. *Family life and school achievement: Why poor children succeed or fail.* Chicago: University of Chicago Press.

Coleman, J. S. 1961. *The Adolescent Society.* New York: Free Press.

Coleman, J. S., and Hoffer, T. 1987. *Public and private high schools: The impact of communities.* New York: Basic Books.

Cusick, P. 1986. A research agenda for understanding low income low (student) performing secondary schools. Seminar presentation at the Seminar on Schools with High Concentrations of Low-income Students. Office of Research, U.S. Department of Education, Washington, D.C.

Doyle, W. 1983. Academic work. *Review of Educational Research,* 53:159–200.

Dwyer, D. C.; Barnett, B. G.; and Lee, G. V. 1987. The school principal: Scapegoat or the last great hope? In *Leadership: Examining the Elusive,* ed. L. T. Sheive and M. B. Schoenheit. Cucamonga, Calif.: Association for Supervision and Curriculum Development.

Epstein, J. L. 1984. Single parent and the schools: The effect of marital status on parent and teacher evaluations. Baltimore, Md.: Center for Social Organization of Schools.

Fillmore, L. W. 1986. Teaching bilingual learners. In *Handbook of Research on Teaching,* ed. Merlin C. Wittrock. New York: Macmillan.

Finn, C. E. 1987. The high school dropout puzzle. *The Public Interest* 87:3–22.

Fordham, S., and Ogbu, J. 1987. Black students' school success: Coping with the burden of acting white. *Urban Review* 18.

Gamoran, A. 1987. The stratification of high school learning opportunities. *Sociology of Education* 60:135–55.

Garet, M. S. and DeLaney, B. 1988. "Students, Courses, and Stratification." *Sociology of Education* 61:61–77.

General Accounting Office. 1986. School dropouts: The extent and nature of the problem. Briefing report. Washington, D.C.: U.S. General Accounting Office.

———. 1987. School dropouts: Survey of local programs. Briefing report. Washington, D.C.: U.S. General Accounting Office.

Good, T. L., and Brophy, J. E. 1986. School effects. In *Handbook of Research on Teaching,* ed. Merlin C. Wittrock. New York: Macmillan.

Gottfredson, G. D., and Hybl, L. G. 1987. An analytical description of the school principal's job. Report #13, Center for Research on Elementary and Middle Schools. Baltimore, Md.: Johns Hopkins University Press.

Graham, P. A. 1987. Achievement for at-risk students. Unpublished paper prepared for Nation At-Risk Seminar on Education of the Disadvantaged, U.S. Department of Education. Washington, D.C.

Greenwood, C. R.; Delquadri, J. C.; and Whorton, D. 1984. Tutoring methods. *Direst Instruction News* 3:4–7, 23.

Hanushek, E. 1977. The production of education, teacher quality and efficiency. In *Educational Organization Administration*, ed. D. A. Erickson. Berkeley, Calif.: McCutchan.

Hawley, W. D., and Rosenholtz, S. J. 1984. Good schools: What research says about improving student achievement. *Peabody Journal of Education* 61.

Heyns, B. 1978. *Summer learning and the effects of schooling*. New York: Academic Press.

Holmes Group. 1986. *Tomorrow's teachers*. East Lansing, Mich.

Hurn, C. J. 1985. *The limits and possibilities of schooling*. Boston: Allyn & Bacon.

Jencks, C. L., and Brown, M. D. 1975. The effects of high schools on their students. *Harvard Educational Review* 45:273–324.

Lee, V. E., and Bryk, A. S. 1988. "Curriculum Tracking as Mediating the Social Distribution of High School Achievement." *Sociology of Education* 61:78–94.

Levin, H. M. 1987. Accelerated schools for disadvantaged students. *Educational Leadership* 44:19–21.

Metz, M. H. 1986. Some reflections on qualitative research concerning low achievement of poor children. Seminar presentation at the Seminar on Schools with High Concentrations of Low-income Students, Office of Research, U.S. Department of Education, Washington, D.C.

National Assessment of Chapter 1. 1986. Poverty, achievement, and the distribution of compensatory education services. Interim report, Office of Research, Office of Educational Research and Improvement, U.S. Department of Education.

———. 1987. The current operation of Chapter 1. Final report, Office of Research, Office of Educational Research and Improvement, U.S. Department of Education.

Applebee, A. N.; Langer, J. A.; and Mullis, I. V. S. 1988. *Who reads best?* Princeton, N.J.: National Assessment of Educational Progress, Educational Testing Service.

Natriello, G. 1986. Restructuring secondary schools for disadvantaged students. Seminar presentation at the Seminar on Schools with High Concentrations of Low-income Students, Office of Research, U.S. Department of Education, Washington, D.C.

Natriello, G.; Pallas, A.; and McDill, E. 1987. In our lifetime: The educationally disadvantaged and the future of schooling and society. Research paper prepared for the Committee for Economic Development Subcommittee on the Educationally Disadvantaged.

Oakes, J. 1987. Improving inner-city schools: Current directions in urban district reform. Santa Monica, Calif.: Center for Policy Research in Education, the RAND Corporation.

Oakes, J. 1985. *Keeping Track: How Schools Structure Inequality.* New Haven: Yale University Press.

OERI Urban Superintendents Network. 1987. *Dealing with Dropouts: The Urban Superintendents' Call to Action.* Office of Educational Research and Improvement, U.S. Department of Education.

Pallas, A.; Entwisle, D. R.; Alexander, K. L.; and Cadigan, D. 1987. Children who do exceptionally well in the first grade. *Sociology of Education* 60:257–71.

Pendleton, A. J. 1988. Young adult literacy and schooling. National Center for Education Statistics, U.S. Department of Education.

Persell, C. H., et al. 1982. *The Effective Principal: A Research Summary.* Reston, VA: National Association of Secondary School Principals.

Ralph, J. 1989. Improving education for the disadvantaged: Do we know how to help? *Phi Delta Kappan* 70:395–401.

Rosenbaum, J. E.; Rubinowitz, L. S.; and Kulieke, M. J. (forthcoming). *Low-income black children in white suburban schools.* Chicago: University of Chicago Press.

St. John, N. 1971. Thirty-six teachers: Their characteristics and outcomes for black and white pupils. *American Educational Research Journal* 8:635–48.

Slavin, R. E. 1988. Students at risk of school failure: The problem and its dimensions. Center for Research on Elementary and Middle schools. Baltimore, Md.: Johns Hopkins University Press.

Stedman, L. C. 1987. It's time we changed the effective schools formula. *Phi Delta Kappan* 69:215–24.

Stein, M. K.; Leinhardt, G.; and Bickel, W. 1988. Instructional issues for teaching students at risk. Pittsburgh, Pa.: Learning Research and Development Center.

Summers, A. A., and Wolfe, B. L. 1977. Do schools make a difference? *American Economic Review* 65:639–52.

Veltman, C. 1983. *Language shift in the United States.* Hawthorne, N.Y.: Mouton.

Willig, A. C. 1985. A meta-analysis of selected studies on the effectiveness of bilingual education. *Review of Educational Research* 55:269–317.

Wilson, W. J. 1987. *The truly disadvantaged: The inner city, the underclass, and public policy.* Chicago: University of Chicago Press.

FACILITATING THE PSYCHOEDUCATIONAL DEVELOPMENT
OF DISADVANTAGED CHILDREN

Norris M. Haynes and James P. Comer

The need to restructure public education to facilitate the academic and psychosocial development of minority children is becoming more recognized as a major educational and social policy issue. Many minority children are from low-income family backgrounds with non-mainstream values and adaptive mechanisms and attend schools reflective of the dominant culture. Thus, they are often impeded by a cultural misalignment between the demands of school and the normative patterns of behavior and adaptation in their family primary social networks.

This paper offers a psychocultural perspective on the development of culturally different and economically disadvantaged children, discusses their unique psychoeducational and developmental needs, and examines the failure of traditional school programs to meet these needs. Included are the description and discussion of a study that was conducted to determine parents' and teachers' assessments of the ability of selected schools to address children's developmental and psychoeducational needs. The study also examined the power of classroom environment factors to predict academic achievement among a group of black children from poor families.

INTRODUCTION

Generally, children from disadvantaged and culturally different backgrounds face more difficulty in adjusting to the traditional school environment than children from higher socioeconomic backgrounds whose families

23

live within the mainstream of the dominant culture (Comer, 1980; Coleman, 1984; Hodgkinson, 1986). American public and private schools to a large extent are structured and organized around mainstream values and norms of behavior. When a child enters school for the first time, the tacit assumption held by school administrators and teachers is that the child has acquired from home at least the basic preparatory social and academic skills that are necessary to function and learn in school.

Teachers are prepared to build upon the developmental foundation they expect to have been laid by the child's parents or guardians during the preschool years. The fact is, however, that in many innercity schools, with large numbers of children from poor families, students arrive with little or no preparation for the school experience. The results very often are poor adjustment and high frustration for both child and teacher (Schraft and Comer, 1985).

The initial experience of failure and feelings of inadequacy which children experience as early as kindergarten set the stage for later problems. These problems often include: being retained, suspended, referred to special education classes, achieving below grade level and dropping out of school. Other consequences of the pressures to achieve and excel academically without the developmental readiness to do so may include deviant social behaviors. The subsequent cycle of failure and reaction by the child becomes a revolving door from which the chance of escape declines with time. The failing child develops into a disillusioned adult.

The problems which confront minority youth in school and in the society at large most often are rooted in the early developmental years. Therefore, the disproportionate representation of minority children among the failures, the dropouts, the maladjusted in middle and high schools is a developmental issue that requires intervention based on child development and psychosocial principles.

Mainstream society, of which the school is a part, is apt to blame the family for failing to provide proper guidance and support. The reality, however, is that the school may have failed to address the total development of the child by focusing narrowly only on instruction and academic development.

An example may serve to demonstrate the misalignment between school expectations and unique cultural conditions. A Puerto Rican school administrator explained that the Puerto Rican child is vested with a certain amount of power within the Puerto Rican family because of the child's fluency in both English and Spanish and the parents' limited ability to speak English. The child very often is called upon to translate and communicate for the parents. As a result, the child, most often a male, assumes a position of power and respect within the family. In school, however, the child loses this power and is often not in a position to obtain it in school-based activities and relationships. Faced with this diminished role in school, the child often reacts in ways construed by teachers to be impudent and counterproductive. This sets in motion a wheel of misfortune for the child who is tagged with a negative label. The label then becomes a self-fulfilling prophecy leading to a downward course in school and in life.

Another example is appropriate. Garibaldi (1985) reported that Black children learn best within the context of a cooperative structure. This learning style is fostered by a family and community tradition of support, caring and sharing. Mainstream society, however, favors individualism and competition. Schools, reflecting mainstream values, encourage an individualistic learning style and competitiveness among students. Thus, many Black children are forced to conform to the dominant style of learning in school. Those Black children who cannot or do not adapt as readily as others are often considered to be underachievers and inferior learners when assessed by mainstream standards.

Researchers have also demonstrated that among Hispanic children (Duda, 1988) and Black children (Evard and Sabers, 1979), from low income families, language differences often account for poor school performance. Wilkinson and Burke (1984) and Willig, Harnish, Hill and Maehr (1983) demonstrated that poor children do worse than middle-class children academically when ethnic background is controlled. Edelman (1986) reported that almost fifty percent of all black children in the United States are poor.

Thus, socioeconomic status appears to be a significant determinant of school success. Coleman and Hoffer (1987) distinguished between disdvantaged and deficient families. Disadvantaged families are those with low incomes. Deficient families are those which are structurally impaired, such as single-parent families. We believe that the critical variable here is not family structure but family functioning. Nonetheless, in both situations, minority children are disproportionately represented. Coleman and Hoffer noted:

> Children from disadvantaged backgrounds and deficient families will make up an increasing fraction of future cohorts of children in the United States. The birth rate of Black and Hispanic minorities is larger than in the past relative to that of non-Hispanic Whites and the fraction of women of childbearing age who are members of these minorities is larger than in the past. The birth rate for women of higher socio-economic status is less then in the past, relative to that of women of lower socio-economic status. (p. 119)

The school should be flexible enough to accommodate the idiosyncratic characteristics of these children while at the same time be able to mold and shape their development in ways that are adaptive and funtional. Hodgkinson (1986), speaking of minority children, asserted, "These children will become tomorrow's adult population. If a third of the United States is non-White, it's important to all of us that that group do well." (p. 8) Writing again about the responsibility of public schools to minority and disadvantaged children, Hodgkinson noted, "To provide an adequate and meaningful education for these children is both a challenge and responsibility for the nation's elementary schools. Each school must adapt to meet the needs of its unique student body." (p. 8)

The potential for conflict between school expectations and non-mainstream children's behavior may be, in part, mediated by school and classroom characteristics and perceptions of what school personnel consider to be important concerns in these children's lives. The greater the agreement between teachers and parents on important issues related to the children's development, the greater the likelihood for a consistent and coordinated program of social development and education. With this in mind, the authors conducted a study to determine the degree of concordance between parents' and teachers' assessments of the school's ability to address the needs of non-mainstream children. The study also examined the relationship between classroom climate and school achievement.

STUDY

Sample

The study sample included 98 randomly selected Black students in grades 3 to 5 from seven elementary schools in an urban innercity school system. These schools had no special programs apart from regular staff development activities and served as control schools in a larger study reported elsewhere (Comer et al, 1987). Sixty eight parents of these children and 25 teachers also participated in the study. The schools were located in low income neighborhoods. All students, based on their parents' income, were eligible to participate in their schools' free lunch programs.

Instruments

Two instruments were used in the study. The School Survey, completed by teachers and parents was developed by the authors as a short, easily administered instrument to assess perceptions of school climate. It contains eight positive descriptive statements about the school. Parents and teachers were asked to indicate the extent to which they agreed with each statement by circling SD = Strongly Disagree, D = Disagree, A = Agree or SA = Strongly Agree. Each statement touched on some area of the family-student-teacher interaction that the authors thought was important. The test-retest reliability coefficients for this instrument are .85 and .87 for parents and teachers respectively.

The other instrument was the Classroom Environment Scale (CES) (Moos and Trickett, 1974). Students were asked to complete this instrument, by indicating on a four-point scale the extent to which they agreed or disagreed with 39 statements about their classroom. The Scale measures nine dimensions of classroom climate. The dimensions are: Involvement, Affiliation, Teacher Support, Task Orientation, Competition, Order and Organization, Rule Clarity, Teacher Control and Innovation. The CES has a test-retest reliability coefficient of .80 and concurrent validity of .70.

Children's scores on the Iowa Test of Basic Skills were also included as a dependent measure.

Procedures

Following the receipt of consent from parents for their children to participate in the study, the CES was administered to the students in small groups over the course of five school days. The parents of these children were mailed a School Survey to complete and return to the research office. The researchers did not want the parent forms returned directly to the school since parents might then have been reluctant to respond as candidly to the questions. Of the School Surveys mailed to parents, 68 (69%) were returned. Teachers of the children also returned their completed School Survey forms to the research office. Of the 30 teachers who received the forms, 25 (83%) completed and returned them.

Analysis

Two separate analyses were performed. First, one way Analyses of Variance (ANOVA) procedures were conducted to examine whether or not parents and teachers differed significantly on their assessment of the sensitivity and concern for children shown by children's schools. An F-test was performed for each of the eight items on the School Survey. Second, a stepwise multiple regression analysis was conducted using children's assessment of their classroom climate on the nine dimensions of the CES as predictors and total score on the Iowa Test of Basic Skills as the criterion variable.

Results

The ANOVA indicated that on all eight items teachers rated their schools higher than parents. Differences were significant on six of the eight items. On the two items where differences were not significant, both teachers and students rated schools very low. Overall, both teachers and parents had fairly low assessments of their school's climate, particularly on those items

TABLE 1
Parent and Teacher Differences on School Ratings

School Climate Categories	Parents		Teachers			
	x	S	x	SD	F	Sig
Concern for Children's Needs	1.4	1.1	2.8	1.1	5.7	.02*
Understanding of Parent's Needs	2.2	1.4	2.8	1.2	4.5	.04*
Parental Involvement in Decision Making	1.6	1.4	2.0	1.5	1.8	.19
Helping Children Build Self-Confidence	1.6	1.5	2.3	1.5	5.5	.02*
Special Help to Slow Children	2.3	1.2	3.0	1.2	6.0	.02*
Relationships Between Parents and Teachers	1.7	1.2	1.8	1.3	.09	.75
Parental Involvement in General Activities	1.8	1.5	2.6	1.5	5.6	.02*
Helping Children Achieve	1.6	1.5	2.3	1.5	5.5	.02*

*Significant Differences

that concerned helping children build confidence and the involvement of parents in schools. These results are summarized in Table 1.

The stepwise multiple regression analysis indicated that of the nine dimensions on the CES, only four were sufficiently strong to be included in the regression model. The strongest predictor of achievement was Teacher Support, $F(1,96) = 14.6$, $p \leq .001$. The second strongest predictor was Involvement, $F(2,95) = 14.9$, $p \leq .001$, followed by Innovation, $F(3,94) = 13.3$, $p < .001$, and Rule Clarity, $F(4,93) = 12.1 \leq .001$. These results are summarized in Table 2.

Discussion

The results of the study indicate that the parents and teachers of the minority and economically deprived children in the present study differed

TABLE 2
Stepwise Hierarchial Multiple Regression of
Classroom Environment Dimensions on Achievement

Classroom Dimensions	B	SEB	Beta	Multiple R	R2	R2 Change	F	Sig
Teacher Support	.26	.06	.35	.36	.13		14.6	.001*
Involvement	.44	.11	.31	.49	.24	.11	14.9	.001*
Innovation	1.6	.59	.23	.55	.30	.06	13.3	.001*
Rule Clarity	.16	.06	.21	.59	.34	.04	12.1	.001*

*Significant F values

significantly in their assessment of the support and sensitivity of their children's schools in addressing the children's psychoeducational needs. The regression analysis further confirmed the importance of classroom climate, especially teacher support and understanding, in determining academic achievement among these children. It should be noted that some of the newly emerging approaches to school reform, especially those endorsed by top-level government officials, stress discipline, homework and rigorous curricula without paying attention to the psychoeducational needs of children from poor families. These approaches ignore the psychoeducational development needs of disadvantaged children.

The discrepancies between teachers' and parents' perceptions of schools' concern for, as well as willingness and ability to address the special psychoeducational needs of disadvantaged children, emphasize the need for the training of teachers to effectively assist these children in adjusting to the school environment. Although other school personnel, such as administrators, psychologists and social workers, were not included in this study, it is reasonable to assume that they too may need to be educated and sensitized. Any such training should include: (1) information on cultural differences, (2) a discussion of problems which the economically disad-'vantaged family faces, (3) the potential transfer of maladaptive mechanisms from the home and community to the classroom and how these should be handled and (4) strategies for creating school and classroom environments that are supportive and caring yet challenging and motivational.

The Yale University Child Study Center School Development Program is designed to focus on the psychoeducational needs of all children and especially minority and disadvantaged children. Briefly described, the program creates a sense of community among school personnel and parents. A process is established in which the interests of the staff, parents' concerns, and students' needs are facilitated and supported. A governance and management mechanism representative of parents, teachers, and administrators establishes mutually agreed upon goals, objectives, and strategies in each school. Home and school are brought together in an alliance and partnership to insure that the education of children takes place within a developmental framework that is culturally sensitive and responsive. The detailed operations of the program are extensively discussed elsewhere (Comer 1980; Comer et al 1986; Haynes et al 1988). The developmental perspective which serves as the basic framework for the program is outlined in Figure 1.

Essentially the perspective recognizes that all children, prior to entering school, are part of a social network. The social network includes the family, church, community and other individuals and groups with whom the child comes into regular contact. This social network exerts a strong influence on the child's psychosocial and cognitive readiness for the school experience. Children whose social networks are not integrated into the mainstream and dominant culture (marginal networks) are not immersed in the values and ways of that culture and are ill-prepared to function within the parameters of the school, which reflects mainstream society.

The task of the school then, is to assist students from disadvantaged backgrounds (marginal social networks) to adjust to the requirements of the school culture. This is accomplished only when the school staff and parents interact in a mutually respectful way.

The School Development Program's perspective identifies five developmental pathways that all children must negotiate successfully to be optimally successful in school and in society generally. These include (1) cognitive-academic, (2) social-interactive, (3) psychoemotional, (4) moral, and (5) speech and language.

The child whose primary social network is marginal is more likely to experience more underdevelopment along these pathways than other children, not because the child's primary social network is inferior to or worse than the more mainstream social network, but because it may be significantly different. Children imitate, identify with and internalize values and behaviors they are exposed to in their primary social networks. School administrators, teachers, psychologists, social workers, counselors and other significant adults in the school become new objects of imitation, identification and internalization.

The potential for conflict between the values and standards of behavior of home and school heighten and the child is at increased risk for self-depreciation, frustration and failure. It is important, therefore, that school personnel be sensitized to the unique circumstances and developmental needs of culturally different children and be able to facilitate their psychoeducational development.

FIGURE 1

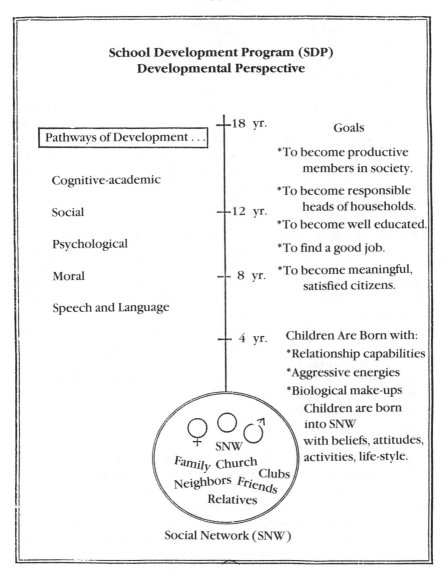

School Development Program (SDP)
Developmental Perspective

Pathways of Development . . .

18 yr.

Goals

*To become productive members in society.

Cognitive-academic

*To become responsible heads of households.

Social

12 yr.

*To become well educated.

Psychological

*To find a good job.

Moral

8 yr.

*To become meaningful, satisfied citizens.

Speech and Language

4 yr.

Children Are Born with:
*Relationship capabilities
*Aggressive energies
*Biological make-ups
Children are born into SNW with beliefs, attitudes, activities, life-style.

SNW
Family Church
Clubs
Neighbors Friends
Relatives

Social Network (SNW)

REFERENCES

Coleman, J. S. and Hoffer, T. (1987) *Public and private high schools: The impact of communities.* New York: Basic Books.

Coleman, J. S. (1984) *Elementary school self-improvement through social climate enhancement.* (Eric Research Document number ED 251961).

Comer, J. P. (1980) *School Power.* New York: Free Press.

Comer, J. P., Haynes, N. M. and Hamilton-Lee, M. (1986). *Academic and affective gains from the school development program: A model for school improvement.* (Eric Research Documents. Number ED 274 750.)

Duda, J. L. (1985) Goals and achievement orientations of Anglo and Mexican-American adolescents in sport and the classroom. *International Journal of Intercultural Relations, 9(2)*: 131–150.

Edelman, M. W. (1987) *Families in peril: An agenda for social change.* Cambridge, MA: Harvard University Press.

Evard, B. L. and Sabes, D. L. (1979) Speech and language testing with distinct ethnic-racial groups: A survey of procedures for improving validity. *Journal of Speech and Hearing Disorders. 44*:271–281.

Garibaldi, A. M. (1976) *Cooperation, competition and locus of control in African-American students.* (Doctoral Dissertation, University of Minnesota) University Microfilms No. 77-12 807.

Haynes, N. M., Comer, J. P. and Hamilton-Lee, M. (1988) The school development program: A model for school improvement. *Journal of Negro Education,* (*57*):11–21.

Hodgkinson, H. L. (1987) *All one system: Demography of Education—Kindergarten through Graduate school.* The Institute of Educational Leadership.

Hodgkinson, H. L. (1986) Here they come, ready or not. *Newsweek,* May 14.

Wilkinson, S. M. and Burke, J. P. (1984) Ethnicity, socioeconomic status and self-concept: Effects on children's academic performance. *Journal of Instructional Psychology 11(4)*: 203–210.

Willig, A. C., Harnisch, D. L., Hill, R. T. and Maehr, M. L. (1983) Sociocultural and educational correlates of success-failure attributions and evaluation anxiety in the school setting for Black, Hispanic and Anglo children. *American Educational Research Journal. 20(3)*:385–410.

APPENDIX A
School Survey
Teacher Version

Below are some statements which may or may not apply to your school. Please indicate the extent to which you agree with each statement by circling either

SD = Strongly Disagree   *D* = Disagree   *A* = Agree   *SA* = Strongly Agree

1. Most teachers in this school care about the educational and emotional needs of the children.   SD   D   A   SA

2. Teachers in this school understand the needs of parents.   SD   D   A   SA

3. Parents are involved in deciding what is taught in this school.   SD   D   A   SA

4. Most teachers in this school help children build self-confidence.   SD   D   A   SA

5. Most teachers in this school give special help to slower children.   SD   D   A   SA

6. The relationship between parents and the teachers in this school is good   SD   D   A   SA

7. This school encourages parent involvement in the day-to-day activities in the school.   SD   D   A   SA

8. Most teachers in this school do their best to help children achieve.   SD   D   A   SA

APPENDIX B
School Survey
Parent Version

Below are some statements which may or may not apply to your child's school. Please indicate the extent to which you agree with each statement by circling either

SD-Strongly Disagree   *D*-Disagree   *A*-Agree   *SA*-Strongly Agree

1. Most teachers in my child's school care about the educational and emotional needs of the children.   SD   D   A   SA

2. Teachers in my child's school understand the needs of parents.   SD   D   A   SA

3. Parents are involved in deciding what is taught in my child's school.   SD   D   A   SA

4. Most teachers in my child's school help children build self-confidence.   SD   D   A   SA

5. Most teachers in my child's school give special help to the slower child.   SD   D   A   SA

6. The relationship between parents and the teachers in my child's school is good.   SD   D   A   SA

7. My child's school encourages parent involvement in the day-to-day activities in the school.   SD   D   A   SA

8. Most teachers in my child's school do their best to help children achieve.   SD   D   A   SA

DEVELOPMENTAL ANALYSIS OF THE RISING TIDE
OF "AT- RISK" STUDENTS

M. M. Scott

THE PROBLEM

Since the publication of "A Nation at Risk" (National Commission on Excellence in Education, 1983) educators have been concerned with the growing numbers of children who either have difficulty in moving through the school system, or who, in fact, do not move through it successfully and drop out. These children are the focus of this paper. For the purposes of this paper, a child who is said to be "at risk" will refer to a child who has an increased probability of learning problems, adjustment difficulties, or of dropping out of school before completing high school.

A number of different problems have been identified with risk of not succeeding in school. Although actual numbers of children in various risk categories vary from report to report, it seems clear that far too many children are experiencing difficulties of one or more types. For example, among the 3.5 million children who entered school in 1986:

(1) 25 percent will live in poverty

(2) 14 percent have teen-aged mothers

(3) 14 percent will be children of unmarried mothers

(4) 15 percent will speak a primary language other than English

(5) 40 percent may live in a broken home before age 18

(6) 10 percent will have almost illiterate parents (Hodgkinson, Mirga, Smith, Trimbach, & Quinn, 1986).

35

These problems and others have been reported and reviewed extensively elsewhere. It is not the purpose of this paper to reiterate these data here. Instead, the purpose here is to examine some of the data in more depth and to attempt to interpret them from a developmental framework.

Underlying Factors

A number of underlying causes have been posited for the substantial increase in numbers of at-risk children during the past decade. These include decline in the quality of public education, a rise in the number of welfare recipients, particularly in multigeneration welfare families, and general breakdown of society in the United States as a whole.

A frequent target as a cause of children's problems in schools has been the substantial changes in family structure in the United States during the past 15 to 20 years. It has been argued that because there are more one-parent families and/or because more mothers work outside the home, more children are experiencing difficulties with learning and development. This presumed explanation is little more than a hypothesis, however, and de-serves a closer look.

A CLOSER LOOK AT FAMILY CHANGES

One of the first problems encountered in an attempt to examine data on children's family living arrangements is that the data are unreliable. Data on children are simply not available in the same ways as they are on adults. For example, children are frequently counted as part of families or as part of households rather than as individuals. Such methods of counting children may substantially misrepresent the facts concerning them. For example, as seen in figure 1, only 31 percent of households and 42 percent of families are married couples with children. While these data are accurate for *house-holds* and *families*, they do not represent an accurate picture of individual children's lives. That is, 75 percent of children still live with two parents.

There are other problems as well. We do not know what proportions of children live with their two biological parents or with other parental com-binations, for example, stepparents, adoptive parents, etc. Data on changes over time in children's family situations are also very difficult to obtain. Finally, data on actual family members with whom the child has regular contact are not the same as those for the normal family. For example, a child may see a noncustodial father fairly regularly. Some children may even see this father as frequently as they did before a divorce.

Once the data problems have been surmounted, an interesting picture emerges of changes in children's family living arrangements between 1960 and 1984. As can be seen in table 1, in 1984 about 75 percent of children lived with two parents. This is a decrease since 1960, when about 87

FIGURE 1
**Graphic Representation of Different Methods of
Calculating U.S. Family Structure (1980)**

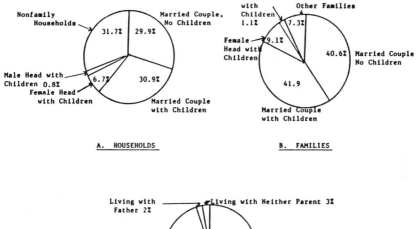

A. HOUSEHOLDS   B. FAMILIES

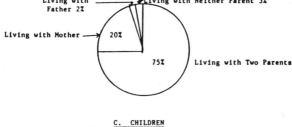

C. CHILDREN

percent lived with two parents. There has been a concomitant rise in percentages of children living with one parent, from 9 percent in 1960 to 23
percent in 1984.

Family structure varies considerably depending on the race of the child.
As seen in table 2, whereas about 81 percent of white children lived with
two parents in 1982, only 42 percent of black children did so. Furthermore,
between 1970 and 1980 the percentage of black children living with one
parent increased from 32 percent to 49 percent. In other words, at the
beginning of the decade about half of black children lived with one parent,
as contrasted with 17 percent of white children who did so.

A third trend in children's family living arrangements is a decrease in
family size. In 1960, 21 percent of families had three or more children,
whereas in 1981 only 12 percent had three or more. A more interesting
set of data, however, were produced by Hernandez and Meyer (1986), who
studied adult-child ratio in homes of both dual and single parents. This
methodology permits some equivalence comparisons from the perspective
of the child, at least in terms of actual numbers, between the two types of

TABLE 1

Percentages of U.S. Children in Various Types of Families: 1960 to 1984

	1960	1970[3]	1980[3]	1984[4]
Living with:				
2 parents	86.8[1]	85.2	76.6	74.9
1 parent	9.0[2]	11.9	19.7	22.6
mother only	7.9[2]	10.8	18.0	20.4
father only	1.1[2]	1.1	1.7	2.2
other	3.5	2.9	3.7	2.5

1. Bureau of the Census. 1960. *Census of population. PC(1)–1C. General social and economic characteristics. U.S. summary.* Washington, D.C.: Government Printing Office. Table 79, p. 210.
2. Estimated from numbers of children in families and subfamilies with various types of household heads. Bureau of the Census. 1960. *Census of population. PC(1)–1D. Detailed characteristics. U.S. summary.* Washington, D.C.: U.S. Government Printing Office. Table 185, p. 459.
3. Saluter, A. F. 1983. *Marital status and living arrangements: March 1983. Series P–20, no. 389.* Bureau of the Census. Washington, D.C.: Government Printing Office. Table D, p. 4.
4. Bureau of the Census. 1984. *Current population reports. Population characteristics. Series P–20, no. 399. Marital status and living arrangements: March 1984.* Washington, D.C.: U.S. Government Printing Office. Table D, p. 4.

TABLE 2

White and Black U.S. Children's Living Arrangements: 1970 and 1982[1]

	All Races		White		Black	
	1970	1982	1970	1982	1970	1982
Percent living with:						
Two parents	84.9%	75.0%	89.2%	80.8%	58.1%	42.4%
Mother only	10.7	20.0	7.8	15.3	29.3	47.2
Divorced	3.3	8.2	3.1	8.0	4.6	9.6
Separated	4.7	5.6	2.8	4.3	16.2	13.6
Never married	0.8	4.4	0.2	1.6	4.4	20.8
Widowed	2.0	1.8	1.7	1.5	4.2	3.3
Father only	1.1	1.9	0.9	1.9	2.2	2.0
Neither parent	3.3	3.1	2.2	2.0	10.4	8.4

1. Select Committee on Children, Youth, and Families. 98th Congress. (May 1983). *U.S. children and their families: Current conditions and recent trends.* Washington: Government Printing Office. Table 2, p. 9.

FIGURE 2

**Percentages of Children with Small, Medium, and Large
Parent-Child Ratios: 1960–1980[1]**

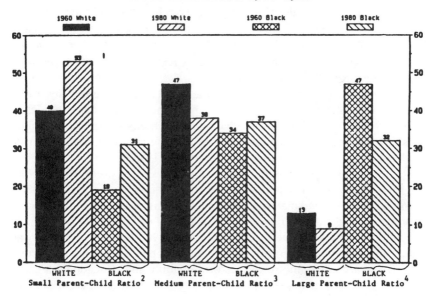

1   Hernandez, D. J. & Meyers, D. E. (1986). Children and their extended families
    since World War II. Paper presented at the meeting of the Population
    Association of America, April, 1986, San Francisco.
2   Small parent-child ratio = 1 or 2 children and 2 parents, or 1 child and 1 parent.
3   Medium parent-child ratio = 3, 4, or 5 children and 2 parents, or 2 children
    and 1 parent.
4   Large parent-child ratio = 6 or more children and 2 parents, or 3 or more children
    and 1 parent.

family structures. As seen in figure 2, there has been a marked improvement
in all children's living situations, if by improvement is meant more adults
available per child. It should also be pointed out that, although this ratio
has improved for black children (decrease from 47 percent to 32 percent
of black children in homes with large parent-child ratios), black children
still lag considerably behind white children (9 percent of white children
live in homes with large parent-child ratios).

Possible Interpretations of the Data

There are several possble interpretations of the above data. One is that
the American family as we know it is disappearing. This conclusion is simply
not supported by the data. First, 75 percent of children still live with two

parents. Second, the marked increase in divorce rates characteristic of the 1970s appears to have slowed or stopped (Norton & Moorman, 1986), and divorce rates actually declined from 1980 to 1985, except for teens. Third, the 1960s saw the liberalization of divorce laws in almost all states (Masnick & Bane, 1980). What may have been happening during the past two decades is a period of adjustment as both parties in a marriage exercised new options. What may be happening in the 1980s is a restabilization as people have begun adjusting to these new options.

A second possible interpretation of the data is that some families are in trouble, and there is some support for this conclusion. What is less clear is exactly which families and for what reasons. One of the greatest changes in family patterns in recent years is the increase in single-parent (usually mother-headed) families. Furthermore, some studies have estimated a child's longitudinal probability of experiencing a single-parent family before age 18 to be between .4 and .6 (Bumpass, 1984; Norton & Glick, 1986). Divorce among second marriages is also high (Bumpass, 1984).

However, while single parentedness has been used as a marker variable for difficulties experienced by families and by children, it may not be the significant variable. Two other factors may be playing a more important role. These are economic resources of the family and educational level of the parent(s). For example, 57 percent of children in one-parent families have family incomes below the poverty line, as contrasted with 25 percent of all children who are poor (Norton & Glick, 1986). Single-parent families tend to have substantially reduced economic resources even if they are not in poverty (Bumpass, 1984). Second, single parents, as a group, also tend to have lower educational levels than do dual parents (Bumpass, 1984). Thus, it might be expected that there would be a lower level of stimulation for children in these homes.

A third possible interpretation of the recent changes in family structure is that some families are coping and adapting to a changed set of environmental circumstances. Again, there is some support for this conclusion. The model underlying this argument is one generated by Ogbu (1981), called a cultural-ecological model of child competence. Ogbu's model is based on three assumptions: (a) that individuals and families genuinely desire success for themselves and their children; (b) that different environments require different sets of behavior patterns to be successful; and (c) that individuals and families are quite astute at observing what is required for success in a given environment and at trying to produce those elements to the best of the knowledge and ability of the individual or family. For example, groups of adolescents and businessmen alike recognize members of their group by cues of dress, language, and behavior. Almost all members of each group can identify the "successful" members, and each member usually tries to do whatever he or she can to be successful, even though the particular behaviors some individuals produce may lead to exactly the opposite result.

This same example holds for behavioral patterns required to be successful in environments as different as, say, a southern Indian Amish community and West Hollywood. Even though the requirements for success are enormously different in the two environments, many cross-cultural researchers have argued that any given newborn child is probably capable of being trained to produce either set of behaviors *IF* the child is socialized into them early and if these roles are accepted by the culture in which the individual lives.

The cultural-ecological model of child competence is presented in figure 3. Ogbu believes that understanding the environment is the key to understanding behavior patterns in various groups. The given environment in which children or families live cues them as to what behaviors will be more likely to lead to success in this environment. People perceive these cues and organize their cultural rules for behavior around these cues. An example that is common to many cultures is the rule most mothers establish, either explicitly or implicitly, that children should stay closer to them when they are in situations that the mother considers potentially dangerous, for example, in a large crowd. In this environment, "success" may require the mother to either protect the child or to issue directions to the child more

FIGURE 3
A Cultural-Ecological Model of Child Competence

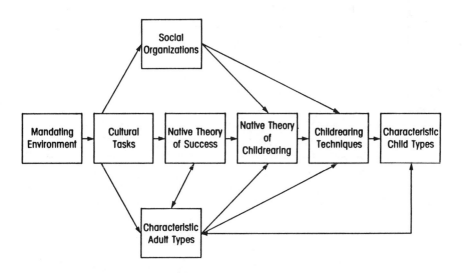

Source: Ogbu, J. U. (1981). Origins of human competence: A cultural-ecological perspective. *Child Development* 52:413–29.

frequently, both of which are more likely to succeed if the child is closer. Collections of these rules or cultural tasks, in Ogbu's terms, then, lead to a native theory of success. From this theory parents and others generate a theory of childrearing. The resultant childrearing techniques eventually produce a characteristic child-type for that culture. In the United States, that child-type is outgoing, gregarious, and high in independence. A number of researchers (cf. Rebelsky & Abeles, 1969; Tulkin, 1972; Caudill & Weinstein, 1969) have found that cultures generate childrearing strategies aimed directly at producing the kinds of adults each culture values. Cultures tend to produce a majority of adults of a type valued, or thought likely to be successful, by that culture. The extent to which these adults actually do succeed then provides a feedback mechanism into the culture. Social organizations and relationships mediate this process.

When this model is applied to the interpretation of changes in family structure, a very interesting picture emerges. The environment requirements for "success" in the United States have been changing substantially in recent years. Three clusters of factors related to success appear important in understanding recent changes in family demography.

The first cluster of factors is related to the decreased number of children per family. Carlson (1986) has pointed out that sheer economics may have produced these decreases. As more two-earner families became necessary in order to survive or to maintain a certain standard of living, the cost of child care and other costs associated with having a child out of the home for larger amounts of time went up proportionally (Hoffman, 1984). There were also fewer tasks for children to do as the economic structure of the country shifted from home-based activities, such as farming, to nonhome-based jobs (Mueller, 1976). In fact, the earlier economic advantage of having large numbers of children has not only shifted, but reversed. A final factor associated with decreasing numbers of children per family has been concern with population growth. With respect to number of children, then, "success" in more recent years has meant producing fewer children, and families have done just that.

A second cluster of factors has been the substantial changes in social roles in the United States. As women began taking new roles in a variety of areas, several things happened. More options opened up for both women and men. Both groups began exercising these options in everything from who washed the dishes to no-fault divorce. These increased options grew out of recognized inequalities and can lead to exciting, interesting, and productive lives for all people. They can lead, as Ogbu's model would predict, to increased coping and adaptation and, ultimately, to "success" in a changed environment. Again, families appear to have very astutely analyzed the environment and set about producing behaviors designed to lead to success in that changed environment.

The data indicate, then, that some families are indeed coping and adapting.

If family living situations become intolerable, people are no longer forced to endure them or make adjustments that may be dysfunctional. If having fewer children appears to be a more successful strategy, families are having fewer. During this recent period when the environment has been changing so rapidly and people have been attempting a variety of behaviors that they hope will lead to success, it is quite likely that a number of these strategies have gone awry. This does not change the fact, however, that, for *some* families, the changes in recent years reflect good coping and adaptation.

The third cluster of factors is related to the fact that the actual day-to-day family living situations of children do not seem to be characterized very well by labeling them "single-parent families." Circumstances vary enormously from family to family; in fact, they may vary more among single-parent families than they do among two-parent families. Such circumstances include the actual (as contrasted with the reported) number of adults in the home, the availability of grandparents, other relatives, friends, and neighbors, and the amount of time the parent actually spends with the child.

Cochran and Brassard (1979) have demonstrated that social network factors such as size and density of the network, variety among its members, frequency of contact, and others strongly influence a child's developmental course. Bianchi and Seltzer (1986) have shown that "the degree to which household structure and composition determine children's access to resources (material and nonmaterial) can only be evaluated in light of knowledge about family relationships both within and across households" (p. 3). They studied a sample of 15,000 children using data from the National Health Interview Survey by the Bureau of the Census. They found that many children continued seeing an absent parent either frequently or at least occasionally, and for children whose parents did not remarry, contact with the absent parent was significantly greater than for children whose parents did remarry. This suggests, again, that the actual family situation is not equivalent to the reported family situation.

FUTURE PROJECTIONS

Projections of future patterns are a favorite task of many demographers and can be very helpful to planners. In the past several decades in the United States, however, the projection business has been one of the most hazardous in all of demography. Since projections of the future are based predominantly on past trends, and since there have been large shifts in the trends in several areas, this has produced substantial errors in projections. This has been particularly true of family projections.

The simple fact is that it is not known what course family patterns will take in the future. One thing that can be said with considerable assurance is that family patterns are now much more complex than they have been in the past and are likely to remain so for a number of years to come. An example may clarify this point. A boy (call him George) is born in 1986 in the United States. When he is 6 years old, his parents divorce. He lives with his mother but continues seeing his father on weekends and in the summer. When George is 12 his mother remarries. George and the stepfather get along well and do many things together. George continues seeing his father, although less frequently, as the father has now moved to California and married a woman with two children. George graduates from high school and enters college. He lives with a woman for two years. He then married another woman and they have a daughter. After several years, George and his wife divorce, but George continues seeing his daughter on weekends and in the summer. Two years later, George remarries. He and his second wife have two more children. During George's life so far, he has lived in nine families either full or part time. Whereas the relationships in some of these families may not have been what George would describe as ideal, in each case there have been people he loved, enjoyed doing things with, and perhaps wanted to continue seeing. This is a substantial change from the situation of several decades ago, in which an individual could expect by George's age to have lived in two or three families at most.

The situation described above for George is surely not true for all children, but portions of it are now true for the majority of children in the United States. Norton and Glick (1986) estimate that a child born in 1986 has a 60 percent probability of spending at least one year in a single-parent family before reaching age 18. Masnick and Bane (1980) predict increases in cross-household family relationships. Some of these experiences produce reduced circumstances, alienation, and a sense of anomie and rootlessness. Others, however, enrich children's lives by providing more experiences, a greater variety of experiences (both of which have been linked to increased cognitive growth), and more (not fewer) adults to serve as role models for children. What does seem clear is that this situation is not likely to go away. Increased complexity of family relations and patterns appears to be the predominant mode of the post-1980 United States. It is complexity that is thought to be the key to understanding the changed environment in which today's children live.

A DEVELOPMENTAL FRAMEWORK FOR VIEWING CHANGES

Extant models of child and human development are thought to be helpful in interpreting the rising tide of at-risk children, particularly with respect to recent changes in family structure. Development, as used here, is defined as intra-individual change over time. It implies a continuing interaction of an individual, who has a particular history, with the environment as it actually reaches that individual at any given point. There are two key concepts in current developmental thinking that appear applicable to children at risk for failure in school and life. One of these is environmental competence and the other is plasticity. Environmental competence refers to the individual's ability to perceive requirements of the environment and to produce responses appropriate to those requirements (Scott, 1987). Plasticity means malleability, i.e., capability of being shaped or molded into new forms. Both of these concepts have implications for understanding the recent increase in numbers of at-risk individuals and for developing effective intervention strategies.

The first concept from the developmental literature that appears helpful is evironmental competence. Human beings seem to have a very strong drive to succeed in whatever environments they find themselves (Ogbu, 1981; Scott, 1987). They appear to be "prewired" to perceive variations in their environments (Pick, 1975) and they appear to be able to produce responses that will increase their probability of succeeding in a variety of different environments. The cultural-ecological model of competence (Ogbu, 1981) is a cornerstone of this argument and has been discussed in detail in an earlier section of this paper. The chief point to be made is that the environments in which children and families have found themselves in the United States in the past two decades have been changing rapidly. There have been changes at virtually all levels of the social order, i.e., the macrosystem, mesosystem, microsystem, and exosystem (Bronfenbrenner & Crouter, 1983). One of the major changes has been in the variety and complexity of family structures. Some families appear to be perceiving the changed environment and coping. For an increasing number of families, however, two problems have occurred. These are low economic resources and low educational level of the parents. These two problems also appear to have risen markedly within the society. Within many families there is only one parent and this parent works. Furthermore, when some families are together, their chief activity is watching television. Studies have shown that (1) amount of interaction decreases during television watching and (2) the type of interaction changes to a lower level (Garbarina, 1975). All these factors translate into less time available for parents to teach their children things traditionally handled within the home, such as values, behavioral rules, etc.

Concomitant shifts have occurred in schools. Factors such as less direct teaching time and lower expectations for students have been criticized as causative in recent decreases in achievement. There also appears to have been a decrease in the teaching of values commonly held by the culture. This decrease has come about as a function of increases in at least rhetorical acceptance of multiple values in a pluralistic society. Such acceptance has the possibility of producing a more complex society, in which the commonly held values are broad in scope and variety among individuals is accepted. In the interim, however, what it has meant practically is that children simply do not get as much information about values and the behaviors exemplifying them in either the home or the school context.

The teaching of values in the home and at school is important in developing environmental competence in the young because values form the mediational framework for determining what "success" means in either stable or changing environments. As Ogbu argues, a culture develops for itself a theory of success based on what the environment actually requires. Values are the means of making these requirements explicit among the adults of the culture and of transmitting them to the young.

What this means with respect to environmental competence in the development of children, then, is that they are growing up during a time of transition, in which marked changes in the environment have occurred and some initial moves have been made to respond to these changes, but there is not yet in place a substantial institutional and societal response (Conger, 1988). It also means that the developmental notion of environmental competence could be a very useful idea upon which to base intervention strategies. If the model is correct, what is now needed is a fairly detailed analysis of the newly changed environment and a set of behaviors designed to lead to success in that environment. Some steps have already been taken toward this end. For example, schools are now focusing more on strategies designed to improve achievement. Concomitant focus on improved parenting strategies is also occurring. A focus on economic productivity and a reorientation of values may also enhance the quality of life for both the individual and the larger society.

Plasticity is the second factor from the developmental literature that appears helpful in understanding increases in numbers of at-risk children. Older models of plasticity suggested that early experiences shaped or molded the child, somewhat irrevocably, for later functioning. It was thought that experiences encountered early in life were critical for certain later performances. For example, enrichment of the experiential background led to later increases in learning (Kretch, 1972; Rosenzweig & Bennett, 1978). It was also thought that certain areas of the brain became increasingly "committed" to whatever material was presented in early life (Penfield, 1972). The findings from these earlier studies are certainly still accurate and valid. It does appear to be true that experiences early in life lay down some important foundations upon which later development is based. What appears to be different is the interpretation of these findings, especially in light of more recent findings. It now appears that the early period in life is still critical, but not exclusive, for certain experiences.

Newer models of plasticity have suggested a more complex picture of the malleability of the child and adult (Gollin, 1981). The early period is still thought to be important, but it now appears that there are other periods throughout the life span during which pivotal development may occur (Oyama, 1985; Scott, 1987). For example, Kagan, Klein, Finley, Rogoff, & Nolan (1979) showed that some Guatamalan children, despite very impoverished early backgrounds of experience (by U.S. standards), could, by the age of 10 or 11, perform as well as U.S. children on some visual-motor and problem-solving tasks. A number of researchers have shown that the capacity of the individual to make major developmental shifts is not set nearly so early as had been thought (Gottlieb, 1983; Greenough, Black, & Wallace, 1987; Kaas, 1987; Pribram, 1986). Diamond (with Hopson, 1984) has, in fact, found that, in animals, significant learning and the accompanying brain changes to support this learning can take place into late life. These studies, then, suggest that our models of plasticity need revision. It still seems to be true that early experiences lay down important foundations for later development, but that considerably less of development is firmly set during the early years than had been thought.

What the concept of plasticity means for understanding the recent rise in numbers of at-risk children and adults is that people have been very responsive. As demands for achievement declined and demands for self-awareness rose, individuals decreased their achievement and increased the awareness of their own needs and those of cultural and ethnic groups to which they belonged. These latter are, of course, very positive changes, but not at the expense of the former.

What the concept of plasticity suggests for future intervention is that there is a considerable likelihood of success in decreasing the numbers of at-risk children and of helping individuals get their lives back on track *IF* the questions and strategies can be framed within the context of the environmental competence factor discussed earlier.

SUMMARY

During the past two decades there has been a marked rise in numbers of at-risk children in the United States. Several factors have been linked causatively to this rise. One of these factors, changes in family demography over the past two decades, was examined in more detail. The data do not support the hypothesis that the American family is disappearing. Some families do appear to be in trouble, but it is difficult to determine exactly which ones and for what reasons. For example, poverty and low educational level of parents appear to be better markers for understanding the problems of children than is single parentedness. Some families appear to be coping and adapting well to the recent changes in the environment. A developmental framework was used to analyze these recent changes. Two concepts appear to be helpful in understanding the changes and in planning intervention strategies. These concepts are environmental competence and plasticity. Environmental competence refers to a natural drive to succeed that is manifested in a variety of ways in different environments and that is mediated by organizational and social systems (Ogbu, 1981; Scott, 1987). Plasticity refers to the individual's capacity to change over time, and newer

developmental models of plasticity suggest that there are recurring cycles
of plasticity throughout the life span (Gollin, 1981).

REFERENCES

Bianchi, S. M., and Seltzer, J. A. April 1986. Children's contact with absent
    parents. Paper presented at the meeting of the Population Association
    of America, San Francisco.
Bronfenbrenner, U., and Crouter, A. C. 1983. The evolution of environmental
    models in developmental research. *Handbook of child psychology.* 4th
    ed., ed. P. H. Mussen. Vol. 1, *History, theory and methods.* New York:
    Wiley.
Bumpass, L. L. 1984. Children and marital disruption: A replication and
    update. *Demography* 21:71–82.
Carlson, A.C. March 1986. Vanishing children: The new home economics.
    Indianapolis Business Journal. (p. 7a)
Caudill, W., and Weinstein, H. 1969. Maternal care and infant behavior in
    Japan and America. *Psychiatry* 32:12–43.
Cochran, M. M., and Brassard, J. A. 1979. Child development and personal
    social networks. *Child Development* 50:601–16.
Conger, J. J. 1988. Hostages to fortune: Youth, values, and the public interest.
    American Psychologist 43:291–300.
Diamond, M. (with J. Hopson). 1984. A love affair and the brain. *Psychology
    Today* 18:62–73.
Garbarino, J. 1975. A note on the effects of TV viewing. *Influences on human
    development.* 2nd ed., Ed. U. Bronfenbrenner and M. A. Mahoney. Hins-
    dale, Ill.: Dryden Press.
Gollin, E. S. 1981. Development and plasticity. *Developmental plasticity:
    Behavioral and biological aspects of variations in development.* Ed. E. S.
    Gollin. New York: Academic Press.
Gottlieb, G. 1983. The psychobiological approach to developmental issues.
    Handbook of child psychology. 4th ed., vol. 2, ed. P. H. Mussen. New
    York: Wiley.
Greenough, W. T.; Black, J. E.; and Wallace, C. S. 1987. Experience and brain
    development. *Child Development* 58:539–59.
Hernandez, D. J., and Meyers, D. E. 1986. *Children and their extended
    families since World War II.* Paper presented at the meeting of the Pop-
    ulation Association of America, April, 1986, San Francisco.
Hodgkinson, H. L.; Mirga, T.; Smith, T. E.; Trimbach, J.; and Quinn, S. 1986.
    There they come, ready or not. *Education Week, 5,* 13–37.
Hoffman, L. W 1984). Work, family, and the socialization of the child. *Review
    of child development research.* Ed. R. D. Parke. Vol. 7, *The family.* Chi-
    cago: University of Chicago Press.

Kaas, J. H. 1987. The organization of neocortex in mammals: Implications for theories of brain function. *Annual Review of Psychology* 8:129–51.

Kagan, J.; Klein, R. E.; Finley, G. E.; Rogoff, B.; and Nolan, E. 1979. A cross cultural study of cognitive development. *Monographs of the Society for Research in Child Development* 44(181):5.

Kretch, D. 1972. Psychoneurobiochemeducation. *Exploring human development.* Ed. H. W. Bernard and W. C. Huckins. Boston: Allyn & Bacon.

Masnick, G., and Bane, M. J. 1980. *The nation's families: 1960–1990.* Boston: Auburn House Publishing Co.

Mueller, J. D. 1976. *Families of the eighties.* New York: Wiley.

National Commission on Excellence in Education. 1983. *A nation at risk: The imperative for educational reform.* Washington, D.C.: U.S. Government Printing Office.

Norton, A. J., and Glick, P. C. 1986. One parent families: A social and economic profile. *Family Relations* 35:9–17.

Norton, A. J., and Moorman, J. E. April 1986. *Marriage and divorce patterns of U.S. women.* Paper presented at the meeting of the Population Association of America, San Francisco.

Ogbu, J. U. 1981. Origins of human competence: A cultural-ecological perspective. *Child Development* 52:413–29.

Oyama, S. 1985. *The ontogeny of information.* New York: Cambridge University Press.

Penfield, W. 1972. The uncommitted cortex, the child's changing brain. *Exploring human development.* Ed. H. W. Bernard and W. C. Huckins. Boston: Allyn & Bacon.

Pick, J. L., Jr. Summer, 1975. Cultural differences in perception. *Newsletter of the Society for Research in Child Development.* pp. 2–3, 12.

Pribram, K. H. 1986. "Holism" could close cognition era. *APA Monitor* 16:6–7, 28.

Rebelsky, F., and Abeles, G. March 1969. *Infancy in Holland and the United States.* Paper presented at the meeting of the Society for Research in Child Development, Santa Monica.

Rosenzweig, M. R., and Bennett, E. L. 1978. Experimental influences on brain antomy and brain chemistry in rodents. *Studies on the development of behavior and the nervous system.* Ed. G. Gottlieb. Vol. 4, *Early influences.* New York: Academic Press.

Scott, M. M. April 1987. *Theory in development: A synthesis for the 1980s.* Paper presented at the meeting of the Society for Research in Child Development, Baltimore.

Tulkin, S. R. 1972. An analysis of the concept of cultural deprivation. *Developmental Psychology* 6:326–39.

ACTIVE AFFECTIVE LEARNING FOR ACCELERATED
SCHOOLS

Robert B. Richardson

PREFACE

One of the golden rules for the practice of Accelerated Learning, according to Georgi Lozanov (1978), has been to maintain an up-beat classroom presentation at all times. The power of suggestion is such that dwelling
upon the mistakes of the past in order to avoid repeating them will tend
to produce outcomes consistent with whatever was dwelled upon; that is,
the mistakes themselves will tend to be repeated. Instead of spending teaching time talking about what *not* to do, more efficient use of the teacher's
time would require him or her to present a simple, well-prepared program
of suggestions for *doing* things, and then to proceed to *do* them with the
students. In other words, and to repeat the first three lines of a song popular
in the 1940s, "Accentuate the positive, / Eliminate the negative, / Latch onto
the affirmative . . ." In keeping with the spirit of Accelerated Learning and
the conditions necessary for its implementation, this paper will not present
analyses of present and/or past errors but rather will attempt to make a
contribution to laying the groundwork for Active Affective Learning (and
Teaching!) adapted to the needs of students served by the Accelerated
Schools Movement.

Consistent with the principles of Accelerated Learning, then, we will do
our best to practice what we teach. We will make it one of our goals to
maintain a consistency and coherence between the form and content of

this paper on the one hand, and the practice we are advocating on the other hand. Accelerated Learning accentuates the positive, the ongoing, and the forward looking and moving at all times. We intend the tone and thrust of this paper to embody these same principles.

WHY EMPHASIZE AFFECTIVE LEARNING?

In their efforts to render the learning process more effective, rapid, and interesting for the learner, Lozanov and those working with him and his ideas in the Accelerated Learning movement have placed more emphasis on environmental and other affective aspects of the learning process than on the cognitive side (see references). While the cognitive side has not been abandoned, and in fact receives considerable attention, by far the most innovative features of Accelerated Learning have more to do with affective considerations than with the cognitive. It is significant that the British professional society for the development of Accelerated Learning in Great Britain is called SEAL (Society for Effective Affective Learning), while its American counterpart is called SALT (Society for Accelerative Learning and Teaching). The two societies work hand in hand, cooperate extensively, and have very similar policies. The goals stressed by both societies lie in the domain of more efficient and effective use of learning time, while the means proposed for attaining these goals, that is, policy changes in relation to traditional teaching/learning situations, mainly involve modifications to the affective components of the learning process.

In the past, whenever modifications to learning schema were under consideration, most attention was given to reformulating and refining cognitive aspects and approaches to the learning process. Since little attention had been paid to the affective components, this area seemed ripe for exploration and exploitation in efforts to increase the efficiency of teaching/learning techniques. Lozanov's argument is to make use of the unused 90 percent of human learning potential. According to the whole-brain approach to learning, the right hemisphere of the brain specializes in affective-intuitive-holistic functions. Combining these three points would seem to indicate rich possibilities in the realm of affective approaches to learning.

WHAT IS AFFECTIVE LEARNING?

Assuming that there is sufficient consensus on the meaning of "learning" among those who will read this paper, we may go on to specify that learning is affective whenever its means or its ends, its causes or its effects, lie in the domain of emotions, feelings, and/or intuition. Affective learning may thus be contrasted with cognitive learning, which implies analytical, verbal, and linear approaches and processes. We can now go on to say that if we accept this definition, all learning is affective. Emotions, feelings, and/or intuition are involved in every act of learning. No one is indifferent to what he or she learns, nor to how it is learned, and of course the bottom line is that even when the learning seems essentially cognitive in nature, people react emotionally, with feeling, and perhaps even with intuition to those very cognitive aspects of learning at some stage of the process.

A very important point is that affective reactions to learning and learning situations may either reinforce the process or inhibit it; in extremely negative cases, such reactions may totally impede the process. Certainly if you feel good about learning something, you will tend to learn it faster and better than if you engage in that particular learning task full of doubts and fears, or even if you feel generally uncomfortable about it. On the other hand, if, for example, you feel confident, at ease, and can readily assume your favorite position while learning, your chances for a successful outcome will be much greater. This may seem obvious at first glance, but a little observation and thought about the relatively little attention accorded to the affective side of learning in schools points to the need for focusing on this aspect of learning design, especially where disadvantaged students are concerned.

"DISADVANTAGED" STUDENTS = "AT-RISK" STUDENTS

"Disadvantaged" children can take particlar advantage of affective learning techniques, especially in the context of the Accelerated School. As we will see more fully in the following sections, mobilizing and properly channeling the affective learning potential of these children is probably one of the most fertile areas to be explored and exploited in the quest for the unused 90 percent of human learning potential. At the same time, a very important affective factor is holding back the vast majority of these students; the factor in question is their own negative self-image, at least insofar as learning is concerned. For most of them, school has been a series of failure experiences, producing low-level or even negative expectations. Part of the job of the Accelerated School is to rebuild the self-image and self-esteem of these students using affectively oriented techniques that will make them feel good, important, and capable of learning. These techniques will be treated more fully in a later section.

At the present time, children whose families and neighborhoods are considered to be culturally and/or economically "disadvantaged" will be "at risk" as students (Levin, 1986). This approximately 30 percent of the nation's children will be subject to hold-backs and early dropouts. As Levin points out, this represents a wholesale waste of the nation's people-potential; not only are we failing to exploit a tremendous potential in brain-power, but, moreover, these people will tend to become clients of tax-supported social services.

What is it about these children that makes them such poor candidates for the learning that schools propose?

Their home life is characterized by the lack of many elements that contemporary school programs take for granted as belonging to the cultural baggage of people in general and to entering elementary school students in particular.

Their attitudes toward language and social exchange represent points of view far different from those that are expected in the classroom. Consider playfulness, for example. Middle-class children tend to play in socially recognizable ways, with all sort of things, including language. However, for the average disadvantaged family, language is for saying things, important things, things that are vital to communicate. When children from such families do play with language, teachers may not recognize that this is what is going on. They may label such activity as mistakes or as attempts to communicate "unacceptable" ideas in "unacceptable" forms. Thus, in kindergarten or first grade, for example, when the teacher asks a question, the answer to which he or she obviously knows, a disadvantaged child may tend to feel that there is something strange or bizarre in such a question that has no point; or perhaps the child will feel that he or she has not understood what it was that the teacher wanted.

Due to cultural and/or economic differences, such a student may not be familiar with, or perhaps not even be aware of, the existence of objects that are considered by our school programs to be familiar to everyone.

Since these disadvantaged students do not possess the prerequisite "baggage" on which the school builds its learning programs, they have trouble answering questions, are rapidly cataloged as "dull," and as time goes by, they fail to understand and therefore fail to remember those concepts and ideas that depend on the assumed entry-level knowledge. Thus they rapidly experience an ever-widening gap between their own achievement levels and those levels expected of children at their age/grade level. These children quickly come to feel that school is a painful experience.

LOZANOV AND SUGGESTOPEDIA

Experience, as well as research, indicates that the affective context within which cognitive teaching strategies are placed, as well as the use of classroom strategies that are affective in nature, can produce significant increases in projected learning outcomes. Herein lies part of the immense contribution Lozanov (1978) made to the field of education. The Bulgarian psychiatrist's two-tiered theory of suggestion: Suggestology, a general theory of suggestion, followed by Suggestopedy,[1] the application of Suggestology to the field of education, proposes that appropriate use of suggestion can create an affective background conducive to more efficient learning, as well as providing a pedagogical framework that is both highly flexible and highly precise about means for adapting to the diverse individuals and constantly varying situations that a teacher must be able to deal with. Suggestopedia may be combined with other compatible approaches to learning as research supplies us with new data and techniques.

WHOLE-BRAIN APPROACH

A case in point is a result of recent research on the functioning of the human brain, which has revealed functional specializations between the right and left hemispheres. The left hemisphere has been shown to process information in a linear, analytical, verbal, cognitive manner, while the right hemisphere handles intuitive, interactive, holistic, affective thought[2] (Ornstein, 1972). Furthermore, both hemispheres show electrical activity while the individual is engaged in learning processes (Hand, 1984a).

Traditionally, teaching has addressed left hemisphere functions almost exclusively, while seemingly ignoring needs of, and functions appropriate to, the right hemisphere. Lessons taught have been judged on the basis of their linear progression from fact to fact, or point to point, the appropriateness of their language, and the logic of their demonstrations. On the other hand, comparatively little attention has been accorded to making lessons attractive and appealing, making them satisfying to the intuitive mind, taking the "big picture" approach, or presenting them in both emotionally and physically pleasing surroundings.

In general, teaching in such a way as to mobilize the entire range of brain functions, from analytical to holistic, will not only promote more efficient traditional-style learning, but also will help provide affective satisfaction and increased learning outcomes for those children whose learning style is more intuitive and holistic than analytical and verbal. At the same time, attention must be given to suggesting and creating a positive affective atmosphere. Some of the affective techniques for insuring an atmosphere consistent with maximum learning potential will now be discussed.

CREATING A POSITIVE AFFECTIVE ATMOSPHERE

Physical Surroundings

The unconscious, suggestive, affective influence of the environment, especially the immediate physical surroundings, cannot be overemphasized. We often tolerate conditions in our schools that we would find totally unacceptable in our homes. Associating intolerable environmental conditions with learning activities does not seem to be the most consistent or effective means of promoting success in the latter.

Perhaps even more important, since much of learning is based on associative processes, as the environmental elements surrounding learning become more pleasing, captivating, and varied, so the learning itself will be quantitatively greater, more enduring in memory, and more rapidly achieved. Treated on this basis, school expenditures for fresh paint, wall-to-wall carpeting, comfortable chairs, etc., represent money spent on the learning process itself rather than simply providing for building maintenance or perhaps even unnecessary frills. Such expenditures may be considered in the same light as they are in the world of business, that is, as necessary for the successful achievement of goals, outcomes, and productivity.

As a practical, right-hemisphere approach to grasping the power and influence of affective elements in our surroundings, just sit back for a moment, relax, and call to mind the image of a classroom. Then contrast this image with that of a living room. Hold the two images side by side long enough to decide which one you prefer. Would you feel just as comfortable in either one? Would you voluntarily go into either one of the rooms for enjoyment? Or would one take precedence over the other?

A physically attractive and comfortable classroom will help the students feel at ease and will enhance their appreciation of the here and now, as well as serving as background for appropriately suggestive teaching aids. A carpet on the floor can do wonders towards warming up a formerly cold, hard, angular atmosphere. Walls and ceilings painted in stimulating shades and colors; furniture that is designed to be comfortable, adjustable, and movable; use of cloth, pillows, cushions, etc., to break up long expanses of metal, plaster, glass, or wood: All of these and other, similar techniques can turn any room into a homelike space for living—and learning. In addition, cloth, carpets, panels, etc., help soften the effects of classroom and exterior noises, thus reducing stress. Potted plants and flowers add a sense of life to any room.

Cushions, carpets, pillows, cloth, etc., also help fill the needs of some students' individual learning styles. Studies in this area (Dunn & Dunn, 1978) show that students vary widely concerning the body positions they find most conducive to learning; Some learn best sitting straight up in a straight-back chair, both feet flat on the floor and both hands on the table. Others find sitting on the floor most conducive to learning, while still others function best from a "Roman banquet slouch" position. The classroom that can comfortably integrate a wide variety of body positions will best promote the joy of learning.

Movement and change of position may be essential for some students' learning styles, and once again, the more a student feels at ease, the more and better he or she will achieve. In general, the more flexible the elements in the classroom, the easier it will be to adapt to individual needs, thereby increasing the potential learning output.

Finally, as a general rule, converting a classroom into a "living room" will go a long way to change boredom and cramps into interest and joy. Where funding is difficult to obtain, or even unobtainable, students and parents can be mobilized to supply materials and labor; this solution carries the added advantage of involving both parents and students in the classroom improvement project—and may often be preferable to a package deal because of the positive effects of this additional involvement.

The walls, ceiling, floors, and furniture can also be used as a background for posters, wall charts, pictures, geographical maps, concept maps, word cards, or other elements that can serve as both direct and peripheral teaching aids. Hopefully, a student who looks around the room will not only have a pleasant experience, but his gaze will also constantly encounter objects that suggest and/or reinforce lesson subject matter.

The disadvantaged student is particularly in need of physical surroundings that suggest a new approach to school and learning. Making an effort to help such a student feel at home is especially important, since he or she is less prepared both emotionally and intellectually for the activities and experiences encountered at school.

Self-Esteem

In order to feel good about learning, you need to start by feeling good about yourself. Self-esteem constitutes a vital prerequisite to the success of any personal activity or project. It is a necessary element for successful living, and is the focal point of numerous psychotherapy programs.

The importance of building self-esteem in children is illustrated by the inspiring Christmas story *The Little Engine That Could*. In addition to the beauty of the story and the intriguing plot, it carries a powerful moral: No matter how small you are, nor how large the job may seem, believing that you will succeed, and following through with appropriate action, will insure a successful outcome. While the message contained in this story is valuable for all children, it contains a vital message for the disadvantaged: You *can* do it (learn); all you need to do is to firmly believe you can.

Self-esteem is at the heart of the advice that Dr. Norman Vincent Peale[3] has spent a lifetime transmitting to the public through speeches, books, and demonstration workshops. Dr. Peale talks about positive thinking and what a powerful mover it is. And to think positively, one must first be positive about oneself.

One very effective means of promoting self-esteem involves recognizing, satisfying, and taking advantage of whatever is unique and individual in each and every student. Birthdays, for example, can be used as a pretext for sharing personal ambitions. Children who speak another language can be called upon to give a sort vocabulary lesson each week—their self-esteem is boosted by playing the teacher's role, and through realizing that their own language is interesting to and valued by the teacher and other students. In the same way, holidays corresponding to students' cultural origins may be celebrated with the help of appropriate students: Cinco de Mayo, Chinese New Year, Tet, Mardi Gras, etc. Parents can bring in food or other interesting things associated with these holidays as part of the parent-involvement programs.

Another technique for promoting self-esteem consists of determining the components of each student's learning style, and then taking appropriate measures to satisfy the needs that correspond to these styles. Dunn and Dunn (1978) have developed a questionnaire that rapidly identifies critical aspects of learning styles. They also point out innovative techniques for organization and layout of classrooms in which the needs of all individual learning styles can be satisfied. All children can learn and can learn rapidly as well; we, as teachers and other interested adults, need to demonstrate our caring for them as unique individuals, since part of growing up involves seeking just this type of recognition. This recognition is also one of the principal keys to insuring that *every* student will successfully complete his or her lessons.

Nothing boosts a student's self-esteem in school more than showing that he or she knows something interesting, something that the teacher values and that the other students will be called upon to use. No student comes to school with a completely blank brain—every student can contribute something to classwork, thus helping build the student's self-esteem. Robert Calfee[4] and his associates in Project Read at Stanford University have developed techniques for teaching vocabulary that satisfy these criteria; the concept to be "expanded" is written on the chalkboard, and students are called upon to tell or describe whatever the concept brings to mind. As the students volunteer words or phrases, the teacher writes them on the chalkboard around the central concept. The teacher groups the words volunteered by the students according to categories, but without naming them. When a sufficient number of new words have been generated, the teacher asks the class why the words were grouped in this way. The category headings given by the students are added to the chalkboard. The chart thus generated by the students becomes basis for further work on vocabulary. Since the students themselves have created this base, they feel an affective involvement in the lesson based on elements taken from their own experience and knowledge.

In general, all children bring a wealth of experience with them into the classroom. Since they have lived and assumed these experiences, the experiences have taken on a positive emotional charge, and to a certain extent have become an integral part of the child. Acceptance of the child as he or she is constitutes the first and basic step towards helping a child maintain and/or create his or her own self-esteem. Thus, if we want to build children's self-esteem, we need to accept *all* experience the child brings along. The teacher's job here is to draw on the students' experiential baggage sufficiently to indicate to the students that their previous knowledge is acceptable, useful, and valued. Of course, in some cases the teacher will need to explain appropriate and inappropriate circumstances for certain words, phrases, or experiences that may be volunteered.

Student Behavior

Any student behavior, no matter how disruptive, outlandish, strange, or otherwise unacceptable, needs to be considered as an appropriate response to someone, something, or some event. By accepting behavior on this basis, the student maintains his or her integrity in the classroom and his or her self-esteem. The student's behavior may need some modification, but any approach to this problem needs to maintain the student as an integral, contributing, and valued member of the class.

Expectations and Outcomes

Closely related to the effects of self-esteem are those of the expectations we have concerning the performances of others. Robert Rosenthal and Lenore Jacobson's study (1968) of self-fulfilling prophecies in the classroom illustrates how important it is for a teacher to hold high expectations concerning all students. Teachers' expectations were shown to be a significant factor in determining outcomes for students.

At the beginning of the school year, Rosenthal and Jacobson, for experimental purposes, arbitrarily identified certain students as showing high academic promise; this information was then communicated to the students' teachers. In fact, these students were chosen on the basis of a random sampling; their educational aptitudes and past performances were widely varied. At the end of the year, the outstanding achievers in those classes were those students whose teachers had believed that they would be successful by virtue of their unfounded identification as "promising." The teachers' expectation of success was a significant factor in determining how well students performed academically.

What happens, though, when teachers are informed, or become aware, that certain students are culturally disadvantaged, economically disadvantaged, or otherwise at risk academically? Statistically, these students are identified as potential low achievers, have difficulty keeping up with classroom work, and have a high probability of falling behind and sooner or later dropping out. Whereas these statistical tendencies are undeniable, there is nothing inevitable about them, provided appropriate measures are taken. When teachers and parents hold high expectations for their students and children, the chances for successful outcomes are dramatically increased.

With disadvantaged students, high expectations are necessary for high levels of achievement. Other techniques can be used to reassure these students of their own value, build their academic self-confidence, and create a climate conducive to satisfactory achievement levels for all.

Goals and Outcomes

Setting goals is a vital and necessary first step in obtaining outcomes. The manner in which these goals are set, however, can be critical in determining whether outcomes will correspond to goals set for the entire class.

Academic achievement goals are most often externally imposed upon teachers and students alike, at least as far as the achievement necessary to successfully complete a given academic level and progress to the next level. When such goals are perceived as predetermined by someone else (such as the State Department of Education), motivation remains essentially on the extrinsic level. In other words, what motivates the students to work toward these goals has little or nothing to do with their own personal ambitions, preferences, and choices in life. Whatever the motivation is, it has been imposed from the outside.

While extrinsic motivation may indeed promote learning, intrinsic motivation (see Martinez, 1987) will produce the most satisfying and lasting experiences for the student, which are integrated into his or her own knowledge, values, and goals in life.

Setting classroom goals in such a way that students become intrinsically motivated to accomplish them takes a little extra time and effort. However, this initial investment will reap very rewarding dividends. Affectively, for example, the joy of learning something that is full of personal significance and meaning for everyone in the class presents a contrast with the task of learning something that someone else has decided needs to be learned. That other person or group may offer extrinsic motivation in the form of good grades or money for a learning job well done, but the effect will never be the same as in those cases where the material to be learned has become personally meaningful to each and every student.

Setting goals for maximum affective enjoyment and personal satisfaction for each student starts with a general discussion about the suggested goal. During this discussion, all points of view, whether favorable or unfavorable toward adopting the given goal, are listened to and thoroughly explored. Then each student is called upon to discuss in what way the proposed goal might fit in with his or her other experiences, goals, and ambitions in life. Discussions about long-term goals, such as for the academic year, semester, or quarter, may well extend beyond one class period and will often provide anchoring points for the subject matter to be learned later. These anchoring points will be pertinent to individual students' past experiences, to their present lives, and to future goals, and will help provide personalized intrinsic motivation.

So far, we have been, implicitly at least, talking about long-term goals. In addition, being affectively effective in the classroom requires attention to short-term goals. When dealing with younger children, and also, as Prichard and Taylor (1980, p. 48) point out, with disadvantaged children, educators must provide short-term, even daily, gratifications. I myself have found that immediate gratification is highly appreciated by all ages and types of students, and very helpful in stimulating them over the long haul.

In order to take full advantage of gratifications, these need to be coordinated with goal fulfillment. Daily moments of gratification for successful goal fulfillment can add considerable warmth, joy, and a sense of caring to the classroom.

But perhaps most important, goals must be set in ways that are challenging and that help insure that everyone can and will (if at all possible) succeed in fulfilling them. One great advantage to short-term goals is that achievement seems easier, and certainly is more imminent, than in the case of long-term goals. The cumulative effect of successes at short-term goals will gradually make the long-term goals seem more attainable, thus increasing levels of enthusiasm and achievement in the classroom. Whenever possible, success in goal fulfillment should be rewarded in ways that go beyond the extrinsic values of grades, money, or other material rewards. Adding points to the total number necessary for holding a special class event would be an example of an intrinsically oriented reward for individual goal achievement (we are, of course, assuming that the class event has been profoundly internalized and desired by all members of the class).

Short-term goals are especially important when teaching "disadvantaged" children. As Prichard and Taylor (1980, p. 48) point out, these students intensely feel the need for immediate gratification. Delayed gratification is very difficult for them—they are hungry for success, and need to be told regularly that they are doing very well. Setting short-term goals, and providing the support and organizational stimulation to insure that all students succeed, is one of the affective keys to successful accelerated learning.

It is often necessary to organize for and set short-term goals in such a manner that they will be fulfilled on the same day they are set. One of the major problems facing teachers and administrators in classroom organization and lesson planning in disadvantaged areas is crystallized in the high rate of absenteeism typical at schools in these neighborhoods. Whenever possible, units of work, or lessons—the basis for short-term goals—would best be chunked in such a way as to be completed within one school day, or one class period. A child's absence will then tend to interfere only with work done on the day or days of his or her absence. Unfinished lessons will be less likely to be left dangling, and the positive affective reinforcements associated with successful goal completion will be more numerous.

Hopefully, as the Accelerated School continues to function through time, this phenomenon of immediate gratification to students for well-learned lessons will become a factor, in and of itself, in reducing absenteeism among disadvantaged students.

Constant goal achievement and constant success will do wonders to build

the students' self-esteem. It has been said that "Nothing succeeds like success!"

Competition

Everybody enjoys winning, but the rules of competition involve losing
as well; some win and some lose. Both outcomes produce affects. Seemingly,
for the winners there is no problem they are affectively stimulated to
continue striving forward. But what about the inevitable losers?

Perhaps the most important consideration for the teacher is the preser-
vation of a satisfactory equilibrium between wins and losses by each individual in the class.

Glasser (1986) points out that by organizing students into teams, and
then having the teams rather than the individuals compete, management
of this equilibrium is greatly facilitated. By redistributing the "stronger"
and the "weaker" members of the class among the various teams, even
those children who might never have won in an individual competition will
from time to time learn what winning feels like by belonging to a winning
team. Reciprocally, and equally important, the stronger members of the
class will have their opportunity to learn how to affectively experience and
assume the consequences of what appears to be a losing situation.

"Right" and "Wrong" Answers

In much the same way that we consider all behavior to be appropriate,
the opposition between "right" and "wrong" answers needs to be thought
through in the context of affectively positive learning. What happens, in
fact, when someone tells you that you are WRONG? Suppose, in addition,
that this person stands in a position of authority in relation to you. The
resulting experience will certainly not be pleasant, especially if this experience tends to be repeated on a daily basis. Such is most often the case
for the disadvantaged child at school. Arriving at school unequipped with
a large part of the cultural baggage that most schools assume as prerequisites
to classroom work, they frequently do not understand the meanings of
words, phrases, and sentences the teacher is using. Sometimes they even
do not understand that one can ask a question to test for knowledge (understanding this is a culturally marked phenomenon!).

On the other hand, children who are accustomed to playing with language
(another, but different, culturally marked phenomenon) have no trouble
situating the significance of the didactic question. But not all children grow
up hearing puns and making them, playing Scrabble, having their parents
test them for knowledge, etc.

Of course, whenever a student produces a wrong answer, we cannot
pretend that the answer is right. Exploring the wrong answer, however, can

lead to a deeper understanding of the subject matter if handled diplomatically. If students produced only right answers, there would be little need to employ teachers! So-called wrong answers, as well as all other responses, provide valuable feedback to the teacher; the student who is not afraid to risk giving a wrong answer will, in the end, obtain the necessary information to modify his or her response. Students' responses tell the teacher how well he or she is teaching, as well as how well the students are learning. Since the Accelerated School is success oriented, a wrong answer will be like a red flag signaling a system failure. The teacher's first job in this situation will be to ascertain why the wrong answer was given, and what led the student to provide that answer.

In short, working through a wrong answer in an effort to determine the causes for its being wrong, and then going on to restructure the lesson in such a way that the right answer becomes obvious can provide invaluable supplemental information to both teacher and students. In any event, such handling prevents hurting a student's pride on one hand, and may also lead to the realization that wrong answers often provide richer and more interesting information than right answers.

Individual Learning Styles and Individual Students

Students have been shown to vary widely in their individual Learning Styles. "Learning Style" is the term Dunn and Dunn (1978) use to designate the set of significant conditions under which a student will learn most effectively. These conditions are expressed as preferences by the students, and have been found to exert an influence on learning outcomes. The authors have identified 18 significant variables, or elements, of Individual Learning Styles; these variables (elements) may be grouped into 4 categories as follows:

1. Environmental Elements: Sound, Light, Temperature, Design (i.e., formal or informal setting). Some of these elements were mentioned earlier in connection with physical surroundings.
2. Emotional Elements: Motivation, Persistence, Responsibility, Structure.
3. Sociological Elements: Peers, Self, Pair, Team, Adult, Varied.
4. Physical Elements: Perception, Intake, Time, Mobility.

Satisfaction of, or denial of, an individual's Learning Style, or even of a small number of its constituent elements, will tend to cause correlative variations in learning outcomes, according to studies carried out by the authors.

Perhaps even more important for the present study are potential effects on the teacher-pupil relationships within a classroom.

A diagnostic instrument, the Learning Style Inventory (LSI) can be administered to students at the outset of a school year. Without going into the details concerning how the evaluations of each individual student are carried out, the simple fact of making an extensive inquiry into the learning preferences of each student acts to crystallize a specific relationship between each student and the teacher. Each student has evidence before his or her eyes that the teacher is interested in reaching him or her as an individual. As the teacher implements the various elements necessary to provide a teaching style that is consistent with the student's learning style, student-teacher confidence increases on the affective level, and later, positive outcomes on the cognitive level reinforce the affective confidence bond.

Dunn and Dunn not only provide an instrument for analyzing Learning Styles, but follow through to provide specific implementation for the various Learning Style needs that are identified by their instrument. Space does not permit a full description here of their contribution. It does appear to be an outstanding approach to solving the daily dilemma of addressing individual needs within a collective setting, and for providing the basis for a sound and positive teacher-student relationship.

Affective Aspects of Lozanov's Design for the Accelerated Lesson

As mentioned earlier, the innovative emphasis in Accelerated Learning has been placed largely on the affective aspects of learning. Lozanov presents a lesson design conceived to mobilize as much as possible of the unused 90 percent of human learning potential. As we run through the lesson design, its affective aspects will be highlighted.

As students arrive in the classroom, music is playing over the stereo system. The selections have been chosen in order to create a specific, previously identified, mood. For example, if the teacher wants to begin a lesson with the students feeling relaxed, music designed to induce relaxation will be played.

When the teacher enters the classroom to begin the lesson, his or her mastery of the subject matter and general self-confidence generate a feeling of confidence. The teacher behaves in such a way that the students know they can have confidence in him or her. When the teacher stops the music, the class is automatically advised that the lesson is about to begin.

The lesson itself begins with the "decoding" phase, in which the teacher familiarizes the students with the lesson material, explaining, illustrating, and furnishing examples as needed. The students are free to ask any questions, and the teacher proceeds to the next phase only when the students feel comfortable with the new material.

Next comes the "Concert 1" phase. The teacher reads the lesson material accompanied by classical music played over the stereo system. The music is chosen for its expressive qualities from movements by classical composers such as Mozart or Beethoven. The teacher's reading is dramatically expressive, and meanings are underlined through gestures, voice intonation, and other theatrical techniques.

The "Concert 2" phase follows. The teacher induces a state of relaxation similar to that experienced just before falling asleep. Baroque music—especially adagio movements rhythmed at 60 beats per minute—is played as the teacher reads the lesson material once again, this time rhythmed not only with the music but also with heartbeat and respiratory rates.

"Concert 2" must necessarily be followed immediately by a break, at least an hour long, to allow memory functions to integrate the input from this half awake, half asleep phase. In practice, "Concert 2" can be scheduled to end at lunch time or at the end of the school day.

Once the break is over, the "activation phase" begins. The teacher actively mobilizes the class to use the material learned during the previous lesson phases. Students play games, sing songs, and participate in role playing, mime, or any other active device that enables them to use the material they have just been learning in appropriate contexts taken from the lesson material.

In a final phase, the "reactivation phase," the material learned in the lesson is actively exploited once again, but this time in new contexts and new situations not covered in the lesson itself. All the activities of the activation and reactivation phases are designed to completely capture the interests of the students. No one is bored; everyone is active and interested in the activities, which not only drive home the elements of the lesson, but are also fun to do in and of themselves.

CONCLUSION

This presentation has provided a representative rather than exhaustive presentation of the affective side of learning and teaching applicable to the Accelerated School. Even with all the resources listed in the references, we still do not have an exhaustive list. In fact, much of what is affective in learning and teaching is specific to the individuals involved. Each student has a different relationship with the teacher, and each class reacts differently as a group. Lozanov was partly referring to this phenomenon of ever-changing relational uniqueness when he said that there is no such thing as affective teaching; there are only affective teachers.

The Accelerated School teacher will need to mobilize as much competence as possible in affective learning techniques, especially since the students come from disadvantaged backgrounds. The most beautiful and rewarding part of mastering and using these techniques is that one is constantly finding new techniques for making a class feel good about learning, about working together, and about living. Each successful Accelerated

School teacher will quickly be able to become a mentor teacher specializing in affective learning techniques.

There is an intimate relation between affective and cognitive learning techniques. In a future paper, the cognitive side will be developed in ways appropriate to the Accelerated School.

NOTES

1. More commonly written and pronounced "Suggestopedia" in the West. "Suggestopedy" is a phonetic transcription of the Bulgarian term coined by Lozanov. The final "y" gave it a typically Bulgarian or Russian consonance, somewhat strange to Western ears and eyes. Very quickly, the term "Suggestopedia," more in harmony with Western usage, supplanted the earlier term.

2. Hemispheric specialization as described here holds true for all right-handed individuals and many left-handed people. However, some left-handed individuals manifest a reversal of the more typical right/left polarization.

3. Norman Vincent Peale, noted author and lecturer. His most famous theme and title was *The Power of Positive Thinking*. The Center for Positive Thinking, P.O. Box 1000, Pawling, NY, 12564, has released a new condensed edition of *The Power of Positive Thinking* (1987).

4. Robert C. Calfee and his associates are compiling a volume entitled *The Book*, based on results of research carried out both at Stanford University and in the school districts practicing Calfee's innovative approaches to reading.

REFERENCES

Bandler, R. 1985. *Using your brain—for a change*. Moab, Utah: Real People Press.

Bandler, R. and Grinder, J. 1979. *Frogs into princes*. Moab, Utah: Real People Press.

Bandura, A., and Schunk, D. 1981. Cultivating competence, self-efficacy, and intrinsic interest through proximal self-motivation. *Journal of Personality and Social Psycholoy* 41(3):586–98.

Bateson, G. 1979. *Mind and nature: A necessary unity*. New York: E. P. Dutton.

Calfee, R. C. 1981–86. *The book*. Unpublished research report, Stanford University.

Caskey, O. L. 1980. *Suggestive-accelerative learning and teaching*. Englewood Cliffs, N.J.: Educational Technology Publications.

Cleveland, B. F. 1984. *Master teaching techniques*. Muskego, Wis.: Connecting Link Press.

Datta, B. April 29, 1987. Building self-esteem in small steps. *Palo Alto Weekly*, 30–31.

Dunn, R., and Dunn, K. 1978. *Teaching students through their individual learning styles: A practical approach.* Reston, Va.: Reston Publishing Co.

Fox, B. 1980. Remedial programs: Some strategies for creating a supportive learning environment. *Reading Horizons* 20(2):147–49.

Gerler, E. R., Jr. 1980. Multimodal education: Affective education and beyond. *Humanist Educator* 18(4):162–68.

Glasser, W. 1965. *Reality therapy: A new approach to psychiatry.* New York: Harper & Row.

———. 1969. *Schools without failure.* New York: Harper & Row.

———. 1985. *Control theory.* New York: Harper & Row.

———. 1986. *Control theory in the classroom.* New York: Harper & Row.

Glickman, C. D. 1987. Good and/or effective schools: What do we want? *Phi Delta Kappan,* 68(8):622–24.

Gold, L. 1985. Suggestopedia: activating the student's reserve capacities. In *English Teaching Forum.* Washington, D.C.

Goodman, P. 1956. *Growing up absurd.* New York: Vintage College Books.

Grassi, J. R. 1985a. *The accelerated learning process in science.* Farmington, Mass.: ALPS Method.

———. 1985b. *An accelerated learning process.* Book 1, *System in mathematics: Introduction to geometry: A curriculum guide for elementary teachers.* Farmington, Mass.: ALPS Method.

Hand, J. D. 1984a. Split-brain theory and recent results in brain research: Implications for the design of instruction. INTUS *New/NUUS* 8(2):9–21. Reprinted from *Instructional development: The state of the art II.* Ed. Bass, R. K. and Dill, C. R. Dubuque, Iowa: Kendall-Hunt, 1984.

———. 1984b. Lozanov's method for study and brain functions (suggestopedia). *INTUS News/NUUS* 8(2):22.

Jacobson, S. 1983. *Meta-cation: Prescriptions for some ailing educational processes.* Cupertino, Calif.: Meta Publications.

Kline, P. 1985. Using suggestopedia to help disadvantaged children to learn. In *Proceedings of the First Internation Conference of SEAL.* Folkestone; SES Press.

Laborde, G. Z. 1984. *Influencing with integrity: Manage skills for communication and negotiation.* Palo Alto, Calif.: Syntony Publishing; Science & Behavior Books.

Labov, W. 1972. *Language in the inner city.* Philadelphia: University of Pennsylvania Press.

Lerede, J. 1980. *Suggerer pour apprendre.* Sillery, Quebec: Presse de l'Universite de Quebec.

Levin, H. M. 1986. *Educational reform for disadvantaged students: An emerging crisis.* West Haven, Conn.: National Education Association.

————. 1987. Accelerated schools for disadvantaged students. *Educational Leadership*, 44(6):19 21.

Lozanov, G. 1978. *Suggestology and outlines of suggestopedy*. New York: Gordon & Breach.

Lozanov, G. and Gateva. 1987. *A suggestopedic training manual for foreign language teachers*. New York: Gordon & Breach.

Maltz, M. 1966. *Psycho-cybernetics*. New York: Simon & Schuster.

Martinez, M. E. 1987. Components of intrinsically motivated learning. Unpublished research paper, Stanford University.

Noddings, N., and Shore, P. J. 1984. *Awakening the inner eye intuition in education*. New York: Teachers College Press.

Ornstein, R. 1972. *The psychology of consciousness*. San Francisco: W. H. Freeman & Co.

Ostrander, S., and Schroeder, L. 1979. *Superlearning*. York: Dell Publishing Co. (French translation, 1980. *Les fantastiques facultes du cerveau*)

Peale, N. V. 1987. *The power of positive thinking*. Pawling, N.Y.: Center for Positive Thinking.

Prichard, A., and Taylor, J. 1980. *Accelerating learning: The use of suggestion in the classroom*. Novato, Calif.: Academic Therapy Publications.

Richardson, R. B., et al. 1963. *Genuine English*. Accelerated English (ESL) for middle school. Paris: I.P.N.

————. 1977. (with Andezian, S., and Zirotti, J. P.). Les enfants des travailleurs immigres et leur parcours scolaire dans l'enseignement secondaire. *Le Groupe Familial*. No. 76:56–61.

————. 1978. *Le langage, la scolarisation et les milieux des enfants de deux milieux defavorises: Francais, et immigres Nord-Africains*. Unpublished doctoral dissertation, University of Paris X, Nanterre, France.

Rose, Colin. 1985. *Accelerated learning*. Great Misseden, Bucks., England: Topaz Publishing Ltd.

Rosenthal, R., and Jacobson, L. 1968. *Pygmalion in the classroom; teacher expectation and pupils' intellectual development*. New York: Holt, Rinehart & Winston.

Schmid, Charles. 1985. Some common denominators in accelerated learning for language and also non-language subjects. In *Proceedings of the first international conference of SEAL*. St. Louis, Mo.: Folkestone; SES Press.

Schuster, D., and Gritton, C. 1985. *Suggestive-accelerative learning techniques: Theory and applications*. The New SALT Manual. New York: Gordon & Breach.

Slavin, R. E. 1983. *Student Team Learning*. Washington, D.C.: National Education Association.

————. 1985. *Learning to cooperate, cooperating to learn*. New York: Plenum Press.

————. 1987. *Cooperative learning*. 2d ed. Washington, D.C.: National Education Association.

Smilansky, M., and Nevo, D. 1979. *The gifted disadvantaged: A longitudinal study of compensatory education in Israel.* New York: Gordon & Breach.

Sonnier, I. L. 1982. Holistic education: Teaching in the affective domain. *Education* 103(1):11–14.

Sproul, D. 1986. Guided imagery in the social studies. In *Practical ideas for teaching writing as a process.* California State Department of Education.

Taylor, J. 1984. The language of feelings: A program in affective education. *Momentum* 15(1):47–49.

Tyler, R. W. 1986. Changing concepts of educational evaluation. *International Journal of Educational Research* 10(1):1–113.

Van Nagel, C. 1985. *Megateaching and learning—Neuro-linguistic programming applied to education.* Vol. 1. Indian Rocks Beach, Fla.: Southern Institute Press.

Vitale, B. M. 1982. *Unicorns are real: A right-brained approach to learning.* Rolling Hills Estates, Calif.: Jalmar Press.

Whitmore, D. 1986. *Psychosynthesis in education: A guide to the joy of learning.* Wellingborough, Northamts., England: Turnstone Press, Ltd.

Williams, L. V. 1983. *Teaching for the two-sided mind: A guide to right brain/left brain education.* New York: Simon & Schuster.

READING INSTRUCTION IN THE ACCELERATED SCHOOL

Jim Barton

BACKGROUND

The Accelerated School, as conceived by Levin (1987), is a transitional elementary school created for a singular purpose—to bring disadvantaged students to grade-level performance by the end of the sixth grade. This boost will allow them to fully benefit from secondary education. The Accelerated School is designed to provide clear instructional goals, advanced learning strategies, meaningful student assessment, and an accelerated curriculum (Levin, 1987).

Because reading is a key learning and thinking tool, it should play a primary role in the Accelerated School. The purpose of a good reading program is to help youngsters become literate individuals who understand the conventions of thinking and communication (Calfee & Drum, 1984). Reading can facilitate thinking. If taught as a process of critical thought, reading can provide the analytical foundation for a lifetime of learning experiences.

An accelerated literacy curriculum requires that learners possess more than the ability to think at the literal level. Students must also learn to draw conclusions and communicate successfully with others about the relationships they find among ideas. Unfortunately, a disturbing pattern in contemporary test scores indicates that little progress is being made in teaching children to use critical thinking skills (Applebee, Langer, & Mullis, 1986). If a student can only "call" words and ferret only superficial meaning out of a text, the student will become intellectually lost in the mid- and upper

71

elementary grades. "Such students enter school with achievement levels that are below those of their non-disadvantaged counterparts, and the disparity in achievement grows over the schooling experience" (Levin, 1987, cf. p. 2, p. 2). Faced with this sense of helplessness, dropping out of school in later years becomes a very attractive option.

The sad fact that many elementary classroom environments are breeding grounds for dropouts is coupled with several other problems currently facing our public school system. First, many school-wide curriculums are so fragmented as to suggest that there is no plan at all. Students cannot be expected to learn with any degree of consistency when academic continuity between grade levels and among subject areas is lacking. Second, the materials for instruction provided to teachers are clearly inadequate. Schools are unlikely to foster informed curriculum decisions when teachers are bound to poorly written textbooks and standardized tests.

How to respond to these challenges? First, teachers can be furnished with the theoretical underpinning for understanding how to develop literate readers and thinkers. Next comes the training to translate these theories into practice in the areas of lesson planning, teaching and learning strategies, and text analysis. The end products are teachers who take charge of the learning process in their classrooms. Students are taught to think critically as part of the process of learning to read, and to gain the skills to share their thoughts with clarity. Teachers see the big curriculum picture, a vision that translates into continuity in lesson planning and consistent expectations of students. Textbook materials become resources for the discriminating teacher rather than a driving force for mediocre instruction. Finally, standardized test results are supplemented by more diagnostic forms of ongoing assessment.

The belief that teacher knowledge is *the* means of student change is the key premise behind the adoption of an accelerated literacy curriculum. Accordingly, the purpose of this paper is to inform the development of powerful teaching strategies for reading instruction at the elementary level. The balance of this document is organized into five major segments. The first section defines the components that make up reading instruction. The second section presents a conceptual background in language development and thinking skills. The third section discusses the implications of these theories for the instruction of "at-risk" students. The fourth section translates the theories into best practice, a theoretically based model of lesson planning for reading instruction. This exemplar offers strategies for developing critical readers. The fifth section closes the chapter with specific recommendations for the adoption of an accelerated literacy curriculum.

It must be stressed that this paper represents a point of departure for beginning to construct a reading program within the Accelerated School. It is most definitely not the final word on the subject of reading. Instead, it is intended to provide some thoughtful first words—a foundation for developing a reading program that creates literate individuals, literate in the fullest sense of the word.

COMPONENTS OF READING INSTRUCTION

Reading instruction can be grouped into three related components: decoding, vocabulary, and comprehension. Each component can be taught separately, but the true test of the proficient reader is the ability to integrate all three so that decoding and vocabulary automatically support the comprehension of material. The ultimate goal of reading is comprehension—without proficient decoding and vocabulary understanding, this goal is not reachable.

Decoding can be defined simply as "the skills and knowledge by which a reader translates printed words into speech..." (Calfee & Drum, 1984, p. 812). Phonics instruction fits squarely into the decoding component. In the past there has been much debate about how phonics should be taught and, in some cases, whether it should be taught at all. Some educators insist that phonics instruction is the key to proficient reading, while others claim that the dissection of words into their constituent sounds interferes with children's attempts to make meaning from text. After thirty years of debate there is substantial evidence pointing to the advantages of early phonics instruction (Calfee & Drum, 1984).

In their review of reading research, Calfee and Drum discuss some of the major issues concerning phonics instruction. First, although a prime difference between poor readers and proficient readers is more fluent decoding skills on the part of the proficient readers, "the advantage of phonics training is typically small, and many students continue to experience comprehension problems, especially in the later grades" (Calfee & Drum, 1984, p. 813). Phonics may help to provide a solid foundation for good reading, but it should not be the only component in beginning reading instruction. Teaching decoding skills in isolation from comprehension is a barrier to the acquisition of other reading skills.

"Reliance on rote drill and practice as the primary vehicle for decoding instruction is probably a mistake" (Calfee & Drum, 1984, p. 813). Rote drill and practice does not aid the reader in transferring skills to new reading situations. Furthermore, most of the drill and practice in classrooms occurs as independent seatwork in workbooks while the teacher is working with other students in a reading group. Anderson (1982) questions the learning outcomes of such practice when students lack any understanding of why they are doing the exercises.

Sensible phonics instruction should emphasize the morphophonemic nature of English spelling. The English spelling-sound system, although complex and somewhat idiosyncratic, contains more consistencies than inconsistencies. Contributions from the Anglo-Saxon, Romance, and Greek languages make up three basic layers of English. If phonics instruction is based on these layers, children will be able to grasp the consistent patterns and apply this knowledge as a tool in their reading and spelling.

The second major component of reading instruction is vocabulary development—knowing the meaning of words. Learning a word "is determined in part by how it is related to experiences of the reader and to other words in the text" (Calfee & Drum, 1984, p. 825). In addition, a word can be known at different levels. Whether a word is understood superficially or with subtlety is determined by the reader's ability to define and recognize its meaning in the context of a passage *and* the flexibility with which the word is used in conversation and writing. Research on vocabulary instruction tends to support "explicit training on strategies for handling words in general rather than training on a particular set of words" (Calfee & Drum, 1984, p. 834). The best approaches teach students both words *and* ways of learning words.

Simply teaching words is not enough to develop better readers. There are a great many words in the English language, and no one teacher could possibly teach all the "important" ones. Also, the constraints of short-term memory dictate the long lists of isolated words are soon forgotten once the weekly quiz is over. As an alternative, when vocabulary lessons are built around a central concept, students can develop precision in word definition and usage. The central concept might be the topic of instruction on a particular day or the central focus in a piece of text. This approach to vocabulary instruction gives students an organized framework to scaffold their thinking. It assists students in their attempts to understand how new words are related to familiar ones. Most importantly, the new words become part of the learner's context for understanding the central concept, leading to increased comprehension.

The final component is comprehension, the real core of reading. Palincsar and Brown (1984, p. 120) have organized comprehension into six major elements:

1. understanding the purposes of reading, both explicitly and implicitly.
2. activating relevant background knowledge.
3. allocating attention so that concentration can be focused on the major content at the expense of trivia.
4. evaluating content critically for internal consistency and compatibility with prior knowledge and common sense.
5. monitoring ongoing activities (to see if comprehension is occurring) by engaging in such activities as periodic review and self-interrogation.
6. drawing and testing inferences of many kinds, including interpretations, predictions, and conclusions.

For instructional purposes, comprehension can be broken down into two subcomponents, narrative and expository comprehension. Narratives have a different central purpose than expository passages. Narratives tell the reader a story, exposition provides the reader with information. Most students arrive at high school with little awareness of this distinction. Flood and Lapp (1986) show that most elementary school basal reading programs devote the bulk of their curriculums to narrative text, even though most high school textbooks are entirely exposition. Consequently, explicit training in the ways that narrative and expository text are different is a vital aspect of comprehension instruction.

Although most children come to school with the ability to tell a story, few can identify the elements that make up a well-developed narrative. Given training in a few fundamental structures, young students can learn to identify the beginning, middle, and end of a narrative, develop a clear understanding of character and setting, and recognize the episodic nature of a story's plot. This structural awareness aids the reader in two ways. First, it provides a consistent framework for organizing and remembering information from a story. Second, the basic structures serve as a scaffold to support the young reader's introduction to more sophisticated literary concepts (i.e., theme, flashback, irony).

Comprehending expository text means more than remembering details from a passage. It also involves the ability to analyze information and make interpretive judgments based on this analysis (Curley, 1986). Many students lack the prerequisite skills for analysis and interpretation—they cannot synthesize and integrate information from a text. Exposition is a foreign language to these students. Training readers to recognize the unique features of expository text is a first step in remediating their difficulties. Calfee and Chambliss (in press) have identified three different genres of expository purpose: description, sequence, and argument. Description presents the attributes of an object, sequence presents a progression of events over time, and argument presents support for an idea. When these text characteristics are taught explicitly, students become capable of using specific text features (i.e., section headings, charts and graphs, italicized words) to identify the essential information in an expository passage.

A THEORETICAL FRAMEWORK

This section of the chapter presents a theoretical base with implications for every aspect of the literacy curriculum. The theories themselves are culled from the fields of cognitive psychology and rhetoric. The special challenge of teaching the at-risk child to read is taken up next, because the theories convey some especially powerful ideas about instruction for disadvantaged children.

Reading Is Thinking!

The reader is not a passive receptacle for the information in a text, but rather an active participant in the making of meaning (Bartlett, 1932). What active processes are taking place in the mind of the reader? Most obviously, some physiological activity is taking place (eye movements, for example). Beyond this sensorimotor activity, the reader is continually building a text for the information in a text as he or she reads. A context is created through the application of personal background knowledge to the new material. The reader engages in the process of making connections—fitting the new information in with prior knowledge. This connecting process leads to critical thinking as perspectives are changed, conclusions are drawn, and motivations are understood. To look at an example, take a moment to read the following passage (Bransford & Johnson, 1972, pp. 722 & 723).

> The procedure is actually quite simple. First, you arrange things into different groups. Of course, one pile may be sufficient depending on how much there is to do. If you have to go somewhere else due to lack of facilities that is the next step, otherwise you are pretty well set. It is important not to overdo things. That is, it is better to do too few things at once rather than too many. In the short run this may not seem important, but complications can easily arise. A mistake can be expensive as well. At first the whole procedure will seem complicated. Soon it will become just another facet of life. It is difficult to foresee any end to the necessity for this task in the immediate future, but then one never can tell. After the procedure is completed one arranges the materials into different groups again. Then, they will be used once more and the whole cycle will have to be repeated.

This selection doesn't make much sense by itself. The words are not difficult, but they probably don't add up to much, if any, meaning. Suppose that the title of this passage, "Doing the Laundry," is supplied. With this title in mind, go back and reread the passage. Notice the connections you are making this time around, presumably because doing the laundry is an activity well within the realm of your experience. Having a context to think within, in this case *laundry*, enables you as reader to connect your past experience with the topic to the information in the text. Meaning is made as you fit the text's information into your prior knowledge. Many student readers fail to comprehend the context they read in their classes because they do not connect the words on the page with their own prior knowledge. Without a context to think within, students feel like you did after your first reading of the laundry passage. The content just doesn't make much sense to them.

The Natural/Formal Language Continuum

This concept is an important way of thinking about language: the Natural/Formal continuum (Freedman & Calfee, 1984; see also Heath, 1983; Scribner & Cole, 1978). All language acts, spoken or written, exist on a continuum between natural language and formal language. Natural language is highly implicit and invites interaction. The phrase "You know?" is a good example of these natural language qualities. This phrase uttered in a conversation between two friends could be completely meaningless to a bystander, but to the friends it is likely to be fraught with intuitive meaning and will serve as an invitation for further discussion.

Another quality of natural language is its tendency to be context bound. It is usually rooted in a particular place and time, probably due to its quality of immediacy. A father who is standing in line at a crowded supermarket and exclaims to his child, "You get over here now!" is providing a fine illustration of this natural language characteristic (as well as temporarily relieving the boredom of his fellow shoppers). In addition, natural language tends to be a uniquely personal means of expression. Anyone who has ever conversed with a small child can testify to his or her idiosyncratic way of using natural language.

Formal language, on the other hand, is highly explicit and more logical than intuitive. Much of the instructional language in content area classrooms falls into this category. Directions are spelled out, utterances are usually rule governed, and few details are left to the intuition of the listener (or reader). Consequently, the context of a formal language act is less rooted in a particular time and place than is the case with natural language. Since more of the "message" is explicitly spelled out when formal language is used, the meaning remains constant regardless of setting. Imagine our same harried parent at the supermarket saying, "Ashley, I must insist that you vacate your position in front of the candy bar display within exactly six seconds and return to stand quietly next to me here in the overcrowded checkout line in this large supermarket in Northern California!", and you can see how a formal language act carries its own context. Precisely because of this explicitness, formal language tends to be memory supported and repeatable. The audience has more specific information to act upon in the making of prior knowledge connections. And so, if the message is coherently presented, there are fewer opportunities for misunderstandings between sender and receiver when formal language is used.

What implications does the natural/formal language distinction have for pedagogy? Almost every child comes to school with the ability to use natural language (Applebee, 1978). In order to succeed academically, students must become adept at understanding and using the formal language of classroom instruction. (This is not to suggest that we wish children's natural language abilities to disappear in the process of acquiring formal language competence.) This task can be accomplished in two ways. First, teachers can lead students to an understanding of the ways that formal language is organized. Second, students can acquire a consistent technical vocabulary as a tool for talking about language. A focus on the development of organizational skills and an emphasis on technical vocabulary are pedagogical tactics that would benefit all teachers' repertoires.

The Importance of Organization for Thinking

The mind likes organization! Research in cognitive psychology suggests that the mind has a natural tendency to chunk information together when it is presented in meaningful units (Miller, 1956). Students are apt to see relationships among ideas when they can think within an organized framework. In addition, research into the nature of human memory tells us that students will remember more information when it is organized and recoded into short-term memory. Miller compares this phenomenon to the process of learning a telegraph code. Initially, the learner hears each telegraph sound as a separate chunk of information. Eventually, the separate sounds become organized into larger patterns and the learner is capable of understanding and retaining more of the message.

For teaching purposes, the point is this: When new information is presented in an organized manner, it tends to be stored and retrieved in a similarly organized fashion. If you make clear connections among the ideas within the context you teach, your students will be able to understand and remember the larger relationships.

Other powerful methods exist to assist the memory process. One such method is the practice of focusing students' attention on one concept at a time. When students are allowed to concentrate on one topic or skill at a time they can master its complexities. When they are given a series of simultaneous directives (e.g., "Finish up yesterday's worksheet on the changes in Earth's climate, discuss the even-numbered questions at the end of the environment chapter, and copy tomorrow's assignment on the solar system from the board. If you have any questions, see me."), their ability to see essential relationships will suffer, as will the teacher's ability to be explicit about expectations.

Another method that promotes the memory process has to do with verbal practice. Ideas that are talked about are more apt to be remembered than ideas that are simply listened to. (Lecturers take note!) Furthermore, many language researchers (notably James Britton and Jerome Bruner) tell us that children can internalize ways of thinking through oral practice at following the steps in the thinking process. Teachers can encourage oral interaction in their classrooms by asking questions that engage students in the practice of verbally following a line of reasoning. This verbal interaction with ideas should not only occur between teacher and student, but among students as well. The fund of background experience students bring to the classroom should not be neglected.

The use of visual structures to show relationships among ideas is another method for facilitating the memory process. A variety of visual structures (e.g., semantic mapping, story graphs) can be employed to integrate student prior knowledge with information in a text. The act of constructing visual "pictures" to show relationships can be an extremely effective learning process, especially when students are the construction workers.

Contrast the implications of these three theories with a "traditional" reading lesson wherein the sole emphasis is placed on the content of a text. When students passively receive new information, they tend to learn isolated details. If they are not trained to see the connections among ideas in the text, they are less able to transfer information from one lesson to the next. In contrast, when students orally practice the process of organizing material into a visual structure, they remember more connected information and the transfer of knowledge and skills becomes a reality.

READING AND THE AT-RISK CHILD

The classification "at risk" includes students with disadvantaged backgrounds, disciplinary problems, learning disabilities, lack of experience with the English language, and chronic absentee problems. It is useful to take an in-depth look at this population, for these students have the most to gain from effective reading instruction.

For many students who come from advantaged backgrounds, formal language thought starts to develop before schooling begins. Their parents and other adults talk with them and listen to them. These advantaged children come to kindergarten and first grade knowing many "school words" and some of the conventions of formal thinking. In contrast, the child who has not been exposed to such early experiences finds school to be an alien environment. Not only are the words different, but the "rules" of communication are different, too. The disadvantaged child must grapple with a new way of speaking *and* a new way of thinking. The child's world has given him or her a natural way of using language and thinking but has not built a bridge to the formal language and thought processes used in school.

One common misconception about this group of low achievers is that they don't have much to say—at least in the classroom. In reality, at-risk students have a great deal of pertinent information to contribute, if their input is seen as useful knowledge by the teacher. *All* children, by virtue of their dealings with the world outside the classroom, have a good deal of information at their disposal. The teacher's challenge is to train students to relate this worldly experience to the classroom curriculum. Lessons that open an avenue for student contribution are tremendously successful in turning passive learners into active participants.

Developing at-risk students' oral language skills can help build the bridge to formal language acquisition. Language researchers (e.g., Britton, 1970) have demonstrated that children can internalize ways of thinking through oral practice at following the steps in a problem-solving process. Led by the teacher's exlicit modeling, students can learn to orally follow the thinking processes of formal thought. Coupled with direct instruction in organizing information, this verbal ability helps the reader to think critically about the content of a text. Ideas that are talked through and organized are more apt to be remembered than ideas that are simply read off a page. Students' formal language thinking abilities improve as they learn to verbally follow the process of using visual structure to organize the information in a text. They learn to retain content and simultaneously internalize such critical skills as sequencing information, making comparisons and contrasts, and inferring cause and effect. In addition, the verbal practice with the processes of formal thought helps students to transfer these skills from one reading situation to the next.

The ability to use organizational patterns of language is especially relevant for children who come to school with little or no English in their language repertoire. These students, as much as any other at-risk group, need to gain a sense of the structure of the English language. Their fluency gains are much quicker if the English language does not appear arbitrary to them. Part of this structural understanding comes from seeing the appropriate connections between English and their native language. A teacher of bilingual students can never make these connections too explicit. Again, the use of visual aids and oral discussion can greatly facilitate the process of learning how language is organized.

DEVELOPING THE ACCELERATED LITERARCY CURRICULUM

The theories in the previous section of this report lead to the incorporation of several major instructional issues into the accelerated literacy curriculum. First, explicit directions must be provided to students to help them gain a clear understanding of the purpose of each learning activity. Second, oral discussions can facilitate the sharing of relevant student background knowledge and take advantage of "group intelligence" for the analysis of a text's content. Third, visual portrayal of the content is an important method for connecting pieces of information from a text together into a coherent organization. Finally, students should be led to internalize the *processes* for analysis as well as the content of a text itself.

The accompanying model for lesson development puts these concepts into practice. This theoretically based model was developed under the direction of Robert Calfee by Project READ at Stanford University. The project is an ongoing collaboration between researchers at Stanford and hundreds of public school teachers in all content areas, grades K through

12. The major goal of Project READ is to increase student literacy skills in reading, speaking, writing, and thinking (Calfee et al., 1981).

READ Lesson Model

Project READ lessons are organized into four clearly delineated segments: Opening, Middle, Closing, and Follow-up. Each segment reinforces not only content, but the organization of this content *and* the process students use to organize the content into an appropriate visual structure. The lesson model is presented below in this format. Each segment is accompanied by a sample selection from a narrative comprehension lesson developed for an upper elementary class.

Each of the learning activities within the body of the lesson are crafted to emphasize a single instruction goal. Explicit directions and clearly spelled-out relationships help students to understand the purpose of these activities. Students engage in the making of meaning through verbal practice at placing the content of a lesson into a visual structure. The utility of student prior knowledge is an important consideration for each lesson. In addition, the teacher highlights technical vocabulary terms (i.e., plot, setting, character) and students are expected to use the terms to reflect upon the meaning of the text.

Opening. The lesson opens with a clear statement of the lesson's goal to the students. The teacher previews the new content to be learned, introduces the visual structure to be used for organizing the content, and models the process students will follow to fit the content into the structure. If this explanation is stated explicitly, the students should now know precisely what they are going to do and why. Students will be motivated to perform if the lesson is described in an interesting manner.

In the accompanying sample lesson, the content is introduced as the characters, setting, and plot of a narrative about mountain climbing. The structure is identified as a web, a semantic mapping technique (Johnson & Pearson, 1984) that is presumably familiar to the students. The process of organizing the content into the structure is described as finding specific information from the story and grouping similar chunks together. The motivation to perform is triggered by the initial discussion on the mountain climbing. Note that students are also informed that the goal of the lesson is to use these chunks of information to better understand the story.

> *Opening Example.* Has anyone here ever climbed a mountain? As you probably know, the art of mountain climbing is not dependent on physical strength alone. You've probably all heard stories of people with physical handicaps climbing mountains. It takes a certain kind of character to make it to the top of a big mountain. "The Man on Top" is a narrative about climbing the toughest mountain

in the world and the types of people who attempt to scale these heights.

All narratives are made up of certain building blocks, and this story is no exception. The building blocks of a narrative are characters, setting, and plot. [List and define these terms on the board.] As we read the story, be on the lookout for details that tell you who the characters are and what they are like, where and when the story takes place, and the important events that occur. After you have finished reading we'll create a web to organize all this information on the story's building blocks. Then, we'll see how knowing information about characters, setting, and plot can help you to better understand a story.

Middle. The middle of the lesson is activity oriented. Here, the content of the lesson is organized into a visual structure. This visual structure is usually created on the blackboard in front of the class. Whenever applicable, student prior knowledge is linked with the new content information in this structure. Students are guided in this activity by the design of the specific structure and through verbal interaction with the teacher (and one another). The students verbally follow the process of organizing the content into the visual structure. This oral interaction may take place as an entire class or in small discussion groups. Students learn a great deal from one another when the group's sum total knowledge on a topic can be accessed, and students contribute more to class discussion when given a visual structure to help focus their thoughts.

A key point to make about the middle of the lesson is this: the students, not the teacher, are doing most of the mental work! They are thinking, talking about their thoughts, and organizing these thoughts into a coherent picture. The teacher serves as a guide to the students' developing thought processes.

In the example, the teacher sets up a basic web structure on the board and elicits two categories of information from the students. First, information about character, setting, and plot details is provided by the students. Second, inferences are made about specific information that is not provided in the text but is necessary to a complete understanding of the three narrative elements. The web, when completed, gives the students an organized picture of the kinds of information they need to glean from a story.

Middle Example. [Students read the story. When they are finished reading, create a web on the blackboard as you elicit information from the students about characters, setting, and plot.] Let's begin with the characters. Who can name one of the characters in this story? Is this person a major or minor character? [Explain the distinction and continue until all characters are accounted for.] On the board I have listed some words that could describe the feelings the characters have in this narrative. [Read and define these words.] See if you can match these feeling words with the characters from the story. Can you come up with other descriptive words of your own for these characters? [Probe for rationale.]

Now, let's turn to the setting. It may not say directly when and where this story takes place, but there are a lot of clues to help us make an educated guess. Does anyone want to speculate what part of the world is the setting for this narrative? What clues did you use to make this guess? What is the name of the town where the story begins? Do the main characters spend the whole story in this town? Where do they end up by the end of the story? Do you think the author who wrote this story wanted the readers to think it took place in the past, present, or future? Why do you think so? About how long did the plot take to unfold from beginning to end? What clues from the story did you use to make your decision?

Okay, now we'll look at the plot of this narrative. Help me to list the important events in the order they occurred in the story. What do you think was the first important event? Why was it important? [Etc.]

Closing. In the closing of a lesson, the content is reviewed and the learning goals are summarized. The teacher probes for the students' mastery of the lesson content, their awareness of the learning process, *and* the name and design of the structure they have used to organize the content. A variety of assessment opportunities are open to the teacher at this point, including the determination of students' capacity to make increasingly sophisticated connections among ideas presented in the content. Again, because the closing of a lesson is conducted orally, the students are led to verbally review the thinking process they have followed as well as the information they have internalized.

In many ways, the closing of a lesson mirrors its opening. In the opening, the teacher explains to the students the learning activity that is about to take place, and in the closing, the students describe to the teacher what they have learned.

In the closing example, the teacher first probes for the technical word for story ("narrative") and then for the name of the visual picture ("a web"). Next, the students are asked to describe the components of the web, how they were organized, and the purpose of the lesson. Finally, the students' understanding of the story content is assessed.

Closing Example. What type of writing are we dealing with today? What structure did we use to organize the story? What are the building blocks of a narrative? What sorts of information do you look for when you want to describe the characters, setting, and plot? In the opening of this lesson, I told you that knowing all this information about the story would help you to understand it better. Let's find out if this is true! [Probe for the connections between character feelings and plot development. Assess students' understanding of the conclusion of the story.]

Follow up. The follow-up to a lesson can take many different forms. The teacher can assign written exercises to help students internalize the content, or this content can be extended and linked to upcoming material through further discussion. The visual structure used in the lesson can be used to organize a new body of knowledge, or the structure can be modified to accommodate new information the teacher wishes to add to the lesson. Alternately, activities can be designed that challenge students to independently follow a line of reasoning similar to the thinking process they employed during the middle of the lesson. Most follow-up activities are creative in nature, stress the development of writing skills, and tie the new information that has been acquired by the students into a larger body of knowledge.

Three follow-up options are presented in this lesson example. The first choice emphasizes transfer of structure by asking students to analyze a new story by organizing its narrative components. The second choice focuses on a more in-depth exploration of either character, setting, or plot. The third choice challenges students to use their newly acquired system for character analysis to write an extension of the story. Obviously, the level of difficulty in the lesson follow-up is heavily dependent on the academic abilities of the students.

Lesson Follow-up.

1. Have the students apply their knowledge of narrative building blocks to a new story.

2. Now that these basic narrative elements have been introduced, pick an appropriate story and teach one element in much greater detail.

3. Have the students create an in-depth character analysis of the major characters and use this analysis to continue the story beyond its present conclusion. The writer's task is to shift the characters into an entirely new setting while attempting to keep the plot events consistent with identified character traits.

The READ lesson model is designed to exhibit three major strengths. First, it encourages explicitness in both language use and intention between teachers and students. Second, a stress on transfer of knowledge and skills is built into the lesson. Third, the stage is set for meaningful student communication rather than rote response.

RECOMMENDATIONS

Many teachers are prisoners of content. They have not been trained to make informed curriculum decisions, so they are forced to rely on teacher manuals and publishers to tell them what to do with their students. In order for students to learn critical thinking skills, their teachers must first have the knowledge to think critically about curriculum development. The informed reading teacher can determine what information in a text is important to stress and how this information fits together coherently. He or she has the ability to choose appropriate methods for showing students these connections among the ideas in a text. He or she has the perspective to teach students the processes of critical thinking, as well as a year's worth of content. Most importantly, the informed reading teacher can help students learn to transfer these developing processes from one learning situation to another.

The following recommendations are provided to assist informed teachers in creating "accelerated" readers in their classrooms. Each technique is based on the concepts of language and thinking development that underlie this paper. The recommendations are as follows:

1. The adoption of a coherent, consistent lesson plan for the purpose of giving and receiving explicit information.
2. An emphasis on verbal interaction with ideas between teacher and students (and among students).
3. The use of visual structures to show how the information in a text is linked to its central themes.
4. The assimilation of technical terms (e.g., sequence, inference) into the student's vocabulary to enhance his or her descriptions of the thinking processes he or she is following.
5. The use of a variety of reading materials to supplement the basal reader and provide clear models for skill instruction.
6. The reconceptualization of assessment as an ongoing opportunity for student diagnosis.

The kind of student change these recommendations promote will not happen overnight. The tools of a critical reader are the ability to find patterns of organization in a text, aptitude in following a process of thought, and the acquisition of a vocabulary that empowers the learner to reflect on his or her thoughts. Children acquire these skills gradually. Over time, the trained reader will strive for more precision in his or her descriptions, search for temporal relationships among events, learn to draw inferential conclusions based on literal evidence, and seek fallacies in the logic of formerly persuasive arguments. In summary, effective reading instruction teaches children to think critically.

REFERENCES

Anderson, L. M. 1982. *Student responses to seatwork: Implications for the study of students' cognitive processing.* Research series no. 102. East Lansing: Michigan State University, Institute for Research on Teaching.

Applebee, A. N. 1978. *The child's concept of a story.* Chicago: University of Chicago Press.

Applebee, A. N.; Langer, J. A.; and Mullis, I. V. S. 1986. *The writing report card: Writing achievement in American schools.* Princeton, N.J.: Educational Testing Service.

Bartlett, F. C. 1932. *Remembering: A study in experimental and social psychology.* Cambridge, Eng.: The University Press.

Bransford, J. D., and Johnson, M. K. 1972. Contextual prerequisites for understanding: Some investigations of comprehension and recall. *Journal of Verbal Learning and Verbal Behavior* 11:717–26.

Britton, J. N. 1970. *Language and learning.* Cambridge, Engl.: Penguin Press.

Calfee, R. C. et al. 1981. *The Book: Components of reading instruction.* Unpublished, generic manual for reading teachers, Stanford University.

Calfee, R. C., and Chambliss, M. J. (in press). The structural design features of large texts. *Educational Psychologist.*

Calfee, R. C., and Drum, P. 1984. Research on teaching reading. In *Handbook on research on teaching.* 3d ed. Ed. Wittrock, M. C. New York: Macmillan.

Curley, B. 1986. Text structure analysis as a model for teaching comprehension skills. Unpublished dissertation proposal, Stanford University.

Flood, J., and Lapp, D. 1986. Types of texts: The match between what students read in basals and what they encounter in tests. *Reading Research Quarterly* 21:284–97.

Freedman, S. W., and Calfee, R. C. 1984. Understanding and comprehending. *Written Communication* 1:459–90.

Heath, S. B. 1983. *Ways with words.* Cambridge (Cambridgeshire): Cambridge University Press.

Johnson, D. D., and Pearson, P. D. 1984. *Teaching reading vocabulary.* 2nd ed. New York: Holt, Rinehart & Winston.

Levin, H. M. 1987. *Towards accelerated schools.* Prepared for the Center for Policy Research in Education of Rutgers University, the Rand Corporation, and the University of Wisconsin.

———. 1987. Proposal to the Rockefeller Foundation for a conference on accelerating the education of disadvantaged students, Stanford University.

Miller, G. A. 1956. The magical number seven, plus or minus two: Some limits on our capacity for processing information. *Psychological Review* 63:81–97.

Palincsar, A. S., and Brown, A. L. 1984. Reciprocal teaching of comprehension-fostering and monitoring activities. *Cognition and Instruction* 1:117–75.

Scribner, S., and Cole, M. 1978. *The psychology of literacy.* Cambridge, Mass.: Harvard University Press.

ACCELERATING ELEMENTARY EDUCATION FOR DISADVANTAGED STUDENTS

Henry Levin

Almost one-third of the nation's elementary and secondary students are educationally disadvantaged, representing a major challenge to the schools. This proportion is rising as new waves of immigration, rising poverty among families with children, and high birth rates augment the disadvantaged population (Levin, 1986). The failure to address the needs of these students will mean increased social and political turmoil, a less competitive economy, higher costs of other social services, and a higher educational sector characterized by rising costs, lower quality, and greater conflict.

The purpose of this paper is to suggest some systematic actions that states might take in addressing the needs of the educationally disadvantaged. Particular attention will be devoted to their current status and the challenge that they present to the states. The paper will describe the elements of a long-term solution that focuses on the elementary school, as well as a set of actions that the states can take to address the challenge.

STATUS OF THE EDUCATIONALLY DISADVANTAGED

For the purpose of this presentation, educationally disadvantaged pupils are defined as those students who lack the home and community resources

Reprinted by permission of the Council of Chief School State Officers to fully benefit from conventional schooling practices and the recent wave of educational reforms. Because of poverty, cultural differences, or linguistic differences, they tend to have low academic achievement and experience high secondary school dropout rates. Such students are especially concentrated among minority groups, immigrants, non-English-speaking families, and economically disadvantaged populations.

Over the last two decades, some progress has been made in improving the education of the disadvantaged (Levin, 1986, pp. 8–9). For example, studies of academic achievement between minority and nonminority students and between low-socioeconomic-status and other students suggest that as much as one-quarter of the achievement gap that existed between these groups has been closed in the last twenty years. Nevertheless, we have reached a plateau in which most of the gap remains, and whatever progress has been made has not been adequate to bring disadvantaged students into the mainstream of educational life in America.

Typically, the disadvantaged child begins schooling with poorer achievement in those subjects that are valued by schools, and the achievement gap widens so that by secondary school such students are performing at two to three years below grade level on the average. This places such pupils at about the twentieth percentile in standard achievement, which relegates them to less demanding courses and remedial work rather than a standard curriculum. High school dropout rates for these students have been estimated at about 50 percent, resulting in an undereducated class of adults, with respect to economic, political, and social opportunities (Levin, 1986).

The latest wave of reforms has not made a meaningful impact on the education of disadvantaged students. As meritorious as these reforms may be for other students, they do not address the specific needs of the disadvantaged. The reforms stress raising standards at the secondary level, without providing additional resources or new strategies to assist the disadvantaged in meeting these higher standards. Any strategy for improving the educational plight of the disadvantaged must begin at the elementary level and must be dedicated to preparing children for doing high-quality work in secondary school. Simply raising standards at the secondary level without making it possible for the disadvantaged to meet the new standards is more likely to increase their dropout rates.

Two of the most typical recent state reforms are the setting of minimum competency standards for a diploma and the raising of course requirements for graduation. Paradoxically, both of these reforms may contribute to increasing dropouts of disadvantaged students, who already have difficulty in meeting the old standards (McDill, Natriello, & Pallas, 1985). Unless the achievement gap can be substantially closed prior to entering secondary school, the higher standards will serve to further discourage the disadvantaged rather than improving their performance.

Dire Social Consequences

In the absence of substantial interventions, the rapidly increasing population of educationally disadvantaged students will ultimately emerge as a large and growing population of disadvantaged adults. The potential consequences of ignoring the needs of these students will affect not only the disadvantaged, but the larger society as well (Levin, 1986, pp. 13–16). These consequences include (1) the emergence of a dual society with a large and poorly educated underclass; (2) massive disruption in higher education; (3) reduced economic competitiveness of the nation, as well as of those states and industries on which these populations have the heaviest impact; and (4) higher costs for public services that are a response to poverty.

1. *A Dual Society.* As the disadvantaged population increases without appropriate educational interventions to improve substantially its situation, this group is likely to form the underclass of a dual society. Composed of racial and ethnic minorities and persons from economically disadvantaged origins, its members will face high unemployment rates, low earnings, and menial occupations. At the same time, the political power of the disadvantaged will increase as their numbers and potential votes rise. The specter of a dual society suggests great political conflict and potential social upheaval.

2. *Conflict in Higher Education.* The implications for higher education are also severe. Larger and larger numbers of educationally disadvantaged will mean that the public institutions of higher education will have to become more restrictive in their admissions criteria, or more devoted to remedial academic work. Either direction is fraught with problems. Substantial remedial activities will require additional university resources, and students will take longer to complete their degrees. All of this means that costs to universities and students will spiral. The increase in remedial functions will alter the character of public higher education, with a tendency to water down the overall curriculum and reduce standards as pressures increase to approve the application of such courses to degree programs.

Alternatively, the universities may seek to restrict admissions through greater reliance on standardized test scores and more academic course requirements so that fewer persons from disadvantaged populations can participate in higher education. Even now, a disproportionately small share of minority and educationally disadvantaged students are eligible to participate in public higher education because of their high rates of dropping out and poor academic records. But these disproportions will be exacerbated by creating an elite system for admissions, a result that flies in the face of the democratic mission conferred upon public systems of higher education supported by tax revenues collected from the entire population. At the same time that higher education would become more exclusive, those who were increasingly excluded would be expanding their political power at both the state and federal levels. Clearly, such a policy will lead to political and social turmoil, both on and off the campuses.

3. *Economic Deterioration.* A further consequence of the present treatment of the educationally disadvantaged will be a serious deterioration in the quality of the labor force. As long as the disadvantaged were just a small minority of the population, they could be absorbed into seasonal and low-skill jobs, or relegated to unemployment without direct consequences for the overall economy. But, as their numbers grow and they continue to experience low achievement and high dropout rates, a larger and larger portion of the available labor force will be unprepared for available jobs. Here we refer not only to managerial, professional, and technical jobs, but to the huge and burgeoning numbers of lower-level service jobs that characterize the economy. Clerical workers, cashiers, and salespeople need basic skills in oral and written communications, computations, and reasoning, skills that are not guaranteed to the educationally disadvantaged. A U.S. government study in 1976 found that while 13 percent of all 17-year-olds were classified as functionally illiterate, the percentages of illiterates among Hispanics and Blacks were 56 and 44 percent respectively (National Assessment of Educational Progress, 1976).

The United States is already facing great difficulties in maintaining a competitive economic stance relative to other industrialized and industrializing nations. As the disadvantaged become an increasing and even a dominant part of the labor force in some states and regions, their inadequate educational preparation will undermine the competitive position of the industries and states in which they work. Employers will suffer lagging productivity, higher training costs, and competitive disadvantages that will result in lost sales and profits. Federal, state, and local governments will suffer a declining tax base and loss of tax revenues.

4. *Rising Costs of Public Services.* The economic losses will come at a time of rising costs of public services for populations that are disadvantaged by inadequate education. More and more citizens will need to rely upon public assistance for survival, and increasing numbers of undereducated teens and adults will pursue illegal activities to fill idle time and obtain the income that is not available through legal pursuits.

The inability to find regular employment that pays sufficiently to overcome poverty will require greater public subsidies to overcome increases in poverty and to counter drugs, prostitution, theft, and other alternatives to legal employment. These developments will reduce the attractiveness of the United States as a place to live, while increasing the costs of public services and the criminal justice system, as well as of public assistance. Pressures will be placed on the middle class to pay higher taxes at the same time that their incomes are threatened by a flagging economy, creating an additional source of political conflict as besieged taxpayers resist tax increases.

State Actions on the Status of the Disadvantaged

This section has reviewed the issue of who the educationally disadvantaged are, as well as their lack of educational progress, the inappropriateness of present educational reforms for meeting their needs, and the consequences of inaction. Each of these areas has important implications for state action.

- ●States need to define clearly the criteria for considering children to be educationally disadvantaged, and to make accurate estimates of their present and future numbers and distribution among school districts. This process should be informed by a standard definition of educationally disadvantaged students, possibly one that is established by the Council of Chief State School Officers (CCSSO).
- ●States need to establish an assessment system that will continuously monitor the patterns of educational progress among these students, with specific attention to differences among the various racial and ethnic subgroups. Indicators that are used in the assessment system should include achievement scores, dropout rates, attendance, teen-age pregnancy, drug use, school violence and vandalism, and a wide range of other appropriate measures. Such an assessment approach should have the capability to delineate areas of both progress and continuing problems. The CCSSO might take the lead in suggesting categories for assessment and a uniform measurement approach.
- ●States need to examine the consequences of the growth of educationally disadvantaged students for state higher education, social equality, economic productivity and employment, and the costs of public services. This information should be disseminated to the population at large, as well as to the political constituencies who will be most affected and to those who can provide political leadership and support for a campaign to address the needs of the educationally disadvantaged.
- ●States need to explore their present strategies for addressing the educational needs of the disadvantaged and consider reforms and interventions that are more appropriate than the earlier wave of reforms of the 1980s. We will explore these issues in more detail in the next section.

WHAT IS WRONG?

If disadvantaged students are unable to improve their educational standing through existing school programs, something is wrong with our present schooling interventions. What is wrong? Disadvantaged students begin their schooling with a learning gap in those areas valued by schools and mainstream economic and social institutions. The existing model of intervention assumes that they will not be able to maintain a normal instructional pace without prerequisite knowledge and learning skills. Thus, such youngsters are placed into less demanding instructional settings—either they are pulled out of their regular classrooms, or the regular classroom is adapted to their needs—to provide them with remedial or compensatory educational services. This approach appears to be both rational and compassionate, but it has exactly the opposite consequences.

First, it stigmatizes them with a mark of inferiority and reduces learning expectations both for them and their teachers. Such students are viewed as slow learners and treated accordingly with negative consequences for student esteem and performance. Second, by deliberately slowing the pace of instruction to a crawl, a heavy emphasis is placed on endless repetition of material through drill and practice. The result is a school experience that lacks intrinsic vitality, omits crucial learning skills and reinforcement, and moves at a plodding pace. It is also joyless.

These two characteristics mean that the disadvantaged child gets farther and farther behind the educational mainstream the longer he or she is in school. That is, the very model of remediation is one that must necessarily reduce educational progress and widen the achievement gap between his advantaged and nondisadvantaged children.

The widening gap in achievement over the school experience would seem to run counter to the philosophy of compensatory or remedial programs. In theory, such programs were established to close the gap. But the fact of the matter is that schools do not focus on the gap per se. That is, there is no time limit established for closing the achievement gap and bringing disadvantaged youngsters into the educational mainstream. Rather, the interventions tend to be procedural and mechanical, without clear goals.

Finally, most compensatory educational programs neither involve teachers and parents sufficiently nor draw adequately upon available community resources. Parents are often viewed as "the problem" rather than being enlisted as a potentially positive influence for their children's learning. Professional staff at the school level are typically omitted from participating in the important educational decisions that they must ultimately implement. Such an omission means that teachers are expected to dedicate themselves to the implementation of programs that do not necessarily reflect their professional judgments, a condition that is not likely to spur great enthusiasm.

In contrast, effective programs must be based upon raising expectations and conferring higher status on the disadvantaged for the learning progress that they will make, rather than on lowered expectations and stigma. These programs must provide vivid examples, interesting applications, and challenging problems rather than emphasizing repetitive learning through constant drill and practice. They must set explicit goals for bringing these students into the educational mainstream, and they must empower teachers and parents to address the specific needs of students. Most important, the approach should incorporate a comprehensive set of strategies that mutually reinforce each other in creating an organizational push toward raising the achievement of students.

ACCELERATED SCHOOLS AS SOLUTIONS

Using these principles, we have designed an Accelerated School for transforming existing schools that have high concentrations of disadvantaged youngsters, a situation typically found in large cities and some rural areas. The Accelerated School is a transitional elementary school that is designed to bring disadvantaged children up to grade level by the completion of the sixth grade. The goal of the school is to enable disadvantaged students to benefit from mainstream secondary school instruction by effectively closing the achievement gap in elementary school.

By bringing children into the educational mainstream, we mean more than bringing them up to grade level in basic skills that are measured by standardized tests. We are referring also to their capabilities in problem solving and communication, as well as their educational aspirations and self-concept as learners. All of these need to be addressed. The approach is also designed to be a dropout prevention program by eliminating the most important single cause of dropping out, serious achievement deficits.

As reflected in the works of Comer (1980) and Goodlad (1984), the stress is on the elementary school as a whole rather than on a particular grade, curriculum, approach to teacher training, or other more limited strategy. Underlying the organizational approach are three major assumptions: First, the strategy must enlist a unity of purpose among all of the participants. Second, it must "empower" all of the major participants and raise their feelings of efficacy and responsibility for the outcomes of the school. Third, it must build on the considerable strengths of the participants rather than decrying their weaknesses.

Unity of purpose refers to agreement among parents, teachers, and students on a common set of goals for the school that will be the focal point of everyone's efforts. Clearly, these should focus on bringing children into the educational mainstream so that they can fully benefit from their further schooling experiences and adult opportunities.

Empowerment refers to the ability of the key participants to make important decisions at the school level and in the home to improve the education of students. It is based upon breaking the present stalemate among administrators, teachers, parents, and students, in which the participants tend to blame each other as well as other factors "beyond their control" for the poor educational outcomes of disadvantaged students. Unless all of the major actors can be empowered to seek a common set of goals and influence the educational and social process that can achieve those goals, it is unlikely that the desired improvements will take place or be sustained (Bandura, 1986; Rogers, 1987).

An accelerated school must build upon an expanded role for all groups to participate in and take responsibility for the educational process and educational results. This requires a shift to a school-based decision approach, with heavy involvement of teachers and parents and new administrative roles (Levin, 1987). It requires information and technical assistance on alternatives as stressed in the New Haven approach (Comer, 1980), as well as a useful system of assessment that can be used as a basis for accountability and for school decision making.

Building on strengths refers to utilizing all of the learning resources that students, parents, school staff, and communities can bring to the educational endeavor (Seeley, 1981). In the quest to place blame for the lack of efficacy of schools in improving the education of the disadvantaged, it is easy to exaggerate weaknesses of the various participants and ignore strengths. Parents have considerable strengths in serving as positive influences for the education of their children, not the least of which is a deep love for their children and a desire for their children to succeed. Teachers are capable of insights, intuition, and teaching and organizational acumen that are lost in schools that fail to draw upon these strengths by excluding teachers from participating in the decisions that they must implement. Both parents and teachers are largely underutilized sources of talent in the schools.

The strengths of disadvantaged students are often overlooked because they lack the learning behaviors associated with middle-class students. Disadvantaged students carry their own unusual assets, which can be used to accelerate their learning. These often include an interest in and curiosity about oral and artistic expression, abilities to learn through the manipulation of appropriate learning materials (as stressed by Montessori, 1965 and Montessori, Jr., 1976), a capability for engrossment in intrinsically interesting tasks, and the ability to learn to write before attaining competence in decoding skills that are prerequisite to reading. In addition, such students can serve as enthusiastic and effective learning resources for other students through peer tutoring and cooperative learning approaches.

School-based administrators are also underutilized by being placed in "command" roles to meet the directives and standard operating procedures of districts rather than to work creatively with parents, staff, and students. In addition, youth organizations, senior citizens, businesses, and religious groups should be viewed as major assets for the schools and the children of the community. The strengths of these participants can be viewed as a major set of resources for creating accelerated schools.

Within the context of a unity of purpose, empowerment, and building on strengths, the Accelerated School utilizes an accelerated curriculum and accelerated instructional strategies to bring all children up to grade level and into the educational mainstream. A major goal is to insure that all students see themselves in a very positive light as productive learners with many future possibilities.

Table 1 shows the prominent features of the Accelerated School, as well as the determinants of student learning that they are designed to affect. This approach shares with the "Effective Schools" literature a focus on the entire school and high expectations (Edmonds, 1979; Purkey & Smith, 1973). It

TABLE 1

FEATURES OF ACCELERATED SCHOOL FOR DISADVANTAGED

FEATURES

● *School-based Governance*

● *Clear Goals*
Students
Parents
Staff

● *Pupil and School Assessment*

● *Nutrition and Health*

● *Curriculum*
Language
Mathematics
Other Areas

● *Instructional Strategies*
Affective Aspects
Use of Time
Peer Tutoring
Cooperative Learning
Homework

● *Community Resources*
Adult Tutors
Businesses
Social Service Agencies

● *Parental Participation and Training*

● *Extended Daily Session*

differs markedly, however, in its emphasis on a staff-based decision model rather than the delegation of all authority to the "instructional leader."

1. *School-based Governance.* The principles set out for the Accelerated School are relatively broad; they can be designed and implemented in a wide variety of ways. The actual choice of curriculum, instructional strategies, and other school policies will be decided by the instructional staff of the school within the latitude set by the school district. These decisions will benefit from the substantial knowledge base that exists on the various dimensions of school programs that have been shown to be particularly effective for disadvantaged students as set out below. But the specific dimensions and their details must be considered, adopted, and molded by the school decision-makers. That is, the decision-making approach is a school-based one, in which those who will be providing the instruction will make the decisions. As the school builds this capacity, it will be important to get parent representatives involved in the decision process as well.

Each school will create its own governance mechanism consisting of a governing body as a whole, a steering committee, and task-oriented committees with particular assignments that will report to the steering committee and the governing body. These groups will be composed of instructional staff, other staff, parent representatives, and the principal of the school. The principal will undertake an important leadership role in identifying problem areas, obtaining pertinent information, coordinating the decision process, and assisting in group dynamics. The principal will also be responsible for obtaining and allocating resources from the school district to implement decisions.

Each school will set out a program that is consonant with the strengths of the district and local staff. In this way, the reform will be developed by those who must implement and evaluate the decisions, a process that is likely to enhance professional commitment. Indeed, the ability of teachers and other school staff to work together to shape the programs that will guide their daily activities is likely to make the school dynamic and exciting from the perspective of educational staff. This participation and accountability are crucial for fully engaging the talents and commitments of educators. Details on shifting responsibilities from district offices to schools, and on the internal organization of schools, are discussed by Levin (1987).

2. *Clear Goals.* In conjunction with the school district and school board, the governing body of the school will establish a clear set of goals for students, parents, and staff with respect to the purpose of the school and its activities. An overriding goal of the Accelerated School is to bring the academic performance of students up to grade level to prepare them for mainstream educational opportunities by the completion of elementary school. The setting of overall school goals should also consider student attendance and participation in school activities; teacher attendance, participation, and morale; vandalism and behavior problems; and school con-

tributions to the community through the performing arts and community service.

Each of the major constituencies will be consulted in setting these goals. The inculcation of school goals among students will serve to create high expectations and to improve their learning through increasing their effort and time devoted to such endeavors. For parents and school staff, the establishment of such goals should serve to raise expectations on the part of those constituencies in a way that will improve the instructional resource climate of the home and school. As collaboration becomes more fully established, new goals will be established and old goals may be modified.

3. *Pupil and School Assessment.* The assessment system evaluates the performance of children at school entry and sets a trajectory for meeting the overall school goal. Periodic evaluations on wide-spectrum, standardized achievement tests, as well as tailored assessments created by school staff for each strand of the curriculum and school goals, will enable the school to see if students are on the anticipated trajectory. Such an assessment system will serve both accountability purposes and diagnostic purposes for improving instruction. In addition, a school-wide assessment system needs to be established to measure progress toward other goals, such as parental involvement, student and teacher attendance, student participation, and so on.

4. *Nutrition and Health.* It is clear that the capacity of children to learn will be heavily conditioned by their nutritional status and health. Children without adequate diet and with dental and health problems are not likely to have the concentration and feeling of well-being that are prerequisite to learning. Especially important are undiagnosed and untreated hearing and vision problems, since virtually all learning activities are centered around these two senses. Schools must work with families and the various social service agencies (public and private) in the community to diagnose and address nutritional and health-care needs of disadvantaged students to improve their capacity to learn.

5. *Curriculum.* Major curriculum features that have been shown to be pertinent include a heavily language-based approach to all subjects, including mathematics (Cuevas, Mann, & McClung, 1986). Language use in all of its forms—reading, writing, speaking, and listening—must be stressed across the curriculum (Barton & Calfee, 1987; Calfee, 1986). An emphasis will be placed on analysis, concepts, problem solving, and applications in all subjects from the early primary grades.

An especially important aspect will be the development of interesting applications that relate to the daily lives and experiences of the children and that demonstrate the usefulness of the tools and concepts that are presented. Students will be asked to discover for themselves applications of the concepts.

Writing will begin early in the primary grades, as soon as students are able to develop even minimal vocabularies. Students will be exposed not only to narrative and poetic forms of language use, but also exposition. Mathematics will be presented through the development of concepts and applications in order to integrate and reinforce the standard arithmetic operations (Romberg, 1986). Science and social studies will also build on the development of analytical skills, problem solving, concepts, and applications in order to provide a stimulating framework for the associative learning tasks. Most important, the students will be active subjects in their learning, rather than passive objects.

Substantial attention will also be paid to the arts and physical activities. These are not only important for full human development, but they are often sources of great intrinsic satisfaction for the participants. Thus, they can serve an important role in making the school a vibrant and attractive experience. The curriculum design is aimed at increasing student capacity through providing conceptual and analytical tools that will enhance the capacity to learn more advanced material while using music, relaxation exercises, visualization techniques and other activities to make the school experience more engaging (Richardson, 1987).

6. *Instructional Strategies.* The choice of instructional strategies must rely heavily on those that will reinforce the curriculum approach and build on techniques that have been effective with the disadvantaged. Most research on these techniques has focused on "pull-out" programs rather than on programs that are integrated into the central organization of school instruction for mutually supportive and cumulative effects (Madden & Slavin, 1987; Slavin & Madden, 1987). The school should stress greater availability of instructional time, as well as its more effective use (Denham & Lieberman, 1980; Fisher & Berliner, 1985). The instructional pace must be adequate to keep students attentive and learning at a rate that is productive, in contrast to the deliberate slowdown usually associated with remedial instruction (Barr, 1973–74; Good & Grouws, 1978). Curriculum and teaching approaches should be used to maintain the interest of students and engage them in active learning. Of special importance in this regard are techniques that are designed to enhance the affective school environment, such as those suggested by Lozanov (1978) and applied by Richardson (1987) to the Accelerated School.

Peer tutoring has been shown to be an unusually effective approach for disadvantaged youngsters (Madden & Slavin, pp. 9–15). Among its advantages are the fact that it is flexible in allowing older children to tutor younger ones or more advanced students at the same level to tutor their colleagues, and that the tutors often learn as much as those whom they are tutoring. Finally, it is an ideal strategy for heterogeneous student groupings, since those who are more knowledgeable are tutors for those who need to master the material.

Cooperative learning is another effective strategy for enhancing learning among diverse groups (Cohen, 1986; Slavin, 1983). Students are given group assignments in which there will be rewards for group proficiency, providing incentives for the more able students to help those who need assistance. Group approaches seem to be relatively effective for disadvantaged students, in contrast with the individual approach that is common in elementary schools.

The use of outside assignments or homework that must be done outside of the classroom is important in teaching independence and self-reliance. Such assignments can be made on a group or individual basis, and they prepare students for later grades, when a high proportion of learning will take place through such study. Even in the first grade, students will be given such assignments. While this strategy focuses on expanding student effort and the amount of time for learning, the other instructional strategies also address the quality of learning resources.

7. *Community Resources.* Accelerated Schools must enlist all of the resources at their disposal to accomplish their mission. Among these are adult tutors who can work with individual students and provide assistance to teachers. An especially rich source of such talent are senior citizens, many of them former teachers, who seek productive activities and social interaction. In addition, local businesses can be enlisted to provide personnel and other resources to assist accelerated schools. Social service agencies can address basic needs of families, including health care, nutrition, and counseling, and youth agencies such as the Boy Scouts and Girl Scouts or Big Brothers and Big Sisters can offer enrichment programs for the young after school, on weekends, and during summers.

8. *Parental Participation and Training.* Parents will be deeply involved in two ways. First, all parents or guardians will be asked to affirm an agreement that clarifies the goals of the Accelerated School and the obligations of parents, students, and school staff. The agreement will be explained to parents, and translated if necessary. Parental obligations will include such supportive roles as insuring that their children go to bed at a reasonable hour and attend school regularly and punctually. They will be asked to set high educational expectations for their children, to talk to them regularly about the importance of school, and to take an interest in their children's activities and the materials that the children bring home.

They will be asked to encourage their children to read on a daily basis and to insure that independent assignments are addressed. They will also be expected to respond to queries from the school. The purpose is to emphasize the importance of the parental role through the dignity of a written agreement that is affirmed by all parties. Students and school staff will also have appropriate obligations regarding their roles, with the understanding that the Accelerated School will only succeed if all three parties work together.

Second, parents will be given opportunities to interact with the school program and to receive training for providing active assistance to their children. Such training will include not only the skills for working with a child, but also many of the academic skills necessary to understand what the child is doing. In this respect, it may be necessary to work closely with agencies offering adult basic education to provide the parental foundation. The parental dimension can improve the capacity and effort of the child, as well as increase the time devoted to academic learning, and provide additional instructional resources in the home (Epstein, 1987; Kelly & Smrekar, 1987).

9. *Extended Daily Session.* An extended session until 5:00 P.M. will provide additional learning time for the youngsters. Following the ending of the normal school session in early or mid-afternoon, the extended-day program would provide a rest period, physical activities, concentration on the arts, and a time for doing independent assignments or homework. During this period, college students and senior citizen volunteers would work with individual students to provide learning assistance. Since many of the children are "latch-key" children, the extension of the school day is likely to be attractive to parents.

IMPLICATIONS OF ACCELERATED SCHOOLS FOR STATES

The case for creating Accelerated Schools for disadvantaged students is compelling. The large and growing numbers of such students, their low educational attainments under present schooling methods, and the deleterious consequences of not intervening for both these students and the larger society represent cogent arguments for drastic improvements in their education. We believe that the principles for creating Accelerated Schools are at hand and that the evidence from similar efforts by James Comer and his associates shows that they can bring disadvantaged students into the educational mainstream (Comer, 1986, 1987). In order for the states to move in this direction, there are a number of policy actions that are necessary.

●The most important implication for the states is to make a clear and stated commitment to accelerating the education of disadvantaged students to bring them into the educational mainstream by elementary school completion. Such a commitment must be reinforced by taking the actions that are necessary to implement an accelerated approach. This may require both new resources and a willingness to reallocate some of the resources that are presently devoted to secondary school dropout prevention, teenage pregnancy reduction, and drug prevention programs. The successful acceleration of learning and elevation of student self-esteem in the elementary years should go far to reduce later problems.

Cost Implications for States

Not all of the dimensions of Accelerated Schools will have cost implications, since much of the effort will require doing different things with available resources. However, the full development of Accelerated Schools will require additional resources for full-program implementation, including such aspects as an extended day and possible summer programs, parental education, and tutoring programs. On the basis of benefit-cost studies, we believe that additional costs will be far outweighed by additional social benefits (Levin, 1972; Catterall, 1986).

●States should recognize that investments in accelerated education for the disadvantaged will have economic and social benefits that far exceed the magnitudes of the required investments. A concerted effort should be made to provide the necessary funding, not only because of the benefits that it confers on the disadvantaged in bringing them into the educational and social mainstream, but because of the benefits conferred upon the state as a whole.

Time Allocation for Changes and for Staff Development

With respect to time, there are two concerns. First is the issue of how long it will take to transform an existing school to a fully accelerated one. Our own view is that this will be a developmental process that should take about six years for an elementary school with a kindergarten and six grades. As school districts gain experience in the approach and benefit from both in-service and preservice training, it may be possible to accomplish the transition in a shorter period of time (e.g., four years). Clearly, the early years must address the establishment of effective systems of staff decision making, assessment, and curriculum goals, methods, and content, and subsequent years can implement additional instructional features of the approach. It may also be useful to transform curriculum for one or two grades each year in this transitional period.

A second aspect of time is finding enough of it during the school year and summer to enable school staff to plan and make decisions and to receive training. The existing school year provides precious little time to make a major transformation of school organization and activities. Perhaps this is one reason for the popularity of instructional "packages" that require only a few hours of staff training, even though subsequent evaluations do provide evidence that such packages are educationally effective. A larger part of the school year and summer must be freed up for school staff to invest in planning and implementation and staff development.

●States should consider ways in which schools can obtain more time for intensive staff development to transform themselves into accelerated organizations. This can be done through providing supplementary pay for summer institutes, as well as more staff development days during the school year in which the schools receive funding for days devoted to such activities.

School Organization

In terms of school organization, it will be necessary to increase both accountability and decision responsibilities of individual schools. This can be done by creating appropriate decision structures at the local school level and by providing the school with the information, technical assistance, and resources to address its challenges, as well as a system of assessment that enables it to evaluate progress. It will also require the school district to shift from a central agency that sets out standardized directions and directives for individual schools to a more service-oriented agency for local school clients. A preliminary model for such changes has been proposed (Levin, 1987).

●States should provide the technical assistance for school districts and schools to modify their forms of organization to give greater decision responsibilities to the individual school. At the same time, school districts will need assistance in creating their own technical services to assist individual schools in their jurisdictions. The states might sponsor research and management studies, which will provide guidelines for the changes as well as consultants to assist individual school districts. An additional set of important products might be a range of conceptual and practical publications that the state could produce to inform a wide audience of the changes and their implementation.

Information and Technical Assistance

It is necessary to establish a capacity for providing information and technical assistance to Accelerated Schools during the developmental phases. While we have created a modest capacity for such assistance under the Accelerated Schools Project at Stanford University—enough to work with two schools—and the beginning of a clearinghouse to support Accelerated Schools around the country, the ultimate support for such schools must be established in the states and the school districts themselves. At the present time, the Stanford University Accelerated Schools Project is working with

Regional Educational Laboratories to expand this capacity.

●States should consider devoting resources to the development of publications and expertise on the various dimensions of accelerated education with special applicability to the disadvantaged and other under-achieving students. States should sponsor more research and research syntheses on these topics, especially on different instructional strategies and organizational aspects. Results could be disseminated widely through both state publications and technical assistance.

Preservice Training

An Accelerated School approach implies very different roles for teachers and administrators. A school-based decision system requires facility in interacting productively in small and large groups as well as in undertaking individual and group problem solving. Instructional strategies and curriculum content for acceleration also presume the existence of knowledge and strategies among educators that are not found in conventional instructional settings or in the curriculum of training programs for teachers and administrators.

●States should review present approaches to credentialing teachers and administrators for working with educationally disadvantaged populations. The Accelerated School approach requires a much heavier emphasis on group dynamics, problem solving, assessment of curriculum and pupil progress, and parent programs than do conventional schools. In addition, teacher and administrator training programs in state universities will need to adopt new courses and training experiences, as well as to establish internships in schools that are dedicated to accelerated learning.

REFERENCES

Bandura, A. 1986. *Social foundations of thought and action.* Englewood Cliffs, N.J.: Prentice Hall.

Barr, R. C. 1973–74. Instructional pace differences and their effect on reading acquisition. *Reading Research Quarterly* 9(4):526–55.

Barton, J. and Calfee, R. 1987. Project READ: Professional knowledge as professional power. Stanford, Calif.: School of Education, Stanford University.

Calfee, R. and Henry, M. K. 1986. Project READ: An inservice model for training classroom teachers in effective reading instruction. In *Effective teaching of reading: Research and practice.* Ed. J. V. Hoffman. Newark, Del.: International Reading Association.

Catterall, J. S. 1986. On the social costs of dropping out of school, no. 86–SEPI–3. Stanford, Calif.: Stanford Education Policy Institute, Stanford University.

Cohen, E. G. 1986. *Designing groupwork.* New York: Teachers College Press.

Comer, J. P. 1980. *School power.* New York: Free Press.

—————. 1986. The Yale-New Haven primary prevention project: A follow-up study. *Journal of the American Academy of Child Psychiatry,* 24(2):154–60.

—————. 1987. New Haven's school—community connection. *Educational Leadership,* 44(6):13–18.

Cuevas, G. J.; Mann, P. H.; and McClung, R. M. 1986. The effects of a language process approach program on the mathematics of a language process approach program on the mathematics achievement of first, third, and fifth grades. Paper presented at the Annual Meeting of the American Education Research Association, San Francisco.

Denham, C., and Lieberan, A. (eds.). 1980. *Time to learn.* Washington, D.C.: National Institute of Education.

Edmonds, R. 1979. Effective schools for the urban poor. *Educational Leadership* 37(1):15–24.

Epstein, J. L. 1987. Parent involvement: What research says to administrators. *Education and Urban Society* 19(2):119–36.

Fisher, C. W., and Berliner, D. C. (Eds.). 1985. *Perspectives on instructional time.* White Plains, N.Y.: Longman.

Good, T. L., and Grouws, D. A. 1978. Curriculum pacing: Some empirical data in mathematics. *Curriculum Studies* 10(1):75–81.

Goodlad, J. I. 1984. *A place called school.* New York: McGraw-Hill.

Kelly, D., and Smrekar, C. 1987. Parent involvement and the accelerated school: A discussion paper. Prepared for the Accelerated School Project, Center for Educational Research at Stanford, Stanford University.

Levin, H. M. 1972. The costs to the nation of inadequate education. A report prepared for the Select Senate Committee on Equal Educational Opportunity. Summarized in Select Committee on Equal Educational Opportunity, U.S. Senate, *Toward equal educational opportunity.* 92d Congress, 2d Session, report no. 92–000. Washington, D.C.: U.S. Government Printing Office.

—————. 1986. *Educational reform for disadvantaged students: An emerging crisis.* West Haven, Conn.: National Education Association Professional Library.

—————. 1987. Finance and governance implications of school-based decisions. Paper prepared for Work in America Institute, Scarsdale, N.Y.

Lozanov, G. 1978. *Suggestology and outlines of suggestopedy.* New York: Gordon & Breach.

Madden, N. A., and Slavin, R. E. 1987. Effective pullout programs for students at risk. Paper presented at the Annual Meeting of the American Educational Research Association, Washington, D.C.

McDill, E. L.; Natriello, G.; and Pallas, A. 1985. Raising standards and retaining students: The impact of the reform recommendations on potential dropouts. *Review of Educational Research* 55(4):415–34.

Montessori, M. M., Jr. 1965. *The Montessori method.* Cambridge, Mass.: Robert Bentley.

———. 1976. *Education for human development.* New York: Schocken Books.

National Assessment of Educational Progress. 1976. *Functional literacy and basic reading performance.* Washington, D.C.: U.S. Office of Education, Department of Health, Education and Welfare.

Peterson, P. L. 1986. Selecting students and services for compensatory education: Lessons from aptitude-treatment interaction research. Paper prepared for the Conference on Effects of Alternative Designs in Compensatory Education, Washington, D.C.

Purkey, S. C., and Smith, M. S. 1983. Effective schools: A review. *The Elementary School Journal* Vol. 83:427–52.

Richardson, R. B. 1987. Active affective learning for accelerated schools. Accelerated Schools Project, Center for Educational Research at Stanford, School of Education, Stanford University.

Rogers, J. 1987. Collective expectations and the education of disadvantaged children. Background paper for the Accelerated Schools Project, Center for Educational Research at Stanford, School of Education, Stanford University.

Romberg, T. A. 1986. Mathematics for compensatory school programs. Papers prepared for the Conference of Effects of Alternative Designs in Compensatory Education, U.S. Department of Education.

Seeley, D. S. 1981. *Education through partnership: Mediating structures in education.* Cambridge, Mass.: Ballinger Publishing Co.

Slavin, R. E. 1983. *Cooperative learning.* White Plains, N.Y.: Longman.

———, Madden, N. A. 1987. Effective classroom programs for students at risk. Paper presented at the Annual Meeting of the American Educational Research Association, Washington, D.C.

II.
MEASURING MINORITY ACHIEVEMENT:
RESEARCH ISSUES

MINORITY ACHIEVEMENT AND PARENTAL SUPPORT: ACADEMIC RESOCIALIZATION THROUGH MENTORING

Henry Trueba
and Concha Delgado-Gaitan

Many minorities have serious educational problems in American schools. Minority student populations (particularly Blacks and Hispanics) are rapidly becoming the majority in some states and in many large cities, such as Detroit, Chicago, New York, Los Angeles, Baltimore, Dallas, and Philadelphia, in which student minorities account for 70 to 90 percent of all students.

INTRODUCTION: THE PROBLEM AND THIS STUDY

In California, for example, 45 percent of Hispanics between the tenth and twelfth grades, and 40 percent before the tenth grade drop out. In Los Angeles, two-thirds of the dropouts are Hispanic or black, and 50 percent of all ninth graders do not complete high school (U.S. Department of Commerce, Bureau of the Census, 1987). We also hear that by the year 2000 approximately one out of every three students will be a minority. There are 13 million children living in poverty (40 percent of all the poor are children—the largest percentage in the last 30 years), and most of these children are minorities living in the Southeast-Southwest poverty belt. Minorities have the largest, youngest, and lowest academically achieving families. And the trend will only continue, since minorities' median age is lower than that of the aging and less fertile mainstream population.

111

Over 70 percent of all Hispanic students attend segregated schools (up 15 percent since 1983), and 63 percent of blacks continue to attend segregated schools (down 13 percent from 1983). Only 2 percent of all Hispanics ever reach college, and only about 1 percent graduate from college or enter graduate school. Dropout rates for blacks and Hispanics are the highest in the country, and range from 40 to 75 percent of entering high school students.

Academic socialization is a process whereby students acquire the competencies necessary to function in the classroom. Academic competencies include not only a high level of proficiency in English, critical thinking skills, and control of the relationship between language and logic, but also social and cultural skills. Whereas academic performance as measured by standardized tests has enjoyed the attention of researchers, the sociocultural abilities and knowledge required for school success—which are obtained through parental mentoring—are less frequently discussed in the literature.

This paper describes the academic socialization of some Chicano and Anglo high school students in La Victoria (a pseudonym), Colorado, through which they acquired the necessary competencies required to succeed in school. We focus on the parents as agents of academic socialization (especially in their role as mentors).

MINORITY ACHIEVEMENT

Failure of students to graduate from high school creates a loss in personal income as well as in governmental revenue (King, 1978; Levin, 1980; Stern, 1985). The actual cost of students dropping out of school far exceeds the investment required to maintain them in public schools (Carnegie Council, 1979). Additionally, some researchers found that Chicano students who graduate from high school but do not continue their education have lower salaries than their Anglo counterparts, and that Chicano students who stay in school often have less earning power than those who drop out (Stern, 1985). The labor market ceiling alluded to by Ogbu (1974, 1978, 1987) may be responsible for preventing minorities from becoming motivated to pursue higher educational goals.

Socioeconomic status, language proficiency, education attainment of parents, cultural factors, and ethnic affiliation are often mentioned as factors contributing to Hispanic school attrition (Steinberg, Blinde, & Chan, 1982; Walberg, 1984). Chicano students with low English proficiency and low socioeconomic status are more likely to leave school than Black or Anglo students in similar circumstances (Bachman, O'Malley & Johnson; Brown, Rosen, Hill, & Olivas, 1980; Casas, Furlong, Carranza, & Solberg, 1986; Rumberger, 1981; Camp, 1980; Marem, 1980.) A study conducted from 1966 to 1970 involving 2,000 boys of varying socioeconomic class concluded that 23 percent of the boys from the lowest socioeconomic strata left school, while only 4 percent from the top strata dropped out (Cook & Alexander, 1980).

Bachman, O'Malley, and Johnson (1971) and Cicirelli (1978) have identified, in addition to socioeconomic status, three family characteristics contributing to the high dropout rates: single-parent families, large number of children, and lack of reading materials in the home. But even keeping these factors under control, Hispanic students continue to leave school at higher rates than their Anglo and black counterparts (Steinberg, Blinde, & Chan, 1982). Hispanic student attrition is probably due to additional factors beyond the low socioeconomic status. Other factors related to Hispanic attrition are truancy, negative peer influence, and low expectations on the part of teachers (Camp, 1980; Carnegie Council, 1979; Cervantes & Bernal, 1977; Cook & Alexnader, 1980; Fox & Elder, 1980; Laosa, 1977).

These studies, however, have not explained adequately the differential performance among Hispanic students from the same lower socioeconomic class. Furthermore, the literature has not dealt with the role of parents as agents of academic socialization used with the relationships between the family and the school personnel during the process of socialization.

This study revealed different reasons why Hispanic students dropped out of school. Some high-achieving students left school for nonacademic reasons, others faced academic problems. Yet most of them remained in school and overcame the same obstacles that pushed others out of school. What is it that makes some students decide to remain in school while others decide to drop out? One salient factor for those remaining in school was the presence of a mentor (often a parent).

Mentors help students acquire sociocultural skills required to interact effectively with teachers and other school personnel, for example in contexts in which students must inquire, seek information, and develop organizational skills to learn. Mentoring as part of the process of academic socialization is similar to the cultural socialization occurring at home: parents transmit knowledge and inculcate values and attitudes deemed essential. Parents can also teach children to view school as a political arena, or as a means to a pragmatic end (get a diploma to get a job), as an unavoidable obligation, or as a challenge and an opportunity. But if parents are marginal elements in the school system and do not acquire a good grasp of its operation, they cannot teach younger children the necessary organizational skills (both cognitive and social) to deal effectively with school demands. There are multiple phases in the process of socialization leading to academic failure that stand in clear contrast to the socialization phases experienced by successful students, regardless of ethnicity and linguistic differences (Kohn, 1983; Sinclair & Ghory, 1987).

In this study, these phases involved family members, peers, school personnel, and community groups. In the case of students who failed to stay in school, the process of socialization led them to disenfranchisement and marginality. The complexity of the process seems to indicate that academic failure is not necessarily the result of lack of ability or motivation. These children learned to feel and act marginal if they were not wanted in school. They learned to seek other rewards outside of the school. Youths showed a number of characteristics that can be interpreted as a preamble to total disengagement from school. To complicate matters more, some students acquired the feelings of marginality in the home before they came in contact with the school.

Often negative attitudes toward school result from inadequate academic socialization. Some students, however, return to school thanks to the intervention of new mentors who help resocialize students for academic success (Delgado-Gaitan, 1986).

THEORETICAL ADVANCES: A SOCIALLY-BASED THEORY OF SCHOOL ACHIEVEMENT

There have been a number of additional theoretical interdisciplinary developments resulting from field-based studies (Trueba, 1983, 1987a, 1987b, in press; Trueba & Delgado-Gaitan, 1988) and dealing with effective interventions by social scientists in schools, and after school hours, with minority children. These interventions have been guided by the work of Vygotsky (1962, 1978) and Neo-Vygotskians (Cole & D'Andrade, 1983; Cole & Scribner, 1974; Cole & Griffin, 1983; Diaz, Moll, & Mehan, 1986; Moll, 1986; Wertsch, 1981, 1985; Boggs, 1985; Tharp & Gallimore, in press).

Within a socially based theory of school achievement, academic failure and/or success are not a personal attribute of the student, but the direct result of structural and psychological contextual factors that permit a child to grow intellectually. Indeed, successful learning always occurs if a child is given the opportunity to engage in socially meaningful interactions within the "zone of proximal development" (Vygotsky, 1978), that is, in contextually meaningful activity settings, through "assisted performance" (with the help of others—those in the same social unit). Vygotsky, interpreted by Tharp & Gallimore, describes assisted performance as the crossroads between learning and cognitive development, whereby "the child performs, through assistance and cooperative activity, at developmental levels quite beyond the individual level of achievement" (Tharp & Gallimore, 1989). Students' commitment to engage in learning occurs during the transition from assisted to independent performance, which can be anticipated by the teacher.

Theoretically, Vygotsky's (1978) notion of the zone of proximal development plays a key role in understanding the socialization/resocialization phenomena. This notion sheds light on the assessment of students' intellectual abilities and the evaluation of instructional practices (Wertsch, 1985). The social and cultural basis of knowledge acquistion is predicated on the psychological and sociocultural functions of the family and social group.

Vygotsky, as interpreted by Wertsch, explained that "any function in the child's cultural development appears on the social plane, and then on the psychological plane" (Wertsch, 1981, p. 162). This process has been described as the process of internalization of cognitive and cultural structures, or cultural socialization, whereby the child moves freely between sociocultural activities and mental activities.

Vygotsky defined the zone of proximal development as "the distance between the actual developmental level as determined by individual problem solving and the level of potential development as determined through problem solving under adult guidance or in collaboration with more capable peers" (Vygotsky, 1978 p. 86). The mentor's role in this study was significant in building the awareness of students, and their ability to deal with the school in a way that allows them to succeed. The relationship between the zone of proximal development and the academic resocialization process through a mentor points to those tasks that students can do with the help of others, in contrast to those they can do alone.

THE STUDY AT LA VICTORIA

La Victoria, an urban community in Colorado of approximately 17,000 residents, was selected as the research site. The families were selected through a snowball process. That is, a key informant in the community volunteered names of families whom she knew through working with the schools, church and community organizations.

The criteria for recommendation included families who had high school students that had dropped out, were high risk, or were high achievers.

The members of ten Chicano families, four Anglo families, and several individual community members were interviewed in their own homes or workplaces, for up to three hours or for a minimum of one hour. Two or more ethnographic interviews were conducted with each participant. Other participants included community leaders, school board members, school administrators, teachers, and church leaders in the Catholic or Lutheran churches in which the families participated. The purpose was to obtain various levels of understanding about the role these participants played in the education of students in La Victoria and how they viewed the issue of dropouts.

Long-term residence in Colorado characterized the majority of these families. Nine of the ten Chicano families interviewed have lived in either La Victoria or other parts of Colorado for several generations. The four Anglo families in the study had resided in La Victoria for over 20 years. Table 1 represents the profiles of the families of the dropout and high-risk students.

TABLE 1
Chicano and Anglo Dropouts/High-Risk Students

Family	Sex	# of Members	Status at time of Study
Salas	M	3	working
Salas	M	4	married, working
Vargas	F	4	married
Avila	M	9	11th (high-risk)
Reyes	F	4	12th (dropped, & returned to alt. school)
White	M	4	married, working
Sands	M	2	working

TABLE 2
Chicano and Anglo High Achieving Students

Family	Sex	# of Members	Yr./Sch.	Academic Track
Gonzalez	M	11	10th	College Prep.
Santos	F	5	Comm. College	Basic
Valles	M	6	9th	Basic
Cerda	M	4	11th	College Prep.
Suarez	F	3	12th	Gifted/College Prep.
Baker	M	3	graduated	Comm. College
Miller	F	5	11th	Basic

These Chicano and Anglo families varied in size, while employment and marital status characterized the individual student's status in each case where the student had dropped out. Only one student had returned to the alternative school after dropping out of the traditional high school. The four males that had dropped out were working while the two women were either married or returned to the alternative school. The young man that was at risk was still in high school and did not have a job at the time but was contemplating quitting school to find employment.

Table 2 represents the family profiles and educational status of high-achieving Chicano and Anglo students. Some of the students were placed in the college preparatory track, while others received high grades but were in the basic curriculum track. That track offered only general education classes that did not prepare students to enter college. Family size in these families varied such that no real pattern existed in this characteristic. Furthermore, gender was recognized only to make the point that both males and females were identified as successful students in the study.

The 1980 census reports that nearly 30 percent of the La Victoria population is Hispanic. The term "Hispanic" is the general category used in the census to identify the population of Mexican and/or Spanish origin. The Hispanic families in the study are identified as Chicano or Mexican. The community is said to be generally middle to low-income level, since more than 12 percent of the households are run by single women parents who work in skilled labor positions or are unemployed. The majority of the employed Hispanic adults hold operational, technical, or service positions.

The La Victoria School District reported a 50 percent dropout rate, which, by their definition, meant that 50 percent of those entering as freshmen dropped out before graduating. The school district was making serious efforts to reduce the high percentage of dropouts. A special task force was established to investigate the problem of dropouts and to propose recommendations to rectify the problem. One of the special programs is the discontinuer transition program, which is designed to bring dropout students back to the high school under an individual course of study for completing their high school requirements. Whereas more Hispanic students than Anglo students drop out of school, the discontinuer transition program attracted ten Anglo students and only two Hispanics in its first year of implementation.

Adequate analysis has not been conducted to determine the reason for these outcomes. The La Victoria School District authorities view high school dropout rates as a complex problem that must be handled separately from the regular classroom activities, that is, students who leave school are "problem students" who need alternative programs. Although the administrators interviewed agreed that students drop out for different reasons, their strategies to correct the problem consist of increasing the accountability of attendance to class and of tracking students into skill classes separate from the regular curriculum. The tendency on the part of school personnel is to consider the dropout issue as a problem inherent in the students rather than a problem related to the instructional process.

Findings: Developing Social Competence

The La Victoria study showed that the choices to stay in school or discontinue are closely related to the significant mentoring of an adult in the student's life. Although the majority of students indicated that school was actually meaningless, the reality indicated that not all students drop out of school. Many of the people who participated in this study believed that the one major reason that they remained in school and were able to overcome severe emotional academic, and social obstacles was their relationship to a special person who served as a mentor in their life and their school career. The role of the mentor was one of an individual who (1) interpreted the school system for the student, (2) persistently encouraged the student and believed in the student's ability, and (3) was actively involved in the school to advocate the student.

The literature defines a mentor in many ways, but usually discusses mentorship in terms of the character of the relationship and the function it serves. A mentor's primary function is to be a parent and peer. This study showed that the mentor was the strongest indicator of what made a difference between students who chose to stay in school and those who dropped out. No significant difference was found between Anglo and Hispanic students with respect to the presence or absence of a mentor. Hispanic and Anglo students who remained in school expressed their thankfulness to the efforts of a significant person who advocated them at times and pushed them when they did not have the confidence to deal with their daily conflicts.

Parents and students expressed their profound dissatisfaction with the content and the method of instruction, which was irrelevant and meaningless in their self-fulfillment. Yet, in spite of their personal or educational obstacles, many Hispanic and Anglo students remain in school and do quite well. The subsequent section presents the concept of mentorship as described by La Victoria students, their families, and teachers. The mentor phenomenon is a strong factor cited by successful students in their choice to stay in school. It was important to see how the mentor functions in the lives of students.

Three major points pertaining to socialization and resocialization are significant in constructing an overview of the schooling process for the students in La Victoria: (1) the type of socialization of attitudes toward school in the home; (2) the resocialization intervention; and (3) the individual's role in resocialization.

Family Attitudes toward School

All students are socialized to a particular orientation toward school. Students that remained in school throughout their career and achieved much experienced a great deal of support from their families to stay in school. The explicit and implicit message from home was that the student was important and that the school must offer the student every opportunity to learn. This message was conveyed through consistent parental verbal acknowledgment of the values of schooling, and through the parents' active involvement in their children's schooling.

Active parents differed in socioeconomic level and educational attainment. Some parents in this category had college educations, whereas others had dropped out of junior high school. In these families, students learned to deal with school-related conflicts because the parents played a strong mentor role. Parents described their persistent interest in their children's schooling as the expected parental behavior. One Anglo parent, Mrs. Baker, related her activities throughout her son's schooling. She had encountered one obstacle after another as she attempted to get the teachers to make a complete assessment of her son's learning abilities when he was labeled "learning disabled." Mrs. Baker was active in her son's schooling since the time he was in elementary school until he graduated from high school. Even after that, she continued to be active as a community member. Her principal form of involvement was in the parent-teacher association (PTA). In spite of her involvement in the PTA, Mrs. Baker felt totally frustrated and isolated from the school whenever she asked questions about her son's academic performance and the school's attempts to place him in a special education class.

> TEXT 1: I don't think as parents that we have a choice on what we have to do to keep our children in school. My son is now in college but it was almost a full-time job to make sure that he got fair treatment at school. It's as if those teachers and administrators felt that students from La Victoria aren't worth much. They also did everything to prevent parents from finding out what they were doing with the students ... I went to a meeting where they were discussing my son's placement into a special education class. I was furious because they had not tested him except in one test and that was not enough to prove to me that he was learning handicapped. At the meeting they [the school personnel] were very impatient and rude whenever I asked for an explanation. My son did not belong in a handicapped class. He had a problem with one eye but he was an intelligent boy, not slow. At the meeting they deliberately tried to keep me from participating in the decision and I kept thinking that if that was the way they treated me, an adult who was not going to be intimidated, I can see why students have so many problems in school.

Mrs. Baker's experiences with the school led her to believe that it was necessary for her to intervene in her son's schooling as much as possible. She felt the alienation as a result of not being able to participate in the decision to place her son in a learning-handicapped class. The frustration Mrs. Baker faced was twofold. First, she felt it was unnecessary for her son to be placed in a special class, because he was intelligent beyond what the school had assessed. Second, her frustration was intensified by the context, which prevented her from expressing her views and from understanding the educators' arguments because of their use of specialized language.

This parent's encounter with the educators was representative of the type of conflicts that parents faced in dealing with La Victoria schools. Parents were typically treated as unwelcome guests. This is where the line is drawn between parents who sustained a consistent active relationship with the schools and those who were so discouraged that they gave up trying to communicate with the school. Mrs. Baker's active role in the school on behalf of her son conveyed the message to her son that his schooling was very important and that he was an intelligent person that deserved the best opportunity possible.

Gerald, Mrs. Baker's son, felt that he was fortunate that his parents, in particular his mother, tried so hard to help him deal with the schooling process. Because he observed how much time his mother spent participating in committees and helping him with his work, Gerald interpreted the parents' role in the socialization process as a symbol of caring. Gerald, as well as his mother, believed that many students have problems in school because their parents do not care about them. Contrary to this belief, the data show unequivocally that all parents cared whether their children succeeded, but the fundamental difference was in the extent to which parents felt capable or powerful enough to intervene in the schooling process.

The strong socialization is essentially a mentorship role played by the parents. This direction toward success in school, which was established in many families in La Victoria, carried an implicit message, that success for these students meant the parents' tenacity in helping the students in the home and getting involved in the schools. The difference between parents who were actively involved in the home and those who were not indicated that parents who did not actively confront the school felt incompetent and unable to make any changes on behalf of their children. These parents played a supportive role in the home and verbally encouraged their children to progress in their studies and to stay in school. Students who had supportive parents at home but had difficulties in dealing with their conflicts in school were oftentimes fortunate enough to find mentors. The mentor intervened in various ways to assist the student in coping with conflicts in school. The mentor was instrumental in the student's resocialization process, which helped the student to recognize the possible options and solutions to school-related problems.

Intervention Strategies at Home

Socialization as has been discussed here occurs in the home and pertains to the students' orientation toward themselves and their schooling needs. Thus, we can ascertain that if students require a different orientation toward themselves and the school, they will need to be resocialized. This concept is presented in this section to interpret the role that adult mentors played in keeping high-risk students in school. Some parents in La Victoria felt that they tried their best to help their children stay in high school. They reminded them to do their work, provided a space to work, and helped them to make decisions about school when necessary. Yet, in spite of these efforts, parents found themselves frustrated when their children developed school-related conflicts that were unmanageable and that eventually caused the students to drop out.

High school students in major conflict with the school often established supportive relationships with significant adults other than their parents. These adults were sometimes alternative school teachers, coaches, or community leaders. Students varied in the time periods during which they had serious conflicts with the school. Some students began to feel isolated and confused in junior high school, whereas others began to feel estranged from school in the first two years of high school. John is an example of a Hispanic student who had conflicts with a teacher and some peers in his freshman year of high school. This group of students felt sufficiently disenchanted with school that they either considered dropping out or actually dropped out.

John Valles is the oldest of four children in his family. His younger brother is in junior high school and is having many problems in school because he is bored. The two younger sisters in kindergarten and in first grade are doing very well because the parents help them to read and support them as much as they can. Although the parents speak only Spanish at home, the children, including John, speak both English and Spanish because their schooling has all been in English. As a student, John was very active in school sports, including track. He also attended weekly teen meetings at St. Mark's Church. Social events were planned by the students that attended and discussions were held by the Catholic Sisters and Brothers.

During his schooling career, John was an average student. He received mostly B's and C's on his report card during most of his elementary school and junior high school years. As a freshman at La Victoria High School, John had become involved with a peer group that thought it was more fun to cut school than attend classes. One day a teacher refused to let John make up a test when he was legitimately absent, and John went with a group of friends who set fire to a trash can on the school grounds. John was expelled and his parents felt hopeless about what they could do to help their son, who seemed to be bored with school and going astray. John's counselor called him into his office soon after the expulsion and asked him if he wanted to participate in a special program through the local state university. The program involved high-risk Hispanic students from the surrounding high schools. The students received guidance about entrance requirements for college from university counselors. This helped the students to prepare for college by taking the appropriate courses while still in high school. John and his parents decided to accept the opportunity to participate in the project for the remainder of his high school career. At the time the study was conducted, he had been in the mentorship project for one year.

TEXT 2: I've been doing OK. I want to stay in school so I can get a good job. The only way is to keep doing my work, I guess, and stay out of trouble.

[To the question on how he would stay out of trouble, John responded:]

I can't listen to my friends like I used to 'cause some of them don't like school and just keep getting into trouble. I have to start listening to the counselor in school unless he tells me that I don't make it. Then I guess I'll have to keep trying harder.

[John clarified how he would deal with the possibility of having counselors or teachers tell him that he cannot make it:]

Well, I think that I probably wouldn't believe him because I do want to make it. My parents want me to make it and they help me all they can. I know there are some teachers over there [the high school] that keep telling me and my friends we'll never be much, but I think I can, 'cause now that other counselor at the college is helping me too, but I guess my parents still want me to find different friends, so I'm trying.

John was depicting the process of resocialization as he described how he was moving from involvement with peers who disliked school to working with his counselor and parents to stay in school. John was also facing negative expectations from some teachers, who wanted John to believe that he was not capable of succeeding. These educators were proven wrong as John began to correct his behavior and engage in his schoolwork. This is a critical point to note, because educators tend to believe that once students begin to pull away from school, their conflict is a permanent condition. Teachers then believe that it is not worth the time and effort to redirect the students' energy. John's case showed that he was interested in doing well, but was not receiving the necessary support and guidance that would focus him into the system.

The intervention on the part of the college mentor was the catalyst in redirecting John's goals. John began to understand how it was possible for him to succeed in a place where he had been failing. In John's case, the mentor role was played by the counselor at the local college. In the case of other students, the resocialization intervention involved teachers, particularly alternative school teachers. In order for resocialization to function between the mentor and the potential dropout, there needs to be a special bond. It is the quality of the bond that leads to the appreciation of school and interest in going to school. John's case also characterizes the student's ability to choose to listen to the mentors and thus assert their individual power to participate in their change.

One alternative high school teacher, who was also a parent in the community, spoke candidly about the different types of dropouts and her role as a teacher. There is a notion on the part of educators and some parents that students who drop out of school do so because they have problems that begin at the moment when they drop out. According to this teacher and parent, Mrs. Lopez, various types of dropouts exist.

Some students do not drop out of school. They leave school because they are pushed out. That means that the students may have trouble in school and the teachers do not provide the necessary help, so the students get bored because they do not understand. Students get tired of waiting around for help. It is easier to leave, especially if they have had to put up with this type of treatment for years.

Another type of dropout is the student who decides that he or she is not going to put up with humiliation by teachers. These students leave the high school, but may return to school through alternative programs. The alternative school and the General Education Diploma (GED) through night school are types of alternative programs. Alternative school teachers, like Mrs. Lopez, in La Victoria had a different perspective than the traditional high school teachers about the students' motives for dropping out because they have to teach students who for whatever reason have left the traditional school system as she states in TEXT 3.

> TEXT 3: Some students leave school because they have financial problems at home and they must help, so they take a break from school and maybe return to the regular high school or find another means to get their GED. Other students might want to break from school because they don't know what they want to do, so they leave and come back when they decide, or they go into the Army and maybe finish up their schooling there.

Mrs. Lopez, an alternative school teacher, provided a typology for why students drop out or are pushed out of school. Students who may even be high achievers are likely to leave school if the conditions are not right. That is, if the school does not have the meaning for them that they seek, they are likely to leave even if their grades are good. Students who may not be getting good grades or doing well in school in general may actually stay in for as long as they meet the minimum requirements.

As a teacher, Mrs. Lopez feels that students who want to do well in school may not have a chance when uncaring and unprepared teachers do not acknowledge or address the academic needs of the students. There appears to be a complex set of factors related to school and the family, which contribute to the student's decision to stay in or leave school. There is a pressing question that underlies the typology suggested by Mrs. Lopez: "If family and personal problems contribute to some of the students' reasons for leaving school then how can we blame the school for the high dropout rate?" Mrs. Lopez candidly shared her views on this particular question.

TEXT 4: By the time they get to alternative school, these students have faced so much failure that they hurt. The challenge is greater to help these young people see themselves for the intelligent human beings that they are. You have to let them know that you're judging their work, not them. As a teacher, I don't care if my students come in smelly or dirty or however they come in. I'm there to teach them not to judge them. Yes, if they are offensive to other students then I'll have a talk with them about hygiene but I'm not going to tell that I won't work with them 'cause they're dirty. If we want them in our classrooms so we can have their minds, then we better be able to deal with them, bad breath and all, just as God made them.

Mrs. Lopez recognized that some students may not be totally conscious of their physical upkeep. However, she felt that once students feel good about themselves and know that they are worth something, then they can deal with those other matters that seem to be social obstacles.

There is a message about teaching in Mrs. Lopez's statement, that is, teachers do not have to view the students' personal limitations as an academic deterrent. Mrs. Lopez is willing to take students where they are and work with them to expand their learning. Thus she is a mentor. This is essentially what the role of a mentor is. Mrs. Lopez acts as a teacher/mentor for students in the alternative school. She acknowledges that her responsibility as a teacher includes recognizing the students' full potential and providing them with the maximum opportunity to execute their skills and talents. She believes that the teacher's role means creating a safe environment in which students can feel competent.

Acceptance is a key aspect of this teacher's responsibility. She knows that she can reach the students by recognizing who they are, their uniqueness, and their needs. She is convinced that most students can perform academic tasks if they have the proper support. Therefore, if students do not have the necessary support in the home or in the high school, she, as a teacher, can still make it possible for them to learn by providing them special moral, intellectual, academic, and human support. Her job as a teacher consisted of becoming a broker between the social milieu (community, school, or home) and the students' peer group. She knew how to stimulate the student in the classroom regardless of the student's home environment and previous experience in school. A key point here is that this teacher understood that students' home problems may contribute to their problems in school, but need not interfere with their classroom learning if the teacher is sensitive to their individual needs. To explain attrition, we need to examine all factors, but we also need to provide opportunity for minority students to be resocialized. They need to begin to see how school is important.

The decision to stay in school or go to school are linked to sociocultural knowledge about schools and the value of learning. This is a Vygotskian (1978) notion of learning with the assistance of a knowledgeable person. The essence here is how culture is transmitted in a case where there is a lack of opportunity for marginal students. Academic knowledge is linked to social knowledge. Vygotsky's theory of advanced psychological processes states that the knowledge is acquired in a sociocultural context when the learner participates through critical inquiry to get information necessary to make decisions.

TOWARD A RESOCIALIZATION MODEL

Resocializing students to succeed in school is a lengthy and complex process. This study showed that the mentor plays a significant role in teaching students to perform competently in their school setting. Consequently, in La Victoria, the presence or absence of a mentor in the students' lives determined how they dealt with school conflicts. The role of mentor in the various stages of socialization is complex and difficult. Table 3, Learning to Succeed: Interactional Contexts and Stages or Socialization (next page, adapted from Trueba, 1988, p. 211), shows how much of the process of academic socialization is affected by factors outside the home. Parents need to regain control of this process and help their children interpret school and street experiences in a way that helps them grow intellectually. The construction of success requires continuous mentoring, guidance, care, and organization in the home.

The role of the mentor must also be understood in its totality rather than in a simplistic manner. In this study, mentorship was shown to occur in various forms and patterns throughout a students' schooling. The most important aspect of mentorship is that the student accepts the message conveyed by the mentor, that is, that the student is a capable and worthy person and that all problems have solutions that can be strategized. The meaning of this message is a powerful source of direction for the students, and for this reason it is critical that students have someone to play this role for them throughout their schooling. However, this study indicated that mentors can also have significant impact on students in the resocialization process. If the student has not had consistent support throughout school and has conflicts in school, a strong possibility exists that a mentor can help the student change his or her direction and choices for schooling.

This study showed that high school Hispanic and Anglo students faced similar serious social, cultural, and economic problems over a long period of time. Such experiences influenced their decision to overcome demanding obstacles and stay in school, or to drop out. It is important to note that the aspirations, expectations, and perceptions that helped to construct a student's choice vary not only among families in La Victoria, but also within the individual families. Diversity exists not only in the type of social and

TABLE 3

Learning to Succeed: Interactional Contexts and Stages of Socialization

		STAGES OF SOCIALIZATION	
		Construction of Success	Outcomes
INTERACTIONAL CONTEXTS	Community	Community-based counseling, legal and mental health services, basic exposure to public institutions (banks, schools, hospitals, etc.) through literacy classes. Message: "America is multicultural and your ethnic community is part of America."	Selective assimilation patterns through active participation in interethnic public activities. Collective presence in various institutional positions and roles.
	School	Use of peer group to reinterpret degradation events and to create a climate of acceptance for cultural differences. Message: "Minority students belong here and can achieve with peer support."	Acceptance of potential success of minority students on the part of school personnel and peer groups. Increasing influence of interethnic peer groups in support of academic success.
	Home	Reach-out efforts to help parents become strong school allies. Friendly communication for the purpose of creating a support system for the minority student. Message: "You and your child belong in our school."	Selective adult support for student. Reorganization of home life style to help student engage in academic work and provide emotional support. Knowledge of the function of school and roles of school personnel.
	Self	On a one-to-one basis, reinterpret past experiences, overcome impact of degradation events, and engage in learning activities through personal relationships with teachers and peers. Discover actual and potential academic skills. Message: "You can succeed if you are willing to seek help."	Redefinition of and acceptance of self. Control over stress and commitment to academic work. Increased cognitive and linguistic skills to articulate abstract thought. Social skills to handle academic problems and engage in learning relationships.

Source: Trueba, 1988, p. 221.

academic problems that students experience but also in the way that they utilize their resources to solve their problem. The variation is explained by the extent to which students are provided the opportunity to learn how to be competent in dealing with school expectations.

Evidence indicates that students do not drop out of school solely as a result of low achievement. Findings in this study confirmed that students are socialized by their families to deal with school. Students who are not taught to understand and deal with the school as a system, or whose parents did not know how the system operates, experienced more conflict in school. These students would still be able to deal with school-related conflicts through the assistance of a mentor. Many of those that are succeeding in school attribute their endurance to the persistent mentorship of a caring and compassionate adult.

A major reason for continuing with school offered by the students was their trusting relationship with a mentor. The absence of such a person in the lives of dropouts was cited as a real gap in their support system. The role of the mentor provided the students with means of interpreting the educational system as an objective institution and in a way that showed faith in the ability of the student. The demystification of the schooling process assisted the students in braving challenges they face with their teachers, the curriculum, and other school academic and social pressures. Mentors manifested their advocacy of students in various ways, including direct intervention with school personnel. Possibly one of the most critical outcomes of the mentors' role was providing the students with a model of self-determination once the students were convinced that their difficulties did not mean that they were personal failures.

If we acknowledge that achievement and social marginality are both learned processes, then we can conceive of a new process of resocialization, which mentors can provide. This new process should include well-designed programs that involve systematic interaction between the school personnel and the members of the family at all levels (Walberg, 1984). This is an initial step in organizing school policy and programs. Possibilities exist for the development of mentorship networks between caring adults and interested students who may be marginal but are capable of performing successfully and staying in school.

Another important function of mentors is to remind teachers and other school personnel of the need to systematically maximize the quality of adult support for students all along their educational career. The level of individual attention given to a student by a significant adult who recognizes the student's potential, believes in the student, and actively engages the student in his or her own learning is critical to the student's development of compentency.

Further research to examine why some students drop out while others are able to persevere and remain in school needs to combine ethnographic methodology and intervention strategies. That is, in addition to examining the problem, the researchers need to work closely with school districts to interpret the research data and form collaborative efforts to assist the local communities in establishing resocialization procedures that will help high-risk students develop self-confidence and constructive educational goals.

REFERENCES

Bachman, J. G.; O'Malley; and Johnson, L. 1971. *Youth in transition: Dropping out—problem or symptom?* Vol. 3. Ann Arbor, Mich.: Institute for Social Research, University of Michigan.

Boggs, S. T. 1985. *Speaking, relating, and learning: A study of Hawaiian children at home and at school.* Norwood, N.J.: Ablex Publishing Corp.

Brown, G. H.; Rosen, N. L.; Hill, S. T.; and Olivas, M. A. 1980. *The condition of education for Hispanic Americans.* National Center for Education Statistics. Washington, D.C.: U.S. Government Printing Office.

Camp, C. 1980. *School dropouts.* Sacramento, Calif.: Assembly Office of Research, California Legislature. ERIC Document Prediction Service, no. ED 191959.

Carnegie Council on Policy Studies in Higher Education. 1979. *Giving youth a better change: Options for education, work, and service.* San Francisco: Jossey-Bass Publishers.

Casas, M.; Furlong, M.; Carranza, O.; and Solberg, S. 1986. *Santa Barbara student success story: Profiling successful and at risk high school students.* Final report submitted to Santa Barbara School Board of Education.

Cervantes, R. A., and Bernal, H. H. 1977. *Psychological growth and academic achievement in Mexican-American students.* Paper prepared for the National Institute of Education. San Antonio: D.C. Development Associates Inc.

Cicirelli, V. G. 1978. The relationship of sibling structure to intellectual abilities and achievement. *Review of Educational Research* 48:365–79.

Cole, M., and D'Andrade, R. 1982. The influence of schooling on concept formation: Some preliminary conclusions. *The Quarterly Newsletter of the Laboratory of Comparative Human Cognition* 4(2):19–26.

Cole, M., and Griffin, P. 1983. A socio-historical approach to re-mediation. *The Quarterly Newsletter of the Laboratory of Comparative Human Cognition* 5(4):69–74.

Cole, M., and Scribner, S. 1974. *Culture and thought: A psychological introduction.* New York: Basic Books.

Cook, M. A., and Alexander, K. L. 1980. Design and substance in educational research: Adolescent attainments, a case in point. *Sociology of Education* 53(4):187–202.

Delgado-Gaitan, C. 1986. Teacher attitudes on diversity affecting student socio-academic responses: An ethnographic view. *Journal on Adolescent Research* 1(1):103–14.

Diaz, S.; Moll, L.; and Mehan, H. 1986. Sociocultural resources in instruction: A context-specific approach. In *Beyond language: Social and cultural factors in schooling language minority students*. Sacramento, Calif.: Bilingual Education Office, California State Department of Education.

Fox, W., and Elder, N. 1980. *A study of practices and policies for discipline and dropouts in ten selected schools*. New York: St. Lawrence University.

King, R. H. 1978. *The labor market consequences of dropping out of high school*. Columbus, Ohio: Center for Human Resources Research, Ohio State University.

Kohn, M. 1983. On the transmission of values in the family: A preliminary formulation. In *Research in sociology of education and socialization*, ed. A. Kerchoff. Greenwich, Conn.: Jai Press.

Laosa, L. M. 1977. Inequality in the classroom: Observational research on teacher-student interactions. *Aztlan: International Journal of Chicano Studies Research* 8:51–67.

Levin, H. M. 1980. *Youth unemployment and its educational consequences*. Policy paper no. 80–92. Stanford, Calif.: Stanford University, Institute for Research on Educational Finance and Governance.

Marem, R. D. 1980. Social background and school continuation decisions. *Journal of American Statistical Association* 75:295–305.

Moll, L. 1986. Writing as communication: Creating strategic learning environments for students. *Theory to Practice* 26(2):102–8.

Ogbu, J. 1974. *The next generation: An ethnography of education in an urban neighborhood*. San Diego: Academic Press.

———. 1978. *Minority education and caste: The American system in cross-cultural perspective*. San Diego: Academic Press.

———. 1987. Variability in minority responses to schooling: Nonimmigrants vs. immigrants. In G. Spindler and L. Spindler (eds.), *Interpretive ethnography of education: At home and abroad* (p. 255–78). Hillsdale, N.J.: Lawrence Erlbaum Associates.

Rumberger, R. W. 1981. *Why kids drop out of school*. Stanford, Calif.: Stanford University, Institute for Research on Educational Finance and Governance.

Sinclair, R. L., and Ghory, W. J. 1987. Becoming marginal. In *Success or failure: The minority student at home and at school*, ed. H. T. Trueba. New York: Harper & Row.

Steinberg, L.; Blinde, P. L.; and Chan, K. S. 1982. *Dropping out among minority youth: A review of the literature*. NCBR report U.S. Department of Education National Institute of Education.

Stern, D. 1985. *Educational attainment and employment of major racial or ethnic groups in California*. A paper presented at the Conference on

Education and Underachievement of Linguistic Minorities, sponsored by the University of California.

Tharp, R. and Gallimore, R. 1989. *Rousing minds to life: Teaching, learning, and schooling in social context.* Cambridge: Cambridge University Press.

Trueba, H. 1983. Adjustment problems of Mexican American children: An anthropological study. *Learning Disabilities Quarterly* 6(4):8–15.

———, ed. 1987a. *Success or failure? Learning and the language minority student.* New York: Newbury House Publishers.

———. 1987b. Organizing classroom instruction in specific sociocultural contexts: Teaching Mexican youth to write in English. In *Becoming literate in English as a second language: Advances in research and theory,* ed. S. Goldman and H. Trueba. Norwood, N.J.: Ablex Publishing Corporation.

———. 1988. Peer socialization among minority students: A high school dropout prevention program. In *School & society: Learning content through culture,* ed. H. Trueba and C. Delgado-Gaitan. New York: Praeger Publishers.

———. (in press). *Raising silent voices: Educating the linguistic minorities for the 21st century.* New York: Harper & Row.

Trueba, H., and Delgado-Gaitan, C. 1988. *School and society: Learning content through culture.* New York: Praeger Publishers.

U.S.Department of Commerce. Bureau of the Census. 1987. *The Hispanic population in the United States: March 1986 and 1987 (advance report).* Washington, D.C.: U.S. Government Printing Office.

Vygotsky, L. S. 1962. *Thought and language.* Cambridge, Mass.: MIT Press.

———. 1978. *Mind in society.* Cambridge, Mass.: Harvard University Press.

Walberg, H. 1984. Improving productivity of America's schools. *Educational Leadership* 4(8):19–27.

Wertsch, J. 1981. *The concept of activity in Soviet psychology.* Armonk, N.Y.: M. E. Sharpe.

———. 1985. *Vygotsky and the social formation of mind.* Cambridge, Mass.: Harvard University Press.

THE PROBLEM OF EDUCATIONAL DEVELOPMENT IN THE INNER CITY

Elaine W. Walker

Education remains one of the primary means of raising the productive capacity of the poor in developed as well as developing societies. Yet, as the historical and empirical evidence have shown, the development of educational structures and their outcomes as measured by the quality of human capital acquired is significantly different for inner-city urban and nonurban sectors, particularly in the United States. The perceived crisis of urban education that this has engendered has led not only to a burgeoning subspecialization within education known as "urban education," but has led recently to bold postures by legislators in some states to wrest control of inept urban educational systems from local control (Braun, 1987).

A recurring oversight in the arguments advanced both in defense of and in critique of current urban systems is the degree of interpenetration by social, economic, and political forces emanating from the larger social structure into these educational systems (Grace, 1984). If, as Grace advocates, urban education must be conceived as the investigation of social, economic, cultural, and political relations as they impinge upon, and are exemplified in, metropolitan educational systems, is there a unifying theoretical perspective that can facilitate such an interpretation? Is there one that can place both the urban system and its institutions within an explanatory framework such that its interlinkage with these wider social forces can be made explicit and testable?

The objective of this paper is to test the utility of the dependency paradigm as a general framework for understanding these interlinkages. The paper focuses particularly on two important concepts—economic and cultural dependency—demonstrating how some of the current ills faced by inner-city urban educational systems may have arisen or have been exacerbated by both. Schematically, the paper begins with an overview of the field of urban education and prevailing paradigms. Second, a presentation of the dependency model is made, followed by an examination of its fit to inner-city urban educational structures on the basis of supportive evidence.

Although the concern with issues pertaining to the education of urban masses dates back to the mid- and late nineteenth centuries (Tyack, 1974; Katz, 1971), the field of urban education did not emerge until the urban crisis was constituted in the 1960s. This crisis represented a coalescence of social and political turmoil coinciding and perhaps exacerbated by the slowing down of the economy. Thus as Sharp noted, "urban education emerged for solving the educational manifestations of the urban crisis, and to redistribute educational opportunity in favor of disadvantaged groups" (Sharp, 1984, p. 64). With a focus on what Sharp defines as distributive justice, the goal became ameliorative in intent, with scant attention paid to the underlying structure of the social system, and no theory of the context of urban schools. Consequently, the educational problems of urban systems within the traditional framework of educational analysis were cast conceptually within a framework that focused on the cultural differences of the urban populace. This framework, in keeping with the earlier sociological analysis of urban social problems in the sociology of Park (1952), Burgess (1967), and others, articulated the problems of education for urban students as the natural deficiencies of these students' homes and cultural backgrounds (Riessman, 1963; Deutsch, 1963). Furthermore, as Bash, Coulby, and Jones (1985) indicated, these empiricisms were marked by a concentration upon the minutiae of urban educational systems, devoid of a strong conceptual frame, and incapable of shedding light on why educational difficulties remained a persistent feature of urban schools.

In contrast, historiographies of urban education in the United States vividly revealed the degree to which narrow class and political interests historically used urban educational systems to pursue their own ends, and as mechanisms of social control (Cohen, 1984; Bowles & Gintis, 1976; Katz, 1968, 1971; Tyack, 1974). Katz's analysis of the school-reform movements in the mid-nineteenth century, in which education was made popular, indicated that, devoid of rhetoric, these reforms served two purposes. First, for the elite, these reforms were viewed as ways of solving the problems of an urban industrial society, while, second, they provided for the middle class the means by which intragenerational mobility could be secured.

The explicit class interests that these earlier reform movements embodied were further expressed in the organizational revolutions that occurred in the public schools in the late nineteenth and early twentieth centuries

(Tyack, 1974). This "revolution," spearheaded by a coalition of university presidents, professors of educational administration, leading businessmen, lawyers, and publishers of newspapers, sought to replace the local ward system with a system of management synonymous with the one that existed in industry. However, these reforms actually served to broaden the spheres of power and control for the school professional. These accounts of the early history of urban education clearly underscored the need to adopt a "critical" approach in studying contemporary urban educational structures, given their historical genesis.

However, the conceptual maps currently used to study and explain the continuing problems of urban educational systems represent a divergence of perspectives, each embodying distinct assumptions and implications for social change. In broad terms, these perspectives may be grouped along the ideological continuum ranging from conservatism to liberalism to radicalism. Briefly discussed earlier in this paper was the conservative perspective, which frames the failure of urban school systems within the deficit paradigm. The argument advanced by this perspective is that the urban school population is culturally disadvantaged and lacks the requisite skills necessary for success in school. The solution to the urban problem lies in the development of educational solutions that will compensate for these deficiencies (Gordon & Wilkerson, 1966). Although culturalist explanations have been discredited by much research (Berger & Simon, 1974; Ryan, 1976; Valentine, 1968), they remain a popular and quick retort of many inner-city urban educators for explaining the failure of urban education.

Liberal perspectives locate the problems of urban educational systems within a multifactor paradigmatic framework. Thus, factors related to the larger urban environment may be deemed important, as well as various organizational and structural features of the urban educational system itself. The fundamental difference between this perspective and the former is the minimization of culturalist explanations by liberals. Proponents of this perspective concede that the urban economy, the problem of scarce resources, and competing interests all impinge negatively upon urban schools (Gittell & Hevesi, 1969; Katzman, 1971). However, there are serious limitations to some of the analyses undertaken in this vein, since there is a tendency to overlook the linkage between the political economy of the city and the functioning of the capitalist economy. For example, Grace (1984) notes that although Gittell and Hevesi addressed the issue of political struggle among various interest groups for control of these systems, the discussion of this issue was disengaged from an analysis of the distribution of power and resources in the larger society.

Similar shortcomings are evident in those analyses that view bureaucratization as a major structural problem (Persell, 1977; Rogers, 1968). Indeed, Rogers went so far as to suggest that the high degree of centralization, coupled with a number of other critical factors, has resulted in organizational paralysis in these systems. Whereas there is no denying the rigidity of the bureaucratic structure of urban educational systems, Tyack (1974) points out that centralization was initially designed to further the interests of white Protestant Americans, although it has been alternatively posited that centralization and bureaucratization were necessary in a system of pluralistic politics (Kaestle, 1973). The evidence indicates that bureaucratic control systems have largely served in many contemporary urban schools to disempower marginal groups (Shapiro, 1987).

Critical interpretations of the problems of education start with the assumption, unlike liberalism, that the reform of these systems is incapable of success within the present configuration of political and economic relations. Within this growing body of pedagogy, four thematic approaches have emerged (Giroux, 1983). First, there is the notion that, given the nature of the linkages between school and the capitalist economy, schooling serves primarily to reproduce the relations of dominance and subordinance that inhere in capitalist production (Apple, 1979; Bowles & Gintis, 1976; Wilcox & Moriarity, 1980). A second pedagogical theme centers on the culturally reproductive role of schooling in the reproduction of power and economic relations through the distribution and affirmation of the dominant culture (Bourdieu & Passeron, 1977). Theories on the role of the state in the structuring of the reproductive functions of the school represent a third approach within critical theories (Corrigan, 1980; Miliband, 1969; David, 1980; Sarup, 1982). Finally, the fourth pedagogical strand of critical theory is grounded in theories of resistance that seek to explicate how the school becomes an arena in which power, resistance, and human agency come together to settle in a struggle for critical thinking and learning (Giroux, 1983, p. 293).

Radical theories of education have been met with sharp criticisms. Giroux (1983) has stringently criticized the reproductive models as offering an overly deterministic view of schooling and leaving no room for understanding human agency. However, Giroux's theory of resistance is also opened to criticism. Giroux argues that a theory of resistance should focus on oppositional behaviors that have emancipatory consequences. These consequences may be gleaned from the subjects' interpretation of their behaviors, or from the theorists' placing these behaviors within the context of historical and relational forces. Specifically, Giroux suggests that radical educators must analyze the counter-logic that informs students' oppositional behaviors. Not clear in Giroux's position are the relationship between emancipatory opposition and conscious formation; the degree to which the struggle against capitalism is turned into a struggle against the state (Castells, 1978) and what this means for "emancipatory opposition"; and the extent to which oppositional behavior may be constrained and shaped by racism and sexism, where the challenge to the system is based on these subordinations and not on a rejection of capitalist relations, e.g., multicultural education.

In spite of the criticisms raised, critical theory has provided us with an alternative theory of education to that embodied in the liberal and conservative perspectives. Although I would acquiesce that understanding the structures of domination, culture, and resistance as they unfold in day-to-day school life is necessary for illuminating the problems of urban education, it provides only a partially perspective picture. The problem of educational development in the inner-city urban communities encompasses an array of factors dealing essentially with issues of political economy, not strictly in the sense as defined by correspondence theories, and race. Although dependency theory does not seek to advance a "theory of education," it complements critical theory by revealing the ways in which the urban school system becomes enmeshed in a set of relationships that reinforce and influence the process of reproduction and resistance.

The dependency model provides a useful analytical framework for understanding the political economy of growth and development among ex-colonial nation states (Devon, 1979; Frank, 1969). Used first to understand the developmental problems of small states in the global system (Girvan & Jefferson, 1971), it has recently been applied to educational development from a comparative perspective (Arnove, 1980; Altbach & Kelly, 1978).

Dependency analysis is rooted in the notions of external economic and political domination, and makes a distinction between the center and periphery. The center refers to those geopolitical states that enjoy hegemonic economic and political power over areas with minimal resource bases and minimal technical and administrative capabilities—peripheries (Watson, 1987). The notion of center and periphery also extends to the domestic societies, with the center of power in these societies exercising dominance over the peripheral or rural areas. The continued dependence of peripheral nations on center economies is posited as being caused by the restructuring of the international division of labor, the redeployment of finance capital to these nations, and the role of domestic factors in reproducing dependency (Watson, 1987). The consequences of these nations' dependency status are reflected in an "interdependence of poverty, low income, low productivity, high mortality rates, urban squalor, economic dependence and illiteracy" (Williamson, 1979, p. 38).

The problem of educational development in peripheral societies is viewed as occasioned by the interconnection of the educational system with the world economic system and the asymmetrical relationships which develop in the flow of cultural capital and economic capital in these societies. Mazrui's (1975) analysis of the cultural penetration of African societies amply demonstrates this accompanying stage to economic dependency. Mazrui argued that the culturally dependent status of African universities, brought about through a reliance on Western nations for (a) criteria for selecting students, (b) content of curriculum, and (c) evaluation of knowledge gained, acted to sustain the culture and values of metropolitan centers in these societies. Thus the indigenous population became socialized to the norms and values of western cultures, which served to consolidate economic dependence (Mazrui, 1975).

Cultural dependency has also been marked by the uneven production of knowledge (Hall, 1978), the dissemination of information—literary colonialism (Altbach, 1975), and the influence of foundation activities (Berman, 1979). Arnove (1980), in a summary of these forms of cultural dependency, notes that knowledge has become a commodity, with knowledge production in the form of published textbooks being controlled by institutions in Europe and North America. The concentration of publishing power in center economies has had implications for (a) the source of scholarly information, (b) the orientation of third-world scholars to publish in prestigious journals of the center, and (c) mass literacy and basic education (Arnove, 1980). More importantly, however, the knowledge produced in third-world countries has been relegated to the periphery of the scientific community, although it has been used by foundations and donor agencies as part of their control structures.

The analysis of cultural dependency and the issues of educational development parallel very strongly the pedagogical themes raised by critical theories of schooling discussed earlier in this paper. For example, the African university's role in distributing the cultures of western societies is consonant with Bourdieu's thesis of cultural reproduction. Similarly, the attempts to counter the cultural penetration of western societies through the diversification of the cultural content of modernity, and through the adoption of alternative "scientism" (Mazrui, 1975, pp. 206–7) underscore Giroux's (1983) notions of oppositional and resistance behaviors as part of the reproductive process. There seems therefore to be an implicit convergence between the language of dependency analysis and critical theories of education. Both stress hegemony and dominance, conflict, and struggle.

In spite of this, the dependency framework has not been extensively applied to understanding educational problems of disadvantaged groups in the United States. However, in the area of race relations, attempts have been made to equate the disadvantageous positions of blacks to those of third-world nations (Blauner, 1972; Carmichael & Hamilton, 1967; Hechter, 1975). These authors have shown that minority groups in capitalist nations have been subjected to similar forms of economic and cultural exploitation as those experienced by the third world. Hechter's (1975) analysis suggests that this occurs in situations where the uneven development of society coincides with distinct spatial units on the basis of culture, and where the people at the core are ethnically different from these at the periphery, both of which lead to a cultural division of labor based on an unequal exchange relationship (see Parkin, 1978, p. 624).

A recent incursion into the problems and issues confronting urban schooling in the United Kingdom noted that the economic statuses of many inner-city communities in those countries approached not only those of third-world nations, as suggested above, but also those existing in the United States (Bash, Coulby, & Jones, 1985). Such similarities between these societies seem to imply the need to place the urban educational system within the context of the relationship between the inner city and both capitalist production and relations, as well as race relations. Although the intent in this paper is to discuss the issue of educational development in the United States, appropriate similarities with other countries will be highlighted.

Comparative data on social and economic conditions in the inner city, metropolitan, and nonmetropolitan areas, as well as the United States as a whole, are presented in table 1. These data indicate that regardless of indices used, conditions are poorer in the inner city than in any other area of the United States. For example, the infant death rate for 1980 in the central cities was 19.4, compared to 13.8 for the United States as a whole, 13.7 in metropolitan areas, and 14.1 in nonmetropolitan areas. Data on the economic position of age-specific groups within these central cities are even bleaker. For example, in 1984, the employment and labor force participation rates for young black males aged 18 to 19 was only 34 percent (Wilson, 1987). The economic precariousness of the young black male in the United States is matched by his counterpart in the United Kingdom. Thus, according to Bash et al. (1985), the employment rates for young black males in the United Kingdom approached 55 percent in some urban areas. These economic and social indicators demonstrate unequivocally that the inner-city communities in these two western industrialized nations are fast approaching peripheral statuses as outlined by Williamson (1979) and discussed earlier in this paper.

The demise of the central city cannot be understood outside of the framework of the capitalist economy and the contradictions inherent in capitalist social formations. In this respect, several factors are worth highlighting. First, both Wilson's (1987) analysis of the inner city in the United States and Bash, Coulby, and Jones's (1985) analyses conducted in the United Kingdom point to the decline of the presence of the traditional manufacturing sector as a major contributing force to the central city's plight. For example, Wilson (1987), in a recapitulation of Kasarda's study (Kasarda, 1986), notes that the urban centers have undergone structural transformation from being centers of production to centers of administration. This transformation has had a deleterious impact on the nature of the labor market in these centers, in so far as the job losses have occurred in those industries and sectors of the labor force that traditionally employ blacks.

Second, as Feagin points out, this process of transformation is inextricably linked to a new round of capital accumulation that has been taking place

TABLE 1

Comparative Social and Economic Indicators for the United States, Central Cities, Metropolitan Areas, and Nonmetropolitan Areas

Type of Community	% Black Resident 1980	Infant Death Rate 1980	Crime Rate 1980	% Unemployed 1980	% Owner-Occupied Dwellings
	11.7				
United States	12.6	13.8	5,893	7.1	64.4
Metropolitan areas	8.8	13.7	—	6.9	61.6
Nonmetropolitan areas	44.8	14.1	—	7.9	73.1
Central cities		19.4	10,615	8.6	50.8

Source: State and Metropolitan Area Data Book 1982: Bureau of Census. Based on a sample of 69 central cities.

in the Sun Belt regions (Feagin, 1986). This has meant that some plants and offices in the Northeast, for example, as well as new capital investments have flowed disproportionally to the South because of lower wages, fewer unions, and a conservative political environment (Feagin, 1986, p. 417). The transformation of the inner city into peripheral economies has also been occasioned by the economic growth of the suburbs, exurbs, and nonmetropolitan areas. Figures provided by Kasarda (1986) and quoted by Wilson (1987) indicate that although the northern urban centers experienced substantial losses in low-skill jobs, between 1975 and 1985, 2.1 million nonadministrative jobs were added. This number, according to Wilson, "exceeded the total number of production jobs available in the combined automobile, steel, and textile industries in this country" (Wilson, 1987, p. 42). Yet most of this growth occurred *outside* of the inner-city urban centers.

A final factor relates to the growing international division of labor, which has been caused by the exportation of jobs from the American economy to the cheap labor market areas in the third world and less developed nations. This expansion of blue collar, low-skill, and white collar production in third-world countries has reduced the numbers of jobs available in the United States both for white and black members of the labor force (Feagin, 1986). Both the economies of the inner-city communities in the United States and those in third-world countries therefore manifest the contradictions of capitalist accumulation. The continued peripheral statuses of both reflect the restructuring of the world economy in terms of the division of labor as well as shifts in capital. The consequence of this is felt not only by the inner-city economies in the form of severe dislocation (see Wilson,

1987; Kasarda, 1986), but also by the economies of the third-world countries (Watson, 1987).

Not to be neglected in our discussion is the fact that the peripheral status of the inner city is overlain by the issue of "race." Indeed, the central city provides the arena in which racial contradictions in the larger social system are most vividly expressed. Inner-city areas in both the United States and the United Kingdom are historically and increasingly composed of poor minorities who have been the victims of structural discrimination. The concentration of the black population in poverty areas in the United States is starkly reflected by data furnished on the increase of the number of poor in the five largest cities. These data show that, whereas between 1970 and 1980 the total white population in the extreme poverty areas increased by 45 percent, and the white poor population by only 24 percent, comparable data for blacks were 148 percent and 164 percent respectively (U.S. Bureau of Census, cited in Wilson, 1987, p. 46).

This social and economic marginalization of the inner-city community and its populations is not independent of educational outcomes. Table 2 presents comparative data on educational achievement in reading and mathematics for 9-, 13- and 17-year-olds by type of community. What these data show is that educational achievement in disadvantaged urban areas not only lags behind achievement in more affluent urban centers, but also behind educational attainment in even extreme rural communities. This trend exists in both reading and mathematics, and despite the fact that the achievement gap is closing, nevertheless persists and must be of some concern.

In understanding the persistence of educational problems in the inner city, its peripheral economic status must be interfaced with aspects of the schooling process, the first of which is its dependence on state and federal government for funding. The extent of this reliance is demonstrated by the data in table 3. Table 3 presents information on the source of revenue for 20 of the largest minority public school systems, as well as aggregate level data for the 120 largest public school systems in the United States. For this larger group, approximately 42.5 percent of revenues for public school funding comes from local taxes. For our sample of 20, only 39 percent of the school budget is raised locally, and in the cases of Newark, Oakland Unified, and Jersey City, this falls to roughly 20 percent.

While most of the state aid received is in the category of equalization aid, some state aids fall under the classification of categorical aid. The principle of equalization grew out of the awareness of unequal educational opportunity structures created by the discrepancies in the economic well-being of poor and nonpoor communities (Ovsiew, 1980). Thus the states assumed the responsibility of providing additional financial aid to poor school districts. Categorical aid, on the other hand, is given to local school districts to meet the educational needs of special populations as mandated

TABLE 2

Comparative Data on Educational Outcomes in Reading and Mathematics for 9-, 13-, and 17-Year-olds by Type of Community

Community Type[1]	Age 9			Age 13		Age 17		
	1974–75	1979–80	1983–84	1974–75	1979–80	1974–75	1979–80	1983–84
			Reading[2]					
Extreme rural	204.0	210.3	205.8	247.9	254.3	255.5	281.3	278.1	282.8
Disad. urban	185.1	186.0	194.4	229.1	241.6	239.6	261.0	258.3	265.9
Adv. urban	226.2	231.9	231.4	271.5	275.2	274.7	301.2	299.1	300.8
All participants	209.6	213.5	213.2	254.8	257.4	257.8	284.5	284.5	288.2

	Mathematics[3]					
	Age 9		Age 13		Age 17	
	1977–78	1981–82	1977–78	1981–82	1977–78	1981–82
Extreme rural	51.1	52.7	52.6	56.3	58.0	57.0
Disad. urban	44.4	45.5	43.5	49.3	45.0	47.7
Adv. urban	65.0	66.3	65.1	70.7	70.0	69.7
All participants	55.4	56.4	56.6	60.5	60.4	60.2

Source: Extrapolated from *Digest of Education Statistics 1985–1986*. Office of Educational Research and Improvements, U.S. Department of Education.

Notes: 1. Disadvantaged urban: students attend schools in or around cities with a population greater than 200,000 where a high proportion of residents are on welfare or are not regularly employed. Advantaged urban: students attend school in or around cities with a population greater than 200,000 where a high proportion of the residents are in professional or managerial positions.

2. Mean proficiency reading score.

3. Mean percent correct.

by state and federal regulations (e.g., compensatory programs, bilingual programs, and programs for special education students).

There are two dilemmas this funding structure poses for the inner-city school district. First, most of the funds received from equalization aid are insufficient to run these systems effectively, since a vast proportion is used to play instructional and administrative salaries, as well as operation costs. Second, aid received through categorical funding is given primarily for "problem" areas. Funds to develop creative and "extra" educational programs likely to benefit all students and not special populations must come from the meager resources of the community. The result is a Hobbesian

TABLE 3

Revenue Sources for 20 of the Largest Minority Public School Systems: 1982–83

(In thousands of dollars)

School System	Total Revenue	Federal	State	Local	Local as % of Total Revenue
Largest 120 School Systems	$25,841,483	$1,491,670	$12,367,021	$10,982,792	42.5
Chicago	1,305,309	176,443	699,606	429,260	32.9
Detroit	630,481	75,926	322,006	232,549	36.9
Philadelphia	657,050	85,157	323,458	266,435	40.6
Baltimore City	345,827	40,679	182,648	122,500	35.4
Orleans Parish	239,117	33,555	109,126	96,436	40.3
Cleveland	275,473	44,160	105,127	126,186	45.8
Atlanta City	202,314	25,711	66,034	110,569	54.7
Mobile	105,734	17,287	57,359	31,088	29.4
East Baton Rouge	168,449	11,957	92,405	64,087	38.0
Newark	223,105	34,303	142,962	45,840	20.5
Greenville, S.C.	102,872	3,678	53,278	45,916	44.6
Cincinnati, Ohio	158,596	19,757	53,017	85,822	54.1
Oakland Unified	165,222	26,932	104,924	33,366	20.2
Birmingham City	94,554	14,832	41,457	38,265	40.5
Charleston, S.C.	92,949	13,354	45,729	33,866	36.4
Norfolk City	94,800	15,593	37,609	41,598	43.9
Flint, Mich.	86,728	6,096	41,590	39,042	45.0
Dayton, Ohio	108,413	15,507	37,843	55,063	50.8
Richmond, Ga.	66,786	7,446	34,156	25,184	37.7
Jersey City	111,345	12,577	68,184	30,584	27.5
					(38.8)

Source: Extrapolated from *Digest of Education Statistics* 1985–1986. Office of Educational Research and Improvements, U.S. Department of Education.

situation in which educational idealism and pragmatic financial concerns are in a state of continual conflict.

This is vividly reflected by recent scholarship, which has expressed concerns about the number of minority students being classified as special education, hinting perhaps of racial and cultural biases (Garner & Lipsky, 1987). Although there is much validity to these concerns, an equally important factor, as cited by one candidate in a local urban school-board election, is "Special Education is where you get the big bucks . . . The more special education students you have, the more money you get" (Kukla, 1987, p. N2). Furthermore, as funds dry up from other sources, special education labeling is used in order to attract additional revenues into the system (Viadero, 1988). For many inner-city urban systems, therefore, their peripheral economies and their continued dependency on state aid as their primary source of funding entrap them in a situation where educational success can mean a significant loss in revenue.

This is not to suggest that there is a deliberate attempt to undereducate students, but rather that it is a paradox of which most urban administrators are aware. In this context, the expansion of educational programing and the nurturance of educational development is extremely limited. For example, in some instances, in order to fund a new educational program, this program has to be tacked 'onto the compensatory program, effectively restricting the population served. However, as the compensatory program grows in size, a certain degree of "tension" ensues between itself and the regular developmental program, partially brought on by the limitations imposed on the extent of interfacing between the two as a result of state and federal guidelines. "Home rule" consequently becomes vacuous in the face of increasing regulations and mandates.

If the peripheral status of the central city economy leads directly to an extensive reliance on state and federal subsidy, it has an indirect impact on the volatile political ecology of school governance in these areas. Indeed, the socialization of conflict that has occurred in many urban school districts (Schattschneider, 1975) has frequently led to a subversion of educational goals (Braun, 1987; Gluck, 1988; Kukla, 1984; Just, 1980). Just's (1980) description of the evolutionary changes in the urban school board shows that the impact of the early educational reform movements between 1890 and 1920 led to a privatization of conflict. Thus, the scope of conflict, and educational governance in principle, were detached from the rest of the political order.

Several subsequent events of a seminal nature led to a broadening of the scope of potential conflict, and significantly altered the political environment of urban school boards. These events included, the 1954 *Brown v. Board of Education* decision, the enactment of the National Defense Education Act, the New York City Teachers' Strike of 1963, and the ESEA legislation, all of which resulted in an expansion of the number of interest groups desiring to be represented in the educational process (Just, 1980). More recently, a new politicization of the school board, especially in inner-city areas, seems to be taking place. As Guthrie (1980) found, "in cities, school board candidates align themselves in election campaign with other politicos. . . . Endorsement by members of Congress or state officials conveys to school board candidates a substantially enhanced measure of name recognition" (as cited by Just, 1980, p. 432).

Whereas there are several reasons underlying the highly politicized nature of the inner-city school board, there are two factors that have direct bearing on this paper. First, the school board provides a base of power from which incumbents may further their political goals (Guthrie, 1980), as well as mount challenges against the political order at city hall. This latter point is demonstrated by the 1984 school board elections that occurred in one of the central-city school districts in the state of New Jersey (Kukla, 1984). In what became a highly contested election, some of the top political forces in the city were pitted against each other. Of the two slates of candidates contesting the elections, one was backed by the mayor, the other by some members of the city council, other high-profile politicos, and a coalition of employee unions and community groups. The aim of this "insurgent slate" as enunciated by its leaders was to win community control of the board and city hall (Kukla, 1984).

The mingling of city hall politics and school board politics raises the question as to who holds the power over schools in the inner city? Braun (1987), in an article addressing this issue, noted that in many inner-city school districts power is wielded by white politicians and power brokers. Unfortunately, however, as the school board becomes enmeshed in the political power structure and struggles of the larger political environment, educational needs and goals are submerged beneath a host of others (Ovsiew, 1980). The ease with which this can take place is facilitated by the generally high levels of voter apathy toward school board elections in inner-city areas. These low levels of citizenry participation in school board elections, coupled with low levels of parental involvement, raise not only the critical issue of accountability, but also result in the vulnerability of these school districts to the ploys and machinations of special-interest groups.

A second factor of considerable import influencing the struggle over the control of the school system is its strategic significance as part of the urban distribution mechanism. Neo-Weberian writers have provided us with some insights into this function of the educational system. Pahl (1975), in particular, has argued that the urban context is characterized by a conflict over scarce resources and allocation. In this arena of conflict, he suggests, the urban bureaucracies play a vital distributive role in the flow of resources. More concretely, in extending Pahl's arguments, in urban contexts where employment opportunities are restrictive, the educational bureaucracy becomes part of the distributive mechanism in the allocation of jobs. That employment opportunities are likely to be restrictive for minority residents in these areas is part of the complex contradictory nature of the central city's economy.

Data furnished by Kasarda (1986) show that whereas there has been a decline in jobs requiring lower education, there has been a simultaneous increase in jobs requiring higher levels of completed education in these urban centers. However, these latter occupations tend to be filled by non-minorities residing both in as well as outside of the central city. The reasons for this trend involve a myriad of factors, not least of which are that (a) these jobs are controlled by corporations with little allegiance to minority residents and the economy of the central city, and (b) the weakness of the educational systems in many inner cities prevents them from easily and quickly meeting the demands for a more indigenous educated labor force.

As part of the urban distributive mechanism, therefore, the educational system is manipulated by politicians and school board members alike, regardless of the way in which the board is constituted. Individuals, both residents as well as nonresidents of the central city and of minority as well as nonminority backgrounds, are rewarded for political loyalty and support with employment at various levels within the educational system. This is reinforced by the assumption that each newly constituted board requires its own administrative team. Since these people are very rarely recruited from a competitive field of qualified candidates, these school systems frequently end up being run by individuals whose qualifications are based less on technical competence and more on political connections. The result is not only a serious credibility gap concerning the competency of the administrators, but great instability in administration and programs. Gluck (1988) cites an example in which the factionalism and struggles on one school board resulted in the elected board going through three acting and "permanent" school superintendents in less than four years.

The systemic roots of educational underdevelopment in inner-city school systems is best illustrated by an examination of the Jersey City school system in the state of New Jersey. Presently, this system is in jeopardy of being taken over by the New Jersey State Education Department. With a population of over 30,000, composed primarily of blacks, Puerto Ricans, and other Hispanic groups, the Jersey City school system has shown consistently weak performance in the areas of reading and mathematics. An analysis of the ills of the school system conducted by the state and discussed in a recent article by Hanley (1988) reveals the extent to which educational development has been stymied by a history of political favoritism and nepotism, and an ever-changing educational environment.

This system has an appointed board, with the mayor exercising considerable political influence over educational governance. In 1981, 41 teachers were dismissed by Gerald McCann after he was elected mayor because they failed to support his candidacy (Hanley, 1988, p. B9). He then transferred 17 principals to the central office in order to create promotional opportunities for other individuals in the schools. After he was ousted in 1985 by Anthony Cucci, these principals were demoted by the newly elected mayor from their jobs at the central office. Meanwhile, the largest high school has had five principals in the last six years (Hanley, 1988, p. B9). Currently, the school superintendent is embroiled in conflict with the school board and city hall after successfully winning a lawsuit to keep his job. He declares, "I'm not kowtowing to politicians." (Hanley, 1988, p. B9). Yet, ironically, when asked to explain why students continue to perform poorly, he blamed the social conditions and environments from which they came (Hanley, 1988).

The generally unstable educational environment in this school system and other inner-city systems is best summed up by a quote from the State Department's report: "Positions are created and abolished and personnel transferred, demoted, promoted and hired with each change of municipal leadership." (As cited by Hanley, 1988, p. B9).

It is important to realize that the economic and political crises of inner-city school systems do not occur independently of their continued cultural domination by the larger social system. Although this dominance is achieved through a complex process, Arnove's (1980) discussion of the facets of cultural dependency suggests three possible ways in which the dominant culture is reproduced: through the control of curriculum and educational materials, evaluation of knowledge, and the production and flow of knowledge.

Several critical discourses on ideology and curriculum have pointed to the tendency for the curriculum to affirm the values of the dominant social and cultural groups and to discredit the experiences of minority groups (Apple, 1979; Giroux, 1981; Lind-Brenkman, 1983). Lind-Brenkman's (1983) recent analysis of big business presence in education, for example, underscored the ability of big business to control curriculum and pedagogy while simultaneously maximizing profit. This group, through their control over the distribution of knowledge, favorably present their interests in various forms of educational materials, while subjecting the interest of other groups to omissions and structured silences (Apple, 1982; Eagleton, 1976; Giroux, 1981). The extent to which this takes place is illuminated by Brown's (1981) analysis of a children's history textbook. Brown discovered that these books were primarily concerned with rural life, contained a strong anti-urban bias, and totally neglected the historical context of urban life. This omission of the experiences of inner-city students in major educational materials is also evident in the standardized instruments used to evaluate their knowledge. Whereas, generally, these instruments have carefully guarded against overt race and gender biases, they have totally overlooked the experiences of students from working-class backgrounds and urban settings.

Of even greater concern in the process of cultural domination is the peripheral status accorded to the knowledge produced by black scholars, as well as critical scholars, by the dominant institutions concerned with knowledge production (Braddock, 1978; Jamison, 1982; Staples, 1984). This status ensures that the dominant pedagogies are not formally challenged within the knowledge community and are not opened up to debate. Although the more obvious and direct consequence of this is felt by black academicians in terms of tenure and their status within academe, its real implication lies in the fact that the education of minority students proceeds on the assumptions regarding pedagogy and learning inherent in the dominant paradigms.

These are several ways in which the peripheral status of this corpus of knowledge is maintained. First, as Staples (1984) points out, works produced by blacks and other critical scholars that generally challenge the dominant paradigms are not published in established white journals. Rather, they have to seek publication in black or critically oriented periodicals. Second, the knowledge itself is subjected to criticism in terms of its scholarly merits. Third, the credibility of these journals is frequently questioned by the dominant university establishments (Jamison, 1982). This ideological function, which established journals and dominant universities perform effectively, controls the kind of cultural capital that flows into the inner-city school systems, and thereby maintains the cultural domination.

Such apparent inequalities in the dissemination of cultural capital and knowledge mirror the experiences that third-world countries face. Altbach's (1975) study of literary colonialism in third-world countries found that these nations enjoyed little autonomy in the area of knowledge production, were relegated to the peripheral international intellectual system, and learned about their own political and economic systems from Western sources. Altbach's observation that this knowledge is suspect for its methodological and ideological biases holds equally for the quality of knowledge concerning inner-city educational structures, generated by the dominant paradigms in the U.S. intellectual community.

The study of educational problems in the inner city has largely been pursued in a piecemeal fashion, disconnected from their associations with political economy issues of the central city. This tendency results from a lack of an overarching framework, which would conceptually link issues in urban education to a social theory of the urban environment (Grace, 1984). Although in this paper I did not attempt to offer a theory of the urban problem, the analysis pursued, based on the dependency mode of inquiry, suggests that urban scholarship in the vein of critical theories of political economy (see Castells, 1978; Harvey, 1973), as well as education (Apple, 1979; Bourdieu & Passeron, 1977; Giroux, 1983), offers the most cogent and promising theoretical formulations.

The distinctiveness of both bodies of thought lies in the central role accorded to the larger political economic and sociocultural forms in determining and influencing conditions at several institutional levels in the central city. This focus does not totally assume a unidirectional and overly deterministic sphere of influence. It is very clear that some urban actors do contribute in their responses to these influences in maintaining the peripheral status of the central city, while others, through their actions, open up the possibilities for change.

It may be quite justifiably asked if taking such a macro-orientation to understanding urban educational systems glosses over human agency as this unfolds at the level of everyday life in schools. The answer is no. First of all, although the school as a social site may appear to be disconnected, superficially at least, from issues of political economy, it is very clear from the work done by resistance theorists that this is not totally so. Willis's (1977) study of working-class males in an English secondary school and

Fine & Rosenberg's (1983) study of dropouts in New York City demonstrate that students' oppositional behaviors were informed by their social, cultural, and political experiences outside of the school environment.

Second, the actions of teachers, principals, and other school personnel, and curriculums and programs in the school, are shaped and influenced in part by the kinds of administration at the central office. To the extent that this administration itself is influenced by forces from the larger economic and political environments of the central city, one may posit that these larger forces also have an indirect impact on the schools through the mediating role of school administrations.

Third, educational pedagogy is not culturally or ideologically neutral. Attitudes toward inner-city students, assumptions regarding learning and whose knowledge is valid, are, the evidence indicates, inextricably linked to the interests of the dominant groups. Many of the pedagogies currently in place in inner-city schools are not of the nature that would transform their peripheral status. On the contrary, in the long run they serve to maintain their economic and cultural domination (Kretovics, 1986; Madhere, 1987).

The goal of the present paper was not to present a pessimistic picture of inner-city school systems, but rather to illuminate why educational problems remain persistent features in spite of numerous programs and research. Several conclusions appear inevitable. First, proposed state takeovers of failing urban school systems may solve some problems, but not all. Second, it is fallacious to believe that more money is the solution to the urban problem. More money in the form of categorical aid becomes an albatross around the neck of many inner-city school districts, burying them in a mire of state and federal regulations reminiscent of the plight in which third-world countries find themselves because of their dependence on the international monetary fund and other world financial institutions. Third, the solution to the crises of inner-city educational systems lies in the solution to the economic demise of the central city, the awakening of a sleeping citizenry, and changes in pedagogical orientation.

The above analyses are suggestive of the agenda that must be pursued by educators and policy makers. It is apparent that scholars interested in the problems of urban schooling must begin to reformulate the field of urban education. In particular, it is clear that factors related to the political economy of the inner city must be brought into models purporting to explain the current ills of these educational systems. Issues such as the political legitimacy of educational governance in these communities, the intrusion of narrow political interests into the educational process, and the impact of these forces on the quality of education that is delivered cannot be successfully understood or redressed without a more expanded conceptual framework of urban education.

It also follows that public policy regarding the education of the inner-city poor has to assume a more holistic focus. Attempts to deal with educational problems have been partial in content and scope. The evidence suggests that school reforms alone are not sufficient to remedy the plight of inner-city residents.

REFERENCES

Altbach, P. G. 1975. Literary colonialism: Books in the third world. *Harvard Educational Review* 45:226–36.

Altbach, P. G., and Kelly, A. 1978. *Education and colonialism.* White Plains, N.Y.: Longman.

Apple, M. W. 1979. *Ideology and curriculum.* London: Routledge & Kegan Paul.

Apple, W. 1982. *Education and power.* London: Routledge & Kegan Paul.

Arnove, R. F. February 1980. Comparative education and world-systems analysis. *Comparative Education Review,* 48–62.

Bash, L.; Coulby, D.; and Jones, C. 1985. *Urban schooling: Theory and practice.* London: Holt, Rinehart & Winston.

Berger, A. S., and Simon, W. 1974. Black families and the Moynihan report: A research evaluation. *Social Problems* 22:145–61.

Berman, E. H. 1979. Foundations, United States foreign policy and African education. *Harvard Educational Review* 49:145–79.

Blauner, R. 1970. *Racial oppression in America.* New York: Harper & Row.

Bourdieu, P., and Passeron, J. 1977. *Reproduction in education, society and culture.* Beverly Hills, Calif.: Sage Publications.

Bowles, S., and Gintis, H. 1976. *Schooling in capitalist America.* New York: Basic Books.

Braddock, J. 1978. Institutional racism in higher education. *Western Journal of Black Studies* 2(4):236–42.

Braun, R. J. November 27, 1987. *Takeover plan protects "all" the children. Star Ledger.*

Brown, J. October 1981. Into the minds of babes: Journey through recent children's books. *Radical History Review,* 25.

Burgess, E. 1967. The growth of the city: An introduction to a research project. In *The City,* ed. R. Park and E. Burgess. London: University of Chicago Press.

Carmichael, S., and Hamilton, C. 1967. *Black power.* New York: Random House.

Castells, M. 1978. *City, class and power.* London: Macmillan.

Cohn, S. 1984. Reconstructing the history of urban education in America. In *Education and the city: Theory, history and contemporary practice,* ed. G. Grace. London: Routledge & Kegan Paul.

Corrigan, P. 1980. Capitalism, state formation, and Marxist theory. London: Quartet Books.

David, M. E. 1980. *The state, the family, and education.* London: Routledge & Kegan Paul.

Deutsch, M. 1963. The disadvantaged child and the learning process. In *Education in depressed areas,* ed. A. H. Passow. New York: Teachers College Press.

Devon, R. F. 1979. *The political economy of peripheral societies: Theoretical themes in the Marxist tradition.* Paper presented at the annual meeting of the Comparative and International Education Society, Ann Arbor, Michigan.

Eagleton, T. 1976. *Marxism and literary criticism.* London: Metheun.

Feagin, J. R. 1986. *Social problems: A critical power-conflict perspective.* Englewood Cliffs, N.J.: Prentice Hall.

Fine, M., and Rosenberg, P. (1983). Dropping out of High School: The Ideology of School and Work. *Journal of Education* 165(3):257–272.

Frank, A. G. 1969. *Latin America: Underdevelopment or revolution.* New York: Monthly Review Press.

Gartner, A., and Lipsky, D. R. 1987. *Beyond Special Education: Toward a Quality System for all Students.* Harvard Educational Review 57(4):367-395.

Giroux, H. 1981. *Ideology, culture and the process of schooling.* Philadelphia: Temple University Press.

———. 1983. Theories of reproduction and resistance in the new sociology of education: A critical analysis. *Harvard Educational Review* 53(3):257–91.

Girvan, H., and Jefferson, O. 1971. *Readings in the political economy of the Caribbean.* Jamaica: New World Group.

Gittell, M., and Hevesi, A. 1969. *The politics of urban education.* New York: Praeger.

Gluck, G. February 21, 1988. *School board shift laced with pitfalls. Star Ledger,* 51.

Gordon, E. W., and Wilkerson, D. H. 1966. *Compensatory education for the disadvantaged: Programs and practices: Preschool through college.* New York: College Entrance Examination Board.

Grace, G. 1984. *Education and the city: Theory, history and contemporary practice.* London: Routledge & Kegan Paul.

Guthrie, J. W. 1980. Emerging politics of educational policy. (Unpublished.) University of California, Berkeley.

Hall, B. 1978. *Knowledge as commodity: The inequities of knowledge creation.* Paper presented at the Conversations in the Disciplines: Universities and the New International Order. State University of New York, Buffalo.

Hanley, R. March 8, 1988. Politics and corruption: Schools under siege in Jersey City. *New York Times,* B8–B9.

Harvey, D. 1973. *Social justice and the city.* London: Arnold.

Hechter, M. 1975. *Internal colonialism.* London: Routledge & Kegan Paul.

Jamison, A. 1982. Black professional journals. *Western Journal of Black Studies* 6(1):50–53.

Just, A. E. 1980. Urban school board elections: Changes in the political environment between 1950 and 1980. *Education and Urban Society* 12(4):421–35.

Kasarda, J. 1986. The regional and urban redistribution of people and jobs in the U.S. National Research Council Committee on National Urban Policy. National Academy of Science.

Katz, M. B. 1968. *The irony of early school reform: Educational innovation in mid-nineteenth century Massachusetts.* Cambridge, Mass.: Harvard University Press.

Katz, M. B. 1971. *School reform: Past and present.* Boston: Little, Brown & Co.

Katzman, M. 1971. *Political economy of urban schools.* Cambridge, Mass.: Harvard University Press.

Kretovics, J. 1986. *Developing a transformative pedagogy: The politics of the hidden curriculum.* American Education Research Association.

Kukla, B. April 9, 1984. *Brown-Stecher-Brown Tea sweeps to victory in school board vote. Star Ledger,* N1.

————. March 30, 1987. Voters hold key to balancing a school board. *The Star Ledger.*

Lind-Brenkman, J. 1983. Seeing beyond the interests of industry: Teaching critical thinking. *Journal of Education* 165(3):283–94.

Madhere, S. 1987. *Global Political Thought and Education Action: Contribution of Freire and Illich. Paper presented at the Conference on Global Political Thinking.* Seton Hall University, New Jersey.

Mazrui, A. 1975. The African university as a multinational corporation: Problems of penetration and dependency. *Harvard Educational Review* 45:191–210.

Miliband, R. 1969. *The state in capitalist society.* New York: Basic Books.

Ovsiew, L. 1980. Home rule is no longer enough. *Education and Urban Society* 12(4):508–28.

Pahl, R. 1975. *Whose city.* Harmondsworth: Penguin Books.

Park, R. 1952. *Human communities.* New York: Free Press.

Parkin, F. 1978. Social stratification. In *A history of sociological analysis,* ed. T. Bottomore and R. Nisbet. New York: Basic Books.

Persell, C. H. 1977. *Education and inequality.* New York: Free Press.

Riessman, F. 1962. *The culturally deprived child.* New York: Harper & Row.

Rogers, D. 1968. *110 Livingston Street: Politics and bureaucracy in the New York City School System.* New York: Random House.

Ryan, W. 1976. *Blaming the victim.* New York: Random House.

Sarup, M. 1982. *Education, state and crisis.* London: Routledge & Kegan Paul.

Schatsschneider, E. E. 1975. *The Semisovereign People.* Hinsdale, Ill.: Dryden Press.

Shapiro, S. 1987. Educational theory and recent political discourse: A new agenda for the left? *Teachers College Record* 89(2):171–200.

Sharp, R. 1984. Urban education and the current crisis. In *Education and the city: Theory, history and contemporary practice,* ed. G. Grace. London: Routledge & Kegan Paul.

Staples, R. March 1984. Racial ideology and intellectual racism: Blacks in academia. *Black Scholar,* 2–16.

Tyack, D. B. 1974. *The one best system: A history of American urban education.* Cambridge, Mass.: Harvard University Press.

Valentine, C. A. 1968. *Culture and poverty: Critique and counter proposal.* Chicago: University of Chicago Press.

Viadero, D. March 2, 1988. *Study documents jump in special-education enrollments. Education Week,* 17.

Watson, H. 1987). Economic dependency and geopolitics: Recurring ideological theories in Caribbean intellectual culture. *New West Indian Guide* 16(3):223–38.

Wilcox, K., and Moriarity, P. 1980. Schooling and work: Social constraints on educational opportunity. In *Education: Straitjacket or opportunity,* ed. J. Benet and A. K. Daniels. New Brunswick, N.J.: Transaction Books.

Wiliamson, B. 1979. *Education, social structure and development.* London: Macmillan.

Willis, P. 1977. *Learning to labour.* Lexington, Heath.

Wilson, J. 1987. *The truly disadvantaged: The inner city, the underclass and public policy.* Chicago: The University of Chicago Press.

THE EFFECTS OF ABILITY GROUPS AND TESTS ON STUDENT VOCATIONAL COUNSELING AND PLACEMENT

J. John Harris III,
Donna Y. Ford,
Frank Brown,
and David G. Carter, Sr.

Few educational issues evoke as much concern and debate as the widespread use of ability grouping. A close review of the literature indicates that few, if any, studies support the validity of its effectiveness and attendant use. Indeed, there is little evidence suporting its positive effects on not only students' learning, but also their motivation, aspirations, expectations, and career choices.

Historically, a major function of school counseling has been the placement of students in ability groups and career-oriented tracks based upon the results of standardized tests. Perhaps the most forceful influence on student vocational choice is the placement of students in such ability groups or tracks. These tracks will not necessarily state who will become a blue collar or white collar worker, but they do separate students into professionally and nonprofessionally-oriented groups—the irony of it all.

Data indicate that most school counselors do very little career counseling beyond the placement of students in ability groups and tracks. Even in schools where there are no counselors, teachers and administrators make extensive use of these practices. When counselors do stress career planning, it is generally after the student has been placed. Thus, becoming a professional or nonprofessional is decided once the student is assigned to the specific track or group. It is assumed that students placed in the higher levels will become professionals, while those assigned to the lower levels will become nonprofessionals. This is rather alarming when one takes into consideration that a disproportionate number of minority students are found in lower ability-level tracks, perhaps 90 to 95 percent. Again, counselors and educators generally use ability or achievement test data to defend their decision, even though such test data may be more a reflection of poor schooling than lack of ability. To this end, low test scores are not necessary indicative of low ability, but rather of other variables that interfere with the demonstration of competence or ability.

This paper will examine the validity or efficacy of ability groups (or tracks) and tests in the placement of minority students, particularly blacks, test fairness, and tests as predictors of school success. Moreover, these issues will be analyzed relative to their effects on vocational counseling and placement of students by decision makers in our schools.

ABILITY GROUPS AND GENERAL ABILITY TESTS

The practice of assigning students to classes, i.e., tracking, based on academic ability is virtually universal in these United States (Cronbach, 1970; Erickson, 1975; Adler, 1982; Boyer, 1983; Goodlad, 1984; Slavin, 1987). The school professional most actively involved in the sorting process is the school guidance counselor. In many instances, however, the counseling function may be relegated to classroom teachers and unit administrators. This is typically the case in schools where districts cannot afford to employ guidance counselors.

Erickson (1975), recalling his experiences as counselor, maintains that guidance counselors serve as gatekeepers and advisors. As advisors, counselors help students advance their academic careers by placing them in enriched educational environments (classrooms); as gatekeepers, counselors serve the system or governmental units by placing students in poor educational environments, which retard their academic growth. In essence, the educational system functions as a sorting mechanism, separating the wheat from the chaff.

Although many educators argue that the role of a school counselor is second only to that of the classroom teacher, others argue that the counselor's role is more important. Kirkland (1971) and Erickson (1975) state that the responsibility goes to the individual who determines the educational environment to which a student will be exposed. Stated differently, schools have the primary responsibility for sorting the nation's [person] power (Kirkland, 1971), and achievement test data just happen to be a convenient mechanism for avoiding complaints from irate parents who question their child's placement (Erickson, 1975). Schools also help in maintaining differential status of population subgroups, and in legitimatizing the dominance of the majority culture (Mercer, 1974; Fordham, 1975).

While there are a variety of ability groupings, the two common forms are tracking and homogeneous grouping. Tracking is the assigning of students to the same academic ability group for all academic courses. Homogeneous grouping is the placement of students in similar ability groups for different academic subjects. An alternative is heterogeneous grouping, which is the placement of students of different ability levels in all academic courses.

Brown and Smith (1976) have found grouping practices to be common throughout this nation. The U.S. Commission on Civil Rights (1974) investigated schools in five southwestern states: Arizona, California, Colorado, New Mexico, and Texas. The commission found that 63 percent of the elementary schools and 79 percent of the secondary schools practiced some form of ability grouping. The study did not include grouping within classes, which may have increased the percentage of students sorted by ability. Moreover, and more consistent with the focus of this paper, the commission found these practices to be more extensive in schools with a high proportion of minority students (75 percent to 100 percent) than in schools with a few minority students (0 percent to 24.9 percent). In essence, the study indicated that minority students were overrepresented in low ability and/or special education classes, and underrepresented in high ability and/or "gifted" classes.

A review of the literature on the advantages and disadvantages of ability grouping does not support claims that ability grouping produces positive academic effects (U.S. Commission on Civil Rights, 1974; Findley, 1974; Kirp, 1974; Slavin, 1987; Oakes, 1988). In practice, its usefulness with high achievers is conflicting, and uniformly unfavorable for improving academic achievement in average or low-achieving groups. Despite the apparent negative effects of ability grouping, the practice is widespread.

Data are readily available that indicate that general ability tests are biased against minorities, as the tests assume that all students, minorities and nonminorities, have had equal access to favorable environments, in school and outside. Furthermore, the tests assume that all students share the same culture, and are equally motivated. In short, the tests appear to operate on a principle of equality, thereby not only failing to place emphasis at points where minorities tend to vary from the majority, but also ignoring situational and chance variables. Despite this, general ability test scores are the educator's or counselor's rationale for the placement of students in a particular group.

Tests, as used here, refer to any general ability or performance test. A test is designed to measure some quality or characteristic of an individual in order to predict how well that individual will perform in school. In this case, the criterion *variable* is school success. The criterion *measure* is the test.

Although educational psychologists agree, for the most part, that general ability test scores are correlated with school success, some psychologists (Williams, 1974; Mercer, 1974; Miller, 1974; Williams, 1981) argue that there are major flaws inherent in most general ability test scores and school success measures. These psychologists believe that such variables do not adequately take into consideration the multidimensional facets that contribute to the makeup of each individual. In essence:

> ... test scores are often invalidly interpreted because they are viewed in isolation rather than in context. Indeed, to the extent possible, test scores should be interpreted in light of the students' motivation, cooperation, and adaptive behavior in the assessment setting—as well as of nontest adaptive behavior in other settings—and in light of the student's family and cultural background, learning opportunities, primary language, handicapping conditions, and whatever other variables are salient in particular instances. But taking context into account implies the need for an even broader array of valid information about students and their circumstances than standardized testing programs typically afford. It suggests the need for comprehensive assessment in context (Messick, 1988, pp. 113–14).

On a different note, Jensen (1980) states that IQ scores are adequate measures of intelligence. Therefore, inequities in the delivery of school services are not considered sufficient to explain differences in IQ test scores (and other ability test scores) between blacks and whites, despite the fact that more blacks attend poor schools in comparison to whites.

Mercer and Williams believe that all ability tests may be the same. Mercer (1974) indicates that Wexman, in his 1967 presidential address before the American Psychological Association, set forth that all ability tests—IQ, aptitude, and achievement—may be used synonymously, and hence, measure that which the individual has learned. Therefore, higher scores increase the likelihood that students will experience academic success in school. Mercer tested black, white, and Mexican-American elementary schoolchildren with the Wechsler IQ scale while controlling for eight measures of family characteristics (Mercer, 1974, p. 86). Upon comparing the test scores, Mercer found that reading achievement scores could not be distinguished from IQ scores. Similarly, Cronbach found a high degree of overlap between IQ and achievement test scores, especially the verbal component of both tests (Cronbach, 1970, pp. 283, 286). In summation, some psychologists state that IQ, aptitude, and achievement tests are no different from other ability tests and therefore are appropriate tools for measuring school success.

Mercer (1974) and Williams (1974) state that the criterion variable—school success—which is used to establish statistical validity for an IQ test score, is the same for achievement test scores. However, either test can only provide prognostic information, i.e., they do not provide diagnostic information. That is, data from these tests do not specify the reason a child's test score is low or high, but rather how well a child is expected to perform in school. The attempt here is not to argue whether IQ test scores or other ability tests measure intelligence, but to consider whether, as a predictive instrument for school success, the tests are (1) culturally fair; (2) adequate school achievement instruments; or (3) social tools designed to deprive certain groups of access to quality education.

Because minority students are overrepresented in the lowest ability classes (inferior educational environments), and because of the general acceptance by psychologists that tests are biased against minorities (Kirp, 1974; Morgan, 1974; Samuda, 1975), the courts have ruled that test scores may not be used by school districts to assign pupils in a manner that results in segregated classes (Morgan, 1974, p. 120). In a lawsuit against the Washington, D.C., public school system, *Hobson v. Hansen*, a federal judge ruled that the use of tests to track or ability-group students was unfair. Judge Skelley Wright stated:

> The evidence shows that the method by which track assignments are made depends on standardized tests which are completely inappropriate for use with a large segment of the student body. Because the tests are primarily standardized and are relative to white middle-class students, they produce inaccurate and misleading test scores when given to lower-class and black students. As a result, rather than being classified according to ability to learn, students are being classified according to their socioeconomic or racial status, or more precisely, according to environmental and psychological factors which have nothing to do with innate ability.[1]

In the Boston Community School District the issue was revisited. In *Morgan v. Kerrigan* (1975),[2] the U.S. District Court took control of the schools and supervised the placement of students.

TEST FAIRNESS

As stated above, a great deal of attention has been focused on test fairness, particularly as test scores influence ability grouping and vocational placement. Miller (1974) and CBS (1975) indicate that ability tests are biased against minorities. For example, Cronbach was asked by Dan Rather, a CBS commentator, the correct answer to an item on an IQ test. The question: If an older child is struck by a younger child, what should be the older child's response? The correct answer was to ignore the younger child. But most black children are taught to strike anyone who strikes them. Cronbach, consequently, replied "The test item is biased in favor of middle-class white norms." Is a black child less intelligent for striking back? Yes, according to this particular test. With tests such as this, an entire generation of young people are being penalized. Consequently, more and more minority students are becoming disenchanted with public schools as they presently exist.

Although Linn (1973) suggests that test fairness requires that two populations of individuals similarly situated have equal test-score means, we must consider whether equal test scores yield equal criterion scores for both groups. The test is biased if, in predicting school success for minority students, consistent nonzero errors of prediction are made for minority groups (Linn, 1973, p. 140). The results of Linn's review of test fairness lead to conflicting data regarding definitions of test fairness.

A suggested remedy, namely culturally biased tests, is a culture-specific test or a culture-fair test (Miller, 1974; Samuda, 1975). A culture-specific test is designed for, i.e., favorably disposed or biased toward, a specific group, for example, blacks only or whites only. A culture-fair test is one that is nonbiased against all groups. The latter test appears more reasonable, especially as culture-fair tests challenge the pervasive myth that the only way to achieve educational equality is through standardization. Despite this, a culture-fair or a culture-specific test will neither improve the educational environment of nor the schools attended by minority students. Although a culture-fair test may not enhance the educational environment, it may indicate that students in poor environments are capable of improved academic performance.

As early as the 1940s, psychologists believed that children who attend poor schools, regardless of race or ethnicity, tend to score low on IQ tests. For example, in 1944 Havighurst found that the IQ test was unfair to poor whites (Kirkland, 1971). Havighurst tested white Midwestern students and found that poor whites fell 20 IQ points below middle-class white students. Other factors are also likely to add or subtract points to or from one's score on a test. These include examiner-examinee relations (Epps, 1974), coaching and test sophistication (Cronbach, 1970), response set (i.e., true-false or multiple choice), language differences (Hall & Turner, 1974), anxiety levels (Kirkland, 1971), and level of aspirations. With deference to black students, the image that emerges is one of black youth with high aspirations but low expectations (Lee, 1985; Oakes, 1988). Simply stated, many blacks aspire to high-level occupations less frequently than whites. Just as importantly, whites expect to enter professional and managerial occupations more frequently than blacks.

It appears that some researchers are placing the blame for poor academic performance on students attending poor schools, rather than on the lack of quality educational *opportunities* for minority students. This statement, made by Havighurst, has been and continues to be largely ignored. Why? Historically, tracking helped to institutionalize beliefs about race and class differences in intellectual abilities and to erect structural obstacles to the future social, political, and economic opportunities of those who were not white or native-born (Oakes, 1986). It seems logical to assume that many academicians have been socialized to give legitimacy to society's sorting process, via the schools, by placing certain individuals or groups into the "have or have-not" categories. In effect, ability grouping stereotypes students as "more able" and "less able" (Oakes, 1988). Indeed, no one can estimate the most deleterious consequences that result from being labeled as such.

SCHOOL SUCCESS

A major rationale for the success of ability tests and their acceptance by the public has been their apparent capability of predicting school success, as well as their resultant psychological advantage in suggesting that the majority group is intellectually superior. It has been argued that the use of ability or IQ test scores to predict academic success is a self-fulfilling prophecy (U.S. Commission on Civil Rights, 1974; Williams, 1974). First, minority students are overrepresented in impoverished educational environments and low-ability tracks, while white students are overrepresented in high-ability group classes and generally enriched educational environments.

Even when educators study the academic achievement of minority students enrolled in white schools, they tend to not indicate ability group categories by race or ethnicity. Hence, placing minorities in poor schools and low-ability groups within schools, while not controlling for such, can lead to a self-fulfilling prophecy. This is quite disturbing when one considers that minorities and the poor are the fastest-growing segments of the school population (Oakes, 1988). Certainly it is this group that has been most adversely or negatively affected by ability grouping.

Williams (1974) argues that predictive measures—ability tests—are biased in favor of whites, and likewise, educational programs are biased in favor of whites. To this end, ability tests and educational programs are biased against blacks. Needless to say, statistical predictions between test scores and school performance must be questioned. Williams suggests that the better the match between the test and the school system, the higher the correlation between the two, and the better the predictive power of the test. Hence, *the quality of the school's program for minorities becomes the main criterion by which predictive validity of IQ and achievement test scores are established.* Williams further suggests a third variable, a moderator variable in which to measure the degree of bias against minorities.

It is well documented that, in general, minority students receive an inferior education from this nation's public schools when compared to nonminority students. This difference in educational opportunity must be more fully taken into consideration when relating predictive variables to criterion variables. The alternative: This nation must provide each child an equal educational opportunity, not only under the law, but also in spirit and in practice.

SUMMARY

It has been generally accepted by psychologists that ability grouping does not fulfill its stated purpose, specifically to enrich the learning potential of students. Even if ability grouping is considered effective, educationally, ability tests (IQ or achievement) are inappropriate tools for use with minority students because they are biased against minorities. In a nutshell, Goodlad and Oakes (1988) state:

> Increasingly, policymakers are troubled by the fact that tracking practices actually restrict students' access to knowledge and that the most educationally impoverished programs are offered disproportionately to poor and minority students. Many suspect that when schools react to individual differences by resorting to tracking, they begin an interactive process that diminishes the educational success of children not in the "top" groups (p. 19).

Despite more than five decades of not coming to fruition, ability grouping practices persist. Again, the authors ask, why is grouping so extensively practiced in this nation's schools? First, homogeneous grouping is perceived by educators as more desirable than heterogeneous grouping, despite evidence to the contrary. That is, supporters assert that the "most able" students require separate educational programs in order to fully develop their talents. Second, these supporters argue that individual needs are more easily targeted and met and students learn more with such grouping. Third, proponents argue that the "most able" require special preparation to become the nation's leaders, especially in sciences, government, and business (Oakes, 1988). Finally, and just as significant, it is considered a helpful tool for resegregating minority students enrolled in integrated schools (Samuda, 1975, p. 111).

Given the data presented, some researchers have suggested that efforts focus upon improving the predictive variable—the test—as a means of diminishing the effects of test bias. In essence, the writers assert that the best estimate of students' learning ability comes from direct observation of the student in a learning environment, rather than from a standardized test. The writers recommend that counselors and teachers receive better training in test development and administration, and become more aware of the possible misinterpretations, and hence, ramifications, of test scores.

In effect, counselors should utilize culture-fair tests. The writers further suggest that educators take into account the myriad criticisms made of tests in the decision of whether to practice ability grouping at all.

The writers also recommend that educators refocus their efforts on improving the schools. Stated differently, concerned educators must take greater strides to ensure minority students equal opportunities, e.g., stimulating educational environments and placement in higher ability groups, particularly as lower-track programs are often detrimental to the students in them. Ample evidence suggests that placement in these programs begins a cycle of restricted opportunities, diminished outcomes, and growing achievement differences between low-track students and their counterparts in higher tracks (Oakes, 1986). Otherwise, as previously stated, the criterion variable—school success—becomes a self-fulfilling prophecy for the predictive validity—the test. Needless to say, efforts to improve both the predictive variable and the criterion variable are important and must continue.

There are many data, supported by empirical evidence, court decisions, and reform proposals, which suggest that tracking has no overall positive effects (Oakes, 1988). Despite these initiatives and corresponding data, ability grouping will be (and has been) with us for some time. The jury is still out on the issue of whether minorities should fight for equality among the different ability groups, for the elimination of ability grouping as defined herein, or for the reestablishment of heterogeneous groups. The latter appears more applicable. For it is in heterogeneous groups that we see multi-ability classrooms, i.e., students of different ability levels in all academic courses (Cohen, 1987). Similarly, Cuban (1975), in a follow-up study to *Hobson v. Hansen*, found that tracking was replaced with "individualized" instruction within class grouping. When the superintendent of schools appeared before the school board to answer questions regarding tracking, he stated that "the tracking system has been eliminated, I hope" (Cuban, 1975, p. 21). The statement requires little explanation.

Notwithstanding this grim picture, continuing professional education programs for educators can do much to change opinions and behaviors by providing educators with information on the proper use and interpretation of test data. In addition, and perhaps more important, educators must be sensitized to the strong possibility that tracking is, to a degree, the dominant mechanism employed by schools for separating students into two career patterns, professional and nonprofessional. Stated differently, one sees a "rich get richer and poor get poorer" pattern of outcome from tracking (Oakes, 1988).

Typically, counselors, rather than parents or students, decide the tests students will take, the ability groups or tracks in which students will be placed, and the courses of study students will be permitted to pursue. Thus, schools function as sorting agents and maintainers of the *status quo*; they use a mantle of scientific inquiry (via testing programs, grouping, and "individualized" instruction) to legitimatize discrimination in the allocation of educational resources to minority students.

It is clear that ability grouping tends to place disproportionate numbers of minority students into lower level tracks and special education classes. Similarly, it is equally clear that the use of ability grouping to resegregate minority students within individual schools is a denial of equal educational opportunity—regardless of the rationale, including the use of achievement tests (Brown & Smith, 1976). If this practice is permitted to continue, greater numbers of minority students will be channelled into lower-level professions—even though they may be desirous and *capable* of employment in a highly technical occupation. Students appear imprisoned in an organizational structure that militates against their own goals. This has been most aptly underscored by Lee (1985), to wit:

> Blacks experience negative anticipatory occupational goal deflection (i.e., incongruence between aspirations and expectations) because, as they proceed through the stages of occupational development, they sometimes find it necessary to compromise occupational aspirations with expectations which is often accompanied by a growing awareness of obstacles [e.g., ability grouping] to reaching occupational aspirations (pp. 28–37).

Such barriers force adolescents to reduce aspirations to expectation levels that are considered more "realistic." This reality squeezes the hopes and dreams of minority youth. For these youth, dreams are not the seeds of reality. The writers stress that these discrepancies must be considered when counseling minority students. Counselors can help blacks overcome vocational restraints by making it possible for them to obtain improved self-esteem, increased motivation, and enhanced vocational skills.

IMPLICATIONS

The concern of the applicability of standardized tests and assessment inventories to minority groups is becoming more and more apparent in the educational and vocational movement. The recurring theme in many studies is that theories in general, including vocational theories, are not applicable to many blacks. Vocational choice is *not* a systematic and orderly process for them, particularly those of lower socioeconomic status—for many, if not most, blacks enter into the labor force earlier, and have higher unemployment rates, fewer role models, periods of sporadic employment, and less chance to acquire quality employment experience and training than their white counterparts. Certainly, then, the career reality of minorities, particularly blacks, does not neatly fit standard vocational theories. Much of this may be a function of ability grouping, which is based upon the results of "normed" tests and measures.

Socioeconomic status and its ramifications place barriers that serve to subvert the opportunity for blacks and other minorities to maximize their career potential and to find satisfaction through wise career decision making. Certainly, this increases the discrepancy between aspirations, motivations, and expectations. We must understand that motivation between majority and minority groups is different, and this difference influences (and may also have a negative impact on) blacks' performance on ability tests and other standardized measures.

Many vocational theories operate on the principle that there is an "equal" chance to attain career goals, and that careers provide intrinsic satisfaction as well as opportunities for self-expression, as supported by Leonard (1985). In a similar vein, Messick suggests that "intrinsic motivation, that is motivation for learning and performance for its own sake, is internally driven and operates in the absence of external reinforcement (Messick, 1988, p. 110). For many blacks, motivation is externally driven, as they have had little opportunity to develop skills, competence, and self-determination. In broader terms, then, such theories fail to place emphasis at points where any blacks tend to vary from the norm, and thus ignore the aforementioned situational and chance variables that restrict and otherwise affect blacks' career aspirations and entry (Leonard, 1985, p. 9).

If education, as well as vocational guidance and counseling, is to become more effective and practical, comprehensive programs must be designed to address these concerns and differences. Comprehensive programs have three main aspects: they assess achievement in relation to student characteristics, in relation to sociocultural environments, and in relation to the quality of instruction (Messick, 1988, p. 114). The writers propose a fourth variable, namely, assessing achievement in relation to the validity and reliability of the test. The writers believe that it is imperative for career education to begin in the primary grades, for it is during these formative years that one's personality and interests develop. Knowledge producers must generate data that assist in reducing the impact of the variance between the ideal, real, and perceived opportunity structure.

Improvements must be made in opportunities for blacks to improve self-concept, increase career awareness, and provide *choices*, otherwise blacks' exposure is limited and career exploration is suppressed or delayed (Perry & Locke, 1985). A systematic means for career exploration is necessary so that black youth can assume a "proactive" vocational stance. This process can be facilitated by needs assessment inventories that provide opportunities for gathering, firsthand, knowledge of the *true*, i.e., self-reported, needs of black students.

Similarly, of utmost importance is that educational professionals and vocational guidance counselors become knowledgeable of which career inventories are most applicable and practical for various racial groups and grade levels. For example, Walsh, Bingham & Sheffey (1986) found that the Vocational Preference Inventory (VPI) and Self Directed Search (SDS) are appropriate for "college-education working" blacks, yet fails to address the predictability and validity of these inventories to "non-college bound, non-working" blacks—of which there are many.

To date, the writers have encountered only two inventories—Ohio Vocational Interest Scale (OVIS) and Career Assessment Inventory (CAI)—designed for the non-college-bound population; however, the issue of socioeconomic status is still relatively ignored. This is not to say that such inventories are worthless or ineffective; rather, they fail to describe the unique career behavior of many blacks and, perhaps, should not be viewed as entirely appropriate guidelines pertaining to the career choice of many blacks. In essence, they may be more helpful when viewed as a data base from which to begin developing better and more appropriate guidelines for assisting blacks.

Vocational counseling must become synonymous with "action counseling" (Dean, 1984). That is, it must focus on change and processes designed to achieve short-term goals (e.g., immediate employment), and teach minorities how to develop an external locus of control, i.e., a greater sense of control over their environment. It is particularly noted that the perception of having little control over one's environment and/or lacking the ability to gain this control is most apparent in the area of employment (Dean, 1984, p. 114). Such counseling has the potential of increasing the intrinsic motivation and/or satisfaction of this population. Action counselors also help blacks locate jobs, and involve parents in the counseling process, which is directive, confrontative, supportive, persuasive, and informational.

The writers cannot stress enough that programs must assist blacks, at an early age and throughout life, in strengthening their self-esteem and motivation. Ultimately, it is expected that the above-mentioned strategies will assist in enhancing self-esteem and improving motivation among this population. For as mentioned earlier, improved self-esteem and increased motivation tend to have positive effects upon test scores. Consequently, the strategies will assist in facilitating the opportunity for gainful employment, and in the elimination of inappropriate decisions in the placement of students by educational and counseling professionals. This has been cogently reiterated by Goodlad and Oakes (1988):

> ... when errors in judgement are made, they are more likely to *underestimate* what children can do. Under these circumstances, the kinds of arguments based on research not favorable to tracking fade in relative importance to compelling ethical concerns. As philosopher Gary Fenstermacher (1983) has argued, "It is possible that some students may not benefit equally from unrestricted access

to knowledge, but this fact does not entitle us to control access in ways that effectively prohibit all students from encountering what Dewey called, 'the funded capital of civilization' " (p. 19).

In the final analysis, the time has come to develop new measures of accountability, as well as standards the measures themselves should meet.

Ability grouping: Has the means ever justified the ends? The decision is up to us as citizens of this nation. The writers believe that this decision, once rendered, may provide a compelling, intriguing, and potentially powerful base from which to have a positive impact on this phenomenon. Such envisioned changes hold the promise of creating new pathways to improve understanding and learning by knowledge producers, helping professionals, and students.

NOTES

1. Excerpted from Judge Wright's statement in *Hobson v. Hansen*, 269 F.Supp. 401–519 (1967). Also see, for example, *Smuck v. Hobson*, 408 F.2d 175 (D.C. Cir., 1969), *appeal dismissed* 393 U.S. 801 (1968); *Debra P. v. Turlington*, 474 F.Supp. 244 (M.D. Fla., 1979), *aff'd in part* 644 F.2d 397 (5th Cir., 1981); *Larry P. v. Riles*, 343 F.Supp. 1036 (N.D. Cal., 1972); *Board of Education of Northport-East, Northport Unified School District v. Ambach*, 436 N.Y.S.2d 564 (Sup. Ct., 1981).

2. *Morgan v. Kerrigan*, 509 F.2d 580 (1st Cir., 1974), cert. denied, 95 S.Ct. 1950 (1975).

REFERENCES

Adler, M. J. 1982. *The Paideia proposal: An educational manifesto.* New York: Macmillan.

Boyer, E. L. 1983. *High school.* New York: Harper & Row.

Brown, F., and Smith, E. 1976. The allocation of educational environment, ability grouping and the law. *Journal of Urban Education* 2(2):201–16.

CBS (Columbia Broadcasting Company). 1975. *The I.Q. myth.* Interview with L. Cronbach. New York.

Cohen, E. 1987. *Denying group work strategies for the heterogeneous classroom.* New York: Teachers College Press.

Coleman, J. 1966. *Equal educational opportunity.* Washington, D.C.: U.S. Government Printing Office.

Cronbach, L. J. 1970. *Essentials of psychological testing.* New York: Harper & Row.

Cuban, L. 1975. Hobson v. Hansen: A study in organizational response. *Educational Administration Quarterly* 2:15–37.

Dean, A. 1984. External locus of control and career counseling for black youth. *Journal of Non-White Concerns* 12(3):110–16.

Epps, E. G. 1974. Situational effects in testing. In *The testing of black students*, ed. L. P. Miller. Englewood Cliffs, N.J.: Prentice Hall.

Erickson, F. 1975. Gateskeeping and the melting pot: Interaction in counseling encounters. *Harvard Educational Review* 45(1):44–70.

Fenstermacher, G. O. 1983. Introduction. In *Individual differences and the common curriculum*, ed. G. O. Fenstermacher and J. I. Goodlad. Chicago: University of Chicago Press.

Findley, W. G. 1974. Grouping for instruction. In *The testing of black students*, ed. L. P. Miller. Englewood Cliffs, N.J.: Prentice Hall.

Fordham, M. 1975. *Major themes in northern black religious thought.* Hicksville, N.Y.: Exposition Press.

Ginsberg, E. 1971. *Career guidance.* New York: McGraw-Hill.

Goodlad, J. I. 1984. *A place called school: Prospects for the future.* New York: McGraw-Hill.

Goodlad, J. I., and Oakes, J. 1988. We must offer equal access to knowledge. *Educational Leadership* 45(5):16–22.

Hall, V. C., and Turner, R. R. 1974. The validity of the different language explanation for poor scholastic performance by black students. *Review of Educational Research* 44(1):69–81.

Jensen, A. 1980. *Bias in mental testing.* New York: Free Press.

Kirkland, M. C. 1971. The effects of tests on students and schools. *Review of Educational Research* 41(4):303–50.

Kirp, D. L. 1974. Student classification, public policy, and the courts. *Harvard Educational Review* 44(1):7–52.

Lee, C. C. 1985. An ethnic group-gender comparison of occupational choice among rural adolescents. *Journal of Non-White Concerns* 13(1):28–37.

Leonard, Y. 1985. Vocational theory and the vocational behavior of black males: An analysis. *Journal of Multicultural Counseling and Development* 13(3):91–105.

Linn, R. L. 1973. Fair test use in selection. *Review of Educational Research* 43(2):139–61.

Mercer, J. R. 1974. Latent functions of intelligence testing in the public schools. In *The testing of black students*, ed. L. P. Miller. Englewood Cliffs, N.J.: Prentice Hall.

Messick, S. 1988. Assessment in the schools: Purposes and consequences. In *Contributing to educational change: Perspectives and practices*, ed. P. Jackson. Berkeley: McCutchan.

Miller, L. P. 1974. *The testing of black students.* Englewood Cliffs, N.J.: Prentice Hall.

Morgan, J. C. 1974. *The schools, the courts, and the public interest.* Lexington, Mass.: Lexington Books.

Oakes, J. 1986. Keeping track, part 2: Curriculum inequality and school reform. *Phi Delta Kappan* 68(2):148–53.

————. 1988. Tracking: Can schools take a different route? *NEA Today* 6(6):41–47.

Perry, J., and Locke, D. C. 1985. Career development of black men: Implications for school guidance services. *Journal of Multicultural Counseling and Development* 13(3):106–11.

Rohwer, W. D. 1975. Learning, race, and school success. *Review of Educational Research* 41(3):191–210.

Samuda, R. J. 1975. *Psychological testing of American minorities*. New York: Dodd, Mead & Co.

Slavin, R. E. 1987. Ability grouping and student achievement in elementary schools. A best-evidence synthesis. *Review of Educational Research* 57(3):293–336.

U.S. Commission on Civil Rights. 1974. *Toward quality education for Mexican Americans: Report 4*. Washington, D.C.: U.S. Government Printing Office.

Walsh, E.; Bingham, R. P.; and Sheffey, M. A. 1986. Holland's theory and college educated working black men and women. *Journal of Vocational Behavior* 29:194–200.

Williams, R. L. 1974. The problem of match and mismatch in testing black children. In *The testing of black students*, ed. L. P. Miller. Englewood Cliffs, N.J.: Prentice Hall.

————. 1981. Culture-specific testing: Part 1. *Journal of Non-White Concerns* 10(1):3–48.

MAINSTREAMING AND INTEGRATION OF EXCEPTIONAL CHILDREN:
A SOCIOLOGICAL PERSPECTIVE

Susan Peters

Americans hold the ideal of wellness—sturdy, healthy bodies and keen, alert minds. Good health, active learning, a wholesome environment, and equality of opportunity make up a considerable portion of American societal ideals. What happens, however, when individuals do not present in their physical well-being the ideal of sturdy and active participation in all that modern life offers? How do schools as mainstream institutions adapt their attitudes and behaviors toward physically handicapped individuals? How do we recognize that difficulties with their full participation in school and the wider society do not reside exclusively within the physically handicapped individuals themselves, but within the broader fabric of experiences created by the environment? How do we sustain a climate of ideal expectations for mental alertness and independent learning in schools while at the same time embracing individual differences as an enhancement of democratic ideals rather than as a problem of assimilation?

The sociological perspective set forth here in answer to these questions is based in part on research of mainstreaming and integration for physically handicapped students (Peters, 1987). It is informed as well by educational policy studies on the questions of equity and equal opportunity for all handicapped school children (Levin, 1975; Mehan, 1981; Reynolds, 1978; Weatherly, 1979). This perspective is also tempered by my own experiences as a person with a severe physical handicap, and by my anthropological training.

When I first began thinking about integration in mainstreamed class-rooms, socialization was not a consideration. Policy issues of equity, cost resources, efficiency, and effectiveness were the dominant concerns. These concerns were framed within the contexts of equal access to programs and services appropriate to children's needs, the effects of cost formulas on equality of education, the role of the federal government, the range of services needed, and kinds of retraining provided to teachers in main-streamed classrooms.

This policy perspective stemmed from years of debating handicapped issues in the political mainstream. I struggled with phrases such as "breaking down attitudinal barriers" and "prejudiced society rife with inequities." I could "see" inequities, and I could "feel" prejudices based on attitudes I encountered in my life as a handicapped person. However, I understood little about why these perceived inequities and prejudices existed.

In the spring of 1983, I began investigating what I then called a "social problems approach" to the problem of understanding why mainstreaming did not always result in positive integration in schools. The questions I had asked previously had to do with the structure of society and people's at-titudes. When I began delving into the work of notable educational an-thropologists, I began to ask how? (Erickson, 1977; Heath, 1982; Spindler, 1963). I began to think about attitudes as an accumulation of values, pref-erences, and unconscious assumptions that were arrived at through social experiences. I recognized that these social experiences were tied up with behaviors. Hence the "social problems approach" meant tying behaviors to attitudes in order to understand the dynamics of mainstreaming.

Still concentrating on attitudes and how they operate to produce behav-iors, I agreed with Peggy Reeves Sanday that my goal must be to "describe the flow of behavior in a way that allows us to comprehend at an emotional level the events set before us and to understand the context motivating these events" (Sanday, 1982). I felt that if I could infer a structure of feelings, attitudes, and values, these could be linked to people's choices, decisions, and behavior. My underlying assumption was that attitudes are the moti-vating forces for behavior.

Pursuing this line of reasoning, the links between attitudes and behavior must then be a process of social interaction or socialization. Socialization is an interplay of expectations and actions between individuals involved in experiencing social events. People constructed their social realities through a reflexive process of assimilation and accommodation in everyday choices of practical action. A sociology of consciousness was being built through these interactions that seemed a good beginning point from which to ap-proach the problem of integration.

These beginning thoughts were refined and adapted through my study of physically handicapped children in kindergarten and first grade main-streamed classrooms.[1] Learning, adaptation, and modification of attitudes and behaviors in integrated classrooms created a joint socialization experience for the well-bodied children and teachers as well as the young physically handicapped children. Two-way exchanges marked the integration of handicapped children with their same-age peers in classrooms that held the goal of enabling all children to participate fully in the initial academic and social learning experiences that would prepare them for successful movement through their years of public schooling. These children and their teachers in a single school, like many others in mainstreamed classrooms throughout the United States, played out in degrees that varied by moment, mood, and membership the expressed purposes of federal mandates calling for integration of handicapped children with their peers.

Integration of physically handicapped individuals involves adjustments within the entire system of education, including the individual within the classroom as well as within the school and community environments. All aspects of socialization and its processes will have to be accounted for in order to address a central problem: What are the effects of the mainstreaming environment on the conditions needed for handicapped children to socialize on an equal level with their peers?

Before responding to this question, this chapter begins by providing an overview of the historical context of mainstreaming. This overview is followed by an explanation of what is meant by mainstreaming and integration and how these can be viewed from a sociological perspective. This explanation leads to the development of socialization theory and its application to mainstream settings. Finally, the effects of socialization as proposed are explored, leading to recommendations for educators seeking to accomplish equity for all children in increasingly diverse classrooms.

MAINSTREAMING: A BRIEF HISTORICAL CONTEXT

The concept of mainstreaming in the United States has its roots in special education—the term used to refer to education of children considered by society to be exceptional in some way. In the nineteenth century, "special education" meant the establishment of special schools, segregated from the mainstream, to deal with those children the medical profession judged defective and unfit for regular classroom instruction and a normal life (Sarason & Doris, 1979; Connor, Rusalem, & Cruickshank, 1971). These schools were established sporadically as a result of local community initiatives and in accord with the prevailing notion of handicap. "A child's handicap was seen as an unalterable characteristic of the child ... given this, and the conviction that the handicapped were different in kind from the rest of children, it made sense to develop separate educational systems" (Hegarty, Pocklington, & Lucas, 1984, p. 8).

In the late nineteenth and early twentieth century, special education became an organized and recognized profession among educators in the United States. Several groups, such as the Convention of American Instructors for the Deaf, the American Association of Instructors of the Blind, and the American Association on Mental Deficiency, organized and applied pressure to the National Education Association (NEA) to create a department within the NEA to meet these children's needs (Sarason & Doris, 1979). Such a department was formed in 1897 and became known as the Department of Special Education. This department was an instrumental force behind the first public school classes for handicapped children in the United States. However, World War I and the Depression interfered with its growth.

World War II and its aftermath had a significant effect on the prevailing notions of handicap and the provision of education for exceptional children. Disabled veterans of the war returned home in large numbers and were visibly leading productive and useful lives. They were a sizable minority whose need for rehabilitation programs began to change attitudes with respect to handicapped people. Spurred by the impetus of returning veterans, parents of handicapped children began to demand access to educational resources for their children in the early 1970s. Many parents felt their children's needs were not being met in segregated schools, where, removed from the educational mainstream, their children received little preparation for a normal adult life (Garwood, 1979). As a result of parental pressure, supported by various special interest groups, Public Law 94-142 was passed and integration became the major issue in special education.

Known as the Education for All Handicapped Children Act, PL 94-142 requires that all handicapped children throughout the United States be afforded an "appropriate education" in the "least restrictive environment." An "appropriate education" ideally translates into equality of opportunity and positive integration of handicapped children with their nonhandicapped peers. The "least restrictive environment" encompasses the ideals of physical accessibility as well as acknowledgment that all bodies and minds must have access to instructional resources that best support the broad array of talents and capabilities represented by society.

Federal policy requires changing environments and behaviors that might seem to be the contradictions of American attitudes toward wellness. Despite these seeming contradictions, the questions of what constitutes an appropriate education and supportive learning environments are fundamental ones for both the general school population and exceptional students in "special" education. Schools are agencies of socialization, transmitting societal goals and values (Parsons, 1983; Dreeben, 1977; Durkheim, 1971). When a handicapped child enters any classroom, teachers and students have an opportunity to become participants in a process of socialization that improves life chances and enhances tolerance for diversity needed for a democratic society to carry out its ideals of equal opportunity for all.

Since passage of PL 94-142, "mainstreaming" has become widely accepted as the way to meet the goals of appropriate education in the least restrictive environment, yet no operational definition of mainstreaming exists (Strain & Kerr, 1981). The most widely accepted conceptual definition is the following:

> Mainstreaming refers to the temporal, instructional, and social integration of eligible exceptional children with normal peers based on ongoing, individually determined educational planning and program process and required clarification of responsibility among regular and special education administrative, instructional, and supportive personnel (Kaufman, Gottlieb, Agard, & Kukic, 1975, p. 73).

This concept of mainstreaming reflects two presuppositions. First is the assumption that certain social benefits will derive from integration. Children with different backgrounds and experiences "will get to know one another better, will learn to get along with each other, and will change the negative attitudes which they have acquired from prejudiced families and communities" (Patchen, 1982, p. 3). Second, equal opportunity will improve academic achievement for handicapped children and thus lead to improved life chances for these children. Life chances are seen as the "child's future ability as an adult to participate fully in the social, economic, and political life of society" (Levin, 1975, p. 217).

Schools teach social skills and academic competence. These two functions are not clearly differentiated, especially in the primary school grades (Calhoun & Elliott, 1977; Dreeben, 1968; Ispa & Matz, 1978; Parsons, 1983). Although mainstreaming stresses the importance of social integration to improve life chances, these chances include preparing children for adult life and the opportunity for economic independence in the job market. However, certain social competencies are prerequisite to academic achievement and to preparation for adult work life. These include learning time-on-task behaviors, acquiring values of achievement, being motivated to learn, developing a positive self-concept, and gaining linguistic ability. Those who learn these social skills and acquire them in integrated classroom settings have a better chance academically (Calhoun & Elliott, 1977; Madden & Slavin, 1982).

Physically hndicapped individuals present a special challenge with respect to social competence and academic achievement. Societal norms emphasize levels of function within a prescribed range of behaviors, capabilities, and developmental markers. Because of the nature of severe handicapping conditions, children with physical limitations often do not have the social and mobility skills exemplified by their same-age well-bodied peers. The gap in levels of development precludes them from playing the same physically active games, communicating at similar levels of proficiency, and from carrying out learning activities independently.

The design of services to assist physically handicapped children and narrow this gap further precludes normalized interactions—or opportunities to interact with their peers through the school day. Self-contained classrooms, different schedules, and separate transportation systems all serve to further socially isolate these children from the general environment.

Societal attitudes toward physically handicapped individuals further heighten differences from the norm. Several studies of teachers' attitudes found negative perceptions of students with special needs (Hegarty, Pocklington, & Lucas, 1984, p. 456). Stereotypic images of physically handicapped children's overall helplessness, tendencies toward overprotectiveness, and fear for children's safety were common responses on the part of teachers in mainstreamed classrooms.

Attitudes of nonhandicapped children toward their severely handicapped peers, on the other hand, have been generally positive (Brady & Gunter, 1985, p. 84–85). However, initial interactions tended toward "over-friendliness" and inappropriate feedback regarding socially acceptable behaviors, resulting in an extension of "the artificial and nonhabilitative 'special' environment to the real world" (Brady & Gunter, 1985, p. 85).

The realities of physical differences and the perceptions of children's overall capabilities based on these differences must be dealt with before children with physical handicaps can acquire the social skills and academic competence needed to function in society. Well-bodied children and teachers in mainstreamed classrooms need to learn ways of behaving that provide a more normalized environment for all concerned.

MAINSTREAMING AND INTEGRATION

The growing concern for human rights and the status of minorities in the United States motivated integration of diverse children from the educational advancement of society as a whole. In the 1950s, the courts began to respond to pressures for integration of racial minorities. In 1954, the United States Supreme Court decided in the case of *Brown v. Board of Education* that segregated public schools are not "equal" and cannot be made "equal," so that equal protection of the laws under the Fourteenth Amendment to the Constitution was being denied to children of racial minorities. The Court further found that segregation of minority children solely because of race "generates a feeling of inferiority as to their status in the community that may affect their hearts and minds in a way unlikely ever to be undone" (Gunther & Dowling, 1970). The right to equal opportunity established in *Brown v. Board of Education* supplied key precedents for integration of handicapped children in general education classrooms.

Feelings of inferiority inherent in segregation of racial minority children were extended logically to the stigma and adverse psychological effects of labeling and placing handicapped children in segregated special education classrooms.

The principles of equal opportunity and the notion of inferiority inherent in segregation provided bases for legal arguments in early special education cases such as *PARC v. Commonwealth of Pennsylvania* (1972) and *Mills v. Board of Education* (1972). In both cases, United States district courts handed down decisions requiring individual states to provide free appropriate education to all children, whether handicapped or not. The case of PARC (Pennsylvania Association for Retarded Children) established the principle that placement in regular public schools is preferable to any other type of placement. The PARC suit led to a consent agreement whereby Pennsylvania education officials agreed to integrate mentally handicapped children with normal children. The case of Mills extended the principle of integration to all handicapped children.

> The court decisions rendered made a significant contribution to guaranteeing educational rights for the nation's handicapped children and fueled the movement for justice. The movement so generated addressed the handicapped child's right to due process and equal protection, to providing children with not just any educational program, but with quality education appropriate to their individual needs, all taking precedence to bureaucratic and professional needs and limitations (Anderson, Martinez, & Rich, 1980, p. 24).

A critical operational result of mainstreaming is integration. A word which since the 1960s has tended to carry heavy emotional values and to have wide varieties of meaning, integration means literally "a process of making whole, of uniting different parts in a totality" (Hegarty, Pocklington, and Lucas, 1984, p. 14). In special education, however, the term has been widely used to mean integration of the handicapped, focusing on this 10 percent of the population as if integration were something done to or by the handicapped themselves and not systemic interaction to form a new educational whole. The focus has also been on physical integration or placement of handicapped children in a regular school. However, physical integration does not in itself lead to desirable social integration and attitudinal shift. Social integration implies resocialization as all children eat, play, and share together in organized classroom activities that support the handicapped child's ability to take a place in society comparable to his or her peers. Also implied is that peers will accept handicapped individuals as part of the diversity endemic to American life.

Court decisions and legislative action have thus far succeeded in providing the opportunity for social integration of handicapped children by requiring their physical placement in mainstreamed or "least restrictive environments" (*Wyatt v. Stickney*, 1972; *Fialkowski v. Shapp*, 1975; *Campbell v. Talladega Board of Education*, 1981). Social mandates have provided moral and conceptual bases for integration of exceptional children and the desire to change intergroup socialization patterns for these children, e.g., the move to deinstitutionalization and provision of community-based services (Biklen & Foster, 1985). If social integration is to take place, children cannot merely be transferred from special schools to regular schools. To put into effect the goal of meeting the needs of handicapped children, their transfer into the mainstream must be accompanied by attention to their social integration into the daily life of regular schools.

HANDICAP AS A SOCIAL CONSTRUCTION

A concept of handicap as a sociological construct developed along with early mainstreaming efforts. This view moved away from focus on handicap as an innate characteristic of the individual to acknowledgment that a considerable part of an individual's handicap was generated by the social environment. In other words, a handicap is not only a particular physical or mental characteristic of the individual child, but also a product of the social environment of work and play for that individual. Labeling, a key feature of the segregative society, condemns a child without acknowledging that a child cannot be handicapped unless professional practices are available to make that judgment. Yet, professional practices are products of institutions that are underpinned by social processes. A label becomes a social fact about a child—"an object with a fixed meaning for the institution, albeit a social product of its own practices" (Mehan, 1981, p. 407).

A logical extension of this notion of handicap as relative to the social environment is the ideology that special education and regular education are neither dichotomous nor fundamentally different. Both exist to further the education of children, so that:

> What is required is that the school adapt its educational provision so as to be able to cater to a wider variety of pupils. This means a highly flexible range of provisions, planned as a whole—since the school is a single entity—but incorporating a multitude of possibilities and not just a simple choice between ordinary and special tracks (Hegarty, Pocklington, & Lucas, 1984, p. 17).

The categorical labeling that is commonly used to identify and place exceptional children reinforces the ethic that handicapped children are "deviant." By the same token, Anthony Platt in his book *The Child Savers* (Platt, 1969) found that juvenile delinquency is an invention of public officials and government agencies. This invention of a term views "troublesome" adolescents as "sick" and "pathological" but goes no further in solving the problem of how to achieve positive social integration for these youths than does the labeling practice that we use as part of the segregative mechanism society imposes on handicapped children. The case of physically handicapped children especially brings out the necessity to separate the label from the child. The fact that a child has physical differences says little about capacity and potential for learning.

If one accepts the view that handicaps are for the most part socially constructed, one must begin by examining the value of equal opportunity. Mainstreaming is essentially a program of socialization in which the value of equal opportunity for all children is carried out through the face-to-face interactions involved in schooling experiences. Equal opportunity must be examined through (1) the contexts of mainstreaming practices—both structure and content; (2) the dynamics of interaction among individuals; and (3) the ways in which behavior and attitudes change as new members are accepted into the mainstream of society. The contexts of structure and content include specific ways activities are organized to promote learning as well as expectations for learning specific subject matter. The dynamics of interaction involve role negotiation and strategies for gaining acceptance as an equal and fully participating member of a group. Changes in behavior and attitudes involve expectations for competence that are grounded in firsthand knowledge of individual capabilities rather than in preconceived notions of ability.

The shapes of mainstreamed environments depend upon federal, state, and local institutional decisions, as well as choices made at the school, classroom, and individual levels of the environment. For federal, state, and local institutions, we need to know the effects of policy mandates and legislative action on mainstreaming in individual schools. Within the schools, we need to know more about the ways teachers, support personnel, parents, and students translate mainstreaming goals into activities of selection, teaching, and testing.

The idea of handicap as a social construction contributes understanding of both the means (e.g., legal mandates, societal resources) and ends (e.g., social conditions) of mainstreaming. Current theories with respect to education of handicapped individuals are dominated by medical, psychological, and administrative approaches. These theories provide "recipe" knowledge and accept as unproblematic what are in fact very complex and debatable concepts of what mainstreaming goals are and how they ought to be carried out (Tomlinson, 1982). A theory of socialization applied to mainstreaming is necessary, not because it gives ready-made strategies, but a body of guiding ideas that in turn gives meaning to the practice of mainstreaming and sustains it. Specifically, asking questions about social structures and social relations inherent in mainstreaming provides an understanding of the behaviors, attitudes, and conditions that underlie practice, suggesting ways practice may be improved.

SOCIALIZATION THEORY DEFINED

The conceptual framework employed here rests on the supposition that schools are agencies of socialization, transmitting societal goals and values (Parsons, 1983; Dreeben, 1977; Durkheim, 1971). The proposed theory of socialization reflects the symbolic interactionist approach most closely. Symbolic interactionists such as George Herbert Mead and H. G. Blumer view socialization as an interactive process among individuals and society. Interactionist theory consists of three basic premises:

> First, human beings act toward things on the basis of the meanings that the things have for them. Secondly, these meanings are a prod-uct of social interaction in human society. Thirdly, these meanings are modified and handled through an interpretive process that is used by each individual in dealing with the signs he/she encounters (Meltzer, Petras, & Reynolds, 1975; p. 54).

According to this theory, socialization is not merely a transfer of values but results in interaction of individuals with the structure of their environment. Individual ability determines and carries with it the possibility for change. The structure places limits or boundaries on human interaction, but within these boundaries, people have room to operate autonomously. Socialization occurs within a "context," or a "particular understanding of culture asso-ciated with a concept of social place" (Wentworth, 1980, p. 2).

Symbolic interactionism considers that "social reality is a creation of social participants, and that social categories and social knowledge are not given or natural, but are socially constructed—a product of conscious com-munication and action between people" (Tomlinson, 1982, p. 19). This view recognizes the significance of individuals and their ability to affect structural institutions through social interaction. When applied to school integration, interactionists would view mainstreaming as a conscious re-structuring of the educational environment.

Socialization is defined here as a process of interaction by which indi-viduals develop attitudes and ways of behaving as a result of their experi-ences within a structured environment. This process includes functional responses that are socially constructed through environmental conditions. Particular environmental conditions contain certain fixed properties (e.g., class size, temporal and spatial relations), but within these properties, in-dividuals may alter certain aspects or respond differentially, thereby mod-ifying their relations to the structure of the classroom environment. The importance of this view of socialization is evident when one considers that mainstreaming constitutes a new social order. The purpose of socialization is seen as inculcating school participants with new ways of thinking and behaving that support the notion of equal opportunity for all children. The Education for All Handicapped Children Act provides integration of non-handicapped and handicapped children as an opportunity for new ways of thinking and behaving—or resocialization into new roles and production of new structural dynamics of class relations.

Socialization is no longer merely the induction of an individual into existing roles, as in the functionalist view, because new roles and relations introduced by laws mandating integration have yet to be worked out. The functionalist definition (internalizing certain patterns of value orientation) works to the extent that society's values and goals are internalized by the majority of its members and have a basis in tradition. The Education for All Handicapped Children Act, while controlling aspects of the structure (i.e., mandating integration) cannot control the social practice involved in carrying out integration. It cannot be assumed that the value of equal opportunity inherent in the law has been internalized and manifested in the behavior of agents of socialization in mainstreamed classrooms, especially considering that the impetus for mainstreaming came from outside the educational system.

The features of educational experience in mainstream classrooms that determine socialization therefore include individuals, structure, and strategies employed by individuals through a process of social interaction. Individuals involved in socialization include handicapped students and their nonhandicapped peers, teachers and other education professionals, parents and family members, and citizens in the community. The structure includes grade level, task organization, subject matter, and group size. Strategies involve ways of communicating expectations based on values and attitudes toward others in the mainstream environment. The degree of influence exerted by individuals depends on a variety of factors that are situational in nature. While some features of the classroom may predominate over others during a period of interaction, the assertion here is that human action will make a difference. If the purpose of socialization is to inculcate in members of a society values and roles consonant with equal opportunity, then socialization must be defined as a mutually interdependent relation of individuals and society, not as a one-sided set of institutionally determined relations. People form attitudes and behavior somewhere in between "a reflective and socially derived interpretation of the internal and external stimuli that are present" (Meltzer, Petras, & Reynolds, 1975, p. 2).

The precise nature of social integration must be understood in order to determine the practices that constitute the implementation of mainstreaming (Strain & Kerr, 1981). Links between individuals and actions, when identified and sorted out, provide the key to the meaning of socialization in mainstreamed classrooms. A dynamic process model of socialization links practices and processes that are important to the study of what goes on in the socialization of mainstreamed children in the context of schools and their larger environments. The practice of mainstreaming referred to as the physical integration of handicapped children with nonhandicapped peers in a school program makes sense only when studied in relation to the processes involved in social integration of these individuals.

SOCIALIZATION THEORY AND ITS APPLICATION TO MAINSTREAMING

The theory of socialization proposed here has not as yet been applied to study of the effects of mainstreaming. Current socialization views of disabled children in mainstreamed classrooms center on stigma management (Goffman, 1963) and "coping" with the "real" world—real being synonymous with "normal" or "able bodied" in the minds of educators and policy makers. Socialization is seen as a one-way street—disabled children must be assimilated by grafting them onto the educational mainstream. Very few researchers study assimilation and accommodation strategies used by the handicapped and nonhandicapped individuals who are themselves involved in the social interaction of mainstreaming.

Mutual Adaptation

The key operant principle in this interactionist definition of socialization is mutual adaptation. Focus on individuals means that socialization can be seen to proceed "through interactions among novices (individuals learning a new role) and agents (individuals responsible for training)" (Cogswell, 1968, p. 12). These interactions among novices (handicapped and nonhandicapped students) and agents (teachers and education professionals) include interpersonal and intrapersonal adjustments within a mainstreamed classroom. The interplay of expectations and actions involved in these interpersonal contacts are defined as accommodation strategies and points of negotiation used by physically handicapped children and their peers as they interrelate.

The idea of mutual adaptation allows us to view socialization as a two-way street. That is, students are socialized to group norms by teachers who transmit values. But at the same time, students—both handicapped children and their peers—influence teachers' expectations and actions through their reactions and responses to their teachers. Students and teachers are thus engaged in rule negotiation and reciprocal accommodations to each other's behavior as socialization interaction is played out in the classroom.

The principle of mutual adaptation means that in order to maximize positive social integration, one must at once be cognizant of students' communicative and physical competencies, task organization, access to resources, and values inherent in making choices. A mainstream program that does not take into account the interplay of these factors may ignore vital linkages essential to the process of socialization.

Interactive Processes

Second, a symbolic interactionist approach suggests that the process in mainstreamed classrooms is interactive. Functional response strategies are socially constructed through manipulation of classroom conditions. These conditions provide ecologies of work and play options that are interdependent with the sources of interpersonal contacts. These sources are defined as ways of dealing with options—reshaping, choosing—that individuals employ based on their communicative and physical competencies. These competencies stem from the resources and values existent in the home and community and are translated into experiences and skills individuals bring to the school environment.

The fact that the socialization process is interactive means that a mainstream program must concentrate on socialization to group norms on the part of all participants; e.g., administrators, teachers, and students. Focus on teacher intervention strategies to promote positive social integration misses the vital fact that students are engaged in a two-way process of socialization. Students and teachers make reciprocal accommodations to each other's differences that must be attended to. Students are agents in their own socialization, so that respect for and equal treatment of each other must be cultivated. This must be done as a general program goal, rather than waiting for specific problems to occur and then reacting on a case-by-case basis. Teachers cannot be everywhere at once. Most social interaction goes unnoticed by teachers. Often, only blatant problems result in direct teacher intervention.

Reflexive Behavior

This interactive aspect of socialization theory is closely related to a third characteristic of the socialization process in mainstreamed classrooms —socialization is reflexive. As students and teachers respond to actions of others, this action is reflected back upon the "agent." Individuals involved in interpersonal contacts experience a process of internalization of values with a resultant change in behavior that affects assimilation and accommodation within one's chosen social milieu. In addition, behavior in a given social interaction sets off a chain of reactions that has cumulative effects. This characteristic of socialization suggests that the timing of interventions in mainstreamed classrooms is important. Teachers and education professionals must consciously plan social integration and continuously monitor its consequences before unintended results become so internalized that major changes are needed, which may be difficult to accomplish.

Fluid Conditions

Fourth, socialization as a process is fluid. Under certain conditions, interactions combine in different ways, leading to positive social integration. In other combinations, the process may lead one down a path of inequality and social maladaptation. Because socialization is fluid, the fact that a single strategy or teacher intervention does not lead to positive social integration in one situation does not mean it will not work in a different situation. This means that classroom alterations can not simply be made across the board. A classroom intervention that works for one child may not work for another. That same intervention may not work for the same child in a different set of task organizations or across grade levels. As with the principle of interaction, the fluidity of the socialization process requires attention to all factors and their combination in a given setting. This attention requires the ability to adapt and be flexible, given differing classroom conditions.

Cumulative Effects

The process of socialization is repetitive. The forces of social structure in mainstreamed classrooms interact with socialization processes and have a cumulative effect on mainstream participants. This cumulative effect results in varying degrees of independence, acceptance, and adaptation for physically handicapped children. The outcome of positive social integration reinforces values and allows access to resources in the school environment that in turn start the integrative mechanisms churning and set the stage for classroom structure and functional strategies to be played out once again.

Because socialization processes involve mutual adaptation, interaction, reflexive behavior, and fluid conditions, the directions these processes take in a mainstream program must be periodically assessed and reevaluated for the degree of access to resources and the degree that values are being reinforced through everyday choices of practical action. Outcomes that are assessed at one point in the program may look quite different several months down the road. Educators cannot expect an "exemplary" program to remain that way or to run a predictable course once implementation has begun.

Socialization theory thus provides a conceptual framework for understanding the dynamics of interaction among individuals and the ways in which societal values and beliefs are internalized by participating members in a social group. Integration of handicapped and nonhandicapped children in classrooms constitutes a new social order and restructuring of class relations. In order for mainstreaming to be successful, the values of equal opportunity and the goal of positive social integration must be internalized and transmitted in classrooms. Socialization theory provides the means for understanding how the task of internalizing and transmitting these values and goals is accomplished. Specifically, it allows us to link attitudes with behaviors, to view all members as participating in reciprocal relations, to recognize the importance of structural contexts, and to incorporate the possibility of accommodation strategies and rule negotiations necessary for implementing the new social order that mainstreaming represents. Attitudes of both handicapped and nonhandicapped students are undergoing mutual adjustments that, when seen through the theory of socialization, allow us to understand the effects of the mainstream environment on conditions needed for these students to socialize on an equal level.

In summary, socialization has come to mean more than strategies and points of negotiation between teachers and students in classrooms. The interplay of expectations and actions in interpersonal contacts forms only a part of a layered web of social interaction. Socialization not only constitutes conscious communication and action between people, but is now defined as a process of interaction powered by individuals within a structured environment. Social consciousness involves functional responses that are constructed through manipulation of environmental conditions—both inside and outside of the classroom.

THE EFFECT OF SOCIALIZATION ON CLASSROOM INTEGRATION

The organization and decision-making processes involved in a mainstream program affect the structure and outcomes of integration and equal opportunity in significant ways. These organizational functions include policy interpretations; personnel selection and training; and informal and formal decision-making processes involved in student placement, preparation, educational planning, and ongoing instructional support. Figure 1 sets forth a model of integration processes in a mainstream environment.

In this model, two groups of conditions are the driving forces external to classroom socialization—resources and values. Resources constitute fiscal allocations and restraints, school curriculum and programs, community socioeconomic level, special materials, personnel, equipment, and facilities. Values include degree of commitment, criteria, and goals of mainstreaming.

The integrative mechanisms in the model link values and resources to classroom interaction components and include policy, roles, and decision-making processes. Participants in mainstream programs develop policies in conformance with values and implement these policies through assigned roles and responsibilities involving both formal and informal decision-making processes that differ by forms of cooperation and communication. Integrative mechanisms are powered by teachers, support personnel, leadership, and parents, as well as by students in the environment. These individuals bring values, allocate resources, and make decisions about students' schooling experiences that provide the props and act as the catalyst for socialization.

These external forces (resources and values) and integrative mechanisms

FIGURE 1
Model of Socialization in a Mainstream Environment

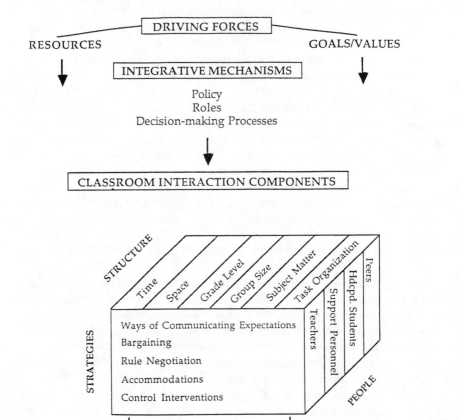

(policy, roles, and decision-making processes) are powered by individuals who shape the boundaries of classroom interaction components illustrated by the three-dimensional box in the model. Outcomes of adaptation, acceptance, and independence operate through these classroom interaction components and are dependent on student and teacher characteristics and ways of managing social interaction.

Mainstreaming as a process of socialization goes beyond strategies and points of negotiation between teachers and students in classrooms. The interplay of expectations and actions in interpersonal contacts forms only a part of a layered web of social interaction. Socialization not only constitutes conscious communication and action between people, but is now defined as a process of interaction powered by individuals within a structured environment. This process includes functional responses that are socially constructed through manipulation of environmental conditions—both inside and outside of the classroom.

A look at the integrative mechanisms and their interaction with resources and values as they impinge upon classroom socialization provides the key to sorting out the totality of conditions needed to effect outcomes of positive social integration for handicapped children and their peers. First, the attitudes and values toward mainstreaming are translated into action of placement and instructional management by teachers, principals, and support personnel. Second, these actions are negotiated over time through assignment of roles. Third, various forms of communication and cooperation are involved in decision making. Teachers and other professionals involved in carrying out the mainstream program have ways of reshaping and choosing options at a program level similar to the reshaping and choosing of socialization experiences employed by students as they interact with each other on an individual level.

IMPLICATIONS FOR EDUCATORS: EQUITY IN THE MAINSTREAMED CLASSROOM

Answering the questions, when integration works, how, and why, depends not on attempting to list factors with "more" or "less" influence, but on understanding the phenomena and interaction of factors involved in the process. Even the most enlightened research on mainstreaming has thus far focused on program instruction and on professional training of teachers and other educators involved in mainstream programs. This focus on educational personnel and actual physical instruction is a natural response to the legal mandates requiring integration. Training, program planning, and curriculum development are tangible and time-limited, and can be accounted for or standardized. An understanding of the process of interaction is far less tangible, ongoing, and cannot be standardized. But as long as education focuses on types of programs, mainstreaming will never be more than a grafting-on process. The kind of integration education accomplishes will be a one-way street. As long as educators view mainstreaming as something that is done to individuals that are labeled as different or special, meaningful integration will never be achieved. Educators can assign labels and react to mandates of mainstream programs, or they can become a part of the process, attributing their own meanings through active participation.

An educational label, if correctly assigned, provides access to services, but gives educators inadequate guidance regarding the individual abilities, skills, and potentials involved in learning. Learning is also much more than academic achievement. Children learn norms and behaviors that are expected in order for them to function in society. Outside of school, many adults who cannot read or who have not received an adequate academic education can still function normally if they have the social skills to interact with others.

Integration requires that for individuals to function in the "main stream," they must learn to get along with each other, respect each other, and care about each other. Ways of accomplishing these goals are largely dependent on individuals. Educators can provide the structure, intervene from time to time, and set the stage for opportunities. Educators can encourage specific norms and behavior through attitudes and role modeling. These strategies all play a part in achieving positive social integration. But in the final analysis, education must enable individuals to carry out socialization processes through their own initiatives as they interact with one another. How is this done?

To achieve social integration of a population of students with differences, the system of education must allow for more heterogeneity within the classroom. Accommodations to allow for a greater range of individual differences requires an open, responsive, and flexible system willing to adapt to change. First and foremost, a mainstream program must be integrated physically, programmatically, and socially. Physical integration is defined as placement of special education children within general education classrooms in a school environment that is free of physical barriers, e.g., narrow doors and steps. Programmatic integration is defined as instruction that allows students to learn from each other within the general education classroom—providing education services to handicapped and nonhandicapped students together in a manner that enhances equal opprotunity. Social integration is defined as learning to accept each other and to treat each other as equal social beings. Integration in its totality means the degree to which people and the physical environment maximize social mixing of disabled children and their peers on an equal level.

In order to accomplish integration, a mainstream program must provide access to resources. These resources, again, must be physical, programmatic, and social. Physical resources must include equipment such as wheelchairs, therapeutic devices, and classroom aides who provide physical assistance when needed. Programmatic resources include appropriate instructional materials and teaching strategies that promote positive social integration within the general education classroom. Social resources include opportunities to interact with participants on an equal level. Operationally, access to resources refers to the degree to which resources provide and support equal opportunity for social interaction.[2]

Integration is a matter of degree. Each level can provide a range of opportunities. The goal is to provide the widest range possible. On a continuum, degree of physical interaction depends partially on the amount of time students are placed in mainstreamed classrooms. Full-time mainstreaming means full-time integration in general education classes and provides the widest range of opportunities for social integration. As children are pulled out from general education classes for special instruction or therapy, the degree of opportunities for interaction lessens exponentially. As children are segregated spatially because of physical barriers, opportunities for social interaction are also lessened.

Degree of program integration ranges from full-time instruction together to full-time instruction in self-contained classes. Because instruction is at once a process and goal of school experiences, the kinds of instruction provided are key components of integration. The organization of classroom learning must at once concern itself with academic achievement and socialization of students. Cognitive skills as well as social skills are interdependent principles in learning, and opportunities for acquiring both kinds of skills must be balanced.

In summary, there is no one type of mainstream and no one right effective strategy for a program. However, the theory of socialization developed here suggests guiding principles for assessing the efficacy and equality of a given mainstream program. Educators can subject a mainstream program to several tests: the range of alternatives it provides, the balance of activities available, and the match of students and programs. These tests should be applied structurally to classroom components as well as procedurally to the internal and external dynamics of the entire system at three levels: physically, programmatically, and socially.

The following questions should be asked regarding the system as a whole: (1) Does the program provide the widest range of alternatives possible? (2) Is there a balance of alternatives? (3) Do program alternatives and balance of alternatives maximize individual student abilities and minimize differences? Degree of positive social integration depends on degree of range, balance, and match that exists. The maximal degree is achieved through flexibility, responsiveness, and willingness to change.

The sociological perspective developed here to understand the mainstreaming process has used the example of physically handicapped young children. The processes and conditions described were applied to a population of children considered "severely handicapped." However, the socialization process is not inherently different for groups with different handicaps. A particular disability may impose limits (such as physical ones), but the process of maximizing a child's potential is essentially the same for all children. A label or a physical handicap is only one aspect of a child. As a group, physically handicapped children are considered one of the most difficult groups to be mainstreamed. If mainstreaming can work for these children, why not for the much larger population of mildly handicapped children? A sociological perspective allows educators the opportunity to work toward equalizing opportunities for an appropriate education for all children, setting the stage for a greater degree of positive integration as children advance to higher grades and out into society.

NOTES

1. For explanation of research methods and specific detail of the study I refer to, see S. J. Peters, *Mainstreaming and Socialization of Exceptional Children*. Ann Arbor, Mich.: UMI Dissertation Information Service, 1987. I chose this particular disability and age group as the focus of my study for two reasons. First, children who are not mentally or emotionally handicapped may be presumed to have the capability to socialize on an equal basis with their peers—the only difference being physical. Second, very young children are presumed to come to school unfettered from the effects of schooling, so that the process of socialization in the classroom may be understood from its beginning.

2. Cooperative learning as an instructional strategy holds much promise for achieving social acceptance of handicapped students and their peers. For an explanation of cooperative learning and its application to handicapped children, see Peters, 1987, chapter 6.

REFERENCES

Anderson, R. M.; D. H. Martinez; and L. Rich. 1980. Perspectives for change. In *Implementing learning in the least restrictive environment*, ed. J. W. Schifani. Baltimore: University Park Press.

Biklen, D. P., and S. B. Foster. 1985. Principles for integrated community programming. In *Integrating moderately and severely handicapped learners: Strategies that work*, ed. M. P. Brady & P. L. Gunter. Springfield, Ill.: Charles C. Thomas.

Brady, M. P., and P. L. Gunter (eds). 1985. *Integrating moderately and severely handicapped learners: Strategies that work*. Springfield, Ill.: Charles C. Thomas.

Brown v. Board of Education, 347 U.S. 483, 1954.

Calhoun, G., and R. Elliott. 1977. Self concept and academic achievement of educable retarded and emotionally disturbed pupils. *Exceptional Children* 44:379–80.

Campbell v. Talladega Co. Board of Education 518 F.Supp. 47 (1982).

Cogswell, B. E. May-June, 1968. Self-socialization: Readjustment of paraplegics in the community. *Journal of Rehabilitation* 34:11–13.

Connor, F. P.; H. Rusalem; and W. M. Cruickshank. 1971. Psychological considerations with crippled children. In *Psychology of exceptional children and youth*, 3d. ed. Ed. W. M. Cruickshank. Englewood Cliffs, N.J.: Prentice Hall.

Dreeban, Robert. 1977. The contribution of schooling to the learning of norms. In *Power and ideology in education*. Jerome Karabel and A. H. Halsey. London: Oxford University Press.

Dreeben, R. 1968. *On what is learned in school*. Reading, Mass.: Addison-Wesley Publishing.

Durkheim, E. 1974. Pedagogy and sociology. In *School and society: A sociological reader*, ed. B. Gosin, I. Dale, G. Esland, D. Mackinnon and D. Swift. London: Routledge & Kegan Paul.

Erickson, Fred. 1977. Some approaches to inquiry in school-community ethnography. *CAE Newsletter* 8(2):58–69.

Erickson, F., and Schultz. 1981. When is a context? Some issues and methods in the analysis of social competence. In *Ethnography and language in educational settings*, ed. Green and Wallat. Norwood, N.J.: Ablex Publishing Corp.

Fialkowski v. Shapp, 405 F.Supp. 946 (DCPa, 1975).

Garwood, S. G. 1979. *Educating young handicapped children: A developmental approach*. London: Aspen Systems Corporation.

Goffman, E. 1963. *Stigma: Notes on the management of spoiled identity*. Englewood Cliffs, N.J.: Prentice Hall.

Gunther, G., and N. T. Dowling. 1970. *Cases and materials on individual rights in constitutional law*. Mineola, N.Y.: Foundation Press.

Heath, S. b. 1982. Ethnography in education: Defining the essentials. In *Children in and out of school*, ed. P.Gilmore and A.Glatthorn. Washington, D.C.: Center for Applied Linguistics.

Hegarty, S.; K. Pocklington; and D. Lucas. 1984. *Educating pupils with special needs in the ordinary school*. Windsor, England: NFER-Nelson.

Ispa, J., and R. D. Matz. 1978. Integrating handicapped preschool children within a cognitively oriented program. In *Early intervention and the integration of handicapped and nonhandicapped children*, ed. Guranick, Michael J. Baltimore: University Park Press.

Kaufman, M. J.; J. Gottlieb; J. A. Agard; and M. B. Kukic, 1975. Mainstreaming: Toward an explication of the construct. *Focus on Exceptional Children* 7(3):1–12.

Levin, H. M. 1975. Education, life changes, and the courts: The role of social science evidence. In *Law and Contemporary Problems: The courts, social science, and school desegregation, part II*, vol. 39, no. 2. Ed. B. Levin and W. D. Hawley. Durham, N.C.: Duke University Press.

Madden, N. A., and R. E. Slavin. 1982. *Count me in: Academic achievement and social outcomes of mainstreaming students with mild academic handicaps*. Office of Special Education, U.S. Department of Education. Grant no. G-00-0194. Report no. 329.

Mehan, H. 1981. Identifying handicapped students. In *Organizational behavior in schools and school districts*, ed. S. B. Bacharach. New York: Praeger Publishers.

Meltzer, B. N.; J. W. Petras; and L. T. Reynolds. 1975. *Symbolic interactionism: Genesis, varieties and criticism*. London: Routledge & Kegan Paul.

Mills v. Board of Education of the District of Columbia, 348 F.Supp. 866 (DCDC, 1972).

Parsons, T. 1983. The school as a social system: Some of its functions in American society. In *Education, policy, and society: Theoretical perspectives*, ed. B. Cosin and M. Hales. London: Routledge & Kegan Paul.

Patchen, M. 1982. *Black-white contact in schools: Its social and academic effects*. West Lafayette, Ind.: Purdue University Press.

Pennsylvania Association for Retarded Children v. Commonwealth of Pennsylvania. 343 F.Supp. 279. DCPA (1972).

Peters, S. J. 1987. *Mainstreaming and socialization of exceptional children*. Ann Arbor, Mich.: UMI Dissertation Information Service.

Platt, A. M. 1969. *The child savers*. Chicago and London: University of Chicago Press.

Reynolds, M. C. (ed). 1978. *Futures of education for exceptional children*. Minneapolis, Minn.: National Support Systems Project.

Sanday, P. R. 1982. Anthropologists in schools: School ethnography and ethnography. In *Children in and out of school*, ed. P. Gilmore and A. Glatthorn. Washington, D.C.: Center for Applied Linguistics.

Sarason, S. B., and J. Doris. 1979. *Educational handicap, public policy and social history*. London: Collier-Macmillan.

Spindler, G. D. 1963. *Education and culture: Anthropological approaches*. New York: Holt, Rinehart & Winston.

Strain, P. S., and M. M. Kerr. 1981. *Mainstreaming of children in schools: Research and programmatic issues*. San Diego: Academic Press, Educational Psychology Series.

Tomlinson, S. 1982. *A sociology of special education*. London: Routledge & Kegan Paul.

Weatherly, R. A. 1979. *Reforming special education: Policy implementation from state level to street level*. Cambridge, Mass., and London: MIT Press.

Wentworth, W. M. 1980. *Context and understanding: An inquiry into socialization theory*. New York: Elsevier Science Publishing Co.

Wyatt v. Stickney, 325 F.Supp. 782 (DCAla, 1972).

III.
SPECIAL EDUCATION

DROPPING OUT: A LOOK AT THE PROBLEM IN SPECIAL EDUCATION

Christine L. Padilla,
and E. Deborah Jay

INTRODUCTION

The dropout problem—students leaving school before high school graduation—has become a national concern because of the costs to the individuals involved and to society as a whole. Significant personal costs stem from forgone income and limited job opportunities for dropouts. In 1984, the median monthly income for persons without a high school diploma was $693, compared with $1,045 for persons with a high school diploma only, and $1,841 for persons with a bachelor's degree (Bureau of the Census, 1987a). In 1985, 32.6 percent of persons without a high school diploma were not in the labor force, compared with 13.9 percent of high school graduates (Bureau of the Census, 1987b). According to a recent estimate, lost lifetime earnings exceed $200,000 per individual dropout and $200 billion for each school class across the United States (Catterall, 1986). The social and economic costs to the nation are due to the mismatch between manpower needs and the training of younger employees, the costs associated with crime and social services attributable to undereducation, and forgone tax revenues associated with higher earnings.

The dropout issue is of particular concern in California because of the high attrition rate for secondary students, a rate that has been increasing more rapidly than that for the nation as a whole (Assembly Office of Research, 1985). Although much research is being directed at obtaining better dropout statistics and developing programs to prevent students from dropping out, most of the research at the state and national level has been conducted on the regular education population. As a result, the extent of the dropout problem for special education students is virtually unknown. This chapter reports a study of dropout rates for special education in California conducted by SRI International for the California State Department of Education. California has the largest number of special education students of all 50 states (over 9% of the total population).

Dropout Rates for the Total Student Population

Past estimates of the national dropout rate have varied fairly widely (Rumberger, 1987). One must therefore be cautious in assessing the extent of the special education dropout problem compared with the overall dropout rate. We report here some relevant findings on dropout rates for the total student population nationally and in California.

National Dropout Rates. Currently, there are three major sources of data on national dropout rates for the total student population: the Bureau of the Census's Current Population Survey, the National Center for Education Statistics's (NCES) Common Core of Data, and NCES's High School and Beyond study. The Bureau of the Census has collected national data on graduation rates for more than two decades. Unfortunately, there is no common definition of what constitutes a dropout, and dropout rates are calculated in a variety of ways among these sources. For example, some are derived from state enrollment figures by grade (e.g., NCES), whereas others are based on interview data (e.g., Census Bureau, High School and Beyond). Dropout rates are reported for age cohorts (e.g., youth age 14 to 15), grade cohorts (e.g., youth in grades 10, 11, and 12), class cohorts (e.g., the sophomore class of 1980), and cohorts of exiters (e.g., youth who exited high school during the 1984–85 school year). Most definitions of dropouts include persons who voluntarily and involuntarily leave secondary school before graduation (e.g., expulsions, youth who age out). Some definitions of dropouts include persons who have received a special diploma or certificate of completion (e.g., NCES), and some exclude them (e.g., Census Bureau). Finally, sometimes *annual* dropout rates are reported, and sometimes *compounded* dropout rates (calculated over a two- and four-year period) are reported.

Using state-level enrollment and graduation figures, NCES estimated the national dropout rate to be 25 percent over a four-year period from ninth through twelfth grade (NCES, 1986). By contrast, the Census Bureau estimated a 15 percent national dropout rate for persons 14 to 24 years of age during a three-year period from tenth through twelfth grade. Interestingly, national dropout rates may be overestimated because as many as 30 percent of dropouts eventually receive a high school diploma or alternative credential (Kolstad & Owings, 1986).

National dropout rates also appear to vary by student characteristics and location. For example, both NCES and the Census Bureau report higher dropout rates for minorities, youth under age 18, and youth living in urban areas.

California Dropout Rates. Reported dropout rates for the total student population in California also vary. Using attrition data as a proxy for dropout data, the U.S. Department of Education (1986) estimated a 36.8 percent dropout rate for the total student population in California, well above the national average of 25 percent. The California Assembly Office of Research reported a 24.9 percent dropout rate for the California student population, also estimated from attrition data (Assembly Office of Research, 1985). The California Department of Education estimated a 29 to 30 percent dropout rate for the total student population based on a variety of data sources (California State Department of Education, 1986).

Recognizing the need for better information on dropout rates, the state of California recently began to collect information from districts on dropouts using a common definition. In 1987, for the first time, the California Basic Educational Data System (CBEDS) collected dropout statistics for the 1985–86 school year on students in grades 10 through 12. These data were analyzed and are summarized, along with our other findings, in the following pages.

Special Education Dropout Rates

The CBEDS data are somewhat limited because no separate information on special education dropouts is included. In fact, information on dropout rates for special education students, both nationally and in California, is limited largely because very little data of any kind have been collected about this population. Moreover, collecting accurate dropout information on special education students is particularly difficult, given the different service configurations that exist to serve these students.

The "Ninth Annual Report to Congress on the Implementation of the Education of the Handicapped Act," released in 1987 by the Office of Special Education Programs (OSEP, 1987), provides the first nationwide statistics on dropout rates for special education students. The data provide a first glimpse at how large the dropout problem is for special education students: states reported that approximately 21 percent of special education students who exited from secondary school during 1984–85 are *known* to have dropped out. However, this estimate may be quite low, because states did not know the status of approximately one-fifth (18 percent) of special education exiters. Moreover, OSEP reported higher-than-average dropout rates for certain disability groups (e.g., 29 percent for emotionally disturbed exiters and 23 percent for mentally retarded exiters). The "Tenth Annual Report to Congress" indicates that 26 percent of special education students who exited druing 1985–86 are known to have dropped out, with particularly high dropout rates for emotionally disturbed (41 percent) exiters. Both learning disabled and mentally retarded exiters also were reported as having higher dropout rates in 1985–86 than in the previous school year, 19 percent versus 26 percent and 23 percent versus 24 percent, respectively (OSEP, 1988).

Although there have been several statewide studies of the transition of special education students (Mithaug & Horiuchi, 1983; Edgar, Levine, & Maddox, 1985; Hasazi, 1984), these have focused on special education graduates and not on all youth in special education. There are relatively few state-level studies of graduation rates for special education students, even though there is evidence that the dropout rate for special education students may be significant. A New Hampshire study, for example, reported an overall attrition rate of 40 percent for special education students and the following rates for various subgroups: 57 percent for the emotionally disturbed, 40 percent for the learning disabled, and 6 percent for the severely impaired (Lichtenstein, 1987). A state study in North Carolina estimated the four-year dropout rate (from ninth to twelfth grade) for disabled youth to be substantially higher than the dropout rate for the total student population (Appelbaum & Dent, 1986). Additionally, a district in Florida that tracks special education students who leave school any time after seventh grade reported that emotionally disturbed students dropped out at a rate of 53 percent, compared with the 37.8 percent estimated statewide dropout rate for special education students other than those with learning disabilities (Project Transition, 1986).

There is evidence that the consequences for dropping out for special education students may be as significant for disabled youth as for other youth, but data are limited on this issue. For example, a study of one urban district in Pennsylvania found that learning disabled dropouts, like other dropouts, have significantly lower employment rates than do youth who obtain a high school diploma (Zigmond & Thornton, 1985). In a 1986 Harris poll, 38 percent of disabled adults who were unemployed attributed their "joblessness" to their lack of adequate education (International Center for the Disabled, 1986).

Research Questions and Data Sources

In the present study, we explored the following research questions in relation to the current student population in California:

- To what extent is there a dropout problem for special education students and how does it compare with that for the total student population? Does it vary by exceptionality?
- What is the relationship between various student characteristics (e.g., placement, ethnicity, age) and the likelihood of dropping out?
- How are district characteristics related to dropout rates for special education students (e.g., do they vary by district size, urbanicity)?

In addition to collecting data to answer these research questions, we also solicited district perceptions of what influences special education students to drop out and information on selected district policies and practices that could influence special education dropout rates.

Two types of data collection activities were performed. In the first phase of the study, *site visits*[1] were conducted in five purposively selected districts or county special education offices. During the site visits, special and regular education instructional staff were interviewed and documents were collected. The main purposes of the site visits were to learn about dropout accounting procedures used for special education students, how special education students are defined, what types of dropout prevention programs are available, and perceptions of reasons for dropping out. Other purposes of the site visits were to determine the feasibility of collecting data in a mail survey using a common definition of *dropout* and to pretest the instruments to be used in the statewide survey planned for the second phase of the study.

For the site visits, a sample of five districts was chosen that reflected variation on each of several dimensions likely to be important in drawing conclusions about dropout accounting procedures and dropout rates for special education students. Criteria for sample selection included district/county size, types of special education students served, urban/rural character, fiscal conditions, and nature of the student population (e.g., ethnicity, poverty level).

Nominations for sites were requested from the State Department of Education (SDE) and from SRI's network of contacts, based on the above criteria. To achieve adequate variation, nominations were checked against the Quality Education Data, Inc. (QED) data base.[2] Table 1 describes the five sample sites selected.

In the second phase of the study, a *mail survey* was conducted of all California high school and unified districts and other special education local planning areas (SELPAs) serving students in grades ten through twelve. As indicated above, CBEDS data also were obtained from the State Department of Education to compare dropout rates for special education students with dropout rates for the total student population.

TABLE 1
Characteristics of Site-Visit Sample

	Site A	Site B	Site C	Site D	Site E
Region of Calif.	Northern	Northern	Central	Southern	Northern
Urban/rural	Suburban	Suburban	Urban	Suburban	Rural
Total enrollment	9,017	15,271	57,925	9,682	1,650
Percent minority	23	52	45	31	59
Poverty level	Low	Medium	Medium	Medium	Medium
(Orshansky percentile)*	(4)	(11)	(19)	(11)	(15)
Type of special education students served:					
Learning handicapped	Yes	Yes	Yes	Yes	Yes
Communicatively handicapped	No	Yes	Yes	Yes	Yes
Physically handicapped	Yes	Yes	Yes	Yes	Yes
Severely handicapped	Yes	Yes	No	Yes	No
Dropout rate for total student population in 1985–86	4.3%	2.1%	12.3%	16.0%	7.0%

*The Orshansky percentile is an index that estimates the percentage of youth in a district that are below the poverty level.

The main purpose of the mail survey was to collect statistically representative data on dropout rates for special education students. Data were also collected on dropout prevention programs, various district characteristics and policies likely to affect dropout rates (e.g., minority composition, graduation requirements, suspension/expulsion policies, and perceptions of reasons for dropping out.

To maximize the precision of estimates obtained from the survey, we decided to survey all of the approximately 400 high school districts, unified districts, and other county offices serving secondary special education students in California. We believed that a 100 percent sample was justified because the universe of districts/county offices was small by survey standards, and the incremental cost of increasing the sample size of a mail survey tends to be small (i.e., most costs are for questionnaire design and analysis). Also, we believed that not enough was known about dropout accounting procedures and dropout rates to develop a more efficient sampling strategy for collecting reliable statewide estimates. The final sample included 373 high school and unified districts and 54 counties that directly served special education students.

Of the 427 eligible districts/county offices, 224 (52 percent) returned questionnaires. However, only 207 of the returned questionnaires were adequately complete for analysis purposes. The response rate varied only slightly by district size: usable questionnaires were returned by 46 percent of very large and large districts, 47 percent of medium districts, and 54 percent of small and very small districts. Approximately 43 percent of counties returned usable questionnaires.

Once the data were cleaned, they were eighted[3] to adjust for district/county nonresponse. Subprograms available in the SAS statistical analysis program were then used to analyze the weighted data. The percentages, means, and medians reported in the text and tables are based on the weighted data. However, the sample sizes reported in the tables reflect the actual number of responding districts.

Information on the number of dropouts for the total student population during the 1985–86 school year provided by each district in California to the State Department of Education (and included in the 1986–87 CBEDS data base) was obtained and analyzed. The following definition of *dropout* is provided in the CBEDS forms:

> Dropouts include students who left the district prior to graduation or the completion of a formal education or legal equivalent—GED or CHSPE—and did not, within 45 school days, enter a public or private educational institution or school program (as documented by a written request for a transcript from that institution).

The same definition of *dropout* was used in the mail survey we conducted on special education dropouts. Although using a common definition eliminated one problem in comparing dropout rates for special education students with those for the total student population, both the mail survey and the CBEDS data may include the following types of measurement error: (1) some districts may not include continuation students or other special populations in their statistics on the total student population; (2) some districts count students who are continuing their education (e.g., trade school enrollees) as dropouts and others do not; (3) districts differ in the amount of effort they spend tracking students (e.g., some districts do not count students who dropped out during the summer because they completed the previous school year); and (4) districts interpret entrance into another educational institution differently (e.g., some districts routinely provide students with a copy of their transcript when they leave school, and therefore do not count them as dropouts). These factors should be considered in evaluating our findings.

FINDINGS

As we discussed previously, dropout rates can be calculated in a variety of ways. To obtain data comparable to those reported annually by California districts and counties to the State Department of Education for all of their secondary students, we used the definition of *dropout* standardized by the California legislature in Senate Bill 65 and now part of the California Basic Educational Data System. CBEDS collects dropout information for all students in grades ten through twelve. However, because special education students may function at a grade level lower than one would expect for their age, secondary students for this study were defined as students age 15 through 22 or in grades ten through twelve.

Data for regular districts were analyzed separately from those for county offices because the two types of administrative units tend to serve different types of special education students (i.e., the county offices are far more apt to serve the severely handicapped than are regular districts), and because they are functionally different (i.e., the county offices serve only special education students). To avoid double counting, districts were asked to provide data only for students they served directly (i.e., they were not to include students sent to a county office, a neighboring school district, or private schools). Counties were advised not to provide data for students for whom they provided itinerant services (e.g., instructional staff who work in the district). All information requested was for the 1985–86 school year, the first school year for which annual dropout data for the total (both regular and special education) student population had been collected.

Statewide Special Education Dropout Rates

Statewide dropout rates were calculated by dividing the total number of students directly served in all districts/counties who dropped out during the 1985–86 school year by the total number of students directly served in all districts/counties at the beginning of the 1985–86 school year. The dropout rates reported for secondary special education students are based on data (weighted to compensate for nonresponse) from the mail survey we conducted. Dropout rates for all secondary students are based on our analyses of data reported by all California districts/counties to the State Department of Education and maintained through the California Basic Educational Data System.

As shown in table 2, approximately 6.6 percent of secondary special education students served in districts and 1 percent of those served in counties dropped out during the 1985–86 school year. As will be discussed later, the lower dropout rate for counties can be explained by the fact that they serve mainly severely handicapped youths, who as a group are less apt to drop out than are moderately or mildly handicapped youths.

Comparison with Dropout Rates for the Total Student Population. The dropout rate for all secondary students (9.0 percent) was slightly higher than for secondary special education students served in districts (6.6 per-

TABLE 2

Status of Secondary Special Education Students and of All Secondary Students at the End of the 1985–86 School Year*

	Secondary Special Education Students Served in Districts	Secondary Special Education Students Served in Counties	All Secondary Students
Completed the school year	80.9% †	93.6%	84.2%
Dropped out	6.6	1.0	9.0
Left district, but did not drop out	12.5	5.4	6.8
Overall attrition	19.1	6.4	15.8
Number of districts/counties for which data were available	172	22	427

*For purposes of this study, secondary special education students were defined as students age 15 to 22 or in grades 10 through 12.

†I.e., 80.9 percent of secondary special education students served in districts completed the 1985–86 school year.

cent) and substantially higher than for secondary special education students served in counties (1 percent).

The true difference between the annual statewide dropout rate for all secondary students and for secondary special education students served in districts may be even smaller than the observed 2.4 percent difference because of measurement error. In some districts "potential" special education dropouts are referred to alternative education programs or continuation schools that do not have classes specifically for special education students. During our site visits, we learned that special education students referred to such programs were no longer considered a part of the special education population when they dropped out. During the 1985–86 school year, districts reported that approximately 5 percent of the secondary special education students they served directly were referred to or enrolled in alternative education programs or continuation schools. Of these, 1 percent were referred to or enrolled in alternative education programs or continuation schools that did *not* have classes specifically for secondary special education students. Additionally, some district and school staff reported that "potential" special education dropouts were placed on "homebound status" rather than being counted as dropouts.

Also, although the annual dropout rate for secondary special education students was less than 10 percent, the dropout rate for a single age cohort compounded each year from tenth grade through twelfth is likely to be significantly higher (probably closer to 20 percent).

Interestingly, the percentage of all secondary students who left the district but did not drop out (6.8 percent) was substantially lower than that for secondary special education students served in districts (12.5 percent) and slightly higher than that for secondary special education students served in counties (5.4 percent). Thus, the attrition rate (the percentage who left the district, including both those who did and did not drop out) was actually higher for secondary special education students served in districts (19.1 percent) than for all secondary students (15.8 percent).

The 1986 study of New Hampshire dropouts cited earlier also reported a higher attrition rate (40 percent) for secondary special education students (ages 15 through 21) than for their nonhandicapped peers (30 percent) (Lichtenstein, 1987). Because the main purpose of our study was to collect data on dropout rates rather than attrition, no data were collected on why special education students have higher attrition rates. For the severely handicapped, poor health may explain the higher attrition rate. For the mildly and moderately handicapped, a variety of other explanations are plausible. Handicapped students may be more mobile than the regular education population (a preliminary finding from SRI's national study of the transition of handicapped youth). Alternatively, some handicapped students return to the regular education program during the year, while others are referred to alternative education programs (as indicated by survey respondents). Finally, some measurement error may have been introduced by respondents who included mid-year graduates in their attrition estimates.

Statewide Dropout Rates by District Characteristics. Next, the relationships between dropping out and three types of district characteristics were examined: size (enrollment), urban/rural character, and poverty concentration. Based on total student enrollment, statewide dropout rates were calculated for very large and large districts (10,000 or more students), medium-size districts (2,500 to 9,999 students), and very small and small districts (fewer than 2,500 students). As shown in table 3, the dropout rates for both special education students and the total student population were the highest in very large and large districts (7.7 percent and 10.3 percent, respectively). The dropout rate increased directly with district size for the total student population, but not for special education students; approximately 5.9 percent of secondary special education students in very small or small districts dropped out during the 1985–86 school year, compared with 4.1 percent of these students in medium-size districts.

The dropout rates for both special education students and the total student population were somewhat higher in urban and suburban districts (6.8 percent and 9.3 percent respectively) than in rural districts (4.0 percent and 7.0 percent, respectively). This finding can be explained by the fact that the very large and large districts, which have the highest dropout rates, also tend to be urban or suburban districts. As noted earlier, several national studies have found dropout rates for the total student population to be highest in urban areas (NCES, 1986; U.S. General Accounting Office, 1986).

As shown in table 3, medium-poverty districts had the highest dropout rates for special education students (9.7 percent) and for the total student population (11.9 percent). By contrast, low-poverty districts had the fewest dropouts (3.5 percent and 6.6 percent respectively). Most other studies of

TABLE 3

Statewide Dropout Rates for Secondary Special Education Students Served in Districts and for All Secondary Students in the 1985–86 School Year, by Various District Characteristics

District Characteristics	Dropout Rate for Secondary Special Education Students Served in Districts	Dropout Rate for All Secondary Students
Size* (enrollment)		
Very large or large	7.7% †	10.3%
Medium	4.1	7.0
Small or very small	5.9	6.0
Urbanicity		
Urban/suburban	6.8	9.3
Rural	40.0	7.0
Poverty level (Orshansky percentile)‡		
Low (10% or less)	3.5	6.6
Medium (11% to 20%)	9.7	11.9
High (greater than 20%)	5.3	7.2
Number of districts/counties for which data were available	183	378

*Very large or large = 10,000 or more students; medium = 2,500 to 9,999 students; small or very small = fewer than 2,500 students.

†I.e., 7.7 percent of secondary special education students in very large and large districts dropped out during the 1985–86 school year.

‡The Orshansky percentile is an index that estimates the percentage of youth in a district who are below the poverty level.

dropout rates have found a direct relationship between poverty level and the likelihood of dropping out—e.g., High School and Beyond (NCES, 1984). One explanation for our findings may be the relationship between district size and poverty concentration in California: in our sample, the very large and large districts tend to have middle-range poverty concentrations.

Also, for special education students, variables others than socioeconomic status may play a more important role in predicting who drops out. For example, one analysis of the High School and Beyond[4] data reported that dropout rates for handicapped youth were explained more by students' grades, achievement level, and academic program than by their background characteristics, such as socioeconomic status (Meyers & Ellman, 1983). One explanation for the direct relationship observed in other studies between socioeconomic status and dropping out among the regular student population is the correlation between socioeconomic status and parental support. However, for special education students socioeconomic status may not be a good indicator of parental support. Clearly, greater demands are placed on families with handicapped children, and socioeconomic status may not be a good measure of parents' ability to deal with children who may be difficult to control or children for whom there is little hope of successful transition to adult life.

Statewide Dropout Rates, by Various Student Characteristics. For purposes of this study, disabilities were grouped as follows: learning handicapped (specific learning disability), speech impaired, communicatively handicapped (hard of hearing, deaf, deaf-blind), physically handicapped (visually impaired, blind, orthopedically impaired, other health impaired), and severely handicapped (severely emotionally disturbed, mentally retarded, multiply handicapped). Learning handicapped students constituted the majority (75.5 percent) of secondary special education students served in districts in the 1985–86 school year (see table 4). Of the remaining 24.5 percent, 12.4 percent were severely handicapped, 5.3 percent were speech impaired, 4 percent were physically handicapped, 2 percent were communicatively handicapped, and 0.8 percent had another primary disability.

Table 5 describes statewide dropout rates for secondary special education students with different primary disabilities. In districts the likelihood of dropping out varied for students with different primary disabilities. Learning handicapped students not only constituted the largest percentage of secondary special education students served in districts, but they also had the highest annual dropout rate (7.5 percent). The next-highest dropout rates were for the speech impaired (4.9 percent) and severely handicapped (4.1 percent). By contrast, only 2.6 percent of the physically handicapped and 2.8 percent of the communicatively handicapped dropped out during the 1985–86 school year. The dropout rate for the severely handicapped would probably have been lower if it did not include the emotionally disturbed

TABLE 4

Profile of Secondary Special Education Students in Districts and Counties in the 1985–86 School Year, by Various Student Characteristics

	Special Education Students Served in Districts	Special Education Students Served in Counties
Primary Disability*		
Learning handicapped	75.5% †	19.2%
Speech impaired	5.3	11.7
Communicatively handicapped	2.0	5.1
Physically handicapped	4.0	6.1
Severely handicapped	12.4	55.6
Other	0.8	2.3
Placement Setting		
Resource room		
Self-contained class	54.0	9.7
Other (mainly designated instructional services)	39.3	76.8
	6.7	13.5
Age		
Under age 18		
Age 18 through 22	81.1	65.4
	18.9	34.6
Ethnicity		
White	55.2	56.2
Black	12.4	11.4
Hispanic	27.4	28.0
Asian/Pacific Islander	4.1	3.4
American Indian	0.9	0.9
Number of districts/counties for which data were available	163–181	21–23

*For purposes of this study, handicapping conditions were grouped as follows: learning handicapped (specific learning disability), speech impaired, communicatively handicapped (hard of hearing, deaf, deaf-blind), physically impaired (visually impaired, blind, orthopedically impaired, other health impaired), and severely handicapped (severely emotionally disturbed, mentally retarded, multiply handicapped).

†I.e., 75.5 percent of secondary special education students served in districts during the 1985–86 school year were learning handicapped.

population, which other studies have shown to have a relatively high drop-out rate.

During our site visits, district- and school-level staff also reported differences in dropout rates by disability. These respondents tended to classify special education students into three groups based on the severity of their handicap: the mildly impaired, the moderately impaired, and the severely impaired. Youth in each of these groups were thought to handle the pressures and experiences of secondary school in a different manner.

District and school staff identified moderately impaired students[5] served in self-contained classes at being most at risk of dropping out, because these students tended to be less integrated with the regular student population than were the mildly impaired, who were served in resource rooms. Because of their placement, the moderately impaired were more apt to be stigmatized and have a lower self-esteem. The moderately impaired tended to be behind academically and, therefore, tended to have less chance of receiving a regular high school diploma. District and school staff felt that moderately impaired students often saw little relationship between their school experiences and their experiences outside of school.

By contrast, district and school staff felt that mildly impaired students were fairly well integrated with the regular education population and that these students benefited from the individualized attention they received in the special education setting (e.g., lower student/teacher ratios, increased counseling). Most staff felt that mildly impaired students had a good self-concept (e.g., they viewed themselves as needing "a little extra help" to graduate and not really being all that different from other students). Respondents claimed that it was this increased attention that has made the difference in reducing dropout rates for these students compared with their "borderline" regular education peers, who they believe make up the largest segment of their schools' dropout population.

Respondents who were interviewed also reported that the severely impaired tended to stay in school until they aged out at 22 because they were usually fairly unaware of the social stigma attached to their placement and because they had few other options. The perception that the severely impaired stay in school longer is supported to some extent by the U.S. Department of Education's statistics on special education exiters. They reported that 15 percent and 31 percent of the multihandicapped and deaf-blind, respectively, aged out of secondary school in 1985–86, while no other handicapping condition exceeded 6 percent (OSEP, 1988).

Unlike in districts, the dropout rate varied less by disability for special education students served in counties (from 0 percent to 2.4 percent). Fewer than 1 percent of severely handicapped, speech impaired, and physically handicapped students dropped out during the 1985–86 school year. Approximately 1.9 percent of communicatively handicapped and 2.4 percent of learning handicapped students dropped out (see table 5). The small-

TABLE 5

Statewide Dropout Rates for Secondary Special Education Students in Districts and Counties in the 1985–86 School Year, by Various Student Characteristics

	Dropout Rate for Special Education Students Served in Districts	Dropout Rate for Special Education Students Served in Counties
Primary Disability*	7.5% †	2.4%
Learning handicapped	4.9	0
Speech impaired	2.8	1.9
Communicatively handicapped	2.6	0
Physically handicapped	4.1	0.8
Severely handicapped	0.6	0
Other		
Placement Setting	6.9	2.8
Resource room	6.6	1.0
Self-contained class		
Other (mainly designated instructional services)	4.4	<0.1
Age	4.9	1.0
Under age 18	14.2	1.1
Age 18 through 22		
Ethnicity	7.6	1.1
White	7.7	0.9
Black	5.6	1.3
Hispanic	3.6	<0.1
Asian/Pacific Islander	7.3	<0.1
American Indian		
	6.6	1.0
Overall dropout rate		
•		
Number of districts/counties for which data were available	157–178	20–23

*For purposes of this study, handicapping conditions were grouped as follows: learning handicapped (specific learning disability), speech impaired, communicatively handicapped (hard of hearing, deaf, deaf-blind), physically impaired (visually impaired, blind, orthopedically impaired, other health impaired), and severely handicapped (severely emotionally disturbed, mentally retarded, multiply handicapped).

†I.e., 7.5 percent of learning handicapped students served in districts dropped out during the 1985–86 school year.

ness of the variation may be due to the fact that the majority of students served by the counties were severely impaired, irrespective of their disability category. For example, although approximately 19 percent of secondary special education students who were served in counties during the 1985–86 school year were classified as learning handicapped, many of these students may actually have severe learning disabilities. The speech impaired (12 percent) and the communicatively handicapped (5 percent) students served in counties may have severe speech or hearing problems or other communication difficulties. The remaining 64 percent of special education students served in counties were classified as severely handicapped (56 percent), physically handicapped (6 percent), or as having another disability (2 percent) (see table 4).

Although respondents in the districts we visited perceived a relationship between placement setting and dropout rates, the survey data indicated that placement setting alone was not particularly related to the likelihood of dropping out of special education in districts. Approximately 54 percent of special education students in districts were served in resource rooms, 39 percent in self-contained classes, and 7 percent in other settings. As shown in table 5, similar percentages of district special education students served in resource rooms and in self-contained classes dropped out during the 1985–86 school year (6.9 percent and 6.6 percent, respectively).

Seventy-seven percent of special education students in counties were served in self-contained classes, whereas only 10 percent were served in resource rooms, and 14 percent were served in other settings. The dropout rate for county special education students was higher for students served in resource rooms (2.8 percent) than that for students served in self-contained classes (1 percent).

Approximately 19 percent of special education students served in districts were over age 18, whereas 35 percent of special education students served in counties were in this age range. In districts, special education students age 18 through 22 were far more likely than special education students under age 18 to have dropped out during the 1985–86 school year (14.2 percent versus 4.9 percent). One explanation for this relationship is that students who are older than their grade-relevant peers tend to be behind academically and therefore have a greater chance of dropping out. Note, however, that age was not particularly related to dropping out of special education in counties, where dropping out may have been more a factor of severity of disability, as discussed above.

Over half (55.2 percent) of special education students served in districts during the 1985–86 school year were white, 27.4 percent were Hispanic, 12.4 percent were black, 4.1 percent were Asian/Pacific Islander, and 0.9 percent were American Indian. Statewide dropout rates for special education students served in districts were the highest for blacks (7.7 percent), whites (7.6 percent), and American Indians (7.3 percent). Approximately

5.6 percent of Hispanics dropped out during the 1985–86 school year. Statewide dropout rates were lowest for Asians/Pacific Islanders—only 3.6 percent dropped out during the 1985–86 school year.

In counties, the distribution of special education students by ethnic group was relatively similar to that for districts: 56.2 percent were white, 28.0 percent were Hispanic, 11.4 percent were black, 3.4 percent were Asian/Pacific Islander, and 0.9 percent were American Indian. Dropout rates were similar for whites (1.1 percent), blacks (0.9 percent), and Hispanics (1.3 percent). Fewer than 0.1 percent of Asian/Pacific Islanders and American Indians dropped out.

District Dropout Rates

Thus far, we have reported statewide dropout rates only. Because statewide dropout rates are determined mainly by the very large and large districts that serve the vast majority of special education students and that also tend to have the highest dropout rates, policies based on statewide dropout rates may be inappropriate for some districts. Therefore, we calculated dropout rates for each district and county. These were calculated by dividing the number of students directly served in each district/county who dropped out during the 1985–86 school year by the number of students directly served in each district/county at the beginning of that school year.

Not surprisingly, dropout rates for secondary special education students varied considerably across districts and counties. They ranged from 0 percent to 89.5 percent for students served in districts and 0 percent to 8.2 percent for those served in counties.[6] However, only 25 percent of districts had dropout rates higher than the special education dropout rate for the entire state (6.6 percent). Approximately 24 percent of districts and 39 percent of counties had no special education dropouts.[7] Only 7 percent of very large and large districts had no special education dropouts, compared with 18 percent of medium-size districts and 39 percent of small and very small districts. In districts that had special education dropouts, the median dropout rate was 4.9 percent. The median rate for counties that had special education dropouts was 2.4 percent.

In comparing district dropout rates with the total student population, we found that in 51.5 percent of districts the dropout rate for special education students was less than 50 percent of the rate for all secondary students. In 27.1 percent of districts, the dropout rate for special education students was between 50 percent and 150 percent of the rate for all secondary students, and in 21.5 percent of districts, the dropout rate was more than 150 percent of the rate for all secondary students. Differences in the dropout rate between all secondary and secondary special education students were not directly related to district size. Medium-size districts were slightly more likely than other districts to have lower dropout rates for special education students.

District Perceptions

During our site visits we found that district and school staff often perceived the dropout rate for special education students to be lower than that for the total student population, even when it was the same or higher. For example, a special education teacher in one high school we visited felt that the dropout rate for special education students was much lower than that for the total student population because only 11 special education students had dropped out in the past year. However, in reviewing the class lists, we determined that the dropout rate for special education students was actually 7 percent, the same rate as that reported for the entire school.

Because special education students represent a small percentage (less than 10 percent) of the total student population, even when district or school staff recognized that the dropout rate for secondary special education students was the same as or higher than that for the total student population, they often did not perceive the special education dropout rate to be a significant problem because the actual number of students at risk each year was small.

Why Special Education Students Drop Out. In the mail survey, special education directors in districts/counties that had special education dropouts were asked to indicate the extent to which they agreed or disagreed (using a 4-point scale, where 1 = strongly disagree and 4 = strongly agree) with various statements about why special education students drop out (see table 6).

Special education directors in districts were most apt to believe that special education students dropped out because they were not doing well in school (mean = 3.2), because they preferred to get a job (mean = 2.8), and because they were not getting along with teachers or students (mean = 2.6). The percentages who somewhat or strongly agreed with these statements were 91 percent, 69 percent, and 58 percent, respectively. Conversely, special education directors were least likely to believe that special education students dropped out because of marriage (mean = 1.6) or because they had to support a family (mean = 1.8). Fewer than 20 percent somewhat or strongly agreed with each of these statements.

As in districts, special education directors in counties were most apt to believe that special education students dropped out because they were not doing well in school (mean = 3.0) and least apt to believe that they dropped out because they had to support a family (mean = 1.3) or because of marriage (mean = 1.5) (see table 7).

Thus, special education students are perceived to drop out for the same

TABLE 6
Perceptions of why Secondary Special Education Students in Districts Drop Out

(Based on 134 to 139 Districts that Had Special Education Dropouts and That Answered Each Question)

	Strongly Disagree	Somewhat Disagree	Somewhat Agree	Strongly Agree	Mean*
"Special education students drop out . . ."					
. . . because they are not doing well in school	4%	6%	52%	39%	3.2
. . . because they prefer to get a job	9	23	50	19	2.8
. . . because they aren't getting along with teachers or students	8	34	44	14	2.6
. . . because their friends or peers drop out	17	28	40	15	2.5
. . . because of pregnancy	33	33	31	3	2.0
. . . because they have been suspended or expelled	39	29	22	10	2.0
. . . because they need to support a family	40	42	16	2	1.8
. . . because of marriage	58	28	13	1	1.6

*Means were calculated on a 4-point scale, where 1 = strongly disagree, 2 = somewhat disagree, 3 = somewhat agree, and 4 = strongly agree. Statements are listed in descending order of mean rating.

reasons that their regular education peers drop out. For example, poor academic performance was reported to be the main reason why students in the High School and Beyond study dropped out of school (e.g., students who were held back a grade were four times more likely to drop out than those who were not). Other explanations of dropping out based on the High School and Beyond data for the regular student population included chronic truancy and delinquency, low self-concept and social maturity, low socioeconomic status, and some type of handicap or limiting condition (e.g., lower intelligence scores) (NCES, 1985).

Characteristics of Special Education Dropouts. In the mail survey, special

TABLE 7
Perceptions of Why Secondary Special Education Students in Counties Drop Out

(Based on 13 to 14 Counties That Had Special Education Dropouts and That Answered Each Question)

	Strongly Disagree	Somewhat Disagree	Somewhat Agree	Strongly Agree	Mean*
"Special education students drop out ..."					
... because they are not doing well in school	7%	21%	29%	43%	3.0
... because they prefer to get a job	15	23	54	8	2.5
... because they aren't getting along with teachers or students	15	31	38	15	2.5
... because their friends or peers drop out	31	31	31	8	2.2
... because of pregnancy	43	29	21	7	1.9
... because they have been suspended or expelled	31	54	15	0	1.8
... because of marriage	46	54	0	0	1.5
... because they need to support a family	69	31	0	0	1.3

*Means were calculated on a 4-point scale, where 1 = strongly disagree, 2 = somewhat disagree, 3 = somewhat agree, and 4 = strongly agree. Statements are listed in descending order of mean rating.

education directors were also asked to indicate the characteristics that mainly described secondary special education dropouts in those disability groups in which they had dropouts. Almost all districts that had special education dropouts had dropouts who were learning handicapped. As shown in table 8, districts that had learning handicapped dropouts were most likely to indicate that these students had poor academic performance (85 percent) and poor social adjustment (71 percent). From 48 percent to 67 percent felt that learning handicapped dropouts were characterized by frequent absenteeism (67 percent), little parental support (67 percent), low participation in extracurricular activities (62 percent), low socioeconomic status (50 percent), and alcohol or drug problems (48 percent). Only 6 percent of districts said that learning handicapped students were non-English-speaking.

Fewer than 25 percent of districts had dropouts who had a primary disability other than a learning handicap. Districts that had speech impaired dropouts, communicatively handicapped dropouts, and severely handicapped dropouts were most likely to believe that these youths had poor social adjustment (60 percent, 76 percent, and 76 percent, respectively). By contrast, districts that had physically handicapped dropouts were most likely to say that these students were characterized by frequent absenteeism due to health or other reasons (66 percent).

Respondents interviewed at the district- and school-level also described

TABLE 8
Percentage of Districts* That Said That Various Characteristics Mainly Describe Secondary Special Education Dropouts in Various Disability Groups

	Learning Handicapped	Speech Impaired	Communicatively Handicapped	Physically Handicapped	Severely Handicapped
Poor academic performance	85% †	32%	72%	27%	44%
Poor social adjustment	71	60	76	26	76
Alcohol or drug problems	48	16	27	7	30
Frequent absenteeism (due to health or other reasons)	67	16	31	66	58
Low Participation in extracurricular activities	62	48	54	53	51
Low socioeconomic status	50	19	19	13	20
Non-English-speaking	6	11	7	0	9
Little parental support	67	32	30	14	26
Number of responding districts	135	25	29	15	34

*Each column includes districts that said they had dropouts with that disability.

†I.e., 85 percent of districts that had learning handicapped dropouts said that these students are mainly characterized by poor academic performance.

special education dropouts as students who were failing academically and who had poor attendance. For example, in one district the special education department chairperson at a large high school felt that special education dropouts from his school were chronic truants who "never dropped into school." The district special education director from that district felt that the special education dropout problem was a symptom of the failure of the school system to serve these students adequately and not a failure on the part of students.

Other respondents who were interviewed characterized special education dropouts as students who did not see the relevance of school to getting a job and who had trouble relating to other students. The lack of parental support also was associated with dropping out. A few district staff said that special education students dropped out because they were pregnant, got a job, or reached 18 and decided to leave school with the rest of their peers. For example, one special education director described dropouts in the following manner:

> They are academically behind by as much as two to four grade levels. Often female students drop out because they are pregnant. Sometimes students say they are dropping out because they found a job. Many dropouts just don't "relate" to anyone in school. Most dropouts do not have a support group at school or at home. Their family situation tends to be very poor.

One special education teacher referred to the stigma of being in special education as being a reason for dropping out:

> Our kids really stand out and that's not acceptable [at this age]. . . . Kids in this school are either in the social group, stoners, or gangs, and special education kids don't fit into any of these.

This teacher also felt that naïveté and the desire for social acceptance have contributed to drug use and pregnancy among her students.

One problem in understanding why special education students drop out is that often they don't give a reason why they are leaving school. For example, one special education teacher said that special education dropouts "just know they don't want to be in school."[8]

Unfortunately, this study collected only perceptions of why special education students drop out. To examine this issue more fully, it would be useful to take a random sample of dropouts (e.g., in districts with high dropout rates), review their student records, and interview them (or their parents) to learn more about why they dropped out.

Dropout Prevention Programs and Other District Practices

In the mail survey, approximately 84 percent of districts reported that they had continuation schools, 58 percent had truancy prevention programs, and 30 percent had dropout recovery/outreach programs. Very large and large districts were the most likely to have alternative schools (93 percent), truancy prevention programs (81 percent), and dropout recovery/outreach programs (57 percent). Conversely, small and very small districts were the least likely to have each of these programs (68 percent, 43 percent, and 17 percent, respectively).

One would expect that the districts that had dropout prevention programs would have a lower dropout rate than districts without such programs. Results of the mail survey do not support this hypothesis—special education dropout rates were positively rather than negatively associated with dropout prevention activities. The reason for this disparity becomes clear if one takes into account two factors: (1) districts with the highest dropout rates are the ones most likely to adopt dropout prevention programs, and (2) although dropout prevention activities may slowly be lowering the dropout rate, they may not lower it to a rate below those of districts with initially low dropout rates. Presumably, very large and large districts were the most likely to have dropout programs, not only because they had higher dropout rates but also because they had more resources with which to address the problem.

Unfortunately, the data collected for this study were not adequate to evaluate the impact of various dropout prevention activities on special education dropout rates. To evaluate their effectiveness, it would be necessary to compare the dropout rates for special education students enrolled in such programs with those for students not enrolled in such programs, controlling for differences in student characteristics.

In addition to dropout prevention programs, we examined a variety of special education policies (e.g., suspension and expulsion policies, graduation policies), the availability of various support services (e.g., vocational education staff trained to work with special education students, vocational education adapted to special education students' needs), and special education practices (e.g., amount of coordination between schools when students transfer) that we thought might affect the likelihood of special education students' dropping out.

There was little or no relationship between the likelihood of dropping out and various suspension and expulsion policies (e.g, whether secondary special education students can be suspended, whether the suspension length is shorter than that permitted for regular education students, whether the Individualized Education Program (IEP) is changed after a secondary special education student is suspended) or graduation policies (e.g., whether a special diploma or certificate of completion is given to special education students who don't meet the same standards as regular education students,

whether special education students are required to pass a minimum competency test) because there was little district variation with respect to these
policies. Also, there was almost no variation in the amount of coordination
between schools when a secondary special education student transfers (e.g.,
whether IEPs are transferred when a student changes schools).[9]

There was either no relationship between various support services (e.g.,
vocational education services, job placement specialists) provided to special
education students and the likelihood of dropping out, or there was a slight
positive relationship due to the fact that large districts were the most apt
to provide special support services to handicapped students and also were
the most likely to have high dropout rates. As with dropout prevention
programs, the aggregate data collected for this survey were not adequate
to examine the relationship between district policies and practices and the
likelihood of special education students' dropping out.

Although the survey data were inconclusive, a common theme that
emerged from the site visits was that education reform and the resulting
increased emphasis on graduation requirements has created greater pressures on the marginal students, which includes the special education population. The emphasis on academics over the past few years has had two
side effects. First, it has made the likelihood of graduation with a regular
diploma even slimmer for students with poor academic performance who,
as a result, see little reason for continuing to attend classes and therefore
don't show up and fall even farther behind.[10] Second, districts have less
flexibility in designing alternative education programs to keep students in
school. Because secondary special education students tend to be several
years behind academically, they may reach 18 well before twelfth grade
and view dropping out and getting a job as a "panacea" for all their problems.[11]

Even though some education reform measures are presenting problems
for certain segments of the school population, a few of the districts that we
visited were finding ways around these difficulties. For example, one district
cross-referenced vocational classes with academic classes to help special
education students fulfill their graduation requirements. Others provided
special education students with additional remedial help for required subjects. In some districts, efforts were made to coordinate the special education curriculum with the regular education curriculum to facilitate
mainstreaming and the satisfaction of graduation requirements.

Respondents who were interviewed felt that increased vocational opportunities might also improve graduation rates for special education students. For example, a special education teacher in one site credited the
improvement in his students' graduation rate (from 8 percent to 33 percent
in the past three years) to his district's new vocational education program
for special education students. Conversely, some teachers mentioned that
vocational education programs for special education students have also

enabled some of their students to find jobs before graduation and have actually facilitated their dropping out.

SUMMARY AND CONCLUSIONS

Our study uncovered considerable variation in dropout rates for special education students in California, depending on how dropout rates were calculated and for which disability groups. The annual (1985–86) statewide dropout rate for special education students served in districts was only 6.6 percent. However, the dropout rate for a single age cohort over a three-year period during high school (from tenth to twelfth grade) is probably closer to 20 percent. In 75 percent of the districts surveyed, the annual dropout rate for special education students was lower than or equal to the statewide dropout rate (6.6 percent). Nevertheless, a few districts had relatively high annual dropout rates of 20 percent or higher. Because the distribution of dropout rates is skewed, averaging dropout rates across districts is likely to be misleading. On the other hand, because statewide dropout rates are determined mainly by the very large and large districts that serve the vast majority of special education students and that also tend to have the highest dropout rates, district policies based on statewide dropout rates may be less appropriate for medium-size and smaller districts.

Additionally, dropout rates reported for the entire special education population conceal the variation in dropout rates for different disability groups. For example, the annual statewide dropout rate for special education students served in districts was 7.5 percent for learning handicapped students, compared with the following dropout rates for other disability groups: 4.9 percent for the speech impaired, 2.8 percent for the communicatively handicapped, 2.6 percent for the physically handicapped, and 4.1 percent for the severely handicapped. Interview respondents indicated the dropout rates vary not only by disability group, but also by the severity of a student's disability within the group (e.g., a student with a severe learning disability may be categorized as learning handicapped).

Both statewide and district dropout rates tend to be higher for the total student population than for special education students. However, the difference in dropout rates may be exaggerated, because in some districts "potential" special education dropouts are referred to alternative education programs or continuation schools that do not have classes specifically for special education students; when they drop out of such programs, they are not included in special education statistics. In some districts, "potential" special education dropouts are assigned to "homebound status" rather than being counted as dropouts. Also, some districts do not count special education students who leave school after the age of 18 as dropouts, even when they do not graduate.

Interestingly, although the statewide dropout rate for secondary special education students served in districts is slightly lower than that for the total secondary student population, the statewide *attrition rate* (the percentage of students who leave the district, including both those who do and do not drop out) is slightly higher. Therefore, attrition rates are a poor substitute for dropout rates.

Our findings on the reasons why special education students drop out of special education are based entirely on the perceptions of special education staff. On the other hand, data from parents of handicapped youth who have dropped out are consistent with these findings (Jay and Padilla, 1988).It is interesting to note that district and school staff indicated that special education students (except for the physically handicapped) drop out for the same reasons (as reported in other studies) that regular education students drop out. Although special education dropouts, like other dropouts, tend to perform poorly and to dislike school, this may be a symptom of an underlying cause for dropping out rather than an explanation for dropping out.

Policy Implications and Unanswered Questions

Our findings suggest that the dropout rate for certain types of special education students may be significant. Although our research focused on special education dropouts within California, findings from this study are consistent with those of the National Longitudinal Transition Study of Handicapped Youth (NLTS) currently being conducted by SRI International for the U.S. Department of Education (Jay and Padilla, 1988). Findings from the Transition study indicate an annual dropout rate for youth in special education who were age 16 and over during the 1986–87 school year that is similar to the rate for all youth in grades 10 through 12 estimated by the Census Bureau.[12] By contrast, the dropout rates for special education exiters reported by the U.S. Department of Education indicate a much higher rate for special education students than for regular education students. A first step toward dropout prevention, therefore, would be to collect better data on special education dropouts by disability and to monitor changes in the annual dropout rate for special education students (e.g., by establishing a uniform definition of *dropout,* calculating dropout rates in the same way, and tracking what happens to exiters).[13]

Because learning handicapped students constitute the largest percentage of special education dropouts and because they also have the highest dropout rates, dropout prevention efforts should be targeted to this group. However, more information is needed, because dropout rates may vary considerably within disability groups as a result of differences in severity.

Also, more information is needed to assess the impact of various district policies, support services, and dropout prevention programs on the dropout rate for special education students. In particular, educational reform policies need to be assessed in terms of the special education population. Increasing graduation requirements may cause dropout rates for special education students to rise. In our study, we found that 88 percent of districts in California that had minimum competence tests allowed special education students to take a modified or different version of their minimum competency test than is used for regular education students to obtain a regular diploma; only 22 percent of districts provided special education students with a special diploma or certificate of completion if they did not meet the same graduation standards or criteria as regular education students. If special education students are no longer given the option of a test modification, graduation rates will probably decline.[14] Analyses of NLTS data indicate that failure to graduate from high school significantly increases the likelihood that special education exiters will fail to become engaged in employment, postsecondary education, or any productive activities after high school (Butler-Nelin, Marder, and Graves, 1989; Wagner 1989).

Our interview respondents felt that the increased emphasis on academics has limited their options to develop programs relevant for potential special education dropouts, such as vocational education programs. This feeling also is supported by findings in a recent report on dropouts prepared by the state Assembly Office of Research (1985): "[Increased requirements and financial pressures] have created a narrow curriculum with reduced course offerings in vocational education, fine arts, and other electives. The result is a curriculum which offers students fewer chances to succeed."

This study was not able to evaluate the effectiveness of various types of dropout prevention programs, and little state-level information on program performance is available. However, the report on dropouts by the Assembly Office of Research suggested that alternative education programs may not be very effective, even for the regular student population. The report characterized alternative programs as "fragmented" and said that they "do not constitute a systematic safety net for dropout prevention or reentry into school."[15] Moreover, most of the dropout prevention programs across the country are based on what the research literature says about why students drop out, but there is very little empirical evidence at the national level regarding the effectiveness of dropout programs (U.S. General Accounting Office, 1986).

Our data from California suggest that a relatively small percentage (5 percent) of special education students are currently being served in continuation schools or alternative programs. Another state study in Florida (Project Transition, 1986) found that very few special education students are included in alternative programs designed to keep youth from dropping out. For example, in Florida, special education youth represent 10 percent of all youth in secondary school, but only 2.4 percent of the youth served in dropout prevention programs. Thus, few special education students appear to be involved in programs that are addressing the dropout problem, and more research is needed on what will work for the special education population. The elements needed to develop a successful strategy of dropout prevention and recovery may require some adjustments to deal with the special needs of the handicapped (e.g., more counseling for emotionally disturbed students versus more academic remediation for learning disabled students). On the other hand, because special education students constitute a small percentage of the total student population (less than 10 percent) it may not be possible for medium-size or small districts—even those with relatively high special education dropout rates—to develop dropout prevention programs specifically for special education students.

Finally, because special education programs theoretically contain many of the same features that effective dropout prevention programs have (e.g., lower student/teacher ratios, individualized instruction), one would expect the dropout rate for special education students to be lower than that for the overall student population. The fact that youth with some types of disabilities are dropping out at the same or higher rates than the national average raises questions that need to be addressed by both policymakers and practitioners: Are there some problems with the adequacy of the implementation of special education programs for these students (e.g., the appropriateness of the curriculum or the support services provided)? Do certain types of schools or educational practices push special education students out of school? Clearly, to formulate policy for all youth in special education and develop specific interventions for those youth most at risk of dropping out, better information is needed on why special education youth (in different disability groups) drop out. In particular, analyses of school context and educational program characteristics, and their effect on the dropout behavior of handicapped youth, are needed to inform the emerging literature on school effectiveness.

Preliminary analyses of the NLTS data have begun to address some of these issues. In an initial analysis of the educational programs and academic achievements of secondary special education students, it was found that specific services do contribute to the school achievement of youth in some disability groups (Wagner and Shaver, 1989). Such results offer promising indications that programs and services reduce the likelihood that students fail courses in school, indirectly improve a student's likelihood of graduating rather than dropping out, and ultimately affect the youth's transition beyond high school. Also, the reasons cited for handicapped students leaving school suggest a group of youth who are disconnected or are growing detached from school. This suggests that researchers and practitioners may need to better attend to the social, as well as the academic, integration of special education students in trying to determine what will help students stay in school and successfully complete high school (Butler-Nalin and Padilla, 1989).

We hope that findings from our research will help to broaden the focus of the research, policy debate, and programming in the dropout arena to include greater attention to the particular needs of special education students.

Butler-Nalin, P., Marder, C., and Shaver, D.R. (1989). *Making the transition: An explanatory model of special education students' participation in post-secondary education.* Paper presented at the annual meeting of the American Educational Research Association, San Francisco.

Butler-Nalin, P., and Padilla, C. (1989). *Dropouts: The relationship of student characteristics, behaviors, and performance for special education students.* Paper presented at the annual meeting of the American Educational Research Association, San Francisco.

Wagner, M. (1989). *Secondary special education students in transition: An overview of descriptive findings from the national transition study.* Paper presented for the Office of Special Education Programs, U.S. Department of Education. Menlo Park, CA: SRI International.

Wagner, M. and Shaver, D.M. (1989). *Educational programs and achievements of secondary special education students: Findings from the national transition study.* Paper presented at the annual meeting of the American Educational Research Association, San Francisco.

NOTES

1. Each site visit lasted from two to three days, depending on the size of the site. In each site, both district- and school-level staff were interviewed. District-level respondents included the special education director, other special education staff, staff involved in continuation and dropout prevention programs, and staff responsible for calculating dropout statistics and completing the CBEDS forms. At the school level, special education staff and staff involved in alternative education and dropout prevention programs were interviewed.

2. QED is a private marketing firm that maintains a data base containing the universe of public school districts in the United States. Information on districts includes such items as total student enrollment, grade levels served by each school in the district, ethnicity of the student population, and demographic characteristics.

3. The following procedure was used to adjust for district nonresponse. Using QED data, all districts in California were divided into strata based on total district enrollment: very large (25,000 or more), large (10,000 to 24,999), medium (2,500 to 9,999), small (600 to 2,499), and very small (less than 600). The weight for each stratum was determined by dividing the total number of districts in the stratum (including responding and nonresponding districts) by the total number of districts in the stratum that had returned a questionnaire. Following are the weights that were used for

each stratum: very large (1.90), large (2.25), medium (2.15), small (1.81), and very small (2.0).

4. The High School and Beyond study contains data for only a single cohort of students (high school sophomores in 1980), who were followed during high school. Also, the only handicapped students included in the High School and Beyond study sample were mildly impaired. However, the study's findings on dropouts are frequently cited, and it remains one of the most current sources of information on why students drop out.

5. There was no real consensus among respondents regarding which disability categories this group constituted, but specific learning disability (SLD), mildly mentally retarded (MR), and severely emotionally disturbed (SED) students were mentioned.

6. The district that had an 89.5 percent dropout rate for secondary special education students was a small district. Dropout rates for very large and large districts ranged from 0 percent to 35.8 percent and for medium-size districts from 0 percent to 22.2 percent.

7. Approximately 64 percent of districts had secondary special education dropout rates less than 5 percent. Twenty-one percent had dropout rates that ranged from 5 percent to 9 percent; 13 percent had dropout rates that ranged from 10 percent to 19 percent, and only 2 percent had dropout rates of 20 percent or higher. Almost all counties (83 percent) had dropout rates that were less than 5 percent.

8. Since there is little money currently available in these districts to follow up on dropouts, no one is really sure what happens to these special education students. Predictions among special education staff were that students that are "street-wise" survive and the rest "live on the margin."

9. Most districts said that secondary special education students can be suspended from schools in their district (99 percent), that the suspension length for special education students is the same as that permitted for regular education students (97 percent), and that when a secondary special education student is suspended, his or her IEP is usually reviewed or changed (62 percent). Only 22 percent of districts give a special diploma or certificate of completion to special education students who don't meet the same standards or criteria as regular education students. Almost all districts (96 percent) require high school students to pass a minimum competency test to obtain a regular diploma. However, most districts that require students to pass a minimum competency test allow special education students to take a modified or different version of the test than that given to regular students (88 percent) and give special education students special assistance (e.g., readers, longer exam time, large-print forms) in completing the test (98 percent). Finally, 88 percent of districts said that when a secondary special education student transfers from one school to another within the district, IEPs and student files and records are always transferred to the new school.

10. The U.S. Department of Education reported that only 43 percent of the handicapped youth in the United States who exited from school during the 1985–86 school year graduated with a regular diploma; another 17 percent graduated from high school with a certificate of completion (OSEP, 1988).

11. McDill, Natriello, and Pallas (1985) examined the influence of school reform policies on the dropout rate and came to the conclusion that reforms directed toward more challenging content and achievement standards may have both positive and negative effects. Although the studies of student time on task offer some hope that greater student effort will lead to greater achievement, this may not be the case for all students under all circumstances. Implementation of a core curriculum of academic standards will probably restrict the variation in school experiences for students, limit the number of dimensions of ability deemed legitimate in the school, and curtail student choice in constructing a program of study (all identified components of successful dropout prevention programs).

12. The Census Bureau defines a dropout as anyone who is not currently enrolled, who has not completed high school, and who was enrolled in the previous year. Based on the October 1983 Current Population Survey, the Census Bureau reported an *annual* dropout rate of 5.2 percent for youth in grades 10 through 12 (Bureau of the Census, 1987c).

13. As a result of the EHA amendments of 1983, OSEP began collecting aggregate state data on the number of handicapped youth who exited from school—the number of youth who received special education and related services during the previous school year but were no longer receiving services. State data are required to be reported according to the reason for exit (including a category for dropouts) for each handicapping condition and for each age beginning at 16. However, because districts often do not know what happens to students after they exit, the quality of the data provided to the state varies considerably.

14. In 1983, 41 percent of California dropouts left twelfth grade because they failed proficiency tests or the courses needed to graduate (Assembly Office of Research, 1985).

15. Two studies of alternative education programs in California show poor success rates for participants. Continuation programs serve almost 20 percent of eleventh- and twelfth-grade students, and only 10 percent of these students graduate (Stern et al., 1986). The Auditor General found that only 11 percent of participants in independent study programs graduated from high school, with an additional 2 percent receiving alternative diplomas (Assembly Office of Research, 1985).

REFERENCES

Appelbaum, M. I., and Dent, C. W. 1986. *North Carolina public high school drop-out study: Extensions and revisions.* Chapel Hill, N.C.: L. L. Thurstone Psychometric Laboratory, University of North Carolina.

Assembly Office of Research. 1985. *Dropping out, losing out: The high cost for California.* Sacramento, Calif.: Author.

Bureau of the Census. 1987a. *Educational background and economic status: Spring 1984.* Series P-70, no. 11. Washington, D.C.: U.S. Department of Commerce.

———. 1987b. *Statistical abstract of the United States,* 107th ed. Washington, D.C.: U.S. Department of Commerce.

———. 1987c. *School enrollment—Social and economic characteristics of students: October 1983.* Washington, D.C.: U.S. Department of Commerce.

California State Department of Education. 1986. California dropouts: A status report. Sacramento, Calif.: Program Evaluation and Research Division.

Catterall, J. S. 1986. Dropping out: The cost to society. *Education* 4(1).

Edgar, E.; Levine, P.; and Maddox, M. 1985. *Washington state follow-up data of former secondary special education students.* University of Washington.

Hasazi, S. 1984. *An analysis of transitional services provided to secondary aged handicapped youth.* Burlington, Vt.: University of Vermont.

International Center for the Disabled. March 1986. *The ICD survey of disabled Americans.* New York: Author.

Jay, E. D., and Padilla, C. L. 1988. Dropping out of special education: Preliminary findings from the national transition study. Paper presented at the annual meeting of the American Educational Research Association meeting, New Orleans.

Kolstad, A., and Owings, J. A. 1986. High school dropouts who change their minds about school. Paper presented at the annual meeting of the American Educational Research Association, San Francisco.

Lichtenstein, S. 1987. Dropouts: A secondary special education perspective. Paper presented at the annual meeting of the American Educational Research Association, Washington, D.C.

McDill, E. L.; Natriello, G.; and Pallas, A. 1985. Raising standards and retaining students: The impact of the reform recommendations on potential dropouts. *Review of Educational Research* 55:415–33.

Meyers, D. E., and Ellman, F. 1983. *Early exits from high school and post-high school transitions.* Washington, D.C.: Decision Resources Corp.

Mithaug, D., and Horiuchi, C. 1983). *Colorado State follow-up survey of special education students.* Boulder, Colo.: University of Colorado.

National Center for Education Statistics. 1984. *High school and beyond, a national longitudinal study for the 1980's. Two years in high school: The status of 1980 sophomores in 1982.* Washington, D.C. U.S Department of Education.

————. 1985. *The condition of education.* Washington, D.C.: U.S. Department of Education.

————. 1986. *The condition of education.* Washington, D.C.: U.S. Department of Education.

Office of Special Education Programs. 1987. *To assure the free appropriate public education of all handicapped children.* Ninth annual report to Congress on the implementation of the education of the Handicapped Act. Washington, D.C.: U.S. Department of Education.

————. 1988. *To assure the free appropriate public education of all handicapped children.* Tenth annual report to Congress on the implementation of the education of the Handicapped Act. Washington, D.C.: U.S. Department of Education.

Project Transition. 1986. *Florida's exceptional students in transition from school to community.* A report to the Florida legislature, Tallahassee, Fla.

Rumberger, R. W. 1987. High school dropouts: A review of issues and evidence. *Review of Educational Research* 57:101–21.

Stern, D.; Catterall, J.; Alhadeff, C.; and Ash, M. 1986. *Reducing the high school dropout rate in California: Why we should and how we can.* California policy seminar final report no. 10. Berkeley, Calif.: University of California.

U.S. Department of Education. 1986. *State education statistics.* Washington, D.C.: Author.

U.S. General Accounting Office. 1986. *School dropouts—The extent and nature of the problem.* Washington, D.C.: Author.

Zigmond, N., and Thornton, H. 1985. Learning disabled graduates and dropouts. *Learning Disabilities Research* 1:50–55.

AN ETHNOGRAPHIC STUDY OF FOUR HMONG STUDENTS: IMPLICATIONS FOR EDUCATORS AND SCHOOLS

Lila Jacobs

INTRODUCTION

An area of growing concern for people involved with issues of equity is the relationship between ethnolinguistically different children and special education (Christensen, Gerber, & Everhart, 1986; Rueda, 1987; Trueba, in press). The number of language minority children placed in learning disability programs is growing in disproportionate numbers. The time has come to search for the underlying causes of this phenomenon and to question the assumptions upon which the diagnoses are being made. Are great numbers of these children really handicapped, or are their cultural differences determining their placement in this category?

This study of four Hmong children describes their encounters in school and their traumas over time as they attempt to belong and participate fully in classroom learning activities. Their low achievement levels are viewed by school personnel as signs of learning disabilities. Using ethnographic research methods, mainly participant observations and interviews (Mc-Dermott & Roth, 1978; Trueba & Wright, 1981; Spindler, 1982; Trueba, 1987), the study focuses on how children become increasingly aware of their differences in cultural values, and attempt to cope with the high levels of stress they experience in school. Teachers, on the other hand, adhere to their own training and values and demand compliance with cultural norms of performance. The Hmong children under study show deep frustration and hopelessness as they fail to engage meaningfully in learning activities. The study offers suggestions for the implementation of educational policy and practice in dealing with culturally different students, and explores possible directions for further research.

SETTING AND METHODOLOGY

The school research site is located in a densely populated community in southern California. Half the population is university students and the other half includes a growing Hispanic community, as well as a community of Southeast Asian refugees. The Hmong people from Laos are part of this latter group.

La Playa elementary school has 591 students (as of 1985). Over half of these students—298 children—have a primary language other than English, with 24 languages included. The largest ethnic group, other than Anglo, is formed by 136 Indochinese students, including 77 Hmong, 31 Laotian, and 28 Vietnamese.

Programs offered by the school include reading and language labs, a learning disability resource program, and Spanish/English bilingual education. Part-time instructional aides are used in the classrooms, as well as student teachers. Two psychological counselors are on site one day per week. The majority of school personnel is Anglo, the exceptions being Hispanic teachers in the bilingual program. There are no Asian adults employed by the school.

The observations took place over a two-month period, during which I was on site daily from the beginning of class at 8:15 until the end of school at 2:30. I also had access to school files, which are included in the analysis.

All interviews were audio-taped, and were conducted with each of the four students and with the two classroom teachers. At school, interviews were also done with the reading specialist, the learning disability resource teacher, the classroom aides, the student teachers, the language specialist, the school psychologist and the counselors. I also spent time in the homes of the students, and their parents were interviewed as well. The parent interviews were done with the help of a translator who is fluent in the Hmong language and also a trained ethnographer.

HISTORICAL BACKGROUND

To better understand the Hmong refugees, it is necessary to include a short historical perspective. The events leading up to the present relocation in California are complex, and they are an integral part of the cultural heritage and the psyche of the community members. The Hmong in this community left Laos after the American troops pulled out and the Hmong military leader, Vang Pao (who had been trained by the American CIA), fled to Thailand (Lee, 1982). Many of the La Playa Hmong made the journey to Thailand on foot, a difficult and treacherous undertaking.

The traumas of survival in these life-or-death circumstances continued into the refugee camp experience. The necessity of satisfying the conditions required by the American Immigration authorities often called for altering roles of wives, ages of children, religious beliefs, and family alliances. The trauma of entering unfamiliar settings and of degradation experiences continue into the resettlement journeys, and persists today in the resocialization process of resettlement (Kirton, 1985).

RESEARCH FINDINGS AND ANALYSIS

The research documents differential participation and skill levels of these four Hmong students in the specific context of their daily school tasks. Pao and Vang, two Hmong boys, were both in classroom number 1, and also together in their reading group and learning-disability class. Chou and Song, the other boy and girl, were both in classroom number two, and in the same reading group and reading lab. The different settings allowed me to observe the students in large and small groups, and working with adults using different teaching strategies.

The theoretical frame used for analysis incorporates a Vygotskian perspective, which uses the zone of proximal development to determine what the student is capable of doing (Cole & Scribner, 1974; Vygotsky, 1978; Griffin, Newman, & Cole, 1981; Trueba, in press). This is determined by the child's experience in a mediated learning situation involving both the teacher (or more knowledgeable peer) and the learner in meaningful interaction. This interaction is impossible if the child is in isolation. Consequently, a strong linkage was seen in the relationship between participation and skill level; high levels of participation increased skill level, and vice versa.

The four case studies reveal some important observations regarding emerging patterns of behavior and themes for discussion:

1. All four children have problems "tuning in" or paying attention and engaging in academic activities. They are bored, uninvolved, spaced out, unaware, and often not participating at all. The causes for the lack of participation are multiple, and it is likely that the lack of participation is the best coping mechanism available to children who do not find the academic tasks meaningful. Remarks made by children that "it is too hard" remind us that instruction is geared in format, content, and delivery to the mainstream child, and that those who do not share mainstream language and culture are left behind at an increasing pace.

2. To compound the problem, these children, to varying degrees, have all been uprooted and traumatized in the process of relocation. The consequences of this have affected their physical and mental health and entire

family systems. Therefore, the efforts to cope with school are only part of the overall adjustment these children are making (McDermott & Hood, 1982; Trueba, 1983, 1985; Delgado-Gaitan, 1986).

3. Directly relevant to the study of learning disabilities in cultural minorities are the findings suggesting that some of these children are classified as learning disabled without a clear notion of the nature of their problems. The definition of learning disability is vague enough to allow for other factors to enter into the diagnosis.

There is a process of "social construction" of consensus among the school personnel. At times, the arguments used to initiate the classification are weak or false. At best, the ultimate argument made is that children cannot function in regular classrooms and cannot respond to instructional efforts conducted in English, with a relatively rigid curriculum, a content that is foreign to other than mainstream children, and a participation structure that tends to isolate or demoralize students who ignore the cultural or linguistic norms of the school.

The school personnel are making serious efforts to meet the demands of these children, but the entire educational process and the pressures on classroom teachers and school psychologists are such that classifying a low-achieving child as "learning disabled" seems the only option available. There are, however, important differences in children's performances to caution psychologists and teachers from using general labels and from accepting the implications attached to such labels.

Other issues that emerged as salient to the study have notable implications for teacher education and school administration (Iannacconne, 1963). Credential programs tend to minimize the need for classroom teachers to see one-to-one contact with students as a viable means of teaching. There is a tendency for teachers to regard one-to-one contact as tutoring, something considered "unrealistic" or "unfair." This mode of teaching is left to the aides, and the result is that the children with the most needs are left to work with the least skilled adults.

Positive reinforcement, cooperative learning, self-esteem, motivation, and the cultural relevance of instructional material also played an important role in the engagement or lack of it for these students. This is apparent in the case of Pao, a ten-year-old boy who had been diagnosed as having a learning disability. In the large classroom group, he had tuned out completely, sitting with his head in his hands and refusing to even look at the teacher. In the smaller reading group, working with the aide or student teacher, he participated in varying degrees but generally was unengaged and unmotivated. Working in a small group with the resource teacher showed a dramatic difference in Pao's abilities, which manifested themselves when he was engaged in meaningful interactions with the teacher and tasks.

HOME AND SCHOOL CULTURE

Another important contribution of this research is the documentation of conflict between values taught at home and those transmitted and demanded by the school. In the Hmong refugee community, the main concern of the family as a cohesive unit has been survival in very basic terms. High rents, medical problems, low income, access to information through translation, and transportation problems have been the major concerns of the family.

Money is a crucial element of survival, and consequently, all adults in a household usually work if they can find employment. This leaves child care and chores to the grandparents and older children, competing with time for study and homework.

Added to this is the fact that most parents do not have a concrete idea of what their children learn in American classrooms, and thus invest the teachers and the schools with a "magical ability" to teach the children "everything there is to know." Although the parents verbally support the importance of school, they have little substance on which to ascertain what would help their children be successful in the education process.

The school experience of the parents has little in common with what happens in the schools their children now attend. The status of teachers in their home country made communication between teacher and parent impossible, and the Hmong parents continue to operate from this frame of reference.

Stories about school in Laos, told to me by Hmong parents, provide insight as to why parents are so happy with American schools. They say that in Laos teachers inflict harsh punishment—making children kneel on pointed rocks or making a friend inflict lashes on another student. Pao's mother sadly told me about her brother:

> In Laos, my brother went to school in the city and the teachers were so mean and they would hit so hard that he would come home crying. That is why he went to be a soldier, and he was killed. Even though the kids haven't gone to school there, we tell them that the teachers here are so nice that even if you don't wash your face or anything, they are still happy to hug you and talk to you.

Lack of English language skills adds to the lack of understanding between parents and teachers. All parents in this study told me that no translator was available during school conferences and that they did not understand what the teachers were saying. This later appeared on school files as, "Parents did not react or seem concerned."

The home language of the four students in Hmong—"American" is used only when children don't want their parents to understand what they are saying. It is significant to note that Hmong, their primary language, does not describe events in the same paradigm as the English language. Thoughts are not divided into equivalent constructs; for example, tenses and plurals are not indicated within the conjugation of verbs.

These distinctions are extremely important, since they lead us to understand that for the Hmong children, learning English when they begin school is not solely the task of learning a new language, but also a new way to view reality—one that does not coincide with the view of their parents and grandparents. The act of learning English thus propels children into a world where they can no longer rely on a single set of values inherited from their cultural background.

IMPLICATIONS OF THE FINDINGS

The data presented have helped to explain the complexity of the adjustment process that Hmong and other minority children have to make in order to be able to learn in our schools. The cultural and linguistic differences are of such magnitude, and they affect so profoundly all instructional activities, that school personnel tend to oversimplify the task of helping these children. Worse still, school personnel tend to find incomprehensible the fact that many of these children cannot function in our classrooms, and consequently surmise that the children must be disabled. In some instances, school personnel have important information regarding the traumatic history of relocation of these Hmong families, but cannot understand why some children take longer than others to adjust.

Children seek to adjust in a number of ways. Some children withdraw and remain isolated, others attempt to overcompensate with anxious overparticipation, while others fight back (Trueba, 1983). The Hmong children are culturally more inclined to select the first two alternatives. A significant implication of this study is that without appropriate intervention by school personnel, the problems of these children will only get worse. Their increasing deterioration in participation and performance levels is observed over a period of time. One reason for this deterioration process is that the emotional cost for children attempting to maintain a high level of engagement in school activities is viewed to yield less and less in terms of learning and success rewards.

As mentioned earlier, to further the problem of adjustment for these students, home support is often well-intentioned but ineffectual due to the parents' lack of familiarity with the culture of American schools. It is apparent that without a viable support system in the home, any student does less well in school. Just as important, the parents who cannot provide that support suffer diminished respect in the eyes of their children, causing a breakdown in traditional family systems.

As the students fall behind in their work, more pressure is placed on them to "catch up." Instead of trying new strategies, the tendency is to "push harder" using the same unsatisfactory methods, thus producing the same unsatisfactory results. When this happens, an amplification of the stress occurs. The image of Song, with her constant overerasing and her manner of speaking in a barely audible whisper, comes to mind. Participating without the skills to perform successfully becomes traumatic, and withdrawal is viewed as a natural response to a painful experience.

The case study of Pao, who will not even look at the teacher, is also a classic example of withdrawal. By cutting himself off from the teacher and the classroom experience, the opportunity to learn is no longer available to him. Withdrawal and isolation are part of the vicious cycle of academic failure, and unless there is a positive intervention, the factor of time becomes a negative variable, and the achievement remains on a negative course of decline.

CONCLUSION

Many issues have emerged from this study that current research must address, such as problems specific to the domain of refugees, educating teachers for cross-cultural classrooms, and empowering culturally and linguistically different parents to take an active role in their children's education.

Specifically, results of this research deal with the policies that govern the learning disability programs in the schools. The current trend of placing language minority and culturally different children in these programs is typified at La Playa School, resulting in an overrepresentation of minority children in these programs. The data reveal a lack of clarity and inconsistency in the use of the learning disability label. The common characteristics of these children is that they do not fit into the parameters of the performance and behaviors expected in the classroom.

Unless there are interventions to halt the cycle of academic failure, alienation and withdrawal will continue to lead to isolation for linguistic minority students, and we will continue to see the dropout process begin even in elementary school. Solutions other than labeling children "learning disabled" must be initiated to allow meaningful mediated learning experiences that are relevant to students, regardless of their cultural backgrounds. The study clearly indicates that students are not individually responsible for their alienation and increased isolation, but that they function as part of a system that includes the entire school and the community, as well as the larger society, and what we observe are manifestations of a systemic failure. Unless this is recognized, and withdrawal and isolation of students are seen as crucial factors interfering with the learning process, appropriate interventions will not be discovered. Rather, we will see more of what is happening now, inaccurate labeling of children in an attempt to rid the classroom of misfits.

234 Lila Jacobs

REFERENCES

Christensen, C., Gerber, M., and Everhart, R. 1986. Toward a sociological perspective on learning disabilities. *Educational Theory* 36(4):317–31.

Cole, M., and Scribner, S. 1974. *Culture and thought: A psychological introduction.* New York: Wiley.

Delgado-Gaitan, C. 1986. Critical consciousness and learning in schools: Education for social change. Unpublished manuscript.

Griffin, P., Newman, D., and Cole, M. 1981. Activities, actions and formal operations: A Vygotskian analysis of a Piagetian task. Laboratory of Comparative Human Cognition, University of California, San Diego. Unpublished manuscript.

Iannacconne, L. 1963. Student Teaching: A transitional stage in the making of a teacher. *Theory into Practice* 2(2):73–80.

Kirton, E. 1985. The locked medicine cabinet: Hmong health care in America. Department of Anthropology, University of California, Santa Barbara. Unpublished dissertation.

Lee, G. Y. 1982. Minority policies and the Hmong. In *In contemporary Laos: Studies in the politics and society of the Lao People's Democratic Republic,* ed. M. Stuart-Fox. New York: St. Martin's Press.

McDermott, R. P., and Hood, L. 1982. Institutionalized psychology and the ethnography of schooling. In *Children in and out of school,* ed. P. Gilmore and A. Glatthorn. Washington, D.C.: Center for Applied Linguistics.

McDermott, R. P., and Roth, D. R. 1978. The social organization of behavior: Interactional approaches. *Annual Review of Anthropology* 3:321–435.

Rueda, R. 1987. Social and communicative aspects of language proficiency in low-achieving language minority students. In *Success or failure: Linguistic minority students at home and in school,* ed. H. Trueba. New York: Harper & Row.

Spindler, G. 1982. *Doing the ethnography of schooling: Educational anthropology in action.* New York: Holt, Rinehart & Winston.

Trueba, H. T. 1983. Adjustment problems of Mexican American children: An anthropological study. *Learning Disabilities Quarterly* 6(4):395–415.

———. 1985. Bilingualism and bilingual education (1984–1985). In *Annual review of applied linguistics,* ed. R. B. Kaplan. Topsfield, Mass.: Newbury Books.

———. 1987. Introduction: Ethnography of schooling. In *Success or failure: Linguisitic minority children at home and in school,* ed. H. Trueba. New York: Harper & Row.

———. (in press). Organizing classroom instruction in specific sociocultural contexts: Teaching Mexican youth to write in English. In *Becoming literate in English as a second language: Advances in research and theory,* ed. S. Goldman and H. Trueba. Norword, N.J.: Ablex Publishing Corp.

Trueba, H. T., and Wright, P. G. 1981. A challenge for ethnographic researchers in bilingual settings: Analyzing Spanish/English interaction. *Journal of Multilingual and Multicultural Development* 2(4):243–57.

Vygotsky, L. S. 1978. Mind in society: The development of higher psychological processes. Ed. M. Cole, V. John-Steiner, S. Scribner, and E. Souberman. Cambridge, Mass.: Harvard University Press.

THE CONSTRICTION OF THE CLASSROOM: THE SUBMERGENCE OF DIFFERENCE.

Steve Harlow

Teaching is impossible. All of the great quests of life begin as impossibilities.

—William Ernest Hocking

This essay will explore key assumptions that have informed the practice of the special education arm of the schools. My thesis is that these assumptions and their resulting practices have aided in the invalidation of the uniqueness and selfhood of the very youngsters special education purports to serve. I will devote attention to the medical model and its shortcomings in dealing with children revealing difficulties. Finally, I will argue that the type of educational experience the youngster with a school-related handicap receives shrinks his self and his agency.

To begin I wish to offer a distinction between true handicaps and school-related handicaps. A true handicap refers to a permanent physical or intellectual condition that places important limits on the individual's ability to handle certain situations. The definition implies that the condition can be shown to exist by objective and verifiable means. The verification process involves both professionally administered tests and collaboration by the individual and/or those who know him best. When dealing with physical or sensory conditions (like blindness or orthopedic handicaps), objective verification does not pose any real difficulty. Here the medical model and its tests appropriately identify and verify the nature of the condition. Using the

237

second part of the verification process—obviousness—the individual and those around him are also aware of the handicap and its limitations. The verification process can also be used in the identification of intellectual handicaps such as severe mental retardation. Here again, medical and psychological tests would reveal that an individual is functioning at a very low level intellectually. The presence of severe mental retardation may not be obvious to the individual, but certainly would be visible to those who know him best.

With most real handicaps, then, the presence of the handicap is known to those who are most familiar with the individual, even before the objective diagnosis is conducted. The handicap is obvious in its presence and in its limitations, and is also present in the totality of the person's environment.

Most of the handicaps that the special education arm of the school deal with do not fulfill the criterion of obviousness or visibility. Such presumed handicaps as educable or mild retardation, learning disabilities, and emotional disturbance are often only visible in the school context. The process of "handicapping" begins as the youngster attempts to meet the social and academic expectations of the school. Difference is not a welcome visitor in the conventional classroom. A student whose needs are not being met is often frustrating to the teacher—either because of the child's seeming inability to learn what is to be learned, or because the student exhibits behavior that puzzles the teacher and others. It is often because of the presumption of biological dysfunction. High activity level, impulsivity, organizational difficulties, poor conduct, and reading below grade level may indeed represent genuine problem areas of student functioning. Framing them as handicapping conditions, however, is not a necessary precondition to helping children come to terms with them.

A disturbing example of the increasing medicalization of the schools is seen in the growth of the number of children diagnosed as having Attention Deficit Hyperactivity Disorder (ADHD). The basic characteristics of the "disorder" are problems with inattention, impulsivity, and hyperactivity. Though ADHD is presumed to be neurologic in its etiology, the necessary signs for its diagnosis are reported to the clinician by the teacher. (It should be mentioned that the functioning associated with ADHD could well be a direct effect of an inappropriate curricular or educational approach. In these situations, relying on the observations of teachers to fortify the diagnosis is to displace responsibility from teacher to child.)

Viadero reports that estimates of ADHD "range from 3 to 10 percent of the 45 million school children mainly boys" (Viadero, 1987, p. 19). The primary treatment of ADHD is the prescription of stimulant medication, usually Ritalin. In fact, from 1985 to 1987 the sales of Ritalin have doubled.

Parents are being persuaded by school officials that Ritalin is necessary to their child's education and adjustment. Viadero quotes Vic Pallos of the Glendale, California, School District: "Education can't prescribe. . . . What the principal and other staff members did do is counsel the parents to have the child evaluated by an outside professional" (Viadero, 1987, p. 19).

> In a similar vein, LeShan (1982) points out that: Those children who object to poor teaching and poor educational theory are turned over to the medical arm of the establishment for drugging and retraining. The belief is that Ritalin will cure them of their objection to an educational system on the brink of disaster (LeShan, 1982, p. 19).

Fortunately parents are beginning to bring legal challenge to school districts who encourage the promiscuous use of Ritalin. At present, however, most parents whose children are taking the drug are neither informed about its significant physical and behavioral side effects, nor are they aware of the fact that Ritalin is not an educational intervention. Advocates of Ritalin talk of its calming qualities, but as many teachers who have had students on the drug will attest, there appears to be a thin line between calming and sedation.

It seems that ADHD is a unique phenomenon of American schools. Koestler (1975) warned that American psychologists have a tendency to find disturbance and abnormal functioning where their British counterparts do not. He concluded that Americans and their mental health practitioners are highly conformist in their viewpoints of differences in behavior. What is hyperactive to American authorities would be attributed to a difference in style by this British counterpart.

While the WISC is not a stethoscope, nor a Woodcock-Johnson a CAT scan (both of which are standardized intelligence tests), they provide the same instrumentation to the medical orientation within the schools. The movement of the medical model into the schools does not rely on the active presence of the medical practitioner. Rather its movement rests on the need to create a tensionless environment in the classroom, to reduce human functioning to simple components (e.g., activity level, intelligence scores), and to quarantine differences. Today's schools operate from a planted axiom that a narrow homogeneity of the regular classroom is necessary to educate efficiently.

A great multiplier effect seems built into the medical model as it seeks to identify present learning and behavioral difficulties. For example, Smith and Robinson (1986) estimate that as much as 20 percent of the school population "has been labeled and served as learning disabled" (p. 236). Bower estimates that 10 percent of the school population "could reasonably be considered as emotionally disturbed [as cited in Kauffman, 1986, p. 252]. There is a strong tendency in the medical orientation to overclassify those who differ from the normal or typical into categories of pathology. Rosenhan explains it this way:

... physicians are more inclined to call a healthy person sick (a false positive: Type II error) than a sick person healthy (a false negative: Type I error). The reasons are not hard to find; it is clearly more dangerous to misdiagnose illness than health. Better to err on the side of caution, to suspect illness even among the healthy (Rosenhahn, 1986, p. 348).

This tendency to see illness and disorder even among the healthy is appropriate and desirable when dealing with possible physical problems. It is, however, quite a different matter when the medical approach focuses on problems that involve social and academic adjustment. Diagnostic classification has social and emotional implications that affect the ways others—students as well as school professionals—will respond to the child.

The question as to why the medical model should become so influential in the determination of how we deal with difference is in part answered by viewing the greater culture. As Zilbergeld has observed, the

tendency to focus on what is wrong and problematic, rather than on total situation or on what is good and problem-free, has become a part of modern sensibility.... We have accepted a fantasy model of well-being and mental health, and therefore of life, that probably cannot be attained by anyone. So we have plenty of deficits to attend to, meaning both that we stay in a constant state of discontent and in continual need of assistance to make things better (Zilbergeld, 1983, p. 20).

The absence of well-being becomes illness. Departure from the norm becomes disorder. Christopher Lasch has stated that the therapeutic community "would abolish the hospital only to make the whole world a hospital" (as cited in Zilbergeld, 1983, p. 94). And the school has become a ward of this great hospital.

In sum, a subtle but thorough transformation has occurred in the schools. When we deal with difference that provokes any type of tension in school settings, the medical model has replaced educational models. With the transformation have come diagnostic categories that essentially keep labeled children from participating in the same educational experience as their nonlabeled peers. But even more than that, the process of sorting freezes the child at the level of objective description with preset limits drawn from the category of disability, while not permitting the process discovery and growth. It is not long before the label replaces the child. With this, an insidious reduction occurs: difference, which the label denotes, becomes equated with inferiority.

If by sorting out difference through the use of school-related handicaps a qualitatively better education—something that could be truly deemed "special"—resulted, then the practice would be defensible. In the final analysis, it is the type of education the child participates in that becomes the touchstone of our efforts. Let us briefly examine the quality of education the child with a school-related handicap receives.

What should we mean by education? Richard Mitchell (1987) has pointed out the importance of framing basic questions with the sense of "should-ness." He points out that in such matters as intelligence, love, or education we are dealing not with questions of fact, but rather with questions of moral consequence. In education we are reminded that our work is with human potential and human struggle. It begins with the meeting of a child with his teacher and classmates. Such a meeting should neither be clouded by labels, nor should it deny the presence of the difficulties a child may bring into a setting. Education does not have as it prerequisites an optimum bioanatomy, a difficulty-free learning style, a compliant disposition, or a harmonious home life.

Education should be an elevating process that enables the child to gain increasing knowledge of self and also a deepening sense of the world. In reality the child designated with a handicap is treated in a way that is quite different than his nonhandicapped peers. First, the child has a specialist (e.g., special education teacher, learning disabilities teacher) who makes the major educational decisions for him. The child may also have a special classroom provided for him and those like him. Both of these factors underscore and reinforce his difference. Knowledge of self is thus distorted. Second, the educational regimen calls for a selection of tasks that the child can readily achieve.

Individual Education Programs (IEP) for most children are legal agreements that guarantee the child's attainment of concrete and uninteresting objectives. Exclusive emphasis is placed on what John Passmore (1980) has described as closed capacities. Closed capacities are those areas of learning that allow for total mastery. In contrast, open capacities are those areas that one can gain a deepening knowledge of and that permit a sense of self-expression, yet cannot be totally mastered (e.g., interpretation, chess, sculpting). Closed capacities, as Passmore notes, are readily converted into routines.

In teaching, staying with closed capacities has the advantage of allowing the teacher to gauge and manage the progress of an activity. The purported value for the student of staying with the easily achievable is a steady current of success. Yet such success is an impostor. To the student, these tasks are unrelated to discovery of self or the world. They are dehydrated of meaning. How can we enable a child who might have attentional difficulties to look and grasp when we pay so little attention to what is alive in him and around him? No, the answer to such a child's difficulties lies elsewhere. In the end, the true value of emphasizing closed capacities for the special student is the predictability that the routine brings. However, curiosity, imagination, and self-expression are not well nourished by routine.

A paradox may be discerned. The special education program focuses upon the problem area of a child's being, while at the same time attempting to create a setting where few problems confront him. The child with a school-related handicap is thought by those who plan and care for him to be unable to handle much of the real world. His special teacher mediates the demands of school and life by drastically reducing them to fragmented and closed capacities. Few accommodations are made by regular teachers to permit adjustment to the regular classroom. Rather than aiding the child in his understanding of and involvement in the world, school removes him from it. In the process, the child is subtly convinced that he cannot handle much of what is ordinarily to be explored and learned. The authority of the school, after all, has mirrored to him that as a child possessing a handicap he can handle so much and no more.

What is denied the child in all of this is his sense of uniqueness and personal experience. As Malcolm Ross contends, "People need to feel whole and must be responsible for their own wholeness. That means they must be helped to make their own sense of the whole of their experience, body and soul, mind and feelings" (Ross, 1978, p. 62). Such is the type of education that should be available to all youngsters, but particularly to those who are experiencing difficulties in school. A piecemeal education that uproots the child from his peers is not conducive to the wholeness Ross describes. Inclusion in the community of the classroom is requisite for the child to come to terms with his uniqueness. Short of that, we are imprinting within the child's conception of himself that he is a member of a special subspecies of students: the handicapped. Difficulties in functioning can be met with patience, flexibility, and accommodation. It is not the absence of struggle and tension that makes us human, but rather the quality of our engagement. With support and understanding, struggle may prove to be a catalyst to gaining self-knowledge and self-agency. Education in this sense is truly special.

REFERENCES

Kauffman, J. 1986. Educating children with behavior disorders. In *Special education: Research and trends,* ed. R. Morris and B. Blatt. Elmsford, N.Y.: Pergamon Books.

Koestler, A. 1975. *The heel of achilles.* New York: Random House.

LeShan, L. 1982. *The mechanic and the gardener.* New York: Holt, Rinehart & Winston.

Mitchell, R. 1987. *The gift of fire.* New York: Simon & Schuster.

Passmore, J. 1980. *The philosophy of teaching.* Cambridge, Mass.: Harvard University Press.

Rosenhan, D. 1986. On being sane in insane places. In *The pleasures of psychology,* ed. D. Goleman and D. Heller. New York: New American Library.

Ross, M. 1978. *The creative arts.* London: Heinenann Educational Books.

Smith, D. D., and Robinson, S. 1986. Educating the learning disabled. In *Special education: Research and trends,* ed. R. Morris and B. Blatt. Elmsford, N.Y.: Pergamon Books.

Viadero, D. 1987. Debate grows on classroom's magic pill. *Education Week* 7 (7):1, 19.

Zilbergeld, B. 1983. *The shrinking of America: Myths of psychological change.* Boston: Little, Brown & Co.

IV.
BILINGUAL EDUCATION

HELPING CONGRESS TO SORT OUT CONFLICTING CLAIMS ABOUT THE RESEARCH EVIDENCE ON BILINGUAL EDUCATION

Eleanor Chelimsky[1]
and Frederick Mulhauser

INTRODUCTION

In a stinging speech in fall 1985, Secretary of Education William Bennett called bilingual education a "failed path," suggested that the federal law establishing a bilingual education program was a "bankrupt course," and claimed that research evidence showed the result of the law was that "too many children have failed to become fluent in English." He proposed major changes in the law lest we "throw good money after bad."[2]

Representative Augustus Hawkins, chairman of the U.S. House of Representatives' Committee on Education and Labor, faced the task of reviewing the same bilingual education law and the same evidence in the 1986–88 session as part of the periodic reauthorization of most federal programs for elementary and secondary education. Issues of when and how to use languages other than English in such settings as state and local government services and publications, or voting assistance, had produced controversy in many parts of the country in recent years. In response, a constitutional amendment was perennially pending in Congress to establish English as the national language. Reauthorization of the federal bilingual education program would be a natural lightning rod to draw the heated charges and countercharges of the advocacy groups.[3]

To sort out one of the obvious areas of controversy the committee would face—over the results of bilingual education—Representative Hawkins turned to the U.S. General Accounting Office (GAO), the investigative arm of Congress, and asked for what one staff member called "an intellectual audit." As that staff member put it, "We often send the GAO accountants to look for any fraud and abuse in the spending of appropriated funds by the executive; this time, we want GAO social scientists and evaluators to check whether there has been fraud and abuse in the Education Department's addition of the research evidence it cites so often." The request was forwarded to the Program Evaluation and Methodology Division of GAO, which had developed approaches to reviewing and summarizing evaluations and research in meeting information requests of committees in such diverse areas as highway safety, women and infants' nutrition, and cancer survival rates.[4]

This chapter reports on GAO's project to develop, in a relatively short time, an objective assessment of the large body of evaluation and research findings on bilingual education. After a brief note on the background of the federal program, the law authorizing it, and the changes proposed by the Department of Education, we outline the design requirements we faced in doing the work, the methods we chose to meet those requirements, and the results we obtained.[5] The chapter ends with an account of the legislative consideration of the native language requirement in the law, and the role of research evidence on effectiveness in the final outcome.

THE FEDERAL BILINGUAL EDUCATION PROGRAM

Part A of the Bilingual Education Act authorizes funds for programs in U.S. schools for children whose English is limited. (Part B authorizes data collection, evaluation, and research; part C authorizes training and technical assistance.) Of the overall appropriation in any year, the act directs the Secretary of Education to reserve 60 percent for programs under part A and to further reserve 75 percent of this amount for programs of transitional bilingual education. The law defined transitional bilingual education as providing structured English language instruction, and to the extent necessary to allow a child to achieve competence in the English language, instruction in the child's native language (20 U.S. Code 3223).

Thus, most school projects under the act must use teaching methods involving some use of native languages other than English. In addition, the act directed the Secretary to reserve 4 percent of the total appropriation for special alternative programs for children whose proficiency in English is limited. These were required to have "specially designed curricula" but did not have to use students' native language. The Bilingual Education Act required that both types of programs have two goals: they must allow a child to achieve competence in English and also meet grade-promotion and graduation standards. In other words, students should not be allowed to fall behind during the time it takes them to develop enough English to do regular schoolwork.

School districts with children whose English is limited do not receive funds automatically. Funds are granted to projects rated highest in national competition. In 1985, as we started our work, from a total appropriation for bilingual education of $139.1 million, the Department of Education awarded about $94.9 million in grants for bilingual programs under part A of the act, including $77.3 million for 538 projects of transitional bilingual education that served about 174,500 students. The department also awarded $5.3 million for 35 special alternative projects that served about 12,000 students. The department estimates that between 1.2 and 1.7 million children 5 to 17 years old live in language-minority households, make substantial use of minority languages, and have limited proficiency in English. Others estimate that the number of children limited in English proficiency is much higher.

As the reauthorization process began, the Secretary of Education proposed to strike from the law the specific reservation of funds for transitional bilingual education. The Secretary and other department officials advocated this change, in part, by citing evaluations of past programs. Specifically, the department believed the research and evaluation results were too ambiguous to support the current legal requirement that most projects use teaching methods involving children's native language. At issue, therefore, was the department's interpretation of what is known about how to teach students with limited English proficiency.

DESIGN AND METHODS OF THE GAO STUDY

Timeliness and objectivity were the two major criteria to be maximized in designing GAO's response to the committee's request. Initial review of the literature in the field showed there were hundreds of program evaluations in the United States and elsewhere, and an extensive body of more general scientific literature on effective conditions for learning first and second languages. The approach used previously in GAO syntheses of research would have required setting criteria to locate an initial group of studies, retrieving the studies, screening them for quality, and then analyzing the acceptable ones for methodology and findings (using quantitative effect-size estimation methods or other ways of aggregation). GAO reached an agreement with the committee that in the time available we could not do a new synthesis of the large mass of material. Therefore, we used reviews of the literature to represent what is known.

The requirement of objectivity was especially important, beyond the general professional standards for both auditors and evaluators, which call for the exercise of independent judgment. In this case objectivity was essential because of the specific controversies that had raged around the program and the related larger issues of language and law. The same large body of research findings had been viewed very differently by advocates for opposing positions. Given the generally supportive views of the chairman of the committee requesting the GAO work, the negative views of the Secretary of Education, concerning the results of native language teaching methods, it was crucial that GAO use a method of interpreting the evidence that would be seen as fair and balanced.

Methodology for GAO's Review

Our objective was to assess the degree of correspondence between research knowledge on bilingual education and statements by Department of Education officials about that knowledge. To do our job as quickly and efficiently as possible, while also attaining the greatest possible degree of objectivity, we used a methodology allowing us to draw on expert opinion, and implemented the work through three tasks.

First, we reviewed specific department statements on bilingual education between 1983 and 1986, and identified all the instances we could find in which research and evaluation were cited in support of claims about effectiveness of current or alternative strategies. From 39 sources we extracted 65 specific statements; after rejecting duplicates, we retained a representative collection of 31 statements.

Second, we searched comprehensively for research summaries or reviews of the effectiveness of different teaching approaches for language-minority students, starting with computerized bibliographic data bases, but also including review of bibliographies, annual meeting programs in the field, and special collections such as the National Clearinghouse on Bilingual Education. From all these sources we obtained 929 references; from abstracts we selected 52 that appeared to analyze multiple empirical studies to draw conclusions about the effectiveness of teaching methods. We retrieved these items, and after review found 29 that analyzed a significant number of studies. We sent the list of 29 to 23 knowledgeable researchers, policy analysts, and others for their review, which allowed us to confirm the adequacy of coverage of our initial list and to add some items.

Retaining 23 reviews published since 1980 for further consideration, we evaluated each on six criteria: (1) balance, or care and impartiality in analysis of the studies under review; (2) breadth of coverage of research on different parts of the United States and different language groups; (3) diversity of teaching approaches covered in the studies reviewed; (4) rigor of approach to locating, selecting, and analyzing the specific studies reviewed; (5) recency of publication; and (6) diversity of learning outcomes analyzed (other than short-term test score gains). We chose some references for unique qualities that went beyond the six criteria. Because the department had done an internal literature review that had been widely cited and discussed, we selected it as our first item. Its methods and conclusions have been commented on in numerous other reviews, and we included one of these. Then, since the department stresses the potential benefits of immersion teaching techniques (where there is no use of the child's native language), and since this approach was not covered thoroughly in either the department's review or the other general reviews, we included two reviews of this method alone, one pro and one con. The other six reviews we selected are in the fields of language learning and various teaching approaches for students with limited English proficiency. The ten reviews we finally selected are listed in the references at the end of this chapter.

Although the shortcomings of studies in the field are widely discussed, we noted that several of the reviews we chose seemed to agree that a sizable body of evidence may be examined for possible conclusions. For example, using criteria similar to those we could have used in screening original studies, two different reviews agreed that 23 specific studies were adequate and could be usefully analyzed.

Third, we talked with authorities (including department officials) nationwide to identify experts who could assess the department's use of research evidence knowledgeably and objectively. We looked for experts who specialized in language learning, in bilingual education, and in reviewing or aggregating social science evidence and drawing conclusions from many studies. We selected ten names. In composing the group, we aimed for representation of diverse research backgrounds, sections of the country, and perspectives on bilingual education policy. Eight were knowledgeable about research and evaluation on language learning and schooling for limited-English-proficiency children; two were knowledgeable about social science cumulation and synthesis. In particular we tried to have a group balanced in terms of fairness to the department. Five of the ten were nominated by department officials, were authors of research publications that the department cited in support of its position, or had testified in support of the department; a sixth had been consulted extensively by the department about research findings in education in the preparation of the department's book *What Works*.

We sent the ten literature reviews in advance to each expert. Then we sent them a structured survey instrument containing the department's statements and our questions asking their opinion of the match between the literature and the statements. The structured instrument clustered the department statements into six topics and then asked the experts to give their views of the department's use of research in each topic area by answering forced-choice questions and writing narratives. The experts worked individually; we did not bring them together to discuss or reach consensus. The GAO report to Congress on the project was based on the experts' written responses to our survey. We did not expand upon the experts' view to draw general conclusions or make recommendations about the law. We explicitly acknowledged that other criteria were pertinent to overall policy on bilingual education programs, including feasibility. We sent the experts a draft of the report and gave them an opportunity to clarify and correct our presentation of their views, and we had an outside evaluation expert review all the experts' written survey responses as well as our draft text for one more check on the faithfulness of our representation of the experts' views.

Strengths and Limitations of the Design

This overall methodology did allow us to provide information much more rapidly than if we had had to locate and review individual evaluation and research studies. By using reviews, we were able to place before the experts extensive and representative examinations of several bodies of literature, including evaluations of diverse teaching methods in school programs and more general research studies on learning a second language. By providing the experts a just-published (March 1986) review of the literature by the Congressional Research Service, we helped ensure that they had a current and independent summary of the state of knowledge along with the other reviews. Two other strengths of the approach were the breadth of search for Department of Education statements and the diversity and knowledge-ability of our panel of experts.

Several limitations were inherent in the indirect approach to the complex topic of claims about methods of teaching for nonnative speakers. Using literature reviews meant that the selection of studies and their interpretation were beyond our control and subject to unknown biases. Using a structured instrument to gather the views of the expert panel meant that we had to accept necessarily brief answers and to forgo more extended comments from them, such as we might have gathered in an interview. Most importantly, our key information base is expert opinion and judgment. While we know that the group we selected brought balance, diversity, and remarkable knowledgeability to the work, we cannot guarantee that a different group might not have given different assessments of the match between research knowledge and Department of Education statements.

THE RESULTS: WHAT THE EXPERTS SAID

Five of the six issues posed to the experts concerned the department's interpretations of research.[6] The most central one concerns the native language requirement and the learning of English. Here the department's statements reflected a stress on English competence as the major educational goal for children in the program, and a concern that time spent teaching in a native language may subtract from time that could be used more effectively in teaching English. Thus the department stated that "past federal policy has discouraged the learning of English and may consequently delay development of English language skills." The advocates of transitional bilingual education disagreed, believing that exposing students to too much uncomprehended English frustrates, fatigues, and discourages them in their efforts to learn the new language. The department believed it unproven that transitional bilingual education was better than other approaches: "the mandated method [using] native language was no more effective than alternative methods of special instruction using English."

Considering this first of two objectives in the law (the law includes keeping up in other subjects as a goal of equal importance with English learning for project students), eight of ten experts disagreed with the department officials' statements. Instead they read the research evidence as sufficient to support the law's requirement of some degree of use of native language (to the extent necessary) in the classroom. They believed this either because it helps students learn English in general or because it strengthens literacy in the native language, which eventually transfers to English reading skill. Four reached their conclusions from the program evaluation literature, especially the meta-analysis by Ann Willig, which found students learned more in any type of program using *some* native language compared to students in programs using none. Four other experts cited broader literature as well. Several made the point that since the law included two goals, it was improper to separate them, to emphasize one above another, or to stress evidence on that one alone. Though these experts might agree that immersion or ESL (English as a second language) methods could effectively teach practical, spoken English, they cautioned that the intent of the law was to bring students to the higher competence needed to handle school texts, abstract ideas, and full academic learning. Of the two experts who considered the department correct that the evidence is insufficient, one judged the evidence poor in quality, while the second questioned its objectivity.

In contrast to the goal of having students in Bilingual Education Act programs learn English, the goal of having them make academic progress in other subjects was rarely mentioned in Department of Education statements. In the few instances we found, the department repeated the claim that the evidence was too inconclusive in these areas (such as math learning) to support the legal requirement of native language use. When the experts responded to our request to judge the evidence for themselves, they were more hesitant this time. Six of the ten believed it adequate to support the law. Sound evaluations of learning in other subject areas are more rare, however, so conclusions about the benefits of native language teaching there are relatively tentative. Several made the point that it was hard to believe that limited-English students' standard academic progress could be maintained, especially as subjects get more difficult in higher grades, without some assistance from native language teaching.

The third area in which GAO probed the experts concerned the merits of alternative approaches, including those the department officials had cited as equally effective if not superior to native language instruction. Indeed, administration officials had routinely interpreted other research as suggesting that there are merits to approaches that do *not* involve the use of children's native language by either teachers or students (sometimes called immersion methods). For example, we found them saying that research on such programs "makes an impressive case" and is "consistently positive." Similarly, the department's leaders interpreted the evidence as showing "alternative programs such as ESL [English as a second language], immersion, or simply Chapter-1-style remedial English are more appropriate for many" children limited in English. Thus, in light of what they considered equivalent results for other methods, department officials stated that "there is no justification to be found for a Federal policy that excludes ESL as an alternative to TBE [transitional bilingual education] (and immersion) as an appropriate instructional method." Of course, if a school district's staff wanted to teach students whose English was limited using immersion methods, or the approach of English as a second language, with no use of the students' native language whatsoever, it was free to do so; the federal bilingual education law does not affect the regular operations of any school.[7] Such programs would not qualify for the federal bilingual program, however. Using their reading of the research as support, department officials wanted to end this exclusion.

Seven of ten experts disagreed flatly with the department's view of research evidence that alternative programs are promising. The basis for their position was the limitation of the evidence available on the subject. First, there are relatively few alternative programs, so there are few evaluations. Second, one body of research, on the alternative of teaching by immersion, was not clearly relevant. Six experts noted that the evaluations of Canadian immersion programs may show success but that the experience is not necessarily transferable to the United States because of differences in the students' backgrounds, families, communities, social status, and schools, and in cultural settings in the two countries. Three experts also suggested that some immersion approaches may not in fact be distinct alternatives, since both the Canadian and some U.S. alternative programs cited by the department appear to involve at least some use of native languages. Finally, two experts raised again the issue of the goals of instruction, agreeing that some alternatives, such as an adequate program in English as a second language, might develop students' English proficiency, as the department states. However, they noted that English as a second language is not a program that teaches other subjects needed for academic progress and grade promotion, as called for in the law's second objective. One expert agreed that research suggested nonnative language alternatives are promising, but did not stress findings about any one approach. Instead, this expert saw a general "suggestiveness in the reviews as a set" in the direction of reduced native language use and benefits to increased time spent learning and practicing English.

The fourth issue that GAO identified in department statements about research concerned long-term educational outcomes of various teaching approaches. In advocating approaches other than those involving native languages, department officials cited data on high-school completion, scores on college entrance exams, and post-high-school education plans and attainments, especially for Hispanics, the largest group speaking a minority language in programs under the Bilingual Education Act. Hispanic students show lower rates of achievement on such measures than other student groups in the U.S. population.

For example, a department official stated that "there is no evidence that language minority children have significantly benefited from the current bilingual program" and then cited the general Hispanic dropout rate. A department report to Congress stated that after 17 years of bilingual education programs, "the condition of LEP [Limited English proficiency] students in our nation's schools had not improved significantly," citing relatively low college entrance exam scores and college enrollments along with high dropout rates for Hispanics. If these associations of outcome data with bilingual programs seem somewhat indirect, a department official made the link more directly in a statement that "for those that have been locked into these [bilingual education] programs, sometimes for years on end, and still at the end of those programs are unable to master English, the frustration level must be a contributing factor to the dropout rate and to the other problems we have with the school." A department fact sheet distributed to Congress acknowledged that "many factors contribute to these problems" but noted that "the persistent educational disadvantage of Hispanic students signals that the Federal programs to aid this group are not achieving what was intended."

Though the department statements suggest chiefly negative outcomes, we asked the experts to address the problem of the adequacy of evidence for any type of claim, positive or negative, about the long-term effects of different teaching approaches for students with limited English. One expert believed there were studies showing long-term effects, and that they were positive. However, seven of the ten firmly rejected the idea that there was any support for connecting bilingual education, either positively or negatively, to later school outcomes. Experts pointed to the multiple problems facing poor language-minority children, and the resulting difficulty in tracing their school results to a single cause such as participation in a bilingual program. We also asked the experts if they knew of any evidence that alternative programs (such as those not using native language) would be any more or less effective in the long term than the current range of bilingual programs. None of the experts cited any such evidence.

We concluded that the limitations of the available evidence dictate caution in making any type of association between bilingual education and general school outcomes for Hispanic youths.

The last query for the experts touched on what statisticians would call "interaction effects," or the possibility that some methods may work for some students. Our review of department statements showed that the administration tended to argue for striking the native language requirement from the law because of the lack of proof that such teaching approaches help *all* students. The department officials would agree that native-language teaching can be beneficial in some situations, but did not pursue this line of analysis to ask if research pinpointed the nature of those situations and whether they were common or uncommon in U.S. schools. Rather, the officials concluded that the research was ambiguous and that since there was no generalized effect, no legal requirement was justified. Department officials cited a World Bank summary of worldwide research to support its position that the law should not overemphasize any particular approach, since no one method is best, and should permit complete flexibility for U.S. educators receiving funds under the law. The department quoted the Bank study as saying "there is not one answer to the question of what language to use . . . but several answers, depending on the characteristics of the child, of the parents and the local community."[8]

We asked the experts, therefore, whether they believed research data could supply answers about approaches that work well for subgroups of students. The question we posed was, "Do you regard the evidence as so ambiguous that no firm conclusions can be drawn concerning the effectiveness of diverse approaches to teaching children limited to their proficiency in English in U.S. schools, with special reference to the role of native languages?" If an expert answered that some conclusions were possible, we asked a follow-up question requesting more detail about the subgroups that seem to profit from particular teaching methods.

Six of the ten experts reading the worldwide literature on language learning disagreed that knowledge in this field added up to ambiguity. That is, they believed that targeted conclusions can be drawn from the research, even if generalized ones are less certain. But, unlike the department, the experts thought that the ambiguous results were at the global level, as the Bank study suggested in its comments on contingent answers to questions of what language to use in teaching. Indeed, it may not make sense to try to find one answer in the research for all situations worldwide; however, with respect to the United States, they thought the evidence was strong enough that the pertinent conditions were present, that native language instruction could be recommended at least for large groups. Four of the six experts identified characteristics of students limited in English who, according to the research, should benefit from teaching approaches that rely on the use of native languages to some extent. The evidence is strongest, according to the experts, that native language teaching will benefit students under three conditions: modest student skill level in the native language, parental interest in native-language teaching, and low status for the native language in the community. In several experts' view, these conditions are met for segments of major U.S. groups such as Hispanics, which in turn suggests benefits to native language teaching for the children.

All policy areas are beset with ambiguities; is this one any worse than any other? Should decisions be any more hesitant here than elsewhere? The department stressed the weakness of the knowledge base in this field as part of the argument that there was not enough basis for the legal requirement of native language use. We asked experts to evaluate the soundness of the knowledge base on bilingual education compared to that on other policy areas they were familiar with. The experts were divided here, but the majority (five of nine answering) said it was no better or worse than other fields they knew. (Four said it was worse, and one did not know other fields well.) This suggests no greater degree of caution in this than in any other field of policy making. When the department's letter commenting on our draft report (discussed below) repeated once again the argument about the error of making policy based on weak research findings on native language programs, we noted in the final report text that the department appeared to have a double standard in judging research. That is, department officials seldom gave equal attention to warning flags about the data on alternative approaches, many of which were raised by the experts we consulted. Problems include the small number of studies on alternatives, the applicability of evidence from the Canadian experiments, done under very different conditions from those in the United States, and the degree of true distinctiveness within "immersion" alternatives, since program descriptions in some of the research reports show that they used native language to some extent.

Several of the experts also reminded us that specific operational problems in creating native language school programs, such as having too few students to make up a native language classroom at a given grade level and the absence of native language teachers or materials, do not invalidate the basic conclusions that can be drawn from the research about the benefits of instructing in native languages when it is appropriate to do so.

THE RESPONSE OF THE DEPARTMENT OF EDUCATION

GAO offered the department the opportunity to comment on a draft of these results. The full text of the comments is included in GAO's report to Congress, as well as a response to each one. The department questioned the report on six different grounds, including our authority to conduct such a review; our conformance with applicable professional standards, especially concerning the qualifications and independence of our evaluators or the experts; our objectives; our methods; our conclusions; and the way we handled the report. The comments were strongly negative in tone as well as substance, calling the report "inept," "not a work of serious or conscientious analysis," and suggesting that it be "radically revised so as to honor the usual canons of scholarship, program evaluation and scientific research." We made a few small changes in the text to reduce the chance of misinterpretation of GAO's work and findings, but in general found no major error requiring correction based on the department's comments on the six topics.

We knew from the time we adopted the design involving selected experts and reviews that the objectivity of each would be open to challenge. As expected, the detailed department comments, after the rhetorical assault of the cover letter, opened with the claim that "the selection of both the experts and the 'studies' given to them for review raises serious doubts as to their objectivity, completeness, and balance." The basis for the department officials' claim concerning the experts was that specific past activities of some members of the group cast doubt on their objectivity. For example, the comment noted that several of the experts had taken stands in opposition to the department and that two were authors or coauthors of items in the readings we provided and one was coauthor of a study that department officials had publicly criticized.

In response, we noted that five members of the group of experts had been cited in department statements in support of its policy positions, one of these had testified in favor of the department's policies, and a sixth is a close consultant to the department on educational research. By the department's logic, if past involvement signifies bias, 60 percent of the experts could have been expected in advance to favor the department's reading of research evidence in bilingual education. However, we did not regard those involvements as disabling. In fact, in a field of public policy with significant controversy during almost two decades (the Bilingual Education Act was first passed in 1968), it was not surprising that experts have at times been advocates. We acknowledged this inevitability and chose a balanced group of individuals with different degrees of involvement in policy debates and with varying substantive views, after seeking nominations from many sources, including the department. We added several experts who had not taken any advocacy role that we knew of. Most importantly, we responded that the prior involvement of experts in policy discussions should not preclude the use of their views, provided that readers are made aware of who the individuals are. We fully disclosed the experts' names and affiliations, as we told them we would do. We did not believe the specific authorship issues the department raised had any effect on the experts' responses to our survey, nor did the department offer any *evidence* of any effect, other than its speculations.

Concerning another major charge in the department's comments about GAO "inaccuracy"—that we had failed to represent their views—we believed we accurately characterized the department in both its policy proposal to abolish the native language requirement, and, most important to our requestor, its use of research evidence to support that position. The department's statements about research in its comments on our report were, in fact, highly consistent with the earlier statements we examined. (In its comments the department reiterated that the research is inconclusive; that native language cannot be generally said to be useful in teaching, although it may be in some cases; and that there is no research base for requiring "only this among the many possible approaches.") All were included in our presentation to the experts, and all were judged by most of the experts we consulted to be inaccurate notions about the state of research knowledge.

CONGRESSIONAL ACTION AND THE USE OF THE REPORT

To obtain views for use in completing the committee's reauthorization, Representative Hawkins chaired a hearing on bilingual education in March 1987, at which GAO testified on its work, along with officials of the department, several local school districts, and a state agency.[9] The first question after the witness statements was to the GAO representative, whether there had been any interference from the committee to direct the study or impair its objectivity. The GAO official said there had been none. The chairman's next question was to the department's representative about the research basis for the Secretary's 1985 claims, which was answered with incomplete citations of various research centers and publications and the summary statement that "there is great debate and we could sit here and duel research back and forth." One member provided dissenting letters from two members of GAO's group of experts, whose views had already been communicated in letters appended to the department's comments on the draft. The letters again put forth the writers' views of the "questionable scientific validity" of the GAO method and "[took] issue with GAO's presentation of the panel survey as representing a consensus among the experts" in light of the writer's count of small margins of agreement on the answers. However, the letters were not made available and were not discussed in the hearing.

The issue addressed in the GAO work, of the effectiveness of native language instruction, was eclipsed by the pragmatic issue of the range of variation (including ESL and immersion) in current school practice and whether greater "flexibility" in the law (i.e., more allowance for nonbilingual approaches) was desired. The possibility of administration support for expanding the overall funds for helping limited-English children, if the share for nonbilingual approaches were raised from the current 4 percent, drew attention. Both the superintendent of schools for Los Angeles County and the head of New York's state school agency spoke of the importance of continued federal emphasis on native language methods. The Californian recalled the earlier decades as he started his career when Spanish-speakers were denigrated, forbidden to speak their tongue in class or the playground, and offered only an ESL program—with overall terrible effect. He warned that he was troubled by the suggestion, repeated now as in earlier years, that ESL could be adequate, and troubled by "the quiet little whispers that really suggest that 'greater flexibility' is a way to avoid becoming involved, a way to avoid becoming committed . . . and a way to work to avoid the problems inherent in establishing a special program for non-English-speaking students."[10]

However, the question was not *whether* the law should permit *some* nonnative language programs to be funded under the act; it already did so (through the 4 percent of the appropriation set aside for special alternative programs), and would continue to do so. Neither such strong personal views as those of the Los Angeles school chief, nor the interpretations of research evidence of effectiveness supplied by the expert group GAO assembled, answered the more pressing question of the committee—in effect, how much flexibility should there be? Perhaps not total flexibility, as the department advocated, but more than the present amount, and to what extent?

Senate views were signaled in the introduction by Senators Clairborne Pell (Democratic chair of the education subcommittee) and Dan Quayle (Republican) of a jointly sponsored bill setting aside 25 percent of the funds for alternatives. Members of the House committee still struggling with their own decisions feared the larger education reauthorization bill would be endangered on the floor if the committee did not present a united front and an acceptable compromise on bilingual education flexibility, and feared as well that the Senate might prevail in a conference if the House proposal was far apart from the Senate's 25 percent.

Under these practical pressures, the effectiveness argument was swept aside and a compromise was crafted that lifted the 4 percent cap on nonnative language programs. The House bill proposed to maintain existing transitional bilingual education programs at their current funded level, but if additional funds were appropriated, after inflation increases for the existing projects, no more than 25 percent of the new funds could go to native-language projects. The rest would be available for alternatives, not necessarily involving native language. The chairman seemed to accept the compromise reluctantly, but in light of the small general support for bilingual education saw it as the "only salvation" of the program and spoke of his hopes for exchanging this greater flexibility for administration support of additional funds for the overall program. He was quoted in *Education Week* saying "I think we have to do away with some emotionalism and be pragmatic" in order to keep the bilingual program "from being stricken altogether." A senior member of the committee, William Ford, Democrat of Michigan, said the compromise was dictated by "political exigencies" and should not be interpreted as proving the merits of "the Secretary's experiment with immersion" teaching methods; "I've seen nothing" to prove that such methods work better than TBE, said Mr. Ford, according to press reports.

But perhaps no evidence would have been useful. A major architect of the compromise, Dale Kildee, Democrat of Michigan, told *Education Week* at the end of the process, "In substance, I certainly believe that transitional bilingual education is a very effective method, but it's not understood [by members of Congress]." In effect, he seemed to be saying, people have made up their minds. He continued, "The anti-bilingual smear job is growing. The attacks are real in both party caucuses. It's not a Democrat-Republican issue . . . I can count votes. I am convinced that this compromise and strategy best serve bilingual education."[11]

The committee's report on their overall bill did not mention GAO's work in the discussion of bilingual education, nor did it raise the issue of effectiveness of various teaching approaches, and several members attached individual statements to the report that went unchallenged though they repeated claims similar to those of department officials that research had failed to demonstrate the superior effectiveness of transitional bilingual education compared to alternatives. The GAO report was cited by one member in floor debate, but generally the whole topic of bilingual education was kept discretely out of view. One Hispanic member from California said that "politeness is the art of choosing among your thoughts" and limited himself to saying that the compromise was "sending exactly the wrong messages" and put dollars into efforts that "show the least evidence of working when there is not enough money for programs that have proven they work well." He acknowledged the "short term political logic" of the proposed compromise.[12] As the full House voted 401–1 for the omnibus education reauthorization bill in May 1987, it certainly seemed that the compromise may have assisted such a smooth passage to approval.

GAO provided its report to a wide range of interested individuals, as usual, and indeed it became one of the most often requested items among the 767 reports GAO issued in 1987. It was frequently cited in press and academic publications in the months after its release in March 1987. As the Senate completed its action on bilingual education, also as part of a larger reauthorization bill, in fall 1987, we provided copies to staff and members concerned with the subject. As signaled by the earlier proposal, the Senate had a long interest in expanding non-native-language funding, and the Senate report explicitly disavowed interest in exploring the effectiveness question.

"This bill," said the report, "does not make a statement as to which instructional approach is better, nor do the Committee Members wish to debate the merits of each type of language instruction."[13] The committee spoke of the need for flexibility, but based it directly on "the needs of schools and school districts that have a multitude of languages represented in their student bodies, but are faced with a lack of bilingual teachers in any but the most common languages." The bill did reaffirm, as had the House bill, the dual goals of English proficiency and academic achievement in other subjects.

But the senators were impressed with practical difficulties of achieving these goals in some settings for limited-English students. Accordingly, the Senate bill permitted the Secretary to reserve up to 25 percent of funds under part A of the act for alternative programs. Furthermore, hesitation about the benefits of native language teaching may have motivated another change in the law, for the first time setting a limit (in most cases to be three years) on the time a student could spend in any federally sponsored bilingual education program.

The committee proposal passed the Senate, with only modest comment in floor debate, in December 1987. Senators repeated such general points as the practical need for greater flexibility and the continued general support for native language instruction in many places where it was practical. Only Senator Edward Kennedy, Democrat of Massachusetts, addressed the subject at length.[14] He reviewed the history of the program and the administration attacks on its effectiveness. He rebutted those with statements of the good outcomes of a Massachusetts state-mandated program. But he, too, turned quickly to the practicality argument and stated that he had data (provided by a separate GAO survey, as it happened) that 25 percent of eligible students were found in districts where "it would be difficult or impossible to implement dual-language programs."[15] The 25 percent compromise figure "recognizes this fact . . ." and "helps insure that all eligible students and their schools have fair access to . . . support" from the bilingual program's funds. He hoped, he said finally, that "by passing this legislation we can lay to rest the confusion and controversy associated with bilingual education and refocus our thinking about language learning in a positive direction." The overall Senate education bill passed December 1, 1987, by a margin as enthusiastic as that in the House, 97–1.

When House and Senate conferees completed the final legislative step of reconciling their differences in the spring of 1988, the Senate plan for expanding alternative program funding from 4 percent to 25 percent prevailed.[16] According to the *Education Week* account of the negotiations, "bilingual education advocates urged House conferees to accept the Senate plan. In return, Senate staff members agreed to accept other House provisions that the advocates favor, such as language limiting the Education Department's ability to alter the program through regulations" such as by changing the definition of eligible students or programs.[17] Thus the House conceded defeat in its attempt to limit funds for alternative programs to only a fraction of any new appropriations. Once again, as in the committee and floor situations, observers believed that a fight, based on effectiveness or any other grounds, for a strong priority for native language instruction was doomed to failure. Said one long-time bilingual education lobbyist, quoted in the same *Education Week* story, the cost of such insistence in the conference could well have been "to give up the future of the bilingual program."[18] With the conference agreement Congress thus finished reauthorizing the program, including the Bilingual Education Act as Title VII of the Augustus F. Hawkins/Robert T. Stafford School Improvement Amendments of 1988, which became law with the President's signature on April 28, 1988.[19]

CONCLUSION

What was the contribution of GAO's work on bilingual education? On one hand, as the decision criterion shifted from the difficult and highly charged one of bilingual education effectiveness, which GAO's report addressed head-on with the experts' views, to the more neutral one of program feasibility, which the report did not address, the report itself faded from view. The larger questions surrounding minority languages apparently remain so divisive that advocates, with the most stake in the evidence of effectiveness, feared defeat in any direct conflicts and pulled back from confrontations and direct arguments. The criteria of debate are set by what most people are willing to talk about, and in the 1987–88 discussion of bilingual education, it appeared that many participants were not eager to "duel research" (as the department's bilingual education head called it) to reach conclusions about what works. The Senate even wrote explicitly in its report that it did not want to enter that debate.

On the other hand, the GAO report signaled that further bald claims of failure for bilingual education wouldn't be credible. The Secretary of Education made no further speeches on bilingual education that we are aware of, so the most patently overstated readings of research were no longer circulated so forcefully. And although advocates may have been disheartened at the small attention paid to the research and the topic of effectiveness, it is possible that in the prevailing political climate, without the experts' probing critique of the department officials' reading of the research evidence, much more sweeping changes in the Bilingual Education Act would have passed, such as the department's initial proposal to drop entirely from the program any requirement of native language use.

Most important, we believe as a result of the GAO report that those who want to adduce a body of research in support of policy positions in the area of first and second language teaching are on stronger notice to do so in a sound manner. Research can rarely provide, and probably should never be considered, a definitive source of policy; thus, it would not be reasonable to judge the impact of GAO's work by whether the policy outcome matched the experts' sense of what the evidence said. But research can be used more or less well, and as the debate opened in 1985, the game of citation was being played rather fast and loose. Now, as a result of the GAO work, Congress has an up-to-date set of views provided by the comprehensive work of the expert panel, so that ad hoc citations of "what the research says" by advocates simply will not be persuasive in themselves. So that research can play its future part as well as possible, *along with* budget concerns, general political wisdom, and the other needed ingredients in decisions, it may thus have been highly useful over the longer term to put before the Congress a new and soundly designed look at the research evidence on bilingual education.

NOTES

1. Eleanor Chelimsky is Assistant Comptroller General for Program Evaluation and Methodology, in the U.S. General Accounting Office (GAO). Frederick Mulhauser is a senior analyst in the same division, and directed the project described in this article. The views expressed in this chapter are the authors' own and should not be interpreted to reflect either the policies or the opinions of the U.S. General Accounting Office.

2. The speech is published as chapter 19 of William Bennett, *Our Children and Our Country.* New York: Simon & Schuster, 1988.

3. For a summary of the policy debate in recent years, see the special report in *Education Week,* April 1, 1987 (pp. 19–50), by James Crawford, "Bilingual Education: Language, Learning, and Politics." A more extensive treatment can be found in Kenji Hakuta, *Mirror of Language: The Debate on Bilingualism.* (New York: Basic Books, 1986). See also J. Crawford, *Bilingual Education: History, Politics, Theory, and Practice.* Trenton, N.J.: Crane Publishing Co., 1989.

4. A summary of the method can be found in U.S. General Accounting Office, *The Evaluation Synthesis,* Institute for Program Evaluation, Methods Paper 1. Washington, D.C.: April 1983.

5. The full report of the study presented in this chapter is in U.S. General Accounting Office, *Bilingual Education: A New Look at the Research Evidence,* GAO/PEMD-87-12BR. Washington, D.C.: March 1987. Requests for copies of GAO reports should be sent to Box 6015, Gaithersburg, MD 20877, telephone 202-275-6241.

6. The sixth concerned a methodological point about the usefulness of broad program labels such as "the transitional bilingual education method" in discussing program success or failure with aggregated evidence from programs that may have varied substantially. The experts' views were mixed on the severity of this problem, but there was no consensus discrediting

the department's use, and the common use by others as well, of terms and program labels in statements about the effectiveness of one "approach" compared to another.

7. Regular school programs for limited-English students are covered by a 1974 Supreme Court decision, *Lau v. Nichols*, which has been generally interpreted as requiring *some* sort of special program for the group. In a case concerning Chinese children in the San Francisco schools, the Court agreed that the regular school program afforded the non-English-speaking minority fewer benefits than the English-speaking majority, since regular instruction was in English and there were no special programs to meet their specific linguistic needs. The Court found this an impermissible discrimination under Title VI of the Civil Rights Act of 1964. The Court did not, however, direct any particular remedy (though it mentioned native language teaching among other possibilities), requiring only that "the Board of Education be directed to apply its expertise to the problem and rectify the situation." San Francisco, in settling the case through a consent decree, did establish bilingual programs for Chinese, Filipino, and Spanish-speaking children. The significance of the case, thus, is that it established that a school district is at risk if it does *nothing* about the special needs of non-English-speaking students; precisely what is to be done, however, remains the district's choice.

8. The Bank review of literature, authored by Nadine Dutcher, was one of the ten provided the experts.

9. See *Reauthorization of Expiring Federal Elementary and Secondary Education Programs: Bilingual Education*, vol. 4. Hearing before the Subcommittee on Elementary, Secondary, and Vocational Education, 100th Congress, 1st Session, on H.R. 5, H.R. 1755, and H.R. 1448. March 24, 1987. Serial no. 100–5.

10. *Ibid.*, p. 32.

11. The press accounts quoted above are found in *Education Daily*, April 23, 1987, pp. 3–4, and *Education Week*, April 29, 1987, p. 19.

12. *Congressional Record*, May 20, 1987, p. H 3782.

13. This and the quotes that follow are from *Report to Accompany S 373, the Robert T. Stafford Elementary and Secondary Education Improvement Act of 1987*, 100th Congress, 1st Session, Senate Report 100–222, p. 79.

14. *Congressional Record*, December 1, 1987, p. S 16785.

15. See U.S. General Accounting Office, *Bilingual Education: Information on Limited English Proficient Students*, GAO/HRD–87–85BR. Washington, D.C.: April 1987.

16. *Elementary and Secondary Education: Conference Report to Accompany H.R. 5*, 100th Congress, 2d Session, House Report 100–567, pp. 365–74.

17. "Conferees Likely to Loosen Rules in Bilingual Law," *Education Week*, March 16, 1988, p. 16.

18. Looking far ahead, some observers took comfort from the fact that the law said only that, from part A funds, the Secretary "*may* reserve not to exceed 25 percent for special alternative" programs; that is, the language is permissive but not mandatory. In this view, a future secretary, more convinced perhaps by evidence of native language teaching effectiveness or implementation feasibility, could decline to reserve the entire 25 percent for non-native-language projects.

19. Public Law 100–297.

REFERENCES

The ten items in this reference list are the ten reviews of literature on the effectiveness of various teaching approaches for children speaking minority languages that GAO sent its panel of experts in June 1986.

A. *The department's review of research.*

Baker, K., and de Kanter, A. 1983. Federal policy and the effectiveness of bilingual education. In *Bilingual Education: A Reappraisal of Federal Policy,* ed. K. Baker and A. de Kanter. Lexington, Mass.: D.C. Heath Co. (A shorter, though very similar, version of the authors' original, unpublished 1981 manuscript.)

B. *Response to the department's review.*

Yates, J., et al. 1982. Baker de Kanter review: Inappropriate conclusions on the effectiveness of bilingual education. Unpublished paper, University of Texas, Austin, Tex.

C. *Reviews on immersion teaching methods.*

Gersten, R., and Woodward, J. September 1985. A case for Structured Immersion. *Educational Leadership* 43(1):75–79.

Hernandez-Chavez, E. 1984. The inadequacy of English immersion education as an educational approach for language minority students in the United States. In *Studies in immersion education.* Sacramento, Calif.: California State Department of Education.

D. *General reviews.*

Dutcher, N. 1982. The use of first and second languages in primary education: Selected case studies. Staff working paper no. 504. Washington, D.C.: The World Bank.

Fillmore, L.W., and Valadez, C. 1986. Teaching bilingual learners. *Handbook of research on teaching,* 3d ed. Ed. M. C. Wittrock. New York: Macmillan.

Holland, R. March 1986. Bilingual education: Recent evaluations of local school district programs and related research on second language learning. Report 86–611 EPW. Washington, D.C.: Congressional Research Service of the Library of Congress.

McLaughlin, B. 1985. Evaluations. In *Second language acquisition in childhood,* 2d ed., vol. 2. Hillsdale, N.J.: Lawrence Erlbaum Associates.

Paulston, C. B. 1978. Bilingual/bicultural education. In *Review of research in education 6,* ed. L. S. Shulman. Itasca, Ill., and Washington, D.C.: F. E. Peacock Publishers and American Educational Research Association.

Willig, A. 1985. A meta-analysis of selected studies on the effectiveness of bilingual education. *Review of Educational Research* 55(3):269–317.

DO BILINGUAL EDUCATION POLICIES
MEET THEIR GOALS?

Armando L. Trujillo

More than 20 years have passed since the enactment of the Bilingual Education Act of 1968. During this period, bilingual education policy and the implementation and design of programs have undergone marked changes. Despite the changing character of bilingual education, the basic assumption and overall goals of this innovative program in the United States have remained virtually intact. According to Paulston, "the major basic assumption which underlies the United States Title VII programs is that of 'equal opportunity' and the belief that bilingual education helps equalize such shortcomings of opportunity" (Paulston, 1978, p. 411).[1] Based on this assumption and others (see note 1), Paulston emphasizes that the perceived long-range goals of bilingual education programs are those of harmonious integration by either economically incorporating or culturally assimilating the ethnolinguistic group into the larger society through the process of equalizing opportunity.

In spite of the fact that the underlying assumption and long-range goals have remained the mainstay of bilingual education policy, little if any research has been done that investigates whether equal educational opportunity as manifested through bilingual education programs really leads to improved economic and social mobility. Most research in bilingual education, as Paulston (1978) has emphasized has been predominantly concerned with pedagogical efficiency concerning language of instruction—using the first language (L1) or the second language (L2) for instruction—and

269

with individual academic achievement outcomes in subject matter knowledge, e.g., science and math, without adequately accounting for how academic achievement or lack of achievement are related to its underlying assumption and long-range goals. To accomplish such a task would require that more effort be placed on relating research on classroom practices and outcomes to the broader societal factors that help to shape those outcomes. It is imperative, therefore, to situate bilingual education within the broader social context of the political economy in order to be better able to relate research on bilingual education policy and practice to the program's assumptions and long-range goals.

Situating bilingual education within a political economy framework also necessitates taking a historical look at the genesis, implementation, and evaluation of bilingual education as an educational reform movement. In order to gain a better understanding of this historical progression, this paper will also seek to situate the corpus of bilingual education within one of the competing traditions of educational research. Pursuing this line of analysis will help us understand the major trends both in research and policy that have taken place in bilingual education during its 21-year history. Paulston (1978, 1980) has provided a useful typology for analyzing bilingual education programs and research. She has made a distinction between studies and programs utilizing structural-functional theory and those using conflict theory. Briefly, she argues that bilingual education programs in the United States have been predominantly influenced and guided by structural-functional theory. As such, programs are predominantly concerned with efficient functioning and improving the technical efficiency of programs that will in turn solve problems of scholastic achievement. In other words, a structural-functional perspective would hold that if bilingual education programs were able to teach English skills efficiently, students' academic achievement would improve.

On the other hand, bilingual education reforms that have aspects of conflict theory define the problem very differently from the structural-functional perspective. According to Paulston, the conflict perspective defines the problem not as "unequal opportunity per se, but rather one of structured inequity of 'persistence of poverty, intractability of inequality of incomes and inequality of economic and social opportunity' " (Paulston, 1978, p. 416). Solutions to educational problems within the program are not sought in terms of technocratic efficiency within the classroom, but rather are seen as occurring outside the program or classroom. Paulston stresses that very few empirical studies have focused upon particular social parameters or explored the relevance of bilingual education across schools and/or across communities, primarily because the majority of programs and research in bilingual education has been guided by structural-functional theory.

Following the typology that Paulston (1978, 1980) has provided for analyzing bilingual education programs and research and relating this to the educational research outside of the arena of bilingual education, I argue that bilingual education in general can be characterized as a liberal-progressive school reform.[2] In brief, this tradition holds the premise that one of the major roles of schooling, in an advanced industrialized country such as the United States, is that of an equalizing process whereby disadvantaged classes and disenfranchised groups, among them ethnolinguistic minorities, are afforded the opportunity for competing with the advantaged classes.

A growing body of literature within the critical theory paradigm shows that schooling and recent experiments in educational reform have not produced equality but rather have served to perpetuate inequality (Apple, 1979l, 1982; Apple & Weiss, 1983; Carnoy, 1982; Giroux, 1983; Willis, 1981a). This critical research tradition faults the liberal-progressive schooling model for its inability to address the issue of the continued reproduction of cultural and economic inequality because it fails to place schooling reform within the broader political and economic context in which it is situated.

Having traced out, in simplistic terms, the competing research traditions, which one characterizes the corpus of bilingual education? Scholars and practitioners may argue that given the historical conditions that led to the legislative mandate for bilingual education, it most certainly must represent a critique to liberal-progressive schooling. It is true that the movement that led to the legislative action mandating bilingual education was critical of the shortcomings of public schooling for ethnolinguistic minority students at the time. However, the calls for change (and this will become more apparent in a later section of this paper) were largely made from within the structural-functional paradigm.

Therefore, despite the political struggle by ethnolinguistic groups that led to the genesis of bilingual education legislation in 1968 and the design and implementation of a few programs that fell under the rubric of maintenance bilingual bicultural programs, there is substantial evidence to show that bilingual education has evolved into a transitional program that emphasizes technical efficiency in the teaching and learning of English. Based on this development and the evidence that Paulston (1978, 1980) has provided, it is reasonable to situate bilingual education within the liberal-progressive camp. Having linked bilingual education to the liberal-progressive tradition, a seminal question to ask of bilingual educators and researchers is, What role does bilingual education, as a recent school reform, play in the continued reproduction of cultural and economic inequality?

The research literature in bilingual education has virtually ignored this question. Yet such a fundamental question needs to be addressed if we are to seriously analyze the relationship between bilingual schooling, "equal opportunity," "cultural diversity," and the goal of improved economic and social mobility. First I will discuss the historical relationship between the liberal-progressive schooling tradition and bilingual education, look at the bilingual education policy shift since 1974, and analyze the limits of the liberal-progressive schooling model. I will then explore the mechanisms through which schooling functions to reproduce unequal class relations characteristic of stratified class structure in the United States. I identify the major premises and most important concepts of the different social and cultural reproduction theories. I also posit that a comprehensive social/cultural/resistance approach provides the best framework for assessing the role bilingual education plays in the reproduction of class inequality among ethnolinguistic minorities at various levels of society. Finally, I apply the most important concepts identified earlier in a brief analysis of bilingual education policy and some aspects of program implementation and practice. An appeal is made to educators and researchers to reanalyze past research in light of this framework, in addition to using it in interpreting future research in this area.

LIBERAL-PROGRESSIVE SCHOOLING AND BILINGUAL EDUCATION

Public education has a long history, especially under the impetus of compulsory tuition-free schooling since the late nineteenth century, in engendering the belief that disadvantaged students from the lower social classes can gain greater opportunity through education in achieving social mobility and full participation in the society's political and economic institutions (Spring, 1982; Tyack, Lowe and Hanset, 1984; Bowles & Gintis, 1976; Willis, 1981a). The ideology of equality through education continues to be a major premise of public education in the United States. This is particularly evident in the numerous educational reforms ushered in during the sixties and seventies by the federal government, which financed them.

These programs included compensatory education, school integration, free-school movement, open classrooms, project Headstart, Title I, the hiring of additional aides and remedial personnel, and bilingual education (Bowles & Gintis, 1976; Cummins, 1986). In general, the aim of these programs, as a number of researchers have emphasized (Tyack, Lowe & Hanset, 1984; Spring, 1982; Bowles & Gintis, 1976; Salomone, 1982; Willis, 1981a; Paulston, 1978), was to enhance the abilities and skills of the "disadvantaged" members of the poor, subordinate classes so that they could come up to par with members of the dominant advantaged classes. Their emphasis has been on increasing abilities and skills, especially in a rapidly expanding economy such as that of the United States, in which advancement within the industrial order is increasingly based upon credentials.

One must keep in mind, however, that many of these programs were enacted in part in response to the social and political upheaval of the sixties and seventies. The Civil Rights struggles among Blacks, Chicanos, and other subordinate minorities vividly illustrate this. At the national level, the federal government responded to the growing demands of the Civil Rights movement by enacting new legislation directed at eliminating discrimination in employment and within public establishments. Within the sphere of education, new legislation and financial support created new educational programs.

Federal aid to education, as Piven and Cloward (1977) have noted, was pegged in the early sixties under the Kennedy Administration as a measure aimed at addressing Civil Rights demands. Salomone (1982) reports that Mexican Americans and other Hispanic groups began, during the decade, to press for a share of the federal aid to education. Given the mounting evidence of low achievement scores, high dropout rates, and poor self-image as reflected in the school performances of racial minority and non-English dominant students, their demands were met with appropriate positive responses by the federal government.

Federal government policies that took form during the sixties and seventies were directed at combating poverty and improving the number of programs in education for the disenfranchised and politically powerless groups. This interest in education follows the progressive line of thought, that is, education is the great equalizer in a society based on an unequal social structure. It is in this ambiance of governmental progressive policy making that we see the genesis of bilingual education specifically aimed at meeting the needs of non-English dominant students.

The Bilingual Education Act of 1968 (Title VII) arose as an amendment to the Elementary and Secondary Education Act (ESEA Title I) of 1965. Salomone reports that the Bilingual Education Act specified criteria aimed at linguistically different and low-income groups: specifically, "the intended beneficiaries of the Act were children of limited English-speaking ability (LESA) between the ages of three and eighteen whose families fell within the Title I poverty guidelines" (Salomone, 1982, p. 32). In short, the Bilingual Education Act illustrates the role the federal government took in assuring equal educational opportunity for linguistically different children and the recognition it gave their native language and culture as legitimate resources for instruction within the classroom (Matute-Bianchi, 1979). While there have been a number of amendments to the original bilingual education law, which reflects the changing national policy with regards to the education of linguistically and culturally different minorities, the overall aim of these progressive educational reforms has been to improve educational opportunity for minority students.

Bilingual Education Policy Shift. Considering the climate in which the enactment of bilingual education took place, researchers have been right on track in arguing that the struggle for bilingual education is a political struggle for educational resources, employment opportunities, and cultural identity (*Bilingual-Bicultural Education,* 1977; Mackey & Ornstein, 1977).

Armed with the mounting evidence that large numbers of racial minority students and non-English-speaking children were experiencing school failure, Chicano, Puerto Rican, Chinese, Native American, and other groups demanded an appropriate response from the government. In response to these demands, the federal government passed the Bilingual Education Act of 1968. Schneider (1976), in her study, states that this new legislation was underlined by arguments of equal opportunity. Matute-Bianchi, as mentioned above, stresses the benevolent role of the federal government in its strategy to assure equal educational opportunity for linguistically different children by recognizing their native language and culture as legitimate resources for instruction within the classroom.

The initial years of bilingual education implementation and design reflect this policy. According to Padilla, the first five years of program implementation reflect a search for equal educational opportunity through experimentation and innovation, i.e., "bilingual programs under the original act could encompass any conceivable combination of time allocation to the two languages of instruction . . ." (Padilla, 1984, p. 100). However, Padilla also stresses that in spite of the fact that Title VII provided wide latitude for experimentation and innovation, the early implementation of bilingual education programs at the local level tended to be of a conservative nature, with emphasis on learning English and assimilating students into the mainstream of U.S. culture.

Nonetheless, the wide latitude in policy was evident in that there were a few programs, especially those implemented by members of the ethnic groups involved, as Paulston (1978) has noted, who referred to these programs as bilingual/bicultural and sought the objective of stable bilingualism with maintenance of the home culture as well as the home language (see Smith & Foley, 1978; Foley & White, 1977; *Bilingual-Bicultural Education*, 1977, pp. 282–85). This wide latitude in policy illustrates the struggle for bilingual education, educational resources, employment opportunities, and cultural identity. Yet, questions concerning the relationship of how the federal government and individual school districts dealt with issues of power, class conflict, and social control has not been adequately covered in bilingual education research. From a theoretical perspective, as pointed out above, this lack of treatment is primarily due to the inadequacy of the structural-functional model. That is, issues of power, class conflict, and social control remain untested because they are concerns that fall outside the paradigm.

Within the arena of politics, however, these issues of power and social control are illustrative of the 1974 amendments to the Bilingual Education Act. Padilla (1984) stresses that the 1974 amendments reflect a fundamental shift in policy away from equal opportunity efforts aimed at effectively trying to restructure schooling (through innovative pedagogy and experimentation) to one emphasizing the onus of change on the individual (primarily done through oral English language assessment). In short, within a period of five years, the appropriate response by the federal government to the demands by Mexican Americans and other Hispanic groups had undergone a fundamental shift, such that the language and culture of the ethnolinguistic groups had lost ground as legitimate resources for instruction.

While legislation and financial support were strengthened in the 1974 amendments the struggle over the social control of bilingual education program design and implementation shifted. Padilla (1984) notes that this was reflected in the new definition of bilingual education, in that emphasis was placed on giving instruction in English and allowing the use of the native language only to the extent that it would facilitate the effective progress of the student through the educational system. Moreover, the definition expressly prohibited teaching a foreign language to English-speaking children, as had been the case under the original act. This fundamental shift in power and social control will be clarified further when we discuss cultural reproduction in a later section of this paper. For now, it is sufficient to note that the new amendment emphasized the use of English and the transitional nature of non-English language instruction. Thus, the benevolent role of the federal government in assuring equal educational opportunity for linguistically different children by recognizing their native language and culture as legitimate resources for instruction was substantially weakened.

The more politically conscious ethnolinguistic groups, who had struggled and obtained some degree of political control of key decision-making bodies such as city councils and school boards, were better equipped to continue the struggle for bilingual, bicultural education maintenance programs (see Smith & Foley, 1978; Smith, 1978; Trujillo, 1978). However, their struggles were made more Herculean with the passage of the 1974 and 1978 amendments to the Bilingual Education Act. Whereas the federal policy established in 1974 did not fundamentally change in 1978, Padilla stresses that the fact of the amendments "reflects the restrictions imposed by opponents of bilingual education to limit in every way possible the number of and types of students who can be served and the length of time that they can receive bilingual instruction" (Padilla, 1984, p. 107). Padilla goes on to say that by shifting the focus from equity through innovative programs to equity by teaching English, opponents of bilingual education had narrowed the focus to issues of equity for the individual student. If one analyzes this policy shift from a structural-functional perspective, the focus is away from systemic change to one of individual change. This is further seen in the push for pedagogical efficiency concerning language of instruction and with individual academic achievement outcomes in subject-matter knowledge.

The shift in policy certainly illustrates how bilingual education as a whole lacks linkages to the broader social, economic, and political issues affecting the schooling of ethnolinguistic groups in the United States. Furthermore, by focusing on individual achievement outcomes, the success of bilingual education programs has been effectively separated from the broader issues espoused in the underlying assumption and goals of bilingual education legislation. This shift also illustrates how at the national level the federal government neutralized the limited power base and control that ethnolinguistic groups may have had in designing and implementing their bilingual programs. In other words, certain ethnolinguistic communities had effectively struggled for bilingual education as an educational resource, with its related employment opportunities, and for cultural identity inherent in maintenance programs, yet the policy shift at the national level effectively weakened their gains.

An inherent contradiction is apparent in the policy shift and the underlying philosophy of bilingual education. On the one hand, there are the underlying assumptions of equal opportunity and cultural diversity, and on the other, there is the goal of improved educational and social mobility. Yet evaluation studies of bilingual education have been overly focused on individual outcomes. In order to better understand the lack of linkages between bilingual education and the broader social, economic, and political issues affecting the schooling of ethnolinguistic minority groups in the United States, the limitations of the liberal-progressive schooling model and the predominant use of structural-functional theory in evaluation studies of bilingual education need to be explored.

Limitations of the Liberal-Progressive Model. Since the mid-seventies, research evidence has been accumulating that brings into question the effectiveness of liberal-progressive schooling reforms (see Bowles & Gintis, 1976; Jencks et al., 1972; Willis, 1981a). Criticism has come from the conservative side of the political spectrum as well as from the left. What has been given particular emphasis is the lack of success that the War on Poverty programs and compensatory education have had in eliminating poverty and discrimination in the United States. A number of national studies have been conducted that pinpoint the limitations of compensatory education. The Rand Corporation study of large national compensatory educational programs concluded that "... virtually without exception ... compensatory educational programs have shown no beneficial results on the average" (Bowles & Gintis, 1976). The Coleman Report of the Office of Educational Opportunity collected statistical information in support of a policy of financial redistribution that would correct educational inequality; however, the evidence "... pointed to the virtual irrelevance of educational resources of quality as a determinant of educational outcomes" (Bowles & Gintis, 1976). In the early seventies, Jencks et al. (1972) published their study, *Inequality,* which reported that even if a school system were made more egalitarian it would have little effect in creating a more equal distribution of income or opportunity.

Bowles and Gintis note that the barrage of statistical studies in the late sixties and early seventies led to a conservative counterattack. This counterattack is typified by the "blame-the-victim" thesis. According to this thesis, poor people are poor because of their intellectual incompetence; their kids and, by extension, the kids of ethnolinguistic minorities fail in school because of deficiencies in their environment, their family backgrounds, or their culture, which we do not allow them to compete with children of the advantaged dominant classes.

Bilingual education as a liberal progressive school reform has also followed this pattern of conservative backlash. This backlash has been fueled by the few national-level evaluation studies conducted—the Congressional General Accounting Office (GAO) Study, the American Institute for Research (AIR) Report, and annual submitted evaluations of Title VII bilingual programs (Troike, 1978; Matute-Bianchi, 1979; Rotberg, 1982). Of these studies, the AIR report is the one most often cited and the one responsible for much of the conservative backlash.

The AIR study, funded under the Office of Education and conducted between 1974 and 1976, evaluated all Title VII Spanish/English projects in their fourth or fifth year of funding. In general, across grades, Title VII students performed slightly lower in English language arts than did non-Title VII students, and at about the same level as non-Title VII students in mathematics, while on the national norms. Title VII Hispanic students scored at about the twentieth percentile in English reading and at the thirtieth percentile in mathematics (Rotberg, 1982). These findings have been used by those opposed to bilingual education to support their argument that bilingual instruction does not significantly improve the academic performance of limited-English-speaking students.

Bilingual educators and researchers have critiqued these national evaluation studies for their numerous shortcomings (see Cardenas, 1977; Gray, 1977; O'Malley, 1978; Troike, 1978; Willig, 1985). However, although the strategy of finding limitations with antibilingual education studies is a necessary endeavor, it places bilingual educators and researchers in an ambivalent position. Because they are forced to defend their position, they necessarily argue that progressive school reforms such as bilingual education do work, that all that is needed is further refinement in the quality of programs, further research to identify the factors and combination of factors that lead to successful programs, and to disseminate these successes to other areas that have not had success. In short, this strategy forces us to work within the structural-functional paradigm and be overly concerned with improved technical efficiency. We need to break away from the limitations of the structural-functional model and become more concerned with factors other than improved technical efficiency.

A few scholars have turned their attention to the content and structure of these studies themselves and found some revealing theoretical limitations. For example, Paulston has conducted a meta-evaluation assessment of a number of research studies in bilingual education and found that "the research findings are not so contradictory if one classifies bilingual education research not according to the findings but according to the theoretical framework used and the consequent identification and interpretation of independent, contextual and dependent variables" (Paulston, 1978, p. 402 . What is revealed in these critiques is the theoretical limitations of liberal-progressive schooling due to an overreliance on the structural-functional or equilibrium model. To paraphrase Paulston, the structural-functional model assumes the need to maintain society in a state of equilibrium through the harmonious relationship of the social components by placing emphasis on smooth, cumulative change. The major limitation of this paradigm is its inability to account for conflict that arises in the social system.

Issues of conflict should be of prime concern in bilingual education, especially given the history and development of this reform movement, the assumption of equal opportunity, and the belief that bilingual education helps equalize such shortcomings of opportunity. The long-range goal of harmonious integration, by either economically incorporating or culturally assimilating the ethnolinguistic groups into the larger society, is oblivious to the fact that such a process will involve conflict.

Approaches that do attempt to analyze conflict, notes Paulston, "emphasize the inherent instability of social systems and the conflicts over values, resources, and power that follow as a natural consequence" (Paulston, 1978, p. 406). These issues are of vital importance in evaluating bilingual education programs with respect to the long-term goals; however, because bilingual education research has predominantly relied on equilibrium theory, it has been unable to address issues such as economic conflict, conflicting values and cultural systems, and conflict arising from oppressive institutions.

The more recent literature arising from a critical perspective, in reaction to the limitations of the progressive-liberal schooling reforms, has made it a point to analyze the role of conflict. Although there are few studies within bilingual education that have been done from a critical theory perspective, bilingual educators and researchers need to be concerned with the broader issues and factors outside of the classroom, for in the final analysis, they come into play within the classroom setting. Given our assumption of equal opportunity and the long-term goal of economic and cultural integration, we need to focus more attention on the interplay of societal factors within the schooling/economic nexus. How can we move to such a task?

We need to draw on those studies that have focused on issues of power, conflict, ideology, and class and economic reproduction. Apple (1978a), for example, is interested in exploring the relationship between school reform, ideology, and class reproduction. In particular, he is interested in how knowledge as expressed in a school's curriculum is related to particular class interests in society. In other words, he is interested in exploring how the ideological control of school knowledge serves the interests of those classes who control economic and political power. These concerns, I believe, can help bilingual educators and researchers conceptualize our roles as facilitators or detractors of equal opportunity and cultural diversity.

A critical look at the role of ideology as it is connected to school curriculum within bilingual education programs can give us clues as to the function it plays in class reproduction within the ethnolinguistic groups it serves. Further research is needed into the complex relationship between bilingual education as a school reform movement and its nexus to economic and cultural reproduction. To do this, we need to draw on those theoretical approaches used by the critics of the liberal-progressive school reforms. This group of scholars have sought answers to more fundamental questions, seeking to expose the basic limitations of these programs elsewhere. Instead of seeking to identify the sources of "failure" by focusing deeper into the family, childhood, individual psychology, or isolated cultural effects (Willis, 1981a), this group has sought to discover the source of inequality within the broader social structure. Their approaches have provided alternative models of explanation, which, in essence, have exposed the myth of the progressive assumptions regarding the role of education in bringing about equality. In the next section, I will briefly review aspects of social and cultural reproduction and resistance theory and explore how this framework can redirect efforts within bilingual education research. In broad general terms, we need to focus on the relationship between the basic assumption and long-range goals of bilingual education by situating it within the economic/schooling nexus.

THEORIES OF REPRODUCTION

Theories of reproduction vary as to focus, yet all of them are concerned with the relationship between schooling and economic life in capitalist societies. Giroux (1981) notes that despite the broad range of reproductive approaches, they can be classified into three major categories. These are theories of social reproduction as exemplified by the work of Bowles and Gintis (1976); theories of cultural reproduction as embodied in the work of Bourdieu (1977), Bourdieu and Passeron, (1977) and Bernstein (1977); and theories of resistance, an approach linked to the work of Paul Willis (1981a, 1981b). The commonality of these positions is that they rely upon macrosociological models to analyze the relationship between schooling and economic activity within capitalist societies. This, in part, may provide the answer to why bilingual educators and researchers have not been drawn to them. That is, the concern within bilingual education, as we have seen above, has been microsociological, i.e, the technological efficiency of classroom instruction.

Reproduction approaches, on the other hand, because they have been concerned with broader issues and factors, have not paid much attention to classroom analysis. Thus, one of the first tasks at hand, if one wants to draw on these approaches, is to identify particular orientations and concepts that can help in an initial analysis of the economic/schooling nexus within bilingual education. In this section, I will limit my analysis to identifying the major premises of the three positions and elaborating on those concepts that hold the most promise in contributing to the bilingual research effort outlined earlier. This strategy has two major advantages: It will minimize an overexposure of new terminology, jargon, and complex theoretical details to the uninitiated, but still identifies the most pertinent concepts.

Social Reproduction Theories. These theories, according to Giroux, are based on the main assumption that "the economy/school nexus represents the most important element in the reproduction of class relationships in industrialized capitalist societies" (Giroux, 1981, p. 4). Social reproduction theories (also known as correspondence theories) are based on the correspondence between the hierarchically structured patterns of values, norms, and skills that characterize the work force, the dynamics of class interaction, and the social dynamics that take place within the school setting. Bowles and Gintis's (1976) work is illustrative of this perspective in that they have sought to reconstruct the role of education in economic life. To them this means that capitalist production and the property relations of the capitalist system require certain educational outcomes.

Bowles (1977) has paid particular attention to the relation between education and the economic expansion of the capitalist system since the decade of the sixties. He argues that schools have evolved in the United States not as part of a pursuit of equality, but rather to meet the needs of capitalist employers for a disciplined and skilled labor force. He stresses that schools accomplish this through their daily social relations of operation by emphasizing discipline, punctuality, acceptance of authority outside the family, and individual accountability for one's work. Aside from stressing the function of schooling in the prroduction of a disciplined and skilled labor force, Bowles makes the connection between unequal schooling and the reproduction of the social division of labor. The operation of the school system itself is seen as perpetuating inequality in education through the mutual reinforcement of class subcultures and social class biases.

As a theoretical advancement over liberal-progressive arguments and cultural deprivation theory, social reproduction theory has drawn attention away from the thesis of "blaming the victim" to broader socioeconomic factors responsible for the continued persistence of poverty and social inequality. This perspective has made it clear that working-class kids fail not because of some inherent deficiency on their part, but because the logic of the system is set up to "reproduce" failure. Education, therefore, functions not for the reproduction of equality, but rather for the reproduction of inequality. Education under this model plays a vital role in maintaining the hierarchical and unequal distribution of labor activity within the economic system of capitalist production.

However, social reproduction theories have not escaped criticism, and such criticism has been quick to point out the limitations of the approach. One of the major criticisms has been that social reproduction theories are too mechanistic and economically determined in that they are overly focused on the macrostructure. Their major weakness is that they have not paid much attention to the internal qualities of schools, as they have neglected the cultural sphere and the lived responses of the classes. Olsen (1981) points out that in overtly focusing on structural elements, correspondence theorists have failed to recognize that schools are places where social inequalities are created and not just reproduced and that, in addition to economics, a range of other factors, such as culture, individual histories, vagaries of the state, and mass movements, help to shape schooling outcomes.

Given the inherent limitations of the social reproduction approach, other scholars have focused on the omitted factors in an effort to better explain the dynamic aspects of social reproduction. As a result, they have gone beyond the simplified and overdeterministic nature of the approach. For a discussion of this advancement, I now turn to cultural reproduction theory.

Cultural Reproduction Theories. Theories of cultural reproduction, like those of social reproduction, are concerned with how capitalist societies are able to reproduce themselves. The focus of concern, however, is with how school culture is produced and legitimated. The cultural reproduction approach places emphasis on the mediating role of culture in reproducing class societies, and in this respect shifts the focus away from the study of economic inequality. According to Giroux (1981), cultural reproduction theories have rejected the premise that schools are mirror images of society and argue that schools are relatively autonomous institutions that are only indirectly influenced by more powerful economic and political institutions. Nonetheless, schools are seen as playing a very important part in the process of class reproduction. Bourdieu (1977) and Bourdieu and Passeron (1977) have contributed to the reproduction approach by focusing on the sphere of culture to explain how schools play an important part in the process of class reproduction. Through the concepts of cultural capital, habitus, and symbolic violence, they are able to show that the reproduction of class inequalities is not as unidirectional and tied to the sphere of economics as the social reproduction theories would have us believe.

In the concept of cultural capital, Bourdieu refers to those different sets of linguistic and cultural competencies that individuals inherit by virtue of their family's class position. Because the school reflects the dominant social relations of a class society, it plays a vital role in legitimating and reproducing the cultural capital of the dominant classes. This process is central to Bourdieu's argument—"the educational system reproduces all the more perfectly the structure of the distribution of cultural capital among classes (and sections of classes) in that the culture which it transmits is closer to the dominant culture and that the mode of inculcation to which it has resource is less removed from the mode of inculcation practiced by the same" (Bourdieu, 1977, p. 493). Since the dominant classes give a certain social value and status to language forms, and to sets of meanings, qualities of style, modes of thinking, and types of dispositions (Giroux, 1981), the cultural capital (high culture) that gets the most social value and status in the schools is that of the dominant classes.

Closely tied to cultural capital is the concept of "habitus" or, as Apple (1978b) puts it, the cultural rules that link economic and cultural control and distribution together. The concept helps to further explain how the social practices of a dominant social structure are reproduced. "The habitus," says Giroux, "refers to those subjective dispositions which reflect a class based social grammar of taste, knowledge and behavior..." (Giroux, 1981, p. 9) or the internalized competencies of the individual. The schools accomplish this because, as Bourdieu says, they appear to be a "impartial and neutral 'transmitter' of the benefits of a valued culture...." Schools perpetuate an ideology of neutrality where no class interests are supposedly being served. Apple states this succinctly: "they [the schools] take the cultural capital, the habitus, of the middle class, as natural and employ it as if all children have had equal access to it" (Apple, 1978a, p. 375). In this respect, they are able to promote inequality in the name of fairness and impartiality for all.

What is actually happening is that such a practice effectively masks a subtle and discriminatory process. In perpetuating the belief that all children are equal, such a practice in implicitly favoring those who have already acquired the linguistic and social competencies to handle middle-class culture. Schools, in short, take as neutral what in essence favors those students who already have access to and control of the cultural capital. This process involves "symbolic violence" against those who do not possess the same cultural capital as reflected in the linguistic and cultural competencies (habitus) perpetuated by the schools. The concept of symbolic violence further exemplifies how schools help to mediate and reproduce, in part, class inequalities.

Giroux underscores the dynamic nature of this process in stating that symbolic violence shows that "class control is not simply the crude reflex of economic power imposing itself in the form of overt force and restraint; instead it is constituted through the more subtle exercise of symbolic power waged by a ruling class in order 'to impose a definition of the social world that is consistent with its interests.'" (Giroux, 1981, p. 80). This is particularly evident in the schooling of ethnolinguistic minority students, as will become clearer in the last section of this paper.

In short, cultural reproduction theory as embodied in the work of Bourdieu and Passeron has sufficiently added to our knowledge regarding the process of reproduction of class inequality. The cultural reproduction model explains the process of cultural production and legitimation, at least among the dominant classes, as well as the role that the supposedly "neutral" school plays in the reproduction of class relations within capitalist societies. Furthermore, this orientation has advanced our understanding of the overall reproduction approach by interjecting the element of human agency. However, despite the advances this model has made over social reproduction, it has not escaped criticism. Giroux (1981) classifies both the social and cultural reproduction approaches as reducing the mechanisms of social and cultural reproduction to the central element of class domination and ignoring other modes of oppression. In order to understand the charges made against the cultural reproduction model we must turn to the third approach—resistance theory.

Resistance Theory. Scholars working within the resistance theory approach have made some major advances over both the social and cultural reproduction models. By contrast, resistance theory includes the issues of conflict and consciousness as the starting point for a critical study of the relationship between schooling and capitalist society (Giroux, 1981). Paul Willis's study (1981a) among working class youth in Britain is exemplary in that it focuses on both the conflicts and tensions that mediate the dominant school culture and the role of the youth counterculture within and outside the school. It also demonstrates how the mechanisms of social and cultural reproduction are an "... ever-repeated creative process" (Willis, 1981, 1981b, p. 60) and are always faced with partially realized elements of opposition.

Furthermore the theoretical model put forth by Willis introduces the notion of cultural production as the creative active agency factor that mediates between the imposed limitations of the broader socioeconomic structure and the lived collective cultural productions that take form under such impositions. The concept of cultural production is an important one for Willis in that, through it, he is able to show that the reproduced social relationship between the classes is actually a "dynamic" and "contested" dialectical process. Through this process, cultural reproduction takes place, but it takes place through the mediating influence of cultural production.

Willis's theoretical framework is a major advancement over both the social reproduction and cultural reproduction perspectives in that it provides the theoretical understanding of how imposed socioeconomic structure and cultural capital mediated through human agency and resistance reproduce social inequality. As mentioned above, the common limitations of the social and cultural reproduction models is that both are too unidirectional and deterministic, for they portray the reproduction of the class relation as "... the downward imposition of meanings about what important social and cognitive knowledge and values are ..." (Apple, 1978, 1978b, p. 497). Willis's study, however, questions this conception in that ethnographically he is able to show that working-class kids, through their counterculture, reject both the social relations of the school and its high culture, but in so doing, they help to reproduce their class position. Perhaps the biggest contribution that Willis has made above and beyond that of Bourdieu and Passeron is that he advances our understanding of how cultural processes become meaningful and creative for the dominated.

The notion of culture under this perspective is much more dynamic. "Culture," says Giroux, "is not reduced to an overly determined, static analysis of dominant cultural capital, i.e., language, cultural tastes, and manners. Instead, culture is viewed as a system of practices, a way of life, that constitutes and is constituted by a dialectical interplay between the class specific circumstances of a particular social group and those powerful ideologies and structural determinants in the wider society" (Giroux, 1981, p. 13).

This particular aspect of resistance theory, I believe, offers us a new theoretical framework that may explain such concerns as a persistent high dropout rate among the Hispanic ethnolinguistic group. Despite the claim and hope among many educators and policy makers that bilingual education programs would help retain minority students in school, the dropout rate among Mexican American and mainland Puerto Rican students remains between 40 and 50 percent, compared to 14 percent for whites and 25 percent for blacks (Jusenius & Duarte, 1982). Yet no study has been done, to my knowledge, that analyzes the persistent high dropout rate among Hispanic youth from the perspective of resistance. It could very well be that a high percentage of youth drop out of school or perform poorly because they have learned that schools offer very little social and economic advancement for them (see Ogbu, 1974).

In summary, the social reproduction model explains the functions of schools from an economic inequality perspective. The cultural reproduction model, especially the concepts of cultural capital, habitus, and symbolic violence, captures the role of culture and helps explain how schools reproduce inequality among groups that are culturally and linguistically different. The resistance model goes beyond these by exemplifying the creative aspects of human agency among subordinated groups. Yet, such cultural creativity may have an inherent contradiction that helps to reproduce class inequality. How then can we use aspects of reproduction theory within bilingual education?

A Comprehensive Approach. The continued interest in the area of social and cultural reproduction in education appears to have entered a new dimension and can offer much to the bilingual research effort. The three major models that have been used in analyzing the relationship between schooling and the continued reproduction of capitalist social relations of production and inequality can be mutually interrelated to achieve a more comprehensive approach. This comprehensive approach can advance our understanding of why and through what mechanisms social inequality is perpetuated within the sphere of schooling, as well as in the interconnected sphere of labor and family. Apple (1981; 1982) has underscored the need for interrelating the approaches so as not to limit the scope of the analysis to the sphere of culture or political economy. He stresses the need to interrelate the analysis on each of the focal areas—culture, mode of production, and objective class structure, in order not to neglect the important and real connections between the economy, ideology, culture, and other aspects of society.

Apple (1982, p. 3) goes on to stress that any serious analysis of each reproduction must account for a number of complex interconnections such as the role of the educational apparatus in roughly reproducing a labor force stratified by sex and class as well as the process of class formation and struggle, capital accumulation, and the legitimation of the privileges of the dominant group. Nonetheless, because the sphere of culture has been shown to have a certain amount of autonomy, it is imperative to take into consideration the role of cultural production and cultural reproduction in its relation to social and economic reproduction.

One caveat in using a macrosociological model, however, is the need to examine the internal qualities of schools and the lived responses of class and gender actors (Apple, 1982) by incorporating the dynamic aspects of resistance theory. Resistance theory links both the imposed macrosociological structure of the economy, politics, and cultural capital and the microsociological responses of actors to such imposition as seen in the interactions of teachers and students, workers and bosses, parents and children, and peer-peer collective responses. It is this interrelation that will account for class struggle not as empty abstractions, but rather as meaningful lived struggles as seen through their social relationships.

In the following section, I argue that this comprehensive perspective can help to illuminate the inherent limitations and contradictions of liberal-progressive educational reform in general, and specifically of bilingual education. This comprehensive perspective can also reorient our focus on the role that bilingual education can play in developing resistance against such imposed limitations.

NEW DIRECTIONS FOR RESEARCH IN BILINGUAL EDUCATION

Reproduction theory, in general, I believe, offers a new direction for bilingual education research. It has advantages over the structural-functional paradigm, the predominant guide within bilingual education, because it incorporates issues of class conflict and power relationships. In this section, therefore, I will present a preliminary analysis of how we can start to apply concepts from reproduction theory to bilingual education to illustrate how this framework can provide a more interesting and enlightened understanding of bilingual education. In addition, by including an analysis of social factors, a more powerful perspective can be obtained to explain the success and failure of such programs.

The concept of cultural capital, for example, can help to explain the shift in bilingual education policy illustrated by the 1974 amendments. As we have seen, the first five years of bilingual education policy and program implementation had recognized the cultural capital (native language and culture) of linguistically different low-income groups as a legitimate resource for instruction within the classroom. Even though the majority of bilingual education programs were conservative, stressing the learning of English and assimilation into the mainstream, as Padilla has stressed, there were still a few bilingual education programs that implemented maintenance bilingual bicultural programs. This flexibility in program policy and practice had initially set in motion a fundamental structural shift within schools with a high percentage of linguistically and culturally different minority students. The original Bilingual Education Act attempted to provide equal educational opportunity through experimental and innovative open-ended programs that could encompass any conceivable combination of time allocation to the two languages of instruction (Padilla, 1984). Furthermore, there was explicit mention of using the history and culture of the ethnic groups involved. Thus, in maintenance bilingual bicultural programs, the cultural capital of the ethnolinguistic group had gained social status and legitimacy as a resource for instruction. The open-ended nature of early bilingual education programs, however, alerted the dominant classes, and conflicts and power struggles for control of the programs set in.

The shift in policy in the 1974 and 1978 amendments, however, reinforced the legitimacy of the cultural capital of the dominant classes and helped to maintain the hierarchical reproduction of the class structure. English instruction, in turn, gained new emphasis as the legitimate resource for maintaining equal educational opportunity. This policy move, of course, was made within the ideology of equal opportunity and with the assumption that once English competence had been achieved, students would have positive linkages to the economic structure. Let us keep in mind, as Bourdieu has stressed, that schools legitimate their actions through the ideology of neutrality and equality for all students. In actual practice, the process reinforces the cultural capital of the dominant classes and masks the subtle ways by which discrimination and inequality are reproduced. For some ethnolinguistic minority students, the shift to equal opportunity through the mastery of English can have devastating effects.

The studies conducted by Cummins (1980) and Skutnabb-Kangas and Toukomea (1976) provide us with vital information as to the potential damaging effects that this policy has on non-English dominant students. Cummins (1980), who has conducted research among immigrant bilingual children in Canada, has found that it takes five to seven years, on the average, for these children to approach grade norms in English cognitive ability language proficiency (CALP). This level is the crucial threshold level necessary for continued high levels of academic development. However, Cummins has also found that immigrant children can acquire a high level of English communicative proficiency in interpersonal situations in a considerably shorter period of time than five years. It follows that having high levels of English oral language proficiency does not imply a commensurate level of ability in using English to learn academic content. Thus, as Skutnabb-Kangas has stressed, "there may be a certain level of L2 [second language] competence (and mother tongue competence which is assumed here to be high) which must be attained to allow the potentially beneficial aspects of becoming bilingual to influence cognitive development" (Skutnabb-Kangas, 1981, p. 223).

The implications of these findings for children who are "... tacitly or openly encouraged to abandon their native language in favor of English before reaching the threshold level..." (Blanco, 1984, p. 189) are that such children are in reality being schooled for underachievement. The current practice within bilingual programs is to limit the length of time in which a child may actually receive bilingual instruction to a three-year period. Although this is sufficient time to acquire conversational English skills, students are unable to master the use of English to learn academic content. Students are exited from bilingual programs generally on the basis of oral language test scores, which do not correlate with later academic achievement. Thus, because of current policy stressing the acquisition of oral English language proficiency above cognitive academic language proficiency, a substantial number of ethnolinguistic minority students may be exited from bilingual programs under the guise that they can now compete on the same level as English dominant students. McCollum and Walker (in press) have looked at the testing procedures for entry and exit criteria in relation to transitional bilingual program policy, and posit that existing testing practices and policies in actuality assure low achievement of LEP students within bilingual programs and their inability to compete with English dominant students after program exit.

The studies of Cummins (1980), Skutnabb-Kangas and Toukomaa (1981), Skutnabb-Kangas (1981), and McCollum and Walker (in press) provide us with vital information as to how program policy regarding the teaching of English and an assessment of language proficiency of LEP students may assure that linguistically and culturally different students are being schooled for underachievement. What we need to do is take the data of these studies and interpret the results within the context of a comprehensive social/cultural/resistance reproduction approach. This new direction provides the framework for linking macrosociological concerns of class reproduction and microsociological concerns of bilingual schooling. It would allow us to go beyond the limitations of liberal-progressive arguments and structural-functional theory and address pressing questions concerning the perpetuation of social, cultural, economic, and educational inequality of ethnolinguistic minorities. Above all, it provides the framework for reassessing the role bilingual education plays in the reproduction of class inequalities. Given the assumptions, long-range goals, and history of bilingual education in the United States, we need to concern ourselves with these issues. The outcomes, however, may hold some troubling contradictions for bilingual educators and policy makers. It may do us well to take heed of what Apple has argued with respect to school reforms: "We may find that the institutional and curricular reforms in which [bilingual] educators place so much hope may be part of a subtle and interconnected set of structured relations that are aspects of economic and cultural reproduction" (Apple, 1978a, p. 386).

NOTES

1. Paulston (1978) has actually identified five assumptions that have guided the implementation, practice, and evaluation of bilingual education in the United States. The first and major one is that of "equal opportunity and the belief that bilingual education helps to equalize such short comings of opportunity" (p. 411). The second concerns the importance of the culture contact situation: "... bilingual education ... includes the study of history and culture associated with the mother-tongue ... [which will lead to] a legitimate pride in both cultures" (p. 411). The third assumption involves teaching method: "an elusive assumption of U.S. bilingual programs is that one method will eventually be found to be more effective than others ..." (p. 412). The fourth assumption is that "... ability and merit influence the attainment of scholastic skills and that once equal opportunity has been provided for by bilingual education, such ability will result in success in school" (p. 412). The fifth assumption is that "there is some relationship between language and cognition ... [such that] language is believed to be the 'vehicle for complex thinking,' [therefore] ... the need to use the language the children know best ... becomes axiomatic ..." (p. 412). In short, Paulston notes that these assumptions that characterize evaluation research on bilingual education in the United States, can be typecast as reflecting two major assumptions: "unequal opportunity" and "cultural diversity." With respect to the long-term goals of bilingual edu-

cation emphasis is placed on either economic integration or cultural assimilation into the larger society through the process of equalizing opportunity. Note that this is the same long-term goal of liberal progressive education.

2. Within the field of educational research, a number of scholars have also provided a useful classificatory typology: liberal-progressive model versus critical theory, which parallels that of Paulston. The liberal-progressive model, as some scholars have dubbed it, is based on structural-functional theory and is closely aligned to liberal democracy. The assumptions that guide this model can be traced as far back as Thomas Jefferson and his view that public education was the hallmark of a democratic society. These assumptions essentially follow the equilibrium model, for emphasis is placed on improving the technical efficiency of schooling, e.g., individualized instruction or remedial reading, or emphasis is placed on changing the home environment or individual psychology of the students. Thus, scholars working within this approach have described schools as socializing institutions that provide students with the values and skills necessary for them to function productively in the larger society (Parsons, 1959; Dreeben, 1968). However, this approach essentially leaves untreated the relationship of the schools to issues of power, class conflict, and social control. The critical theory approaches, on the other hand, have criticized the liberal-progressive model for portraying schools as apolitical and neutral. Scholars working within this approach have illuminated the political nature of schools by pointing to the role that schools play in reproducing the inequalities of wealth and power that characterize the existing society. The major approaches within this tradition are those emphasizing social reproduction, cultural reproduction, and resistance theory.

REFERENCES

Apple, M. 1978a. "Ideology, reproduction and educational reform." *Comparative Educational Review*, 23(3):367–387.

Apple, M. 1978b. "The new sociology of education: Analyzing cultural and economic reproduction." *Harvard Educational Review*, 48(4).

Apple, M. 1979. *Ideology and curriculum.* London: Routledge & Kegan Paul.

Apple, M. 1981. Reproduction, contestation, and curriculum: An essay in self-criticism, *Interchange*, 12(2–3):27–47.

Apple, M., (ed.). 1982. *Cultural and economic reproduction in education.* London: Routledge & Kegan Paul.

Apple, M. and Weiss, L. 1983. *Ideology and practice in schooling.* Philadelphia: Temple University Press.

Bernstein, B. 1977. *Class, codes and control, vol. 3: Towards a theory of educational transmission.* London: Routledge & Kegan Paul.

Bilingual bicultural education: A handbook for attorneys and community workers. 1977. Cambridge, Mass.: Center for Law and Education.

Blanco, G. 1984. Equity, quality, and effectiveness in bilingual education. In *Equity and educational excellence.* New York: New Jersey Coalition for Equity.

Bourdieu, P. 1977. Cultural reproduction and social reproduction." In *Power and Ideology of Education,* eds. J. Karabel and A.H. Helsey. New York: Oxford University Press.

Bourdieu, P. and Passeron, J. 1977. *Reproduction in education, society and culture.* Beverly Hills: Sage Publications.

Bowles, S. 1977. Unequal education and the reproduction of the social division of labor. In *Power and Ideology in Education,* eds. J. Karabel and A.H. Helsey. New York: Oxford University Press.

Bowles, S. and Gintis, H. 1976. *Schooling in capitalist America: Educational reform and the contradiction of economic life.* New York: Basic Books.

Cardenas, J. 1977. AIR evaluation of bilingual education. *Intercultural Development Research Association Newsletter,* pp. 1–3. San Antonio, Texas.

Carnoy, M. 1982. Education, economy and the state. In *Cultural and economic reproduction in education,* ed. M. Apple. London: Routledge & Kegan Paul.

Cummins, J. 1980. The entry and exit fallacy in bilingual education. *NABE Journal,* 4(3).

Cummins, J. 1986. Empowering minority students. *Harvard Educational Review,* 56(1):18–35.

Dreeben, R. 1968. *On what is learned in school.* Reading, MA. Addison Wesley.

Foley, D. and White, R. 1978. Revitalizing the bilingual-bicultural reform movement through community-based approaches. Paper prepared for Southwest Educational Development Laboratory, Austin, Texas.

Giroux, H. A. 1981. Hegemony, resistance, and the paradox of educational reform. *Interchange,* 12(2–3):3–26.

Giroux, H. A. 1983. *Theory and resistance in education.* South Hadley, Mass.: Bergin & Garvey Publishers.

Gray, T. 1977. Response to AIR study "evaluation of the impact of ESEA title VII Spanish-English bilingual education program." Arlington, VA: Center for Applied Linguistics.

Jusenius, C., and Duarte, V. L. 1982. *Hispanics and jobs: Barriers to progress.* Washington, D.C.: National Commission for Employment Policy.

Jenks, C., M. Smith, H. Acland, J. Bane, D. Cohen, H. Gintis, B. Heyns, and S. Michelson. 1972. *Inequality: A reassessment of the effects of family and schooling in America.* New York: Basic Books.

Mackey, W. R. and Ornstein, J. 1977. *The bilingual education movement: Essays on its progress.* El Paso, Texas: Texas Western Press.

Matute-Bianchi, M. E. (1979). The federal mandate for bilingual education. In *Ethnoperspectives in bilingual education research, vol. 1: Bilingual* educátion in public policy in the United States, ed. R. V. Padilla. Ypsilanti, MI: Department of foreign Languages and Bilingual Studies.

McCollum, P. and Walker, C. L. 1990. The assessment of bilingual students: A sorting mechanism in *Readings on Equal Education, 10: Critical issues for a new administration and congress,* ed. S. S. Goldberg. New York: AMS Press.

Ogbu, J. 1974. *The next generation: An ethnography of education in an urban neighborhood.* New York: Academic Press.

Olson, P. 1981. Rethinking social reproduction. *Interchange,* 12(2-3):1–2.

O'Mally, J. M. 1978. Review of the evaluation of the impact of ESEA title VII Spanish-English bilingual education program. *Bilingual Resources,* 1(2):6–10.

Padilla, R. 1984. Federal policy shifts and the implementation of bilingual education programs. In *The Chicano Struggle,* eds. J. Garcia, T. Cordova, and J. Garcia. Binghamton, N.Y.: Bilingual Press/Editorial Bilingual.

Parson, T. 1959. The school class as a social system: Some of its functions in American society. *Harvard Educational Review,* 29(4):297–318.

Paulston, C. B. 1978. Rationales for bilingual educational reforms: A comparative assessment. *Comparative Education Review,* 22(3):402–419.

Paulston, C. B. 1980. *Bilingual education theories and issues.* Rowley, MA: Newbury House Publishers.

Piven, F. and Cloward, R. 1977. *Poor people's movements. Why they succeed. How they fail.* New York: Vintage College Books.

Rotberg, I. 1982. Some legal and research considerations in establishing federal policy in bilingual education. *Harvard Educational Review,* 52(2):149–68.

Salomone, R. 1982. Public policy and the law. Legal precedents and prospects for equity in education. Report submitted to the Race, Sex, and National Origin Desegregation Assistance Centers. New York University, Rutgers University, Columbia University.

Schneider, S. G. 1976. *Revolution, reaction or reform: The 1974 bilingual education act.* New York: L.A. Publishing Co.

Skutnabb-Kangas, T. 1981. *Bilingualism or Not: The Education of Minorities.* Clevedon, England: Multilingual Matters.

Skutnabb-Kangas, T. and Toukomaa, P. 1981. *Teaching migrant children's mother tongue and learning the language of the host country in the context of the sociocultural situation of the migrant family.* Helsinki: Finland, Finnish National Commission for UNESCO.

Smith, W. E. 1978. *Mexicano resistance to schooled ethnicity: Ethnic student power in south Texas, 1930–1970.* Doctoral dissertation, the University of Texas at Austin.

Smith, W. E. and Foley, D. E. 1978. Mexicano resistance to schooling in a south Texas colony. *Education and Urban Society,* 10(2).

Spring, J. H. 1982. *American education: An introduction to social and political aspects.* White Plains, N. Y.: Longman.

Troike, R. 1978. Research evidence for the effectiveness of bilingual education. *NABE Journal,* 31(1):13–24.

Trujillo, L. 1978. *The quest for Chicano community control: A case study.* Doctoral dissertation, University of California at Berkeley.

Tyack, D., Lowe, R. and Hanset, E. 1984. *Public schools in hard times: The great depression and recent years.* Cambridge, Mass.: Harvard University Press.

Willig, A. C. (Winter/Spring, 1981–82). The effectiveness of bilingual education: Review of a report. *NABE Journal,* 6(2&3):1–19.

Willis, P. 1981a. *Learning to Labor: How working class kids get working class jobs.* Morning side edition. New York: Columbia University Press.

Willis, P. 1981b. Cultural production is different from cultural reproduction is different from social reproduction is different from reproduction. *Interchange,* 12,(2–3):48–67.

THE ASSESSMENT OF BILINGUAL STUDENTS: A SORTING MECHANISM

Pamela McCollum
and Constance L. Walker

To understand the nature of the relationship between American public schooling and its language minority children, one must trace the evolution of testing in the education of limited and non-English-speaking children. For it is there that we see the patterns of exclusion, denial, indifference, and frustration that have characterized attempts to serve linguistically and culturally different students.

This paper will examine the policy implications of assessment practices that affect limited-English-proficient students. In order to set the stage for the discussion of current practices in language assessment, the purposes of testing in schools will be delineated, followed by an examination of the social construct of testing. In this way, language assessment can be viewed as a branch of a larger testing system—having common ties, yet developing distinct characteristics of its own. The development of second language testing practices and their outgrowth from foreign language pedagogy will clarify the major characteristics of language testing. A discussion of current practices in the testing of linguistically different children will alert the reader to those language assessment issues that affect and have implications for decisions far beyond the purely linguistic.

Once the framework of language assessment has been constructed, the major thesis of this paper will be offered: the development of language assessment practices in response to legislative, judicial, and administrative needs has resulted in the misuse and misapplication of testing that serves to perpetuate the underachievement of language minority students. Such assessment must be viewed in the context of the sorting of minority students by an education system that uses testing as a legitimate means of classification, in effect reproducing an existing system of underachievement and underemployment.

TESTING AND MINORITY STUDENTS

Perhaps the first hint of the relationship between the world of testing and language minority students became evident with the application of intelligence testing to immigrants at the turn of the century. Results of this testing supported the notion of a "bilingual handicap," in that individuals with dual language skills were expected to demonstrate lower intellectual functioning. Although later research has refuted such beliefs, citing the cognitive advantages of bilingualism (Peal & Lambert, 1962; Cummins & Gulutsan, 1974; Lambert, 1977; Duncan & DeAvila, 1979), vestiges of such beliefs have yet to be completely eliminated from American society.

Continued testing of minority students with standardized testing measures produced predictable results: below-average achievement, retention at grade levels, classifications of learning disabilities and mental retardation. Mercer (1974) found the public school system to be the primary labeler of mental retardation in the community, and pointed to an extreme over-representation of Chicano and black students in programs for the mentally retarded. Like many who have examined the relationship between minority students and schools, she found that "standardized testing provides a mechanism for blaming children and their families when the educational program of the school fails." (Mercer, 1974, p. 137). Over time, a legitimization of failure that test scores provide serves to exclude students from schools, with little effort to assist or retain students who are at risk.

Despite years of caution against the application of traditional testing practices to minority children, in the 1980s, testing is the focal point for decision making concerning language minority students. When language differences were not considered, widespread achievement testing served to legitimize institutionalized beliefs concerning minority students. The emphasis on the language needs of such students led to a concurrent focus on the testing of language as the way in which to determine need for assistance. In that way, language assessment has become the primary means of placement and monitoring in bilingual, English as a second language, and mainstream classrooms in states serving large populations of limited and non-English-proficient students. More recently, both language *and* achievement measures are being used in order to reach a consensus concerning eligibility, appropriate program placement, and progress.

What has been the nature of language assessment as the foundation for testing language minority students? What are the implications of a dual assessment system for achievement in school? How might these testing practices relate to a larger societal agenda with respect to schooling and minority students?

LANGUAGE EDUCATION AND TESTING

In order to examine the foundations of language assessment, we must begin by tracing changes in linguistic theory and the influences of these changes on second language teaching. For it is from the pedagogy of language instruction that patterns of language testing have evolved. Understanding the nature of language teaching and its requisite testing will enable us to critically examine the influences of language assessment as applied to bilingual students today.

Departing from the study of classical languages, language teaching reform movements in the late 1880s attempted to free modern languages from traditional constraints. Yet foreign language education continued to be viewed in a narrow sense, with reading skills seen as the major attainable goal in secondary schooling. While the period 1920–1940 saw criticism of language teaching practice and students' lack of proficiency, the testing of language at that time was largely haphazard, without reliance on any genuine principles of language structure or psychometric restrictions. Adults were the major learners of second languages—in international settings they were literate adults studying English as a Foreign Language in order to gain entrance to higher education, while American college students studied foreign languages in programs where oral language proficiency was rarely achieved. Both groups were generally middle- or upper-class individuals who were already "achievers," and for whom academic success was not related to foreign language proficiency.

The 1940s and 1950s saw the advent of both structural linguistics and behaviorism in psychology. Structuralism argued that structural analysis of the language formed the basis of curricula, and in combination with behaviorism influenced developers of the audiolingual methodology of second language pedagogy. Testing also reflected the structuralist influence, with language skills measured indirectly through paper and pencil discrete point tests. Spolsky, cited in Oller (1979), calls this period of language testing the "psychometric-structuralist" era, when testing became a "science" and the influences of psychometric principles were applied to language assessment. More attention was paid to how testing was done than to what was tested, with the nature of tests and testing receiving greater emphasis than the language skills supposedly under scrutiny. Specified structural phonological and lexical points were examined in isolation, with the resulting term "discrete point" describing this focus. The opposite orientation, "integrative testing," purported to measure global or communicative language ability.

The rapid growth of linguistics (in particular, psycholinguistics in the 1950s and sociolinguistics in the 1960s) brought about many changes in language teaching and testing. New technology, new organizational structure for language teaching programs, alternative methodology, and teacher training efforts coalesced into the expanding field of foreign language education in the United States and English as a Foreign Language programs in Great Britain. Linguistics continued to influence language testing and teaching through the work of Chomsky (1957). Transformational generative grammar offered a different kind of influence than had structuralism. A closer relationship between language and thought in Chomsky's view contrasted with the behaviorist perspectives of language in isolation and as habit, and began to influence theories of second language (L2) acquisition. Language teaching was influenced to adapt more eclectic methodology that took into account learner variables, affective variables, and instructional settings. More importantly, fundamental questions concerning the nature of language and language learning were raised, which in turn had implications for language teaching and testing.

Movement away from an emphasis on linguistic skills alone characterizes more recent trends in linguistic research, second language teaching, and language testing. Termed "communicative competence," the proficiency movement attempts to describe, teach, and test language from a functional perspective: language is communication, it can be learned in communicative contexts, and language tests should approximate situations and tasks that are real. It is possible that the communicative movement in second language teaching and testing was inevitable. Dissatisfaction with foreign language teaching in the United States has been legendary in that, after several years of study, it was not expected that students could satisfy routine communicative demands in real-life situations through the second language. Sociolinguistic research contributed to the development of a communicative perspective, in that rules for social language use were seen as part of language competence. Emphasis on the social, functional, and contextual uses of language brought new meaning to the refinement of the term "language proficiency." Discussions of the meaning of language proficiency began to include a more holistic view of proficiency, a communicative competence far greater than simple linguistic proficiency.

The proficiency movement has sought to expand upon communicative views of language for both teaching and testing second languages. The latest advances in adult language assessment are evident at the college/university level, where outgrowths of the Foreign Service Institute's oral interview, together with the American Council on the Teaching of Foreign Languages (ACTFL) guidelines, are provided a structure for the development of curriculum and testing procedures. The ACTFL/ETS Proficiency Guidelines have pioneered the developed of generic and language-specific goals in the four language skills and culture, and are forming a foundation for curriculum development, testing, and teacher training.

The testing of pragmatic communication can be expected to influence the nature of language instruction in classroom settings, and continued efforts at refining global language assessment measures will eventually affect the language assessment of school-age children who are bilingual. At this time, the assessment of the language of minority children has not yet reached the level of sophistication available for adult L2 learners. Much of this can be attributed to the sociopolitical and administrative requirements placed upon the assessment of limited-English-proficient children. While there is a need for more appropriate methods for testing oral language, educational programs have been constrained by factors that impede the use of perhaps more accurate methods of assessment. The following section will outline the nature of language assessment in bilingual education, examining such factors and their implications in a larger social context.

LANGUAGE ASSESSMENT AND BILINGUAL EDUCATION

Like many education programs that evolve from legislative initiative or judicial mandate, bilingual education was funded without several ancillary areas to guide its early policy and implications. Early years of bilingual education funding suffered from lack of research concerning instructional methodology and effectiveness, lack of teacher training, and lack of materials and resources. In addition to problems in implementation, there were no adequate means of identifying which children were eligible for services. The growth in programs serving limited-English-proficient students required instruments that would measure the nature of English proficiency in order to determine the need (or lack of need) for service. Federal and state legislation concerning bilingual education, as well as court decisions, began to mandate testing that would determine eligibility as well as allocate funds and services. Bilingual education was seen as an equity issue—if language minority children could understand and produce English, they would then be able to participate in the educational process and compete with English-speaking peers. The focus on their language "deficit" meant many years of erroneous preoccupation with language as the problem and the belief that increased levels of English proficiency was the solution.

The absence of research in the area of second language learning by minority children combined with lack of information on effective language testing for bilingual learners resulted in a void that was filled by legislative and judicial mandate. What was not known to linguists and educators—how to accurately assess English language proficiency and potential for successful participation in classrooms—was made incumbent upon practitioners serving bilingual students. Policy concerning languages of instruction and remediation was now set by legislators and judges, as opposed to linguists or language educators. The implication of such policy was left to school personnel, and the race was to find the best language tests. The emphasis was on fast, efficient screening of limited- and non-English-proficient students, and early tests simply attempted to measure speaking ability in English. The proliferation of tests of language ability, language dominance, and language proficiency was nothing short of phenomenal. With millions of unserved bilingual children in the nations' schools, and a virtual absence of measures for assessing them, the testing bandwagon began to roll. Results were predictable: "Some tests sprang full grown from the brows of their authors during weekend fits of innovation, or so it seemed" (Bernal, 1982, p. 3). School-wide and district-wide testing, heretofore a responsibility of testing and guidance specialists, was, in the area of language assessment, often relegated to nontesters—teachers and aides—who were called upon to administer measures to bilingual students.

The emphasis on oral language proficiency measures came in part from a federal definition of students in need as "limited English speaking," later to be amended to the term "limited English proficient" (LEP). Tests were developed to correspond to guidelines developed in the wake of the 1974 *Lau v. Nichols* decision requiring school districts to serve limited-English-proficient students. Such guidelines stressed the primacy of oral language development, and the need for judgments concerning the relative proficiency of a student's language ability in English and the non-English language. Early measures of oral language proficiency were quasi-integrative in that they were based on oral language but were scored with discrete point scoring systems. These measures all purported to test language ability in English, yet subsequent research (Ulibarri, Spencer, & Rivas, 1981) has found little correlation across tests in their ratings of students' English language proficiency classifications. More importantly, it became evident that such measures did not predict later academic achievement. This is an interesting finding, given that determination of English language competence was earlier thought to be crucial to decision making concerning eventual academic success. It was thought that understanding a language meant that academic achievement in and through that language would follow. Although the use of such tests continues, studies have found that teacher estimates of language competence are a better predictor of a student's eventual academic success (Ulibarri, Spencer, & Rivas, 1981).

The reliance on oral language testing during this period was interesting, in that English proficiency was examined in isolation from school learning, yet any demonstration of proficiency in oral English was thought to be generalizable to success in academic classroom settings. More recent studies have questioned whether tests of grammar and phonology are accurate predictors of the ability to function in a classroom setting through English (Cummins, 1979, 1980, 1984). Students who are placed in English-speaking classes generally fail to achieve at the same levels as their English-speaking counterparts, even though they have been determined by proficiency measures to be "English proficient." Cummins has outlined the distinctions between surface-level oral language proficiency and the level of language skill necessary to perform cognitive skills in decontextualized situations, and believes that five or more years may be necessary for a student to develop academic language proficiency.

Although increased criticism of oral language measures has made educators more aware of their inherent problems, they still form the basis for decisions concerning the entry and exit of language minority students from programs of ESL and bilingual education. More recently, these tests have been used in combination with standardized achievement measures in order to determine need for ESL instruction or readiness for reclassification to a mainstream classroom setting. Ironically, standardized tests of achievement in English, previously avoided due to cultural and linguistic bias, are now used as yardsticks with which to measure the increasing academic skills of bilingual students. Some researchers argue that in fact standardized achievement tests given in English, rather than a language proficiency test of English skills, are far more indicative of the language skills necessary for achievement at a particular academic level (Troike, 1983).

TESTING AND BILINGUAL STUDENTS

Clearly the growth of testing in bilingual education (as in education in general over the past 20 years) has resulted from a need for program evaluation of specially funded school programs. Citizens demand performance data on schools, and accountability requires that tests serve monitoring and evaluative functions rather than serving as motivators for students. In meeting the role of public accountability and instructional monitoring, tests have come to be used as administrative mechanisms by which educational policies are implemented.

Where minority students are concerned, the use and misuse of tests has been documented extensively, particularly with respect to standardized testing measures and intellectual functioning. While such work will not be repeated here, it is important that we also consider particulary the misuse of tests where policy decisions concerning culturally and linguistically different children are concerned. As mentioned earlier, the policy of avoiding standardized tests for language minority students has been reversed in order to determine need for a special program. In the same way that the roots of educational testing lie in the efforts to evaluate the success of schools rather than monitor the performance of individuals (Resnick & Resnick, 1985), the evaluative concern for assessing programs serving language minority students has resulted in a return to standardized testing. The use of standardized measures in conjunction with language assessment requires that cut-off scores on tests determine entry and exit criteria for bilingual program participation. Despite the protest of some educators concerning the seemingly careless designation of such scores, "technical warnings about the arbitrary nature of cutoff scores are dismissed by politicans as irrelevant psychobabble" (Madaus, 1985).

Language testing policies, while varied, reflect solutions at the state level for achieving the most accurate estimate of LEP children's language proficiency, their need for placement in, or their readiness for exit from, bilingual programs, and their chances for subsequent academic success in English-only classrooms. Those involved in language proficiency assessment, from the level of state departments of education to the classroom teacher, acknowledge the inadequacies of the measures that are currently available and argue for more accurate methods for detemining language proficiency levels and facilitating the placement and exit of children from bilingual programs. Skutnabb-Kangas suggests that by continuing to focus on the need for improved test construction, we are diverting our efforts and are missing the central issue regarding the education of language minority children:

> Psychological tests used for sociolinguistic and educational purposes have been discussed as though their purpose had been the technical, linguistic one of revealing exactly where and how immigrant children's linguistic ability is deficient. The problem that should be discussed is *why* immigrant children do so badly, worse than majority children, in different kinds of measurement of linguistic ability and school achievement, and what the long-term consequences of this may be (Skutnabb-Kangas, 1981, p. 218).

The following discussion will examine this question and the role of language proficiency testing in programs serving LEP students from a broader perspective, drawing on work in sociology, economics, and educational philosophy.

EDUCATIONAL REFORM AND THE EQUALIZATION OF RESOURCES

Bilingual education existed in many parts of the United States from the turn of the century until roughly World War I, when a combination of public xenophobia and English-only legislation brought it to a close. It reemerged in 1968 with the passage of the Bilingual Education Act. The impetus for its reappearance came from several areas: (a) recent gains in civil rights had heightened public consciousness concerning the needs of linguistically and culturally different students; (b) minority spokespersons were successful in bringing political pressure to redress minority taxpayers whose children were receiving a second-class education due to language barriers and racist attitudes in schools (Cohen, 1985); (c) it was seen as a way to alleviate the stress that large numbers of immigrant Cuban children had placed upon the public schools, particularly in Florida; and (d) the development of compensatory education models required some educational response to those students identified as underachieving due to language differences. During the sixties, the "War on Poverty" was attempting to equalize the distribution of social and economic resources—education was thought of as the "great equalizer," and large-scale compensatory education programs such as Head Start and Title I were instituted with the goal of improving the quality of education for minority students and ultimately increasing their economic mobility. Patterned in the image of compensatory schooling, the original bilingual education legislation espoused educational equity as its primary intent.

Studies in the late sixties and early seventies that investigated the effects of compensatory educational programs showed that they had not accomplished their goal of improving the academic achievement of minority students. The Coleman Report (1966), mandated by the Civil Rights Act of 1964 to provide support for the policy of financial redistribution to overcome educational inequity, showed that educational resources were not determinants of educational success. In a similar vein, the Rand Study, which examined the effectiveness of educational programs, stated that ". . . virtually without exception all of the large surveys of the major compensatory educational programs have shown no beneficial results on the average" (Averch et al., 1972, p. 125). Other social science research at the time dedicated itself to the relationship of egalitarian schooling to increased opportunity and subsequent job mobility. The work of Jencks et al. (1972, 1979) demonstrated that equalizing educational opportunities would do little to equalize the distribution of income, that the economically advantaged received twice the economic benefits from education as did the disadvantaged. It was also found that blacks, even those with a high school education, would probably not receive any increased economic benefits from education. The effects of these evaluation studies of compensatory education programs, which were largely negative, and the research that questioned the premise of equalizing the distribution of opportunities and resources through education severely challenged the liberal-progressive philosophy of egalitarian reform. As a result, a conservative backlash occurred, which resulted in beliefs, policies, and practices that sought to place the onus for school failure on the individual child. This trend was further strengthened by a reliance on psycho-educational testing, which strove to isolate those personal qualities of the individual that would be predictors of success or failure. It seemed reasonable to expect that if children were privy to special programs that employed unique treatments, and still failed to achieve, there must be something inherently wrong with the child, his family background, and/or his culture.

Jensen (1971), who took the most severe position, placed the failure of liberal-progressive experiments in compensatory education on the genetic inferiority of the poor. He stated that inequality in society existed and would persist due to inherited intellectual abilities or deficiencies, regardless of the type and quality of education provided. Others (Banfield, 1968; Moynihan, 1967) attributed the poor academic performance of minority children to their impoverished family background, believing that social circumstances did little to foster attitudes and values that would prepare them to compete with middle-class children. In the case of language minority children, bilingualism was posited as the main factor accounting for low levels of academic performance in school.

All of these "personal trait" rationales, such as intelligence, family background, cultural mismatch, and bilingualism, which situate the cause of school underachievement within the learner, serve several purposes. First, they reinforce the "diagnostic perscriptive" model, which calls for testing to identify and label the problem even when the construct being tested is not fully articulated nor are valid and reliable instruments available to measure it. This can lead to a self-fulfilling situation wherein both the child and the teacher are influenced by ambiguous labels that do not contribute to, and in many cases further hinder, the educational progress of the child. Second, the pathology models contribute to perpetuating the status quo, avoiding the examination of existing school curricula and the appropriateness of testing policies. Finally, personal trait rationales for underachievement lock one into a very narrow focus, which excludes the examination of the interaction of socioeconomic and political factors. While personal trait theories are probably still the most commonly given explanation for why minority children fail to achieve on a level with majority-group children, they are much too simplistic to account for such a complex and pervasive phenomenon. The following section presents two alternate explanations to account for minority children's school performance, situates them in the context of bilingual education in the United States, and questions the role played by language proficiency testing and program policy decisions.

SOCIAL REPRODUCTION THEORY

In examining the complexity of evaluating education, Michael Apple (1979a) pointed out that school curriculum failure generally cannot be explained, because schools are seen as discrete institutions that exist apart from the social and economic forces around them, and because they use input-output methodologies to measure success. In the seventies, others (Althusser, 1972; Bernstein, 1977; Bowles & Gintis, 1976; Bourdieu & Passeron, 1977) began to take a more macrosociological approach, which included forces outside the school, in an attempt to explain why special educational treatments did not result in increased student achievement or social mobility. Bowles and Gintis (1976) offered an alternative explanation for minority children's poor school performance by analyzing the relationship of schools to the economy. They posited that schools in capitalist countries produce workers who will later occupy positions in a highly stratified job market that is determined by market, property, and power relationships within the economic system. Schools mirror the power relationships that exist in the larger society and perform a social sorting function that corresponds to the highly stratified work force of the capitalist system. According to this theory, "Schools legitimate inequality through the ostensibly meritocratic manner by which they reward and promote students, and allocate them to distinct positions in the occupational hierarchy" (Bowles & Gintis, 1976, p. 11). While the manifest school curriculum presents one program of study, the hidden curriculum inculcates some students with a class consciousness that prepares them to occupy higher positions in the job market similar to those occupied by their parents. Usually minorities and students of low socioeconomic status do less well and eventually are relegated to the same low paying, low-status jobs as their parents. Therefore, within this framework, schools are seen as the main agent responsible for reproducing the existing social order. According to Bernstein (1977) and Bourdieu and Passeron (1977), the transmission and assessment of knowledge are crucial determiners of the reproduction of class relationships in industrial societies.

If one analyzes bilingual education within this perspective, there are many parallels. First, bilingual education was reestablished at the same time as the large-scale compensatory education programs of the sixties. The original legislation also espoused as one of its goals the equalization of educational opportunities for linguistically and culturally different children in order to bring them into the social mainstream and increase their chances of economic mobility in later life. While manifest curriculum includes dual language instruction, close examination of what is actually implemented at the school level shows that the curriculum is one that emphasizes English instruction, with only lip service paid to native language instruction. The exit of students to English-only classrooms (usually after a period of three years) in effect serves to limit the very assistance that may be necessary for success in school.

National statistics attest to the lack of educational gains for U.S. linguistic minority students, and analysis of the achievement of Hispanic students (Duran, 1983) identifies continual patterns of underachievement. Examination of the achievement levels of Hispanic high school sophomores and seniors from the 1980 High School and Beyond longitudinal study (Nielsen & Fernandez, 1981) shows that in the areas of mathematics, reading, and vocabulary achievement, all Hispanic subgroups (Mexican American, Cuban, Puerto Rican and other Latin Americans) scored about one standard deviation below white non-Hispanics. The 1980 Census data show that language minority youth, ages 16 to 24, are one and a half times more likely than their English-speaking peers to leave school before obtaining a high school diploma (Cardenas, Robledo, & Waggoner, 1988). Whereas studies of Hispanic student achievement have increased during the past 50 years, only recently has work begun to focus on the sociopolitical determinants of educational outcomes, as well as the interaction between child and school (Au & Mason, 1981; Barnhardt, 1982; Erickson & Mohatt, 1981; McCollum, 1980) that may produce underachievement and continual patterns of school failure (Walker, 1987).

Several important points need to be made concerning the relationship between existing practices of bilingual education in the United States and the continuing underachievement of Hispanic students. Only a small proportion of eligible Hispanic students are served by bilingual programs. Thus the great majority of students limited in their English proficiency receive either English as a second language services or no assistance at all. Where assessment practices are in place to determine need for bilingual or ESL services, such practices have been found to be based on inappropriate understanding of the relationship between language and learning (Cummins, 1984). The inadequacy of testing procedures eliminates many students who actually do need help, and often misclassifies those who are determined to be in need of the program.

The transitional nature of bilingual programs and the various policies at the state level that govern language testing may very well be contributing to the continued failure of language minority children. Research evidence (Cummins, 1976, 1979, 1984; Skutnabb-Kangas & Toukomaa, 1976) indicates that in order for children to reap the benefits that accrue to bilingualism, a certain threshold level of L2 competence must be achieved. Whereas transitional programs may allow sufficient time to acquire L2 oral language proficiency, the ability to use decontextualized language for academic purposes may take up to 7 years to acquire (Ramsey & Wright, 1970; Cummins, 1980). Other work cited by Duran (1983) supports this thesis by contending that several years of instruction in the native language are necessary to develop cognitive structures that will allow for achievement in English.

Although there is a wide variation in the bilingual instructional models and curricula used, children generally do not develop literacy skills in their native language due to the emphasis placed on the rapid acquisition of English in order that they be placed in English classrooms as soon as possible. The majority of the language proficiency measures currently being used to establish entry/exit criteria are based on a communicative competence model of language proficiency that emphasizes oral proficiency over literacy. As a result, children are exited from bilingual programs on the basis of oral language proficiency scores, without well-developed native language skills or sufficient exposure to English to develop the ability to use decontextualized language for cognitive academic purposes (Cummins, 1980). They are, in effect, being placed in double jeopardy by the transitional nature of bilingual programs and language assessment policies that exit them with sufficient skills to allow them to achieve on a par with their English-speaking peers. If research data are to be believed concerning the cognitive benefits of bilingualism and the need for both first language development and sufficient development of cognitive-academic language proficiency, current assessment and instructional policies are structured to perpetuate the continued failure of language minority students. Therefore, many students who are exited from bilingual programs as English proficient on the basis of oral language proficiency scores fall further behind grade-level norms as they continue through school (Mazzone, 1980), thus increasing the differential between minority and majority student academic performance.

More recently, many states use a combination of oral language proficiency scores in conjunction with subtest scores from standardized achievement tests in an effort to assess the child's ability to achieve in an all-English-speaking classroom. The language testing policy that is in effect in the state of Texas provides a good example. Bilingual program entry/exit criteria (desired proficiency levels for oral language proficiency test performance and percentile scores for standardized achievement battery subtests) are determined by the state. School districts are free to choose testing measures from the list of state-adopted tests for use in their schools. Limited-English-proficient (LEP) children who score at the fortieth percentile on the reading and language arts subtests of the district-adopted standardized achievement test, and who also score at appropriate levels on the district language proficiency measure are automatically exited from bilingual education programs. Those who score below the twenty-third percentile on the achievement measure subtests qualify for entry. Those, however, who score between the twenty-third and the fortieth percentile fall into a gray area that requires that the Language Proficiency Assessment Committee (LPAC), made up of administrators, teachers, parents, and a language specialist (where available), convene to decide whether the child should be exited from the program. No further testing is done at this point.

An LEP student performing at the twenty-third percentile in reading and language arts could therefore conceivably be judged to be prepared to participate in all-English instruction. Is performance at the twenty-third percentile on the same achievement tests considered adequate for a native-English-speaking child? Of course not. In this case, the child would most likely be considered at risk, and would probably be retained and/or referred for special services. One has to question why this disparity exists and what function it serves.

Although very low, the standards for bilingual program exit used in Texas are stringent when compared to policies and standards that are in effect in other states, where LEP students are exited to English-only classrooms after reaching the equivalent of the twentieth percentile on an oral language proficiency test. The trend toward school decentralization has caused many states to provide only broad policy guidelines regarding LEP students' participation in programs. Increasingly, individual districts design their own assessment and reclassification procedures, which conform to state guidelines and suggested performance levels. Rarely do district standards exceed state-suggested minimum performance levels. Table 1 outlines exit requirements designated for eight states, with attention to the percentile levels of performance required to exit elementary LEP students from bilingual and/or English as a second language (ESL) programs.

By examining reclassification criteria for exiting children from bilingual programs, it becomes clear that a dual set of standards is in operation—one that determines what is acceptable achievement for language minority children, and one that applies to the achievement of native-English-speaking children. At one level, these dual criteria serve to sort children within and among programs in the school. But at another level, such standards function to place language minority students at a disadvantage which may never be overcome. The transitional nature of bilingual programs, and the practice of exiting children from programs on the basis of oral language proficiency scores coupled with low scores on standardized achievement tests, are compounded by the lack of emphasis on native language development and literacy in most bilingual programs. These practices, together with institutionalized lower expectations for achievement by the use of arbitrary percentile minimums, may very well create a permanent underclass of students within the school population. The results of such differential expectations for minority and majority students have been well documented (Rosenthal & Jacobson, 1968; Rist, 1970; Leacock, 1979). For those who choose to remain in school, successive years of failing to learn the manifest academic curriculum result in repeated assessment and continued relegation to the class of underachievers. This transmits the subtle message that they are less capable than their language-majority counterparts. Furthermore, they come to believe that their failure to achieve at acceptable levels is due to their language, their culture, and their own inability to succeed. Skutnabb-Kangas, in reference to the education of immigrant children in Sweden, concludes that

> Since the children officially have the same opportunities as majority children, especially with an immigrant policy of the Swedish type, and since they have internalized the norms that tell them that they are being given equal opportunities with the majority children, it becomes more difficult to see that they are still the victims. But they are nonetheless *being made* scapegoats for the system. They

TABLE 1

Sample Program Exit Criteria for Elementary Bilingual Education and/or ESL Programs*

Location	Objective Measures		Subjects Used	Exit Criteria	
	OLP†	Standardized Tests		Automatic Exit	Possible Conditional Exit
Texas-state mandated criteria for all	X	X	District-Adopted Achievement Battery -language arts -reading	40th%	23rd–39th%
California, i.e., San Diego	X	X	CTBS -reading -math -language	36th%	31st–35th% (with parental consent)
Colorado, i.e., Denver	X	X	ITBS -reading -language arts	30th%	
Illinois, i.e. Chicago	X	X	ITBS -reading -language arts	above 1 S.D. below the mean	
Minnesota-all districts	X	X	District-Adopted Achievement Battery -language arts	above ⅓ S.D. below the mean	
New York-recommended state cut-off	X or	X		equivalent of 23rd%	
New York City‡		X		equivalent of 20%	

begin to *believe* that they must be inferior and that their poor performance is their own fault, since the system is fair to them. Minority children will begin to explain to themselves that they are simply not as capable as the majority children, and that is the reason they do not do well in the system (Skutnabb-Kangas, 1981, p. 314).

This consciousness, inculcated by the school and fostered by policy dictating the scope of programs and testing practices, effectively creates an agenda for underachievement and later underemployment for language minority students. While espousing a policy of equality, the system may very well help to produce the actual stratification of social order required by the existing economic structure.

A MODIFIED EXPLANATION: RESISTANCE THEORY

While correspondence theories or theories of social reproduction can help account for the underachievement of language minority students, using them as the sole analysis may be somewhat flawed in that they are too deterministic. Belief that the goal of the school is to develop a class consciousness that simply reflects the needs of the economic system ignores the fact that those within the school, both teachers and students, actively construct the reality they experience, thereby reproducing or contesting the system. Apple (1979b) criticizes correspondence theory because it views the schools as "black boxes," which take input (students) and process it through curricula to produce output (workers). He states that "This neglects the type of cultural forms and meanings that actually exist in schools . . . schools do more than simply process people; they help create and make legitimate (sometimes in contradictory and paradoxical ways) forms of consciousness that are dialectically related to a corporate society like our own" (Apple, 1979b, p. 104).

Resistance theory is more explanatory than correspondence theories in that it unites the macroperspective, the relationship of the school to the economy, with the microperspective, the relationship between teachers and students within the school. This is done by using an ethnographic methodology to study how students become labeled underachievers, how they may resist learning the manifest and hidden curricula, and how they contest not having the proper "cultural capital" to succeed within the system. Within this framework, students from advantaged backgrounds are seen as bringing values with them to school that allow them to excel. They accept the values of individualism and competition, which the school rewards, and therefore they achieve. Furthermore, since those values are also rewarded in the work place, at higher levels of employment, this group ultimately goes on to occupy positions similar to others of their social class. One study that exemplified this approach is Paul Willis's *Learning to*

Labor (1977), which studied a group of working-class males, known as the Lads, in a secondary school in an industrial town in England. Willis examined how the Lads resisted the academic agenda, rejected school knowledge (mental labor), and thus sealed their fate by assuring that they would only be prepared to accept physical labor in industry once they had graduated. Although school promised self-betterment and economic advantage as outcomes, this contrasted sharply with the real-life experiences of the Lads' family and friends, who had gone through school. The Lads' behavior seemed to reaffirm their belief that school would not allow them to get much further than they already were. Thus their behavior was a form of cultural resistance, which contrasted sharply with that of the "ear'oles" who, by virtue of their class background, were able to accept the values of the school, follow the rules, and achieve. This group, by accepting the mental labor in school and the dominant class ideology, was prepared to pursue mental work after graduation. Within this framework, it is evident that the basic requirements of the economic system are contradictory, yet the system is reproduced due to an autonomy of culture within the educational system.

Analyzing the underachievement of language minority students using the resistance theory perspective is advantageous in that it forces one to rethink some critical issues. First, one must acknowledge that schools are not isolated from the values and socioeconomic forces that exist outside them. Second, *premises*, one must question why the success of bilingual programs has been reduced to one issue—that of the rapid acquisition of English. As Paulston (1976) has suggested, other factors—school attendance, job statistics, etc.—should be examined in order to judge program effectiveness. Third, resistance theory accounts for the complexity of human interaction within social systems and draws attention to what occurs in schools. Erickson (1985, 1987) examines such interactions in order to more clearly identify the complex forces at work in teaching and learning settings with culturally and linguistically different students. A call is made for more culturally responsive education to prevent further educational estrangement and failure. In a similar vein, Cummins (1986) speaks to the empowerment of minority students and provides suggestions for breaking their present patterns of underachievement.

It is clear that we need to examine the role that current language proficiency testing policy and program exit criteria play in sorting children in school so as to reproduce an existing social order. In reference to U.S. immigrants, Spener (1988) argues that transitional bilingual education fulfills an economic need by preparing them for low status, low paying jobs. Their record of academic underachievement and resultant perceived inferiority serve to legitimize limited employment opportunities. Spener's argument is also applicable to native U.S. ethnolinguistic minorities, who are also socialized by transitional bilingual education to have lowered expectations for success in school and later life.

The recent "educational excellence" movement, heralded by the publication of *A Nation At Risk* in 1984, and followed by best-sellers such as *The Closing of the American Mind* (Bloom, 1987) and *Cultural Literacy* (Hirsch, 1987), criticizes present-day education, calling for a return to traditional values, a unified curriculum, and across-the-board improved standards of excellence. Proponents of the movement view increased educational standards as the road to producing a more skilled labor force and maintaining parity with foreign economic markets. The movement, which focuses on teaching canonical forms of knowledge, is driven by assessment that informs the re-teaching of skills. Interestingly, one area of schooling that has not been targeted for increased standards is bilingual education. On the contrary, policy guidelines and exit criteria have been loosened, contributing to earlier program exit. Once in English-only classrooms, students who are not prepared to compete academically are confronted with even higher educational standards in the general curriculum, which serve to guarantee their underachievement and entry into low-level jobs.

Previously cited research evidence should encourage us to begin to reevaluate the effects of transitional bilingual programs and current language assessment policies on language minority students and the role they play in maintaining hegemony within society. These effects need to be examined in light of actual classroom achievement, as well as the long-term success of schools in educating language minority students. Rather than continuing to focus our efforts on the development and construction of better and more complex language assessment instruments, much larger questions involving assessment need to be considered. For example:

- Given that we are in the throes of an educational excellence movement, why are bilingual program exit criteria not raised, allowing students to develop native and English language skills to levels that would allow them to compete with native-English speakers?
- In light of research evidence regarding the levels of language proficiency requisite for bilingualism to be beneficial, why does policy promote early exit from bilingual programs?
- Why do we accept institutionalized lower expectations for language minority students than for native-English speakers?

If after reflecting upon and evaluating these and related issues one accepts that these policies are not in the best interest of minority children, then the only alternative is to actively work toward changing them. In the interim, more qualitative longitudinal studies are needed to document how assessment policy may function to sort language minority children both academically and socially. Information can be used to guide informed testing and program policy decisions that may ultimately help to ensure equality of educational opportunity.

REFERENCES

Althusser, L. 1972. Ideology and ideological state apparatuses. In *Education: Structure and society*, ed. B. Cosin. New York: Penguin Books.

Apple, M. April 1979a. *Doing social evaluation in education.* Paper presented at the Competing Aims of Program Evaluation Meeting, Urbana-Champaign.

————. 1979b. What correspondence theories of the hidden curriculum miss. *The Review of Education* 5(2):101–12.

Au, K., and Mason, J. 1981. Social organizational factors in learning to read: The balance of rights hypothesis. *Reading Research Quarterly* 17(1):115–52.

Averch, H., Stephen, C., Donaldson, T., Kiesling, H., and Pencus, J. 1972. *How effective is schooling? A critical review and synthesis of research findings.* Santa Monica: The Rand Corporation.

Banfield, E. 1968. *The unheavenly city.* Boston: Little, Brown & Co.

Barnhardt, C. 1982. Tuning-in: Athabaskan teachers and Athabaskan students. In Cross-cultural issues in Alaskan education, vol. 2, ed. R. Barnhardt. Fairbanks: Center for Cross-Cultural Studies, University of Alaska.

Bernal, E. 1982. *Tests of language dominance and proficiency: A sampler and a critique.* Unpublished manuscript, Bilingual Special Education Consortium, Department of Special Education, University of Texas at Austin.

Bernstein, B. 1977. *Class, codes and control. Vol. 3: Towards a theory of educational transmission.* London: Routledge & Kegan Paul.

Bloom, A. 1987. The closing of the American mind. New York: Simon & Schuster.

Bourdieu, P., and Passeron, J. 1977. *Reproduction in education, society and culture.* London: Sage Publications.

Bowles, S., and Gintis, H. 1976. *Schooling in capitalist America.* New York: Basic Books.

Cardenas, J., Robledo, M., and Waggoner, D. 1988. *The undereducation of American Youth.* San Antonio: Intercultural Development Research Association.

Chomsky, N. 1957. *Syntactic structures.* The Hague, Netherlands: Mouton.

Cohen, A. 1985. Bilingual education. In *Beyond basics: Issues and research in TESOL,* ed. M. A. Celce-Murcia. New York: Newbury House Publishers.

Coleman, J. S., Campbell, E. G., Hobson, C. J., Partland, J., Mood, A.M., Weinfeld, F. B., and York, R. L. 1966. *Equality of educational opportunity.* Washington, D.C.: U. S. Department of Health, Education and Welfare.

Cummins, J. 1976. The influence of bilingualism on cognitive growth: A synthesis of research findings and explanatory hypotheses. *Working Papers on Bilingualism* 9:1–43.

———. 1979. Cognitive/academic language proficiency, linguistic interdependence, the optimal ages question and some other matters. *Working Papers on Bilingualism* 19:197–205.

———. 1980. The entry and exit fallacy in bilingual education. *NABE Journal* 4(3):25–60.

———. 1984. *Bilingualism and special education: Issues in assessment and pedagogy,* Boston: College-Hill Press.

———. February 1986. The empowerment of minority students: A framework for intervention. *Harvard Educational Review* 56(1):18–35.

Cummins, J., and Gulutsan, M. 1974. Bilingual education and cognition. *Alberta Journal of Educational Research* 20:259–69.

Duncan, S., and DeAvila, E. 1979. Bilingualism and cognition: Some recent findings. *NABE Journal* 4:15–50.

Duran, R. 1983. *Hispanics' education and background: Predictors of college achievement.* New York: College Entrance Examination board.

Erickson, F. 1985. School literacy, reasoning and civility: An anthropologist's perspective. *Review of Educational Research* 54(4):525–46.

———. December 1987. Transformation and school success: The politics and culture of educational achievement. *Anthropology and Education Quarterly* 18(4):335–56.

Erickson, F., and Mohatt, G. 1981. Cultural organization of participation structures in two classrooms of Indian students. In *Doing the ethnography of schooling,* ed. G. Spindler. New York: Holt, Rinehart & Winston.

Hirsch, E. D. 1987. *Cultural literacy: What every American needs to know.* Boston: Houghton Mifflin Co.

Jencks, C., Smith, M., Aclard, H., Bane, M. J., Cohen, D., Gintis, H., Heyrs, B., and Michaelson, S. 1972. *Inequality: A reassessment of the effects of family and schooling in America.* New York: Basic Books.

Jencks, C., M. Corcoran, J. Crouse, D. Eaglesfield, G. Jackson, K. McClelland, P. Mueser, M. Olneck, J. Schwartz, S. Ward, J. Williams. 1979. *Who gets ahead?: The determinants of economic success in America.* New York: Basic Books.

Jensen, A. 1971. *The I.Q. argument.* Peru, Ill.: Library Press.

Lambert, W. 1977. The effects of bilingualism on the individual: Cognitive and sociocultural consequences. In *Bilingualism—psychological, social, and educational implications,* ed. P. A. Hornby. New York: Basic Books.

Leacock, E. 1979. *Teaching and learning in city schools.* New York: Basic Books.

McCollum, P. 1980. *Attention-getting strategies of Anglo-American and Puerto Rican students: A microethnographic analysis.* Unpublished doctoral dissertation, University of Illinois, Urbana.

Madaus, G. F. 1985. Test scores as administrative mechanisms in educational policy. *Phi Delta Kappan,* May:611–17.

Mazzone, E. 1980. Current trends in Massachusetts in the assessment of language minority students. In *Georgetown round table on languages and linguistics,* ed. J. E. Alatis. Washington, D.C.: Georgetown University Press.

Mercer, J. 1974. A policy statement on assessment procedures and the rights of children. *Harvard Educational Review* 44(1):125–41.

Moynihan, D. 1967. *The Negro family.* Cambridge, Mass.: MIT Press.

Nielsen, F., and Fernandez, R. 1981. *Hispanic students in American high schools: Background characteristics and achievement.* Washington, D.C.: National Center for Educational Statistics.

Oller, J. Jr. 1979. *Language tests at school.* New York: Longman Publishers.

Paulston, C. 1976. Bilingual education and its evaluation: A reaction paper. In *Bilingual education, current perspectives, Vol. Linguistics,* 1977.

Peal, E., and Lambert, W. E. 1962. The relation of bilingualism to intelligence. *Psychological Monographs,* 76:1–23.

Ramsey, C. A., and Wright, E. N. 1970. *Language backgrounds and achievement in Toronto schools.* Toronto: Board of Education for the City of Toronto.

Resnick, D. P., and Resnick, L. B. 1985. Standards, curriculum, and performance: A historical and comparative perspective. *Educational Researcher* 14(4):5–20.

Rist, R. 1970. Student social class and teacher expectations: The self-fulfilling prophecy in ghetto education. *Harvard Educational Review* 40:411–451.

Rosenthal, R., and Jacobson, L. 1968. Pygmalion in the classroom: Teacher expectation and pupils' intellectual development. New York: Holt, Rinehart & Winston.

Skutnabb-Kangas, T. 1981. *Bilingualism or not: The education of minorities.* Clevedon, England: Multilingual Matters, Ltd.

Skutnabb-Kangas, T., and Toukomaa, P. 1976. *Teaching migrant children's mother tongue and learning the language of the host country in the context of the sociocultural situation of the migrant family.* Helsinki, Finland: Finnish National Commission for UNESCO.

Spener, D. 1988. Transitional bilingual education and the socialization of immigrants. *Harvard Educational Review* 58(2):133–53.

Troike, R. C. 1983. The influence of public policy on language assessment of bilingual students. In *Issues of language assessment: Vol. II. Language assessment and curriculum planning,* ed. S. Seidner. Springfield, Ill.: Illinois State Board of Education.

Ulibarri, D. M., Spencer, M. L., and Rivas, G. A. 1981. Language proficiency and academic achievement: Relationship to school ratings as predictors of academic achievement. *NABE Journal* 5(3):47–80.

Walker, C. 1987. Hispanic achievement: Old views and new perspectives.

In *Success or failure? Learning and the language minority student,* ed. H. T. Trueba. New York: Newbury House Publishers.

Willis, P. 1977. *Learning to labor.* New York: Columbia University Press.

V.
DESEGREGATION

THE EVOLUTION OF THE SCHOOL DESEGREGATION MOVEMENT AND ITS IMPLICATIONS FOR EQUITY AND EXCELLENCE

Charles B. Vergon

Few movements have lasted as long, generated as much controversy, or had as great an impact on American public education as the school desegregation movement. The past decade, however, has been a period of reassessment and redirection. In many respects it has been a period of paradoxes both in Supreme Court pronouncements and school desegregation practices.

Whether the movement is approaching another set of historic crossroads, at which fundamental choices are made that will serve to characterize its future, is open to debate. What is less subject to debate is that the past and present periods through which the movement has evolved have had implications for educational equity and excellence, just as will the future course of the movement. However, rather than speculating about the course and implications of desegregation policy in the year 2,000—something far more appropriate for a futurist than a precedent-bound lawyer—the purposes of this article are far more modest. They are twofold. One purpose is to provide a historical overview of desegregation policies, approaches, and priorities through an analysis of the legal developments and strategies that have brought us to the present crossroads. The other is to suggest the implications of the past decade of reassessment and redirection on equity and excellence today, and over the next decade.

A HISTORICAL OVERVIEW OF THE SCHOOL DESEGREGATION MOVEMENT

The schooling of blacks and other minorities in the United States has undergone substantial change in terms of goals and means over the past century. Much of this change has been associated with the school desegregation movement and the various stages through which the movement has passed. While any attempt to characterize and suggest starting and ending dates for periods of complex and continuing social action is inherently simplistic, such characterizations may provide a convenient means of reviewing the social forces and legal precedents contributing to fundamental changes in desegregation policy and approaches over time, as well as the tempo of such changes. The desegregation movement is divisible into four major periods: the transition to a new standard (1850–1954); massive resistance (1955–1967); meaningful progress (1968–1973); and reassessment and redirection (1974–1986).

The Transition to a New Standard (1850–1954)

The quest for educational opportunity among blacks in America dates from their arrival in this country (Woodson, 1919). Yet the history of the education of the minority child has been one of exclusion, segregation, and inequality (Weinburg, 1977).

Prior to the Civil War, virtually none of the over 1 million black slave children in the United States were enrolled in the public schools. The less than 2 percent of all black children who did attend school during the period were freed Negro children attending "Negro schools" scattered across the

FIGURE 1
Overview of the School Desegregation Movement

Transition to a New Standard	Massive Resistance	Meaningful Progress	Reassessment and Redirection
1850–1954	1955–1967	1968–1973	1974–1986
exclusion			
	nullification	implementation (South)	
segregation			limitation
	circumvention		
equalization			
	minimalization		redirection
desegregation		translation (North)	

North. Even after the adoption of the Emancipation Proclamation and the ratification of the Thirteenth, Fourteenth, and Fifteenth Amendments, few blacks were immediately afforded access to any type of formal public education. It was not until 1870 that the proportion of black children attending school approached 10 percent, from which it increased to 33 percent by 1880, a level at which it remained through 1900 (Bond, 1934, p. vii).

As the policy of excluding blacks from any public educational opportunities was diminishing in the late 1800s, the practice of segregating them for such schooling was gaining governmental support. States enacted laws expressly prohibiting students of different races from attending common schools. The policy of providing separate public services gained additional force with the Supreme Court's 1896 decision in *Plessy v. Ferguson*. In *Plessy*, the Court approved Louisiana's practice of providing separate but equal public transportation for its black and white citizens. This decision and the separate but equal doctrine it embodied ushered in a period during which the comparability of educational opportunities and the equalization of resources between black and white schools were the principal goals of constitutional litigation. This transitional period, which began in 1896, would not end for nearly half a century.

The initial application of this doctrine to the field of public education came in 1899, just three years after *Plessy*. Blacks petitioned the Court to intercede in a Georgia community's decision to temporarily suspend the operation of a black high school due to economic circumstances, while continuing the high school serving whites. Noting the circumstances of the case and the interest of the state in educational matters, the Court, in *Cummings v. Richmond County*, declined to issue an injunction barring the black school's closure.

At the turn of the century such dramatically unequal levels of public monies and educational opportunities were increasingly common as blacks lost their political clout through disenfrancisement. It was not uncommon—even for states that had provided substantially equivalent public support in 1870—to spend from two to three times as much for the education of a white child as for a black child in the opening decades of the 1900s (Bond, 1934).

Cases challenging the availability or allocation of educational resources did not reach the Supreme Court again for several decades, at which time they began yielding results different from *Cummings*. In 1938, the Court ruled unconstitutional Missouri's policy of paying the tuition of qualified black students to attend law school in an adjacent state, rather than operating a law school for blacks within its own jurisdiction (*Gaines v. Canada*). A dozen years later, in 1950, the Court declared that although the state of Texas provided a law school for blacks within its borders, the education attainable at that institution was not substantially equivalent to that afforded white students at the University of Texas (*Sweatt v. Painter*). In reaching this conclusion, the Court noted tangible differences between the schools, including the size and quality of their law libraries and faculties, as well as the limited opportunity provided black students to associate with whites who represent the vast majority of the legal practitioners and jurists in the state.

The importance of individual associations and intellectual interaction as an ingredient of equal educational opportunities was cited by the Court in another 1950 decision. In that case, the Court struck down an Oklahoma requirement that blacks admitted to white colleges sit in certain rows in classrooms and at separate tables in the college library and cafeteria (*McLaurin v. Oklahoma*).

This progression of cases, methodically pursued over more than a quarter of a century by civil rights organizations, provided the foundation for the Supreme Court's pronouncement in 1954 of a new policy governing race and education in the United States. In its historical *Brown v. Board of Education* decision, the Court declared state-sanctioned segregation inherently unequal and a denial of the constitutional rights of black children. The effect of this decision was to establish a new standard providing that schools should be operated on a nonracial or desegregated basis in the 17 southern and border states that then required or permitted the separation of students by race.

Yet the Court did little in *Brown* to elaborate on this standard or how school districts were to satisfy it. Instead, the Court scheduled a separate hearing the following term devoted exclusively to the question of remedy. Neither, however, did this second *Brown* decision provide specific prescriptions for school districts or courts to follow. Instead it set out general principles to guide them in formulating plans and evaluating remedies on a case-by-case basis. Among these principles were (1) that the local school board was primarily responsible for developing and implementing a desegregation plan; (2) that it must make a prompt start and proceed with all deliberate speed in doing so; and (3) that good faith would be the standard by which school district progress would be judged. The decision also established that district courts were to retain jurisdiction over the cases and apply equitable principles in facilitating the dismantling of the dual school systems. Although far from definitive, this new standard of school desegregation represented a substantial, if not radical, departure from the previous standards, which had successively provided for the total exclusion of blacks from public education and for their later admission to inferior and strictly segregated public schools. Thus it was not unpredictable that the new standard would be met with massive resistance.

Massive Resistance (1955–1967)

Segregation in public education was absolute in most southern and border states in 1954. Public resistance to the new standard of racially desegregated education was pervasive across the region. It would last well over a decade and take a number of forms, including overt attempts to nullify the policy, covert measures to circumvent its application, and informal as well as formal strategies to minimize its effect or delay its ultimate implementation.

In the immediate aftermath of *Brown,* state officials and private citizens attempted to nullify the Supreme Court's commands. Various states adopted interposition statutes directly challenging the supremacy of the Constitution and federal authority to interpret and enforce it. Citizens, joined by elected officials in communities such as Little Rock, attempted to nullify the new desegregation standard in practice through public demonstrations of hostility and open defiance of the law.

With such nullification maneuvers thwarted by court action and the intervention of federal marshals, resistance turned to more subtle modes of circumvention or minimalization. Ten states, including Tennessee, adopted facially-neutral pupil placement statutes requiring students to seek admission to schools other than those to which they were previously assigned (*Northcross v. Board of Education*). Placement committees operated to maintain the status quo of racial segregation by employing selection criteria that were frequently only thinly disguised surrogates for student race. In other states, such as Virginia, public schools were closed in the face of imminent desegregation. State resources were then transferred to private, segregated academies and tutition grant programs instituted to benefit their white student clientele (*Griffin v. Prince Edwards County*).

As these and other attempts at circumvention were blunted by an increasingly impatient judiciary, school districts in the mid-1960s began advancing minimal desegregation plans designed to have little impact on existing levels of segregation. The effectiveness of many such plans frequently was dependent on the voluntary participation of students. Such "freedom of choice" plans, as they were called, proved singularly ineffective, as demonstrated by the experience of 37 parishes in Louisiana over a four-year period in the mid-1960s (*Hall v. St. Helena Parish*). During that time, only 2 of 266,233 whites exercised their freedom of choice to enroll in formerly black schools, thus placing the burden to achieve whatever desegregation would be realized squarely on blacks, a pattern repeated wherever such voluntary techniques were employed.

Even in those districts where school officials assumed responsibility for reassigning students, plans were frequently phased-in, one grade per year, thereby forestalling meaningful desegregation for up to an additional school-age generation. And finally, in states such as Virginia and North Carolina, districts facing impending court orders sought to splinter themselves into several independent school systems with the effect of minimizing the degree of desegregation that would otherwise be achievable by means of countywide plans (*Wright v. Emporia* and *U.S. v. Scotland Neck*).

As a result of such measures, pupil desegregation moved across the South at an almost imperceptible pace between 1954 and 1964. The number of blacks attending schools with whites increased at an average rate of only about 1 percent a year, with over 89 percent of black students in the 17-state southern and border region attending all-black schools during the 1964–65 school year. Within the 11 states of the old Confederacy, only 2.25 percent of black students attended schools with whites a decade after *Brown* (U.S. Civil Rights Commission, 1967).

Although only southern and border states had explicit statutes in 1954 requiring or permitting racial segregation in the schools, school segregation was not purely a southern phenomenon, either at the time of *Brown* or a decade later. In 1968, for instance, 60 percent of all black students in the 32 northern and western states were enrolled in predominantly minority schools (U.S. Civil Rights Commission, 1975).

Meaningful Progress (1968–1973)

The initial decade of desegregation litigation had consisted of the issuance of negative injunctions striking down various barriers thrown up to block the admission of blacks to formerly white schools. It has done little to require districts to take affirmative measures to ensure that blacks and whites were enrolled in common schools on an equal basis.

The Supreme Court's impatience with the rate and degree of desegregation became increasingly evident during the 1960s. As early as 1963, the Court hinted that the time for all deliberate speed "was running out" (*Griffin v. Prince Edwards County*, p. 234). Run out it did in 1968, when the Court, in *Green v. New Kent County*, declared that desegregation must be accomplished "now." Its resolve was underscored a year later, when the Court, in *Alexander v. Holmes County*, emphatically commanded desegregation "immediately." In elaborating on this standard, two Justices noted in a concurring opinion in *Carter v. West Feliciani* that:

> [I]n no event should the time from the finding of noncompliance with the requirements of *Green* to the time of actual operative effect of relief, including the time for judicial approval and review, exceed a period of approximately eight weeks (p. 293).

The Court upheld the mid-year implementation of a faculty and student desegregation plan in this case, and in another case required the implementation of a plan within three weeks to coincide with the opening of school (*Jefferson Parish v. Dandridge*).

In addition to picking up the pace with which school districts were required to respond to the obligations set out in *Brown*, the Court proceeded in *Green* to spell out a new standard for evaluating the legal adequacy of pupil desegregation plans. Rather than assessing them on the basis of the school district's good faith, desegregation plans were to be hereafter evaluated on the basis of their effectiveness, or, in the language of the Court, whether they "promise to realistically work, and work now." In striking down a proposed freedom-of-choice plan, the Court went on to require that school authorities use the most effective means reasonably available to achieve the maximum amount of desegregation possible in light of local community conditions.

As a result of the rulings in *Green* and *Alexander* requiring the immediate implementation of effective desegregation plans, a 59 percent increase in the number of black children attending school with white students was registered in the South between 1968 and 1972. More than 1 million blacks entered majority white schools for the first time during this four-year period (U.S. Civil Rights Commission, 1975, p. 47).

In 1971 the reasonable means of pupil reassignment which school districts would be obligated to employ to achieve the maximum amount of desegregation possible were further delineated by the Court in a case involving the Charlotte-Mecklenburg schools in North Carolina. In *Swann v. Charlotte-Mecklenburg,* and a series of companion actions decided on the same day, the Court approved and required the use of race-conscious pupil reassignment techniques, including the affirmative gerrymandering of geographic attendance boundaries, the pairing and clustering of schools, and the transporting of students to schools other than those serving their immediate neighborhoods.

The years between 1965 and 1972 represent a significant watershed in the implementation of school desegregation policy in the United States, especially in the South. Not coincidentally, they also represent a watershed in terms of judicial approach and strategy. The issuance of negative injunctions and the approval of voluntary desegregation measures through the early 1960s gave way after 1965 to increasingly affirmative injunctions requiring mandatory reassignment measures that were to be judged by their objective effectiveness rather than the subjective good faith of their proponents. The simultaneous adoption of Title VI of the 1964 Civil Rights Act also contributed to the unparalleled progress achieved in the South, although the development and enforcement of administrative measures was neither immediate nor vigorous (Orfield, 1969; National Center for Policy Review, 1973).

While community after community desegregated across the South, educational segregation remained a fact of life for blacks in the schools of the North and West. Seventy-one percent of the black students in the 32 states comprising these regions attended predominately minority schools in 1970 (U.S. Civil Rights Commission, 1975, p. 47). This continuing segregation was largely due to a legalism rooted in the Fourteenth Amendment. Since northern and western states had never enacted or had previously abandoned segregation statutes, it was necessary for black plaintiffs to demonstrate that the segregation they experienced was somehow attributable to purposeful state action. In 1973 the Supreme Court heard its first northern school case, declaring in *Keyes v. School District of Denver* that segregation traceable to the purposeful policies and practices of local school officials was no less offensive to the Constitution than the segregation commanded by state statute in the South. Thus northern districts were also under a legal obligation to remedy segregation resulting from purposeful public policies. Furthermore, the Court reasoned that once purposeful segregation was proven in a significant portion of a northern school district, a presumption would arise that any other segregation in the district was the result of similar intentional action, thereby necessitating a systemwide desegregation plan.

The Court's ruling in this case implicitly approved segregation findings and desegregation orders issued between 1969 and 1973 in cases involving more than a score of northern and western communities from Pontiac to Pasadena. For the first time, two decades after *Brown*, the new standard had been translated beyond a mere regional policy. The decade of massive resistance in the immediate aftermath of *Brown* had been followed by five years of meaningful progress between 1968 and 1973, with the promise of even broader desegregation in the years to come.

Reassessment and Redirection (1974–1986)

Desegregation continued in the North and West after 1973, but the progress was neither as rapid nor as widespread as initially anticipated. After *Keyes* came a series of other northern cases that shattered the Court's tradition of unanimity in matters of race and schooling. New complexity was introduced into both the violation and remedy aspects of school desegregation litigation with the redefinition or addition of concepts such as "discriminatory intent," "interdistrict segregation," and "incremental segregatory effect." As well as confounding lower courts, the new principles and technical standards confused local school officials, and redirected, if not totally diverted, the plans and actions of school systems that had yet to desegregate. In many respects, the period between 1974 and 1986 was one of reassessment, particularly of the issue of pupil desegregation, and one of redirection toward a broader, multidimensional concept of the unitary school, with an emphasis on quality rather than mere equality.

One of the major legal issues that slowed the momentum of school desegregation in the early 1970s was the Supreme Court's reassessment of the appropriate standard for determining segregatory intent, one of the essential elements of an equal protection violation. In cases involving police hiring practices in the nation's capital and zoning ordinances in the suburban Chicago community of Arlington Heights, the Court rejected the notion that segregatory intent could be inferred merely from the natural, probable, and foreseeable consequences of public actions. Instead, the Court announced a substantially more stringent standard, requiring the evaluation of factors including (1) the historical background and specific sequence of events leading to the decision; (2) the contemporaneous statements of decision makers or records of their actions; (3) the procedural regularity or irregularity of the action; (4) the consistency or inconsistency of the action with usually important or controlling substantial considerations; and (5) the racial impact of the decision (*Washington v. Davis* and *Village of Arlington Heights v. Metro Housing Corporation*). Based on its rulings in these nonschool cases, the Court vacated and remanded half a dozen school desegregation cases to lower courts between 1975 and 1976 for further findings on the issue of segregatory intent. Although the lower courts almost universally reaffirmed their prior findings of intentional segregation using the Supreme Court's more strict standard, attention was diverted for 6 to 18 months from remedy formulation to relitigation of the underlying constitutional violation.

Simultaneously, the Court was being asked to reassess the limits of its equitable authority in fashioning school desegregation remedies. In *Swann*, and again in *Keyes*, the Court alluded to the equitable principle that the nature and scope of the remedy should be reasonable in relation to the constitutional violation. In 1974 the Court focused additional attention on this principle when rejecting a proposed metropolitan desegregation remedy for the city of Detroit and up to 52 suburban districts. The 5–4 decision in *Milliken v. Bradley* held that federal courts lack the authority to order interdistrict relief except upon a showing of purposeful governmental actions with an interdistrict segregatory effect. Although denying such relief in Detroit, and temporarily discouraging metropolitan desegregation actions such as would subsequently be approved in Wilmington, Indianapolis, and St. Louis, among other communities, the primary consequence of the decision was to rivet the attention of school officials and their attorneys on the legal limits of desegregation relief.

While the application of this principle linking violation and remedy appeared reasonably manageable in the context of interdistrict actions, its translation into the remedy formulation process in more conventional, single-district desegregation actions caused considerable confusion. Much of the confusion centered on the meaning and application of the concept of "incremental segregatory effect," as explicated by Justice Rehnquist in a 1977 appeal brought by the Dayton public schools. The appeal in *Dayton v. Brinkman* challenged the appropriateness of a systemwide desegregation plan required by the Sixth Circuit of Appeals. The opinion reasoned that since equitable remedies are intended to restore individuals to the position they would have otherwise enjoyed but for the unconstitutional actions of public officials, school desegregation remedies should be limited to correcting the "incremental segregatory effects" of proven misconduct. Because such an analysis was not reflected in the record below, Dayton's systemwide desegregation plan was remanded for further consideration. As happened when the standard for proving discriminatory intent was clarified, the Court received a number of school district petitions asking that lower courts be required to reassess the appropriateness of their prior rulings. In this instance, they requested that the scope of the remedial plans proposed for Columbus, Milwaukee, Omaha, and Los Angeles be reevaluated in light of the Dayton ruling.

Within 24 months the Dayton case was back before the Supreme Court, along with a companion case, *Columbus Board of Education v. Penick*. In both cases, the Supreme Court affirmed systemwide desegregation orders, ignoring almost completely the "incremental segregatory effect" test it had formulated less than two years previously. These decisions, and several made earlier in the decade, provoked one commentator to lament the Supreme Court's "vagueness and vacillation" and the "sea of murky technicality" that characterized its desegregation decisions in the 1970s (Kirp, 1982, p. 285).

The result of this vagueness and vacillation was both practical and symbolic. Practically, it required plaintiffs to expend more time and resources in demonstrating a constitutional violation and then in justifying the scope of pupil reassignment warranted by the facts, be it either intra- or inter-district in nature. Because plaintiffs were largely successful in demonstrating discriminatory intent and proving official conduct with systemwide, and in some instances even inter-district segregatory effect, the Court's vacillation tended to slow rather than halt the process of pupil desegregation between 1974 and 1979. Perhaps more significant than the practical effect of this period of reassessment was its symbolic impact. It cast doubts on the national policy of school desegregation, creating uncertainties not only among school districts and the public, but also the lower federal courts responsible for interpreting and applying the policy.

However, the reassessment and limiting of pupil reassignment remedies was not the only major development influencing desegregation policy in the mid-1970s. The Detroit metropolitan desegregation case triggered not only a reassessment of the scope of inter- and intra-district pupil reassignment plans, but also a redirection in the nature of remedies that would be sought subsequently in cases involving urban school districts. Faced with the prospects of a Detroit-only plan that would leave the district predominately minority and without the expanded resources or political leverage that a metropolitan plan would have provided, school district officials and plaintiffs focused their attention on clarifying the concept of the unitary school and redefining the content and contour of an effective remedial plan in light of contemporary community conditions.

The foundation for a broad remedial regime had been laid over a 20-year period. In *Brown II* (p. 300), the Court had noted that merely opening the doors of formerly white schools to blacks would require consideration of means to overcome "varied local obstacles," including those associated with "the physical condition of the school plant, the school transportation system, personnel ... and the revision of local laws and regulations. ..." In 1955 the Court advised district courts to consider petitions for faculty desegregation simultaneously with those seeking pupil reassignment (*Bradley v. Richmond*). The Supreme Court in *Green* further defined the indicia of a segregated school system, noting that in the school district before it:

> Racial identification of the system's schools was complete, extending not only to the composition of the student bodies ... but to every facet of school operations—faculty, staff, transportation, extra-curricular activities and facilities (p. 435).

Focusing on the nature and priority of a district's remedial obligation in such circumstances in 1971, the Court observed in *Swann:*

> When a system has been dual in these respects, the first remedial responsibility of school officials is to eliminate invidious racial distinctions. With respect to such matters as transportation, supporting personnel, and extra-curricular activities, no more than this may be necessary. Similar corrective action may be taken with regard to the maintenance of buildings and the distribution of equipment. In these areas, normal administrative practice should produce schools of like quality, facilities, and staffs (pp. 18–19).

One additional factor that characterizes a dual system was identified in the 1973 *Keyes* case: the perception of the community and the school administration. Where a building is perceived as black or inferior, irrespective of its actual racial composition or objective equality, it is nevertheless "segregated" from a constitutional standpoint. This is, at least in part, because citizens will make decisions regarding residence, and school officials regarding student assignment and resource allocation, based on such perceptions.

Thus, by 1974, the seven components of a unitary school system had been sketched out. In addition, the Court had identified two dimensions or requirements associated with each component, namely that they be operated on a nonracial or desegregated basis and provide comparable educational resources to black and white children (Figure 2). A new dimension was added to the concept of the unitary school system in 1977 as the result of the second Detroit desegregation case.

In *Milliken II* the Supreme Court acknowledged the authority of federal courts to not only require remedies that afford comparable and desegre-

FIGURE 2
**Components and Dimensions of
The Supreme Court's Unitary School Concept**

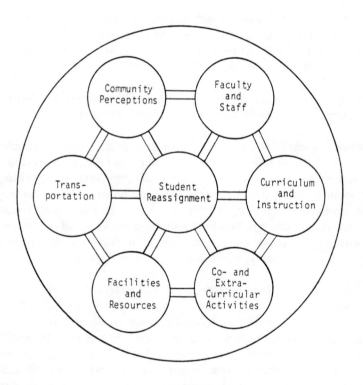

DIMENSIONS

purpose	-	principle
accessibility	-	desegregation
comparability	-	equality
remediation	-	equity

gated educational experiences, but also ones that compensate for and remedy the effects of past unlawful segregation and discrimination. Although such compensatory or remedial relief was considered an integral part of equitable remedies in other contexts, and had been employed on a limited basis in a few southern desegregation cases, it was only in the context of the Detroit case that it became a centerpiece of remedial plans in the mid-1970s.

Late in 1974 the federal district judge presiding over the Detroit school desegregation case ordered the district to submit a desegregation plan for his consideration. The Detroit Board of Education responded early in 1975 with a comprehensive remedial proposal consisting of 13 educational components, as well as a traditional pupil reassignment plan. These ancillary or educational components provided programs focusing on reading and communications, multicultural and bilingual education, vocational and technical training, co-curricular and enrichment opportunities, guidance and counseling services and testing practices, a uniform code of student conduct, the in-service training of staff, and school-community relations activities. Some of these components represented entirely new initiatives; others reflected the revision or expansion of preexisting programs.

District Judge Robert DeMascio incorporated these educational components in the court's August 1975 remedial order and assessed against the state co-defendant half the cost of four components, specifically those pertaining to reading, counseling, testing, and staff training. The state, however, contended that the proposed educational components could not be ordered by the court. The state reasoned that since the constitutional violation involved the segregation of students, the remedy must be limited to pupil reassignment.

The Supreme Court ultimately rejected this argument, noting that equitable principles only require that a federal court decision "... directly address and relate to the *condition* offending the constitution" (emphasis in original). Elsewhere in its opinion the Court observed that "discriminatory student assignment policies can themselves manifest and breed other inequalities..." and that "federal courts... cannot close their eyes to inequalities... which flow from a longstanding segregated system." Finally, the Court declared that:

> Pupil assignment alone does not automatically remedy the impact of previous unlawful educational isolation; the consequences linger and can be dealt with only by independent measures (*Milliken II*, pp. 287–88).

Justice Burger identified three factors that federal courts should take into account when fashioning desegregation decrees involving such independent measures or ancillary components:

[First] ... the nature of the desegregation remedy is to be determined by the nature and scope of the constitutional violation. The
remedy therefore must be related to the *condition* alleged to offend
the Constitution. . . . Second, the decree must indeed be *remedial*
in nature, that is, . . . designed as nearly as possible to restore the
victims . . . to the position they otherwise would have occupied. . . .
Third, the federal courts in devising a remedy must taken into
account the interest of state and local authorities in managing their
own affairs (*Milliken II,* pp. 280–81).

The addition of this "remedial" dimension to the unitary school concept
represented a major development in two respects. First, it affirmed the
equitable principle that justice may require differential treatment of groups
that are, at a certain point in time, unequal because of purposeful governmental actions. Second, it shifted the focus of the unitary school, from mere
access to desegregated schools and comparable inputs to a more nearly
outcome-oriented measure of equity; specifically, it meant that the remedy
should restore blacks to the position they would have occupied if they had
not been subjected to public-sanctioned discrimination.

Even though the Court expressly observed that the district court's order
in *Milliken II* was not a blueprint for other cases, the imprimatur of the
Court on an expansive remedial regime, plus the prospects of a nonschool
district party assuming a substantial portion of the associated costs, all but
drowned out the Court's admonition. In successive cases at the federal
district court level, the *Milliken* regime was proposed and contended for
by school district after school district, and in some instances by plaintiffs
and even the court's own operative experts and masters. Between 1976 and
the early 1980s federal district courts had ordered, and appellate courts
had affirmed, comprehensive remedial orders for school districts serving
Boston, Benton Harbor, Cleveland, Columbus, Detroit, Indianapolis, St.
Louis, and Wilmington, Delaware, among other northern and western communities. (For illustrative cases, see *Morgan v. Kerrigan, Evans v. Buchanan,
Berry v. Benton Harbor, United States v. Board of School Commissioners
of Indianapolis,* and *Liddel v. Board of Education of St. Louis.* For commen-
tary, consult Kalodner & Fishman, 1978; Willie & Greenblatt, 1981; Hawley,
1983; Vergon, 1985).

In review, the 1970s were a paradoxical period for the Supreme Court
and the school desegregation movement. While the Court was reassessing
and limiting the scope and availability of pupil reassignment remedies in
some cases, it was at the same time in *Milliken II* greatly expanding the
nature and availability of ancillary relief, including educational components
designed to remedy the effects of past segregation and discrimination and
complete the transition to a unitary system. Acting together, these developments served to redirect attention in the 1980s away from pupil deseg-

regation and toward educational quality components with potentially significant policy implications for the future of both pupil segregation and educational excellence.

IMPLICATIONS FOR EQUITY AND EXCELLENCE

These developments have several important implications for pupil seg-regation or access to common schools. The period of reassessment has effectively reversed the era of meaningful progress and turned the clock of the desegregation movement in the direction of the once-rejected doc-trine of separate but equal, although it would be premature to characterize recent developments as a return to this earlier standard.

Federal court action, however, does not appear likely to bring about substantial levels of new pupil desegregation in the near future. When this lack of new initiatives is coupled with current population trends and res-idential patterns, it is clear that blacks, Hispanics, and whites are likely to attend schools that are increasingly unrepresentative of the pluralistic na-tion in which they will live and work. Given the increasing proportion of blacks and the growing concentration of Hispanics in urban communities, only metropolitan-wide plans, implemented on a broad scale, will effectively bring about meaningful levels of desegregation and interracial contact across the North and West, as well as in a number of southern communities. Variations of such metropolitan plans exist in communities such as Benton Harbor, Indianapolis, St. Louis, and Wilmington by virtue of federal court order, and in Boston and Milwaukee as the result of legislative inducements. These plans represent relatively isolated situations. Their national impor-tance consequently has more to do with demonstrating the feasibility of such educational constellations than achieving a detectable decline in the overall levels of segregation, as evidenced by the fact that 17 of 24 large city school districts reported enrollments of more than two-thirds minority students in 1982 (National Center for Educational Statistics, 1985, p. 4).

While the implications of recent developments are clearly negative in terms of equity, as measured by access to racially representative schools, the impact of these developments on ensuring comparable educational resources is less clear. The impact may vary depending not only on the district in question, but also the referent selected for measuring compar-ability. For instance, a typical pupil reassignment plan implemented during the period of meaningful progress guaranteed not only that each building contained blacks and whites in rough proportion to their presence in the entire district, but also that whatever the quality of the educational program, it would be distributed evenly among whites and blacks. To the extent that white students found the quality of their new school facility or program to be less than that to which they were accustomed, improvements could be expected, thereby ensuring the comparability of schools and, in some instances, enhancing the overall quality of the school district's program.

In those situations where desegregation is less than districtwide and one or more racially identifiable schools remain under the plan, comparability may only result when the court uses its legal leverage to obtain the inclusion of specific measures—independent of pupil reassignment—to ensure resource equalization. However, to the extent that the court lacked the authority to require the desegregation of such schools because of the absence of proof of intentional segregatory actions, the court may be equally unable to order the equalization of resources in such buildings except upon a showing of intentional inequality in their allocation. With the exception of this presumably limited second type of situation, equity as measured in terms of the comparability of resources between schools that serve racially-mixed and minority-identifiable populations in the same district is reasonably assured by the standards in effect in the 1980s.

Viewed from a broader perspective, such equity may be an illusion, since it is predicated exclusively on intra-district comparisons of equality. In many urban areas—where racial, ethnic, and language minority students are increasingly concentrated—severely eroded tax bases must finance all or part of a variety of public services including education. In such school districts, bounded by the constraints of *Rodriquez v. San Antonio* and *Milliken I,* the guarantee of comparability may represent little more than the equal distribution of grossly inadequate resources and inequitable opportunities. As minorities represent a dramatically expanding segment of the U.S. population, the continuance of such interdistrict inequalities will represent a drain on the development of human capital at the same time that educational quality takes on new significance in a competitive global economy.

Historically, the issue of quality as contrasted to equality has held little legal sway in the desegregation movement. The Supreme Court's introduction of the "remedial" or third dimension of the unitary school concept, however, has served to link an educationally focused goal of "overcoming the effects of past segregation and discrimination" with an outcome-oriented measure of its satisfaction, "blacks occupying the position they would have enjoyed but for prior unconstitutional conduct of public officials." The arguable effect of this standard should be to require that plans be judged on their quality or effectiveness in overcoming the effects of systemic educational neglect, just as pupil desegregation plans have come to be judged by their objective success rather than protestations of good faith.

The implication of this development and the comprehensive remedial regimes associated with it go beyond comparability to an actual increase in the number, nature and quality of educational services provided to minority children. There are some causes for optimism that quality and excellence may be advanced through such regimes in the 1980s. First, we know more today about programs and approaches that work in making education effective than we did a decade ago. The effective schools research reported during the period has yielded an uncommon consensus regarding correlates that enhance instructional outcomes (Benjamin, 1981; Brophe, 1979; Edmonds, 1979). Equally as important has been the widening public recognition of research and experience documenting that minority schools can be centers of excellence. Second, remedial plans have also benefited from a growing base of research regarding effective strategies for introducing desegregation and institutionalizing equity in educational organizations (Hawley, 1983; Smith & Downs, 1973; Chesler et al., 1978). Third, organizational leadership has passed to minorities in many of the nation's largest districts, providing a greater sensitivity to and priority on meeting the needs of the victims of past discrimination. Fourth, the courts, assisted by their own experts and masters, have demonstrated an increasing sophistication regarding schools as complex social organizations and the nature and range of strategies that may need to be employed to facilitate organizational change, accountability, and compliance (Kirp, 1981; Starr, 1981; Wasby, 1977). These strategies include extraordinary measures to marshal resources and interject significant sums of new money to support broad programs of educational improvement (Vergon, 1985). Finally, it is important to note that although the number of school districts desegregating has diminished over the last decade, the proportion of districts and students covered by comprehensive educational plans has increased substantially during this period.

To the extent that plans designed to overcome the effects of past discrimination are fundamentally different from those instituted to provide equal access and comparable resources to black and white students, both educational equity and excellence may be benefited. Will these comprehensive, educationally focused plans have such salutary effects? Will these programs of quality be more readily or effectively implemented than those earlier ones that sought more modest goals using simpler means and requiring the cooperation of fewer partners? (Kirp, 1981, 1982; Kalodner & Fishman, 1978, Yudof, 1981). If implemented, will such programs have the intended impact and desired outcomes? If not, can the schools adapt rapidly enough and courts retain jurisdiction long enough to permit the development and implementation of programs that work? If adapted and sustained, will such programs of demonstrated quality and excellence stabilize urban school systems and revitalize enrollments, making desegregation once again both legally feasible and politically viable?

There are, of course, no definite answers to these questions. Furthermore, history suggests that the course of the school desegregation movement in the immediate future may not depend or even wait on the answers to these questions. Nevertheless, proponents must work to see that these questions are answered in the affirmative for the benefit of today's children and the prospect of a national policy that recognizes the interaction and synergism of equity and excellence in American education.

REFERENCES

*Chuck Vergon is an attorney and associate professor of education law and policy, The University of Michigan School of Education. Reprinted with permission from The Journal of Equity and Excellence 24,1 (Fall 1988).

Cases

Alexander v. Holmes County Board of Education, 396 U.S. 19 (1969).

Berry v. School District of Benton Harbor, 515 F. Supp. 344, aff'd 698 F.2nd 813 (6th Cir. 1983).

Bradley v. School Board of Richmond, 382 U.S. 103 (1965).

Brown v. Board of Education (I), 347 U.S. 483 (1954).

Brown v. Board of Education (II), 349 U.S. 294 (1955).

Carter v. West Feliciani, 396 U.S. 290 (1969).

Columbus Board of Education v. Penick, 443 U.S. 449 (1979).

Cooper v. Aaron, 358 U.S. 1 (1958).

Cummings v. Richmond County Board of Education, 175 U.S. 528 (1899).

Dayton Board of Education v. Brinkman (I), 433 U.S. 406 (1977).

Dayton Board of Education v. Brinkman (II), 443 U.S. 526 (1979).

Davis v. School Commissioners of Mobile, 402 U.S. 33 (1971).

Dowell v. Board of Education of Oklahoma City, 795 F.2d 1516 (10th Cir., 1986).

Evans v. Buchanan, 447 F.Supp. 982, aff'd 582 F.2d 750 (3d. Cir., 1978), cert. denied 446 U.S. 923 (1980).

Gaines ex rel Missouri v. Canada, U.S. (1938).

Goss v. Board of Education of Knoxville, 373 U.S. 683 (1963).

Green v. New Kent County School Board, 391 U.S. 430 (1968).

Griffin v. School Board of Prince Edwards County, 377 U.S. 218 (1963).

Hall v. St. Helena Parish School Board, 417 F.2d 801, cert. denied, U.S. (1969).

Jefferson Parish School Board v. Dandridge, 404 U.S. 1219 (1971) (In Chambers).

Keyes v. School District of Denver, 413 U.S. 189 (1973).

Liddel v. Board of Education of St. Louis, 567 F.Supp. 1037, aff'd in part, 731 F.2d 1294 (8th Cir.), cert. denied 105 S.Ct. 82 (1984).

McLaurin v. Regents of Oklahoma, 339 U.S. 637 (1950).

Milliken v. Bradley (I), 418 U.S. 717 (1974).

Milliken v. Bradley (II), 433 U.S. 267 (1977).

Morgan v. Kerrigan, 401 F.Supp. 216, aff'd 530 F.2d (1st Cir.), cert. denied, 426 U.S. 935 (1976).

North Carolina State Board of Education v. Swann, 402 U.S. 43 (1971).
Northcross v. Board of Education of Memphis, 302 F.2d 818 (6th Cir.), cert. denied, 370 U.S. 944 (1961).
Pasadena Board of Education v. Spangler, 427 U.S. 424 (1976).
Plessy v. Ferguson, 163 U.S. 537 (1896).
Reed v. Rhodes, 455 F.Supp. 569, aff'd in pertinent part, 607 F.2d 714 (6th Cir.), cert. denied 445 U.S. 935 (1982).
Riddick v. School Board of Norfolk, 784 F.2d 521 (4th Cir., 1986).
Rodriquez v. San Antonio School District, 411 U.S. 1 (1973).
Swann v. Charlotte-Mecklenburg Board of Education, 402 U.S. 1 (1971).
Sweatt v. Painter, 339 U.S. 629 (1950).
United States v. Board of School Commissioners, 506 F.Supp. 657, aff'd 637 F.2d 1101 (7th Cir.), cert. denied 449 U.S. 838 (1980).
U.S. v. Montgomery County Board of Education, 395 U.S. 225 (1969).
U.S. v. Scotland Neck City Board of Education, 407 U.S. 484 (1972).
Village of Arlington Hts. v. Metro Housing Corp., 429 U.S. 252 (1977).
Washington v. Davis, 426 U.S. 229 (1976).
Wright v. Council of City of Emporia, 407 U.S. 451 (1972).

Books and Articles

Benjamin, R. 1981. *Making schools work.* New York: Continuum.
Bond, H. 1934. *The education of the Negro in the American social order.* Englewood Cliffs, N.J.: Prentice Hall.
Brophe, J. 1979. Advances in teacher effectiveness research. East Lansing, Mich.: Institute for Research on Teaching.
Center for National Policy Study. 1974. Justice delayed and denied. Washington, D.C.: Catholic University Law School.
Chayes, A. 1976. The role of the judge in public law litigation. *Harvard Law Review* 89:1281–1316.
Chesler, M., Bryant, B., and Crowfoot, J. 1978. Institutional changes to support school desegregation. *Law and Contemporary Problems* 42(4):174–213.
Dentler, R. 1978. Desegregation planning and implementation in Boston. *Theory into Practice* 17(1):72–77.
Edmonds, R. 1979. Effective schools for the urban poor. *Educational Leadership* 37:15–18, 20–24.
Hawley, W. 1983. *Strategies for effective desegregation.* Lexington, Mass.: Lexington Books.
Kalodner, N., and Fishman, J. 1978. *Limits of justice: The court's role in school desegregation.* Cambridge, Mass.: Ballinger Publishing Co.
Kirp, D. 1981. Legalism and politics in school desegregation. *Wisconsin Law Review* 924–69.
———. 1982. *Just schools.* Berkeley: University of California Press.

National Center for Educational Statistics, 1985. *The condition of education: A statistical report.* Washington, D.C. U.S. Department of Education.

National Center for Policy Review, 1974. *Justice delayed and denied.* Washington, D.C.: Catholic University Law School.

Orfield, G. 1969. *The reconstruction of southern education.* New York: Wiley.

———. 1978. *Must we bus? Segregated schools and national policy.* Washington, D.C.: Brookings Institution.

Smith, A., Downs, A., & Lachmon, M. 1973. Achieving Effective Desegregation. Lexington: Lexington Books, D. C. Heath Co.

Starr, M. 1981. Accommodation and accountability: A strategy for judicial enforcement of institutional reform decrees. *Alabama Law Review,* 399–440.

U.S. Civil Rights Commission. 1967. *Racial isolation in the public schools.* Washington, D.C.: USCCR.

———. 1975. *Twenty years after Brown v. Board of Education.* Washington, D.C.: USCCR.

Vergon, C. 1975. The dialectics of desegregation: Twenty years on the road to equal opportunity. *Desegregation and beyond,* ed. Moody and Vergon. Ann Arbor, Mich.: University of Michigan.

———. 1985. Trends in school desegregation litigation and the financing of remedial decrees. In *Education law update,* ed. Jones and Semler. Topeka, Kan.: National Organization on Legal Problems in Education.

Wasby, S., D'Amato, A., Metralier, R. 1977. *Desegregation from Brown to Alexander: An exploration of supreme court strategies.* Carbondale: Southern Illinois University Press.

Weinberg, M. 1977. *Minority students: A research appraisal.* Washington, D.C.: National Institute of Education.

Woodson, C. 1919. *The education of the Negro prior to 1861.* Washington, D.C.: The Associated Publishers.

———. 1922. *The Negro in our history.* Washington, D.C.: The Associated Publishers.

Willie, C. and Greenblatt, J., eds. 1981. *Community politics and educational change.* White Plains, N.Y.: Longman.

Yudof, M. 1981. Implementation theories and desegregation realities. Alabama Law Review, 32:441–464.

EDUCATION REFORM: DESEGREGATION AND UNFULFILLED PROMISES IN ST. LOUIS

James E. Walter

Historically, most education reform movements have been initiated out-side of education and usually focus on some real or presumed deficiency in our society. For example, in the 1930s, political and social progressives saw education as a means for democratizing society.[1] In the 1950s, the scientific and the military communities assumed education was the means for ensuring our nation's scientific and technological superiority and thus our military defense.[2] In the 1960s, social and political liberals put forth the promise that education could eliminate poverty.[3] Now, in the 1980s, leaders in business and industry see education as the means for maintaining our nation's economic position in the face of foreign competition.[4]

As with most social reform movements, those in education have tended to overlap each other, with the newer movement both overshadowing and shaping the latter stages of the prior one. Education reforms do not usually result in all of the expected benefits. For example, concerns in the 1960s with social issues of poverty and justice overshadowed concerns in the 1950s with world-wide technological superiority. At present, a presumed declining position in the world marketplace overshadows issues of social equity. While progressive education did transform the schools in several ways, the changes in the schools did not have as much impact on society as its proponents envisioned.

Public school desegregation as a reform movement was intended as one means for moving toward a desegregated society. Like other reform move-

337

ments, proponents of the desegregation movement have lost sight of the *initial* impulse that energized and sustained the movement.[5] It has, moreover, taken on many characteristics of the "business" ideology that has been part of education since the 1920s[6] and provides the foundation for the current educational reform. This concern for conditions favorable for business has affected how desegregation is now "managed." the "success" of court-ordered plans is now being measured in much the same way a corporation's success is measured—simply in terms of numbers or percentages and monetary costs.

This discussion focuses on the premise that reform movement goals are seldom fully achieved. The thesis here is that conditions of education for blacks are *not* substantially improved after a court-ordered remedy has been implemented than they were before the suits were initiated.[7] The St. Louis desegregation case provides a current situation in which to test that thesis. The plan ordered by the court in 1983 anticipated that in 1988 only about 15,000 black students (of the approximately 30,000 in 1983) will be in one-race schools. Midway in the plan, there was little evidence to suggest that this case will result in improved conditions for the majority of black students in the St. Louis public schools.

Following a brief review of the history of the St. Louis desegregation case, a progress report will focus on the educational conditions for black students in the St. Louis public schools. The discussion will then assess the case in terms of some of the ideals of justice that undergird American society. The closing comments will provide a summary and synthesis of the article.

THE ST. LOUIS CASE[8]

In 1980, the Eighth Circuit Court of Appeals reversed the District Court's decision and ruled that both the St. Louis Board of Education and the State of Missouri had violated the due process clause of the Fourteenth Amendment. In 1983, the District Court ordered a voluntary interdistrict settlement plan. The 1980 intra-district remedy addressed the finding of liability for the St. Louis Public Schools and the State of Missouri. The 1983 interdistrict voluntary remedy addressed the need to increase opportunities for a desegregated education for black students in the St. Louis public schools. Both remedies, which were essentially upheld on appeal, constituted a fairly complex plan.

The intra-district portion of the plan provided for "integrated"[9] schools and magnet schools. The district, which had only K–8 elementary schools and high schools, implemented middle schools as one means for creating other settings that could be desegregated. There were also provisions for improving instructional programs and home-school-community relations for the entire district. The court ordered part-time "integrated" programs and a wide variety of compensatory and enrichment programs for the 30,000 students that, in 1980, remained in all-black schools.

The inter-district portion of the plan provided for transfers of black students from St. Louis to suburban schools and of white students from the suburbs to the magnet schools in St. Louis. Procedures were established for transfer students to take full advantage of the programs, including extracurricular activities, in the suburban districts. A teacher-exchange program was also included. Designed as a five-year effort, the plan included provisions for improving the quality of education in all schools in the St. Louis public schools, with additional resources to be utilized in the all-black schools.

An independent monitor will evaluate all aspects of the implementation of the plan after 1988, the fifth and final year of the inter-district plan. On the basis of the number of black students transferring into the suburban districts in relation to a "plan ratio," some districts have been awarded final judgment that they have satisfied their pupil desegregation obligation. They have not, however, been released from an obligation to maintain their plan ratios, to continue to accept and assist transfer students, and to assist those from their district who may want to transfer to the magnet schools in St. Louis.

A Progress Report

Since the presumed benefits of desegregating schools should accrue to black students, the focus of this section will be on assessing the educational conditions for black students that remained in the St. Louis public schools and for those transported to suburban districts. The first assessment will be related to the proportion of black students that are in desegregated schools. The second assessment will consider the level of implementation of special programs for the remaining all-black schools as measured by comparing expenditures with budgeted amounts. The final, less quantitative, assessment will focus on evaluations of the quality of education in the all-black schools.

Proportion of Black Students in Desegregated Schools. The standard for desegregation cases was established over 30 years ago in *Brown v. Board of Education of Topeka.* The Supreme Court determined that different educational systems, regardless of their presumed equality, are inherently unequal. Wolters[10] argues that the Supreme Court in *Brown* called for racial mixing as a remedy. Subsequently, remedies in desegregation cases have been predicated on the standard that black and white students must attend the same schools. In the St. Louis case, the Appeals Court noted that a "strong presumption exists against the Constitutional propriety of one-race schools...."[11] Against this standard, most school desegregation efforts fall short, including St. Louis.

In the St. Louis plans, the desegregated settings within the city and in the suburban area did not, in 1986–87, accommodate a majority of the black students.[12] Within the city, only 23 percent of the black students were enrolled in integrated and magnet schools. The voluntary transfer of students into suburban, predominantly white, schools increased the number of black students in desegregated settings. When the figures about black students transported to the suburban school districts were put into the equations, some 44 percent of all of the black students in the St. Louis school district were in desegregated settings. In other words, about 56 percent of black students in St. Louis remained in one-race schools. The overwhelming majority of students remaining in the one-race schools were concentrated in the city's north side, where the poorest reside. When viewed from this perspective, the desegregation efforts were even less fruitful.

Not even did the arrangements for desegregation fall short of the *Brown* standard, they became less viable. For demographic reasons, there could not be an increase in the number of desegregated schools in the city. Because white students did not transfer to the magnet schools in the city in sufficient numbers, there were no openings for black students. As suburban districts achieved their plan goals and ratios, they received final judgments from the court. These judgments required them to maintain their ratios and goals, but did not require them to recruit additional transfer students, although the districts were required to accept transfer students above their ratio or goal.

Level of Special Program Implementation. Most desegregation cases do not result in remedies where all of the black students attend schools with white students. St. Louis is no exception. Recognizing this, the Appeals Court noted that ". . . a court must find that the existence of one-race schools is justified in light of particular facets of the case and the feasibility of other desegregation techniques. When no other feasible desegregation techniques exist, the specific remedial programs for students in the remaining one-race schools may be included as a means of ensuring equal educational opportunity."[13]

As a means of ensuring equal educational opportunity, the St. Louis plan incorporated a wide variety of programs and special conditions that were to be implemented in the all-black schools. In general terms, the special programs and conditions provided for increasing home and school communications, lowering pupil-teacher ratios in the all-black schools below the ratios in the integrated schools, hiring instructional coordinators, after-school and weekend remedial programs, summer school, a variety of motivational experiences, additional on-school-time instructional opportunities, and so on.

A major provision of the plan for the all-black schools was the "Schools of Emphases," in which each school developed its own special emphasis to be applied to all areas of the curriculum and serve as a focus for the schools. Some examples include ancient cultures, aerospace, journalism, and career exploration. These special efforts held promise for improving the conditions of education in the all-black schools.

A comparison of expenditures with budgets for the inter-district plan reveals[14] that spending was less when compared to budgeted amounts for all-black schools. In 1984–85, the spending level for all provisions of the plan was 86 percent. For the provisions for the all-black schools, the spending level was 53 percent. Although the gap narrowed considerably in 1985–86, the overall spending rate was lower than in the previous year.

In terms of implementation of the special provisions for the all-black schools, the St. Louis public schools did not fully implement the court order. Of 11 special provisions of the inter-district portion of the plan, 3 were not implemented at all in three years. As a matter of policy, the St. Louis Board of Education reduced the pupil-teacher ratio city-wide without the further reduction in the ratios in the all-black schools as mandated by the plan. The Appeals Court ordered that the provision be observed beginning in the 1986–87 school year. In recent budget proposals, the St. Louis public schools requested that certain special provisions be eliminated from the intra-district plan and did not budget for three programs in the inter-district plan. The court denied the requests and ordered the omissions restored. The State's filing for reconsideration was denied and the matter was appealed, further delaying the implementation of provisions for all-black schools.

Quality of Educational Programs.[15] Recognizing that in St. Louis there were not going to be sufficient desegregated settings for all of the black students, the Appellate Court ordered, in February 1982, the District Court to attend to the quality of education in the all-black schools. A Committee on Quality Education for Non-Integrated Schools was established in May 1982. One of its major responsibilities was to evaluate the quality of education in the all-black schools.

The evaluation was designed with indicators of quality that were conceptually not dependent upon any particular programs or clusters of programs being implemented. This approach was taken so that quality could be accounted for in both the presence of the court-ordered programs and other activities in both the individual schools and the district. Fourteen indicators were conceptualized and organized into input measures, process measures, and output measures. Sample elementary and middle schools were randomly selected from high-, middle- and low-performing all-black schools on the district's standardized test. Three of the five all-black high schools were selected on the same criteria. Samples of convenience of parents, students, teachers, and administrators were selected for surveys, interviews, and classroom observations. Analysis of records, including student absence rates and test scores, provided additional data.

Evaluation of the all-black schools in St. Louis indicated that both the content and methods in these schools was much like Anyon[16] described for schools serving the unskilled and semiskilled. In her study of schools serving students from different social classes, the curriculum and instructional methods commonly used in schools serving unskilled or semiskilled working classes were what might be called "shallow" or "thin." In these schools there was an emphasis on basic skills and simple intellectual operations and memory work. By contrast, the curriculum in schools serving children from elite executive homes can be characterized as "thick" and "rich." Students in these schools were engaged in higher order intellectual skills and exposed to problem-solving instructional methods.

While the formal and express portion of the curriculum in the St. Louis schools was driven by the content in the items of a nationally standardized test and a state-wide criterion referenced test, the informal or hidden curriculum was driven by a set of desires held by the staff for black students. Interviews with a sample of the professional staff in each of the sample schools revealed a very strong desire for the students to acquire the social behaviors perceived as necessary to succeed in a working, middle-class, white setting. It was also driven by a perceived need for these students to experience settings outside those in which they live and go to school. Discipline efforts, according to the respondents, were aimed at helping students learn self-control (i.e., nonphysical modes for dealing with differences of opinion), punctuality, social amenities, and responsibility for getting work in. For many of the staff interviewed, field trips were of value not so much for what was at the end of the ride but for the broadening effects that come from seeing and experiencing different settings.

Although there might be no argument with having students learn basic skills (assuming that is what is measured by the tests) and certain socially acceptable behaviors, and experience other kinds of settings, it certainly can be argued that the students deserved a much "thicker" curriculum than they were getting. Interviews with informants from several of the suburban schools suggested that voluntary transfer students attending suburban schools were being exposed to a much richer curriculum than existed in the sample of all-black schools from which data were gathered.

In terms of test scores (which were only one indicator of quality), the scores of students in the all-black schools were improving. Data from both interviews and record analysis contain some indications that some unusually remarkable gains in scores in some schools probably reflected two conditions. One was the district's emphasis on raising test scores and relating personnel evaluations to student achievement. The second was the narrowing of the curriculum to focus on the content of the tests.

In many schools there were very interesting and valuable experiences being planned and implemented for the students. An Effective and Efficient Schools Program based on the work of Edmonds and Brookover and Lezotte[17] was supported in part by desegregation funds. The increase in achievement scores in the program schools was higher than the increase in nonprogram schools.[18] The School of Emphasis program required by the desegregation plan for the all-black schools only and, as noted earlier, somewhat underfunded, gave the school staffs some discretion in planning and organizing interesting and "thicker" curricula and learning experiences. These activities were in many cases interrelated with the regular curriculum.

In terms of considerations of quality, there were several indications that the education being given to the students in the all-black schools was, relatively speaking, less enriching than it could and perhaps should have been. The curriculum could have been richer and "thicker," so that students could be exposed to a much wider range of knowledge and more opportunities to learn a wider range of skills. A wider range of instructional techniques could have been used. Students should have been engaged in learning higher order intellectual skills.

Are the St. Louis Plans Just?

Implicit in the question, "Are the St. Louis plans just?" is the assumption that they are, just because they have been found to be Constitutional by the courts. While some actions may be legal and acceptable to the courts, they are not *ipso facto* just. In protecting the rights of minorities, the U.S. Constitution operationalizes a form of distributive justice.[19] In this context, the burden of correcting a Constitutional violation should favor the plaintiffs, and unequal distributions should favor the least advantaged.

Perhaps the most obvious indication that the St. Louis plans, and any others that depend upon transportation as part of the remedy, are not just is the fact that black students nearly always are the ones transported. Black students gave up attending schools near where they live in much larger proportions than did white students. Black students experienced the dissonance of becoming accepted into the culture of a different racial setting and socioeconomic class; white students did not.

Parents also were faced with increased burdens. If parents wanted to or had to visit their child's school, attend open-house, or have a parent-teacher conference, they most often had to find their own transportation. For many of the parents, the only transportation was a taxi or bus or imposing on a friend. Even when communicating over the phone, the parents experienced communication problems that arose out of their class/culture differences.

To be sure, the professionals in the host schools were confronted with new and unusual experiences presented by the transfer students. These students had to be socialized into the values and norms of the host schools, and until that socialization process was completed, usually within about two school years, the professionals had to deal with dissonance that they do not ordinarily have. Even so, the dissonance was only within their professional role. For the transfer students, the dissonance was much more personal and thus more intense. In other words, the burden imposed by the transfer students on the professionals pales by comparison to the burden desegregation plans imposed on the transfer students.

A key aspect of the St. Louis plan is the financial incentives. Under this aspect of the plan, the host school districts received an amount of money equal to the per-pupil costs in that district. The sending district also received an incentive equal to one-half of the per-pupil costs for that district. The consequence of all of this was that several of the relatively wealthy school districts' budgets were substantially enhanced by the incentive payments. While the host schools should not be expected to absorb the costs of educating transfer students (these schools were never found guilty of contributing to segregation in St. Louis), the St. Louis plan created a situation in which justice for black students was treated as a commodity; it was purchased from school districts serving primarily white students.

The distribution of funds for desegregation favor the most advantaged. Funds received by the host schools go into the schools' general fund, not to programs for the transfer students. As noted earlier, the funds made available to the St. Louis schools for the all-black schools are not being spent at the same rate as for other parts of the desegregation plan.

With the assumption that justice is realized when the burdens and resource distribution favor the plaintiffs, the St. Louis desegregation plan is not a just remedy. The burden falls most heavily on the parents and students. The funds accruing to the wealthier districts benefited students already advantaged, while funds that could have benefited the least advantaged were not spent fully on their behalf.

CONCLUSION

There is no question that some of the transfer students have benefited from their experiences. They have been exposed to a much more substantive curriculum than they were likely to have encountered in their home schools. For the most part they adjusted well to their new schooling environments. Not unexpectedly, there were reports of negative and positive incidents. In some situations, transfer students are presumed to be learning disabled and are assigned to and kept in the lowest reading groups, and an undue proportion are treated as disciplinary problems. In other schools, however, individual teachers and building staffs are conscientiously attempting (not necessarily with full understanding) to accommodate the transfer students and treat them equitably.

The court has ruled that the plans implemented by the various parties and the court's administrative committees are constitutionally acceptable. The various arrangements, such as for transportation, and the financial incentives are legal and approved by the court. The target goals set by the parties of the settlement agreement will probably be realized; at least progress in the 1986–87 school year looked promising.

When the St. Louis plan is analyzed from the perspective of those who developed it, the plan can be said to be "working." Generally, this is intended to convey that when actions are compared to what was planned, there is a high level of congruence, with one notable exception. The quality of education being provided students who remain in all-black schools is something less than desirable from an educational perspective.

When the St. Louis plan is compared to the promise once held out for desegregation, it suffers badly. The plan does not meet the standard anticipated in the *Brown* decision; less than half of the black students were in desegregated settings. The vision of *Brown* that black students would attend schools with white students held forth the promise that *all* black students would benefit by such a condition. Provided other burdens would not be imposed on the plaintiffs, that condition had the promise of being a just settlement. Thirty-four years after *Brown,* the struggle for an intangible ideal of justice has been replaced by a willingness to settle for the tangible and practical. From this perspective, whatever ideal "good" may come from the current plan is secondary. The plan might satisfy the court and the various parties to the case, both plaintiff and defendant. The essential point remains: Justice has not been served.

NOTES

1. Lawrence A. Cremin. 1961. *The transformation of the school: Progressivism in American education, 1876–1957.* New York: Alfred A. Knopf.

2. See, for example, Hyman Rickover. 1959. *Education and freedom.* New York: E. P. Dutton.

3. Diane Ravitch. 1983. *The troubled crusade: American education, 1945–1980,* Chapter 5. New York: Basic Books.

4. National Commission on Excellence in Education. April 1983. *A nation at risk: The imperative for educational reform.* Washington, D.C.: U.S. Government Printing Office.

5. Desegregation in Transition. November 1986. *Education USA* 24:97.

6. Raymond E. Callahan. 1962. *Education and the cult of efficiency.* Chicago: University of Chicago Press.

7. Raymond Wolters. 1984. *The burden of Brown: Thirty years of school desegregation* Knoxville, Tenn.: University of Tennessee Press.

8. The following section is based on several Court documents: Adams v. United States, 620 F.2d 1277 (8th Cir.) *cert.* denied, 449 U.S. 826, (1980); Liddell v. State of Missouri, 731 F.2d 1294 (8th Cir.) *cert.* denied, 105 S.Ct. 82, (1984); Liddell v. Bd. of Educ., 667 F.2d 643 (8th Cir. 1981) *cert.* denied 454 U.S. 1081, 1091 (1982); Liddell v. Bd of Educ., 693 F.2d 721

(8th Cir. 1981); *Desegregation Plan of the Board of Education of the City of St. Louis* (St. Louis, Mo.: U.S. District Court of the Eastern District of Missouri, 1980); *Settlement Agreement* (St. Louis, Mo.: U.S. District Court of the Eastern District of Missouri, 1983).

9. In this article, the term "integrated" is used as the court uses the term, to mean a class of schools that meet the court's criterion for having a mix of black and white students. The term is used here in this technical sense and not in a larger, sociological sense. They are desegregated settings in the same way that the magnet schools and the metropolitan schools are desegregated settings. Hereafter, the use of the word "integrated," when in reference to schools, is meant to refer to a specific class of schools within the St. Louis public schools.

10. Wolters, p. 5.

11. *Liddell v. State of Missouri.*

12. *Eleventh report of the city board under paragraph 14 of the court's order of May 21, 1980.* October 1985. St. Louis, Mo.: St. Louis Board of Education; *Thirteenth report of the city board under paragraph 14 of the court's order of May 21, 1980.* October 1986. St. Louis, Mo.: St. Louis Board of Education.

13. *Liddell v. State of Missouri.*

14. Faith A. Sandler. October 1986. Comments for panel discussion—Current status of the St. Louis plan. Paper delivered at St. Louis University Law School conference, School Desegregation: Results and Prospects, St. Louis, Mo.

15. The author was the court-appointed educational expert to the Committee on Quality Education from 1982 to 1985. The material in this section is based on Kenneth Keiser and James E. Walter. 1984. *Evaluation design and methodology for the evaluation of non-integrated schools.* St. Louis, Mo.: Committee on Quality Education, Federal District Court of the Eastern District of Missouri; James E. Walter and Kenneth Keiser. 1984. *Measures related to the fourteenth dimensions of quality schooling: A concept paper for the evaluation of non-integrated schools.* St. Louis, Mo.: Committee on Quality Education, Federal District Court of the Eastern District of Missouri; James E. Walter and Kenneth Keiser. 1984. *A report of findings from evaluation data gathered in the fall of 1984 in the non-integrated schools of the St. Louis public schools.* St. Louis, Mo.: Committee on Quality Education, Federal District Court of the Eastern District of Missouri; James E. Walter and Faith A. Sandler. 1985. *Findings from evaluation data gathered in the fall of 1985 from the non-integrated schools of the St. Louis public schools.* St. Louis, Mo.: Committee on Quality Education, Federal District Court of the Eastern District of Missouri.

16. Jean Anyon. 1983. Social class and the hidden curriculum of work. In *The hidden curriculum and moral education: Deception or discovery,* ed. Giroux and D. Purpel. Berkeley, Calif.: McCutchan.

17. Ronald Edmonds. October 1979. Effective schools for the urban poor.

Educational Leadership 37:15–24; Wilbur B. Brookover and Lawrence W. Lezotte. 1977. *Changes in school characteristics coincident with changes in student achievement.* East Lansing, Mich.: College of Urban Development, Michigan State University.

18. Rufus Young, Jr. 1986. *Effective and efficient schools program: End of year report, 1985–1986.* St. Louis, Mo.: St. Louis Public Schools.

19. John Rawls. 1971. *A theory of justice.* Cambridge, Mass.: Harvard University Press.

VI.
EXAMINING THE CONSEQUENCES
OF INEQUALITY

IMPLEMENTING EDUCATIONAL OPPORTUNITY
PROGRAMS AT THE COMMUNITY COLLEGE LEVEL

Judith S. Kaufman
and Anna F. Lobosco

For 1986–87, the Governor and the Legislature of New York state approved $400,000 to strengthen and/or establish counseling and tutoring support services for EOP (Educational Opportunity Program) qualified students at three community colleges, on an experimental basis. The funds also included moneys to evaluate each of the approaches developed by the colleges in order to facilitate the development of a model program that could be replicated in other community colleges within the SUNY (State University of New York) system.

The concept and practice of funding counseling and tutoring services for EOP students in state-operated institutions of higher education is well established and has been shown to be effective. The recently released Legislative Commission of Expenditure Review (LCER) report of SUNY's Educational Opportunity Program at state-operated four-year campuses indicated that tutoring significantly increased EOP student persistence and success in completing a college program. Funding for counseling and tutoring has not been made available previously to community colleges in the SUNY system. While the majority of the SUNY community colleges do have a history of supporting EOP's, this support has been limited to direct student aid.

During the summer of 1986, the Office of Special Programs of SUNY/Central Administration sought proposals from established community college

EOP's. Of particular interest were courses of study and programs that emphasized tutoring and counseling services independent of specific course demands for at-risk students. It was requested that courses in which EOP students fared least well and courses that were avoided be identified in the proposals. Once these courses were identified, the proposals were to show the relationship between student needs and suggested remedies. Minimum criteria used in the selection process were (1) existence of an established EOP with a full-time director; (2) development of a counseling and tutoring model that would promote self-confidence, time management, study skills, and academic and personal growth among EOP students; (3) structuring the counseling and tutoring programs so that they would be both diagnostic and prescriptive in nature; (4) determination of ideal interaction that should occur between faculty, counselors, tutors, and students, and exploration of effective ways to train and orient faculty and program staff to new methods and strategies for effective service delivery; (5) development of methods for evaluating program effectiveness; (6) development of methods that would encourage student participation in counseling and tutoring; and (7) development of a model program with potential applicability to other community colleges in New York State.

Three campuses were selected to participate in the program and receive additional funding to enhance existing program efforts. These three institutions were Erie Community College, serving 545 EOP-funded students and another 500 to 550 EOP-designated students (students who are eligible for support services but receive no funding); Monroe Community College, serving 245 students; and Suffolk Community College, serving 195 EOP students. Each of these programs had designed a unique service delivery program to meet the needs of the local EOP student population. The programs included varying degrees of supplemental instruction, academic tutoring by professional and peer tutors, student and faculty-staff orientations and workshops, and eclectic diagnostic and counseling support, which covered the financial, academic, emotional, social, and career planning needs of students.

During the summer of 1987, a formative assessment was conducted by the Evaluation Consortium to evaluate the different approaches employed across the three EOP sites. Major issues concerning implementation arose during and subsequent to this evaluation; this paper addresses three of these issues within a socioeconomic perspective of the community college movement and within the framework of implementation theory. The three issues to be explored are (1) the unique needs of community college students; (2) the impact of the EOP and the students it serves on the more general college community; and (3) inter-systemic concerns highlighted by conflict between the practical concerns at the local level and state-wide expectations.

Even with a high level of state and local support, input, and commitment to the funded program, these three contextual issues are formidable concerns in need of consideration with regard to their effects on program implementation and desirable outcomes for the target population. The issues outlined above fit neatly into an ecological perspective that considers the impact of program implementation on ascending levels, beginning with student needs and culminating with state-level response to those needs.

THE UNIQUE NEEDS OF COMMUNITY COLLEGE STUDENTS

Open-door policies, initially begun in the late 1960s and early 1970s in response to minority demands for equal access to higher education, have attracted larger numbers of students experiencing educational and economic disadvantage. EOP's are designed to meet the needs of these students by easing their transition process into academic life and promoting greater academic success. However, in meeting objectives of increased retention, achievement, and higher graduation rates, certain difficulties encountered in serving this population affect program implementation and success.

Specifically, finding effective methods for initiating and maintaining contact with potential and current EOP students was identified as a persistent problem in the formative evaluation. For example, all of the programs studied provide orientations, tutoring, counseling, and workshops for EOP students. Many of these services are mandatory, and despite personal contact, notices in school newspapers, posters, letters, and word of mouth, they are poorly attended. At orientations, which are considered essential to initiating contact, students receive information on financial aid and the details of the various EOP services; they are also informed of their responsibilities and obligations as EOP students. In some of the programs, students who have not attended an orientation are informed that they will not receive their stipends until they have met with their EOP counselor. When this fails, counselors must resort to intensive counseling over the telephone. At one campus included in the evaluation, only 10 to 20 students showed up for an orientation.

Workshops addressing such topics as financial aid, academic survival, coping with social services, and improvement of self-concept are also poorly attended, despite an expressed student interest. To increase participation, counselors regularly contact students to remind them to attend, or workshops are offered during class time, or on Saturdays.

Student participation in tutoring is also low and is considered to be essential for students who might otherwise fail their courses. At two of the campuses, tutors are only serving about 30 to 40 percent of the students who signed up for the service, even though it is mandatory for many of them, or strongly encouraged by counselors.

Amid the variety of outreach methods mentioned above, no one technique was identified as particularly successful. Additionally, the students are reluctant to admit to academic disadvantage and do not seek appropriate support assistance. Overall, considerable difficulty in identifying and maintaining contact with program students represents a challenge to implementation efforts.

In order to understand factors affecting outreach efforts to program students, we begin this section with a discussion of the historical context of the broader community college movement. The broken promises of this movement provide a basis for understanding the current experiences of EOP students and why outreach efforts have not been particularly successful. We contend that the effectiveness of EOP programs not only rests on meeting the immediate needs of students, but necessitates an approach that includes recognition of the social and economic factors influencing EOP students.

HISTORICAL ANALYSIS

The existence of EOP's in higher education reveals a consistent discrimination experienced by minorities and the poor within the American system of education. Taylor (1985) notes that there are three perspectives through which this discrimination has been explained. The first is a social-economic perspective; its proponents argue that inequalities in educational outcomes are a direct reflection of a class-based society where the upper classes maintain their positions of wealth and power through systematic oppression of the lower classes. From an economic viewpoint, the schools serve a maintenance function "by developing lower-class children to be better workers and middle-class ones to be better managers in the corporate economy and by reproducing the social relations of production in the schools to inculcate children with values and norms supportive of capitalist work organization" (Carnoy & Levin, 1976, p. 10). On this basis then, any attempts to achieve educational equity are necessarily contingent on a fundamental restructuring of society.

The second explanation reviewed by Taylor lays the blame for educational inequality on the schools. Taylor states that "this approach suggests that remedies might be found by analyzing school practices and pedagogical methods. It acknowledges that societal factors influencing income, class status, etc., will still loom as obstacles but within the school itself a more equitable environment can be created" (Taylor, 1985, p. 12).

The third perspective cited by Taylor incorporates an approach that "blames the victim." Its conservative proponents claim that the inability of minorities to academically succeed is due to their own lack of motivation. The opportunities for equality exist; all students need to do is take advantage of them. A more extreme version of this perspective, exemplified by Jensen (1969) and Herrnstein (1973), attributes failure to heredity. It is readily apparent that this view leaves little room for educational remedies.

EOP's are clearly rooted in the second perspective. They have been developed on the belief that equal academic outcomes can be achieved through compensatory efforts within the educational institution. But it is maintained that effective implementation of these programs, particularly with regard to students, cannot succeed without cognizance of the first perspective: the social structures that created a need for these programs in the first place. The recent history of the community college movement will serve as a vehicle to elucidate at least some of the social structures that have contributed to the current needs of poor and minority students and their attitudes toward educational support services. As Taylor states, "successful retention programs tend to address the factors that create the problems" (Taylor, 1985, p. 14).

The unprecedented growth of community colleges that occurred during the 1960s can be traced to the introduction of the GI Bill following World War II. During the seven years in which benefits were available under the bill, 7.8 million veterans enrolled in some form of post-secondary education, and of that number over 2 million attended institutions of higher education (Ravitch, 1983). The colleges and universities, which prior to the enactment of the bill had mainly served an elite class of students, now found themselves deluged with veterans from all socioeconomic classes. This overcrowding, along with predicted advances in science and technology, led the President's Commission on Higher Education (under Truman) to recommend a greatly expanded system of higher education (Ravitch, 1983).

Generally, the commission recommended the "democratization of education." Ravitch summarizes their findings and states, "The ultimate educational goal of the American people, the commission urged, should be 'an educational system in which at no level—high school, college, graduate school or professional school—will a qualified individual in any part of the country encounter an insuperable economic barrier to the attainment of the kind of education suited to his aptitudes and interests' " (Ravitch, 1983, p. 16).

While there was much support for the ideas contained in this report, there were widespread fears among the academic elite that such expansion would compromise the standards and quality of higher education. The solution to expanding higher education while maintaining an elite academic community is clearly evidenced in the commission's recommendation of a "rapid expansion of two-year community colleges (not junior colleges),[1] which would 'fit into the community life as the high school has done' " (Ravitch, 1983, p. 16). That this goal of expansion was more than realized is commented on by Shor:

There was a gold-rush quality to this scene of social development. In the 60s, two-year campuses sprouted like boomtowns, at the rate of one every ten days.... Virtually overnight, a headlong rushing economy created and peopled an educational frontier. This new line of growth became known as the 'community college movement'; it was set up especially for working students (Short, 1987, p. 4).

The intent of Truman's commission, the "democratization of education," was not achieved; to be sure, any citizen could pursue post-secondary education, but the promise of the reformist movement of the 1960s, education as the "great equalizer," was not realized. The prominent issues of poverty and racism stood, and still stand, in direct contrast to this promise, and the possession of a community college degree merely increased skills, without corresponding increases in social status for the student. The class divisions of society were simply reproduced in the system of higher education. In 1971, 27.2 percent of the students attending two-year public colleges came from families earning less than $8,000. Another 34.8 percent came from families earning between $8,000 and $12,499. At the other end of the spectrum, 41.8 percent of the students attending private universities came from families earning over $20,000, while only 10.6 percent of these students were from families who earned under $8,000 (Bowles & Gintis, 1976). As Bowles and Gintis note, this system of higher education "reflects both the social status of families of the students and the hierarchy of work relationships into which each type of student will move after graduation" (Bowles & Gintis, 1976, p. 209).

This trend toward expansion and stratification of higher education continued and intensified during the 1970s, and as Bowles and Gintis note, was "facilitated without undermining the elite status and function of the established institutions" (Bowles & Gintis, 1976, p. 208). An excerpt from the Carnegie Commission on Higher Education (1967–1973) reveals the intentionality behind this trend.

> [Elite] institutions of all types—colleges and universities—should be protected and encouraged as a source of scholarship and leadership training at the highest levels. They should not be homogenized in the name of egalitarianism. Such institutions, whether public or private, should be given special support for instruction and research, and for the ablest of graduate students; they should be protected by policies on differentiation of functions.[2]

This brief history of the community college movement reveals that its inception was an effort to ostensibly equalize higher educational opportunities for the masses without a corresponding equalization of their socioeconomic status. The common analogy of the Band-aid is usefully applied: Whereas the community college as Band-aid is meant to cure or at least cover up the discriminatory practices present in higher education, its permanence as an institution also reveals that these inequities still exist. The application of a further, but necessary, Band-aid in the name of EOP's is additional evidence that the community college has failed in its function to obscure the racial and social discrimination it is meant to cover over.

Making tutoring and counseling services available to EOP students, and the commissioning of a formative evaluation to assess the effect of those enhanced services, is evidence of an attempt to deal with the inequities that exist. The EOP directors, particularly at urban community college campuses, indicate that a much broader portion of the community college student population would benefit from the grant funded services offered by the EOP's. One director indicated that virtually every student at her urban campus could technically be considered EOP-eligible, but the size of the program is limited by the monitoring agency and the campus fills its allotted spaces under a "most demonstrated need" policy. This awareness of the unique needs of the community college population could signal a growing commitment to full opportunity policies and a more informed awareness of the needs of disadvantaged students.

THE CURRENT EXPERIENCE OF EOP STUDENTS

During the 1984–85 academic year,[3] almost 68 percent of the first-time freshmen EOP students at 20 community colleges in New York State had gross family incomes under $7,000 (the total enrollment for that year was 4,023). Over 38 percent of these students were black, 11 percent were Hispanic, over 42 percent were white, fewer than 4 percent were Asian, fewer than 1 percent were Native American, and almost 4 percent comprised the category of other. Additionally, 57 percent of these students were women and 43 percent were men. With regard to age, 46 percent were under the age of 23, 28 percent were between the ages of 23 and 29, and 26 percent were 30 or over.

Eligibility for services and the average EOP stipend of $275 per year vary to some extent from program to program, but generally students must be low income ($7,600 a year or less for a one-member household), and have a high school grade average in the C range or lower, or hold an equivalency diploma. Additionally, EOP services and grants are, for the most part, available to only full-time day students.

Many of the students at the three community colleges included in the evaluation are either on some form of public assistance, or work to meet their expenses. With regard to public assistance, student status can compromise the receipt of social service funding. For example, students are not eligible for food stamps, and if a student is not referred to a school by social services, he or she may lose all of their public assistance. Additionally, students can lose that assistance if they are not in approved programs of study that have high rates of placement following graduation.

It is clear that EOP students must overcome many obstacles before they even get to school; once in school they must juggle class schedules with social service appointments, jobs, and children, and allot time for their studies. In addition, many of the women enrolled through EOP must arrange for, and cover the expenses of, adequate childcare.

These EOP students have come to the community college to pursue the "American dream." They want better jobs, they want higher earnings, and, as Shor states, "they are looking for learning that means dignity, brings respect, and restores them from the low self-image imposed by school and culture" (Shor, 1987, p. 13). But, once they get to college, these students begin to realize that they are what Shor calls "higher education's third-class citizens. . . ."

> The cheap facilities, bad food, and bureaucratic rigmarole signal that college is one more impersonal institution set up for them by someone else. So, they hold back, withdraw, resist. A succession of experiences through the institutions of American life has left them with [institutional] personalities. They have accumulated injured pride, fear of failure, need for recognition, self-doubt, cagey watchfulness, and unpurged anger. This psychology of defensive withdrawal develops over a long period of time through their institutional transactions. . . . Worker students entering school's doors walk through a membrane that triggers their institutional behavior. Their action in this setting is marked by silence, submission or sabotage (Shor, 1987, p. 34).

The EOP is designed to lessen this acknowledged institutional impact on students by detouring them around the characteristically impersonal and regimented procedures. The admissions, registration, and financial aid processes are all personalized in an attempt to reach the student before the institution does. At orientations, segregated for EOP students, information is disseminated concerning the wide variety of support services that will help these students persist in their studies and reach the ultimate goal of graduation. They are told that they will have responsibility and personal freedom to take full charge of their lives, and that they have the potential and ability to succeed. They are also told that with the variety and amount of support available to them, "*you have no excuse to fail. If you fail, then it was your choice to do so.*"[4]

EOP students are promised freedom, dignity, respect, and a chance to raise their low self-esteem, but the actions and intentions of program personnel and planners, though well-meaning, contradict these promises. The EOP is designed to compensate for the educational and cultural discrimination these students have experienced. Yet, ironically, they are told that they, and not the institution, will be responsible for their failure if they reject the offer of support. Other contradictions are evident in the offer itself: orientations are mandatory; counseling is mandatory; tutoring is mandatory in some of the programs for those students who are in danger of failing; certain classes are mandatory; and career and placement testing is mandatory. In one program, students are required to sign a document known as the "Twelve Commandments of EOP"; this document cites class attendance and involvement in program activities as requisite for continued EOP participation and support. Generally, these mandates are intended to insure participation so that students will fully benefit from the support provided by the EOP, but on the basis of their rate of participation, this control appears to be more alienating for than supportive of students.

Understandably, this orientation toward requirements and structure is consistent with the current focus of education in the United States. The "back to basics" movement in education today, which requires demonstrated competence in required core subjects, is a response to a perceived deficiency in the basic skills of students coming out of both public and higher education in the 1960s and 1970s, when students had far fewer core requirements to satisfy in pursuit of their diplomas and degrees.

With specific reference to the EOP, this imposition of regimentation and structure is based on a belief expressed by program personnel that failure to meet obligations is a general feature of the EOP population. Thus, they must force students to participate with the proviso that if they fail to meet their obligations, they may jeopardize their EOP status and funding. The idea that students must be coerced into accepting what is ultimately good for them is not critically examined, and thus program personnel do not confront the contradictory ideas of control and personal freedom. As a result, the difficulties in maintaining contact with EOP students are attributed to a number of other important, but secondary, factors. The newness of the programs was most often cited in the evaluation; with time, it was predicted that the newly implemented services would become familiar fixtures on campus and therefore would be utilized more often. Personnel also recognize that many of the EOP students fail to participate because they experience inordinate demands on their time. Another acknowledged factor is practical: students are in the program because of the financial aid they receive, and counselors must convince them that they have academic needs as well as financial ones; it has never been fashionable to acknowledge a deficiency. Students at community colleges are usually commuters; this not only impedes communication, but prevents socialization and the formation of a cohesive community among EOP students. Finally, these programs serve between 200 to 1,000 students, and counselors can only maintain consistent contact with those students who demonstrate the greatest academic need or the greatest willingness to use program offerings.

All of these factors are important considerations, but they cannot entirely account for the lack of participation among 50 to 70 percent of the EOP population. Counselors note that among those students they reach are some who are motivated and serious about their studies; these students would probably seek out support without the encouragement of program staff. For some students who were initially resistant, observation shows that, once involved in the program, they realize concrete benefits in terms of higher grades and increased self-confidence, and are thus inclined to take greater advantage of the services.

For students who are not convinced of the benefits associated with full involvement in the EOP, some state that they simply do not have the time, motivation, or energy to participate in the array of services available to them. For returning students, school is, for the most part, a priority, but their jobs, children, and interactions with social services cannot be deferred. Other students are simply unaware of the various services—or are resistant to using them. For example, some students feel they do not need tutoring. These students feel that they need only to put in some extra work. Other students say that they have bad study habits that cannot be changed through tutoring. Some students explicitly react against the authoritarian nature of the programs.

The majority of EOP students are poor, female, black, and Hispanic. Most, it is safe to say, have rarely experienced a sense of power over their own lives. In their primary and secondary schooling they have been tested, tracked, and counseled; these "objective" methods have been used as evidence to indirectly tell these students that they, and not the institutions, are responsible for their inability to achieve. These students, particularly those who are returning, come to the community college for something different; perhaps with the idea and the promise that they can take control of their lives. Soon, though, they are confronted with an institution that bears a striking resemblance to the high schools they have emerged from. In the words of Shor, "they hold back, withdraw and resist."

If EOP's are to succeed for these students, they must begin by providing them with an educational environment that is fundamentally different from those in which they have already experienced failure. The counselors, tutors, and administrators we spoke with in this evaluation all work from the belief that EOP students can succeed, but their methods of providing support do not allow students to succeed on their own terms. They are not allowed to take control or assume a legitimate responsibility for their own successes and failures.

Rogers and Shoemaker (1971) describe three types of decisions in relation to implementing an innovation.[5] The first is optional, where an individual decides to use an innovation regardless of the decisions of others involved. The second is a collective decision, where individuals agree by consensus. The third is an authority decision, where an innovation is forced by someone in authority. The researchers note that the third decision results in faster initial adoption of the innovation, but the changes are more likely to be discontinued. In regard to the EOP, the second approach appears to be the most promising.

It will be difficult to relinquish the rules and regulations that have been successful with a portion of students, but they can be partially replaced with a closely knit community of faculty, students, counselors, tutors, and administrators who are all engaged in cooperative rather than coercive support. Some brief suggestions include capitalizing on the experience of second-year EOP students. In a recently evaluated EOP, second-year students were recruited and paid $10 an hour to serve as "peer partners" to incoming freshmen. Their responsibilities generally included guiding new EOP students through the process of socialization to facilitate their sense of belonging in the college community. These partners also familiarized students with available resources, and assisted them in the "self-diagnosis of problems" so that they could seek appropriate assistance. Along these same lines, second-year students can serve as an invaluable resource at orientations and recruitment fairs. The development of a weekly EOP student newspaper and student-run daycare are also realistic possibilities. We maintain that if control and responsibility are not merely given lip service, but concretely enacted at all levels of service, more students may be drawn into the program. They will legitimately experience their success (or failure) as their own.

THE IMPACT OF THE EOP ON THE COLLEGE COMMUNITY

The issue of cooperation, raised above, re-emerges when considering the next issue of implementation: the impact of the EOP and the students it serves on the general college community. At this level of implementation, cooperation is considered a given; program administrators are well aware that for the EOP to function effectively, cooperative efforts are required of EOP staff and other campus support services such as admissions, financial aid, faculty, and academic departments. Additionally, administrative support can decidedly affect implementation outcomes. During the course of our evaluation, several issues relevant to cooperation were identified. They are detailed below and further discussed within two interrelated contexual issues: the conflict between developing a self-contained EOP and integration with existing services, and the issue of full opportunity for all community college students. The latter issue reveals a common perception among college personnel that EOP students are representative of all community college students. It is only through the application of strict admissions criteria that they are singled out. Therefore, it is difficult to justify intensive support exclusively for this small population of students without making it available to the broader student population.

Relationship with Campus-Wide Administration

Miles (1983) asserts that when administrators are committed to an innovation, they will assist by providing supports such as direct assistance, in-service training, equipment, and materials. This level of commitment is clearly evident in the administrative support provided to the EOP's included in this evaluation. Since grant funding from the state only provides for the salaries of counselors, some tutors, limited materials, etc., each of the EOP's are dependent on their institutions for a substantial portion of monetary support. For example, office space, supplies, telephones, and the salary of the EOP director are institutionally supported. Additionally, EOP students benefit from specially funded programs available to the more general student population.

Apart from financial considerations, the administration must provide support in terms of facilitating productive liaisons with other campus services. Of the three EOP sites included in this evaluation, two were well established within the larger college community and had been providing tutoring and counseling in addition to financial aid. The third had only been providing service in the form of direct student financial aid. Administrative support was much more crucial for the third program in helping it to achieve visibility and priority in the institution.

Relationships among EOP Staff

Berman and Pauly (1975) note that ongoing training in the initial stages of implementation and frequent meetings relate to the success of an implementation. Along these same lines, Fullan and Estabrook (1973) observe that users must play an active role in the entire process of innovation and, Fullan and Pomfret (1977) emphasize that personal interaction, in-service training, and other forms of people-based support are crucial to implementation. All of these views are emphasized by program personnel to a greater or lesser extent in their EOP's. Their work is guided by a holistic philosophy and a team approach, where, ideally, tutors, counselors, faculty, and students are working in concert to meet the practical, personal, and academic needs of the EOP population.

On a practical level, this approach requires frequent meetings and in-service training between all support staff to discuss individual students and more effective ways of providing services to students, but due to the part-time schedules of many staffers and the multiple duties of full-time ones, this type of interaction is rarely possible. As a result, EOP counselors must play a central role in coordinating the activities of support staff by communicating with tutors and faculty on an individual basis. This adds to the already heavy workloads of counselors, and further results in feelings of isolation among some tutors and faculty. For example, tutors expressed a need to become more integrated with the program; they feel excluded from the team approach, and feel they are perceived as simply providing some extra remedial services. Some faculty members also expressed a desire to become more involved. Conversely, other support staff do not feel a need to become more involved; they have substantial contact with counselors and because of their part-time status and tight schedules, they are unable to devote additional time to the program.

This conflict between practical concerns and ideal practice is present in one form or another in all of the evaluated programs, and is not easily resolved. A program director suggested that a position be created for a counselor/coordinator, whose responsibilities would be equally divided between counseling students, arranging meetings, and providing training for support staff.

Relationship with Faculty and Academic Departments

Cooperation with academic departments and individual faculty members is crucial to the EOP in providing effective assistance for students. Instructors provide feedback on student progress to counselors and they must work with tutors in varying capacities. On a departmental level, cooperation is needed in designing and offering developmental courses for EOP students. Additionally, faculty must be willing to participate in training seminars on how to effectively work with EOP students. The necessity for faculty education is explicitly revealed in the following observation by Shor:

> ... the elite training of community college teachers, in universities where few worker-students are enrolled intensifies the cultural clash of the classroom.... Between worker-students and professors, the stark difference in needs and styles is most often painful and destructive, sometimes productive, and even comic (Shor, 1987, p. 19).

The facilitation of reciprocal relationships with academic personnel poses some difficulties. Generally, faculty who exclusively consider themselves content specialists must be willing to serve in a remedial capacity and work with other support personnel and learning specialists in a cooperative atmosphere that is historically foreign to teaching professionals (Lortie, 1975). Related to this are territorial issues, and inevitably conflicts arise between the needs of the EOP and the traditional domains of faculty members. An example here concerns some resistance over the hiring of tutors, which was largely handled through the EOP. Academic departments customarily do their own hiring, and the EOP was perceived as overstepping their own and departmental boundaries. The quality of tutors hired, and their demonstrated ability to work with faculty and students, helped diminish the degree of faculty resentment. Other problems concern biased attitudes among some faculty members; they feel that EOP students are not "college material, and are therefore a waste of time and a waste of taxpayers' money." Other faculty are reluctant to enter into a cooperative relationship with the EOP because it necessarily entails additional expenditures of time and effort.

As noted above, administrative support has been and is invaluable in creating an environment that facilitates effective working relationships between faculty, departments, and program personnel. This has helped to ease some of the difficulties, but program personnel must continually devote a variety of resources in promoting an "EOP awareness" among faculty members. They are actively engaged in faculty education concerning EOP goals, services, and the needs of EOP students, and try to emphasize that the benefits afforded to students and academic staff far outweigh the additional demands on faculty time and energy.

Relationship with Admissions and Financial Aid

The ability to identify EOP students early in the semester is essential; most students who drop out of the community college do so in the first two weeks of the semester, a period considered the most difficult time for adjustment.[6] The admissions office on one campus plays an important role in this identification process by screening for eligibility and routing applications to the EOP office. But on the remaining campuses it is generally up to students to contact the EOP office if they think they are eligible. This creates unnecessary work for program personnel who must maintain contact with admissions to monitor new and returning applicants, who would otherwise be missed during the first few weeks of the semester. Attempts by the EOP to build closer liaisons with the admissions office include the establishment of computer link-ups between the two offices, and the development of quick screening methods at registration so that eligible students can be immediately assisted by EOP representatives.

With regard to financial aid, EOP counselors bypass the financial aid office and generally handle most of this work for the students. In most cases, they actually complete forms for students, requiring only their signatures before they are sent in. It is assumed that the financial aid office does not have the time or the resources to provide this kind of personalized attention for EOP students. But, this assumption increases the workloads of counselors, and further demands that they keep abreast of continually changing regulations and new sources of aid for students. Since this area of expertise is already within the purview of financial aid officers, it may be more expedient to provide specialized training for these personnel in meeting the particular needs of EOP students. Again, this arrangement can be promoted through the support of campus administration.

Broader Issues of Implementation

Amid the need to integrate and forge cooperative relations with other support services on campus, there is an opposing tendency to develop a somewhat self-contained EOP where redundant services (i.e., financial aid, career counseling, tutoring, remedial courses) are developed within the EOP exclusively for EOP students. EOP personnel reason that their deeper and more informed understanding of the needs of EOP students render them more capable of providing these supports. But if, as argued in the previous section, students are given more responsibility and control, and campus administrators and faculty are truly educated concerning the needs of disadvantaged students, then this kind of segregated support would eventually become unnecessary.

This is related to the second issue concerning full opportunity for all community college students. EOP personnel and the more general college community perceive the needs of EOP students as being only minimally different from the needs of the student population at large. This makes the issue of separate procedures for EOP students even more problematic. The EOP cannot begin to serve the needs of the entire student population. If their population is really not that distinctive, then, again, the priority of the EOP should lie with educating the entire college community to the needs of disadvantaged students. At present, changing the behaviors of EOP students assumes a higher priority than education of campus support personnel. We advocate a rethinking of priorities; a greater effort should be geared toward eliminating the discriminatory practices of various institutional components instead of concentrating the entire effort on altering the behavior of the EOP population. In this way, the Band-aid of EOP will not become a permanent fixture on the community college campus, but will eventually become an active agent for institutional change.

INTER-SYSTEMIC CONSIDERATIONS

The third issue for consideration concerns the interaction between the local and state-wide systems of service delivery. The conflict between the political agenda at the legislative level and the practical implementation at the local level is not unique to the establishment of counseling and tutoring support services within EOP's at community colleges in New York State; it is a problem that plagues the development, initiation, and maintenance of all innovative services and service delivery systems.

The evaluation documented several notable problems during the first year of funding for enhanced EOP support services. Outside of basic academic concerns, the problems noted were classified as administrative. Largely, however, they stem from the inter-systemic nature of this funded program. The differing perspectives of the levels within the service delivery system often saw different interpretations of program and student needs; the state level personnel functioned from an adminstrative, executive, policy-formulating position, while the local program personnel were concerned with the practical programmatic implementation portion of the policy process. The major concerns were related to urgent and unrealistic time frames for implementation of the funded services that posed distinct problems; gaps in mutual understanding of the local and the larger frame of reference and noncomplimentary views of program ownership; and conflict between local need for program flexibility and the standardization that necessitates constraints on EOP funded service availability.

Time Frames

Proposals were sought and approved during a three-month span between the completion of the 1985–86 academic year and the beginning of the 1986–87 academic year; funded programs were expected to be in place for the 1986–87 academic year. The late notice of grant approval and lack of adequate planning time posed severe problems for each of the three programs. Hiring staff, obtaining adequate space, purchasing of necessary materials and equipment for the tutoring component, and building relationships with faculty were noted difficulties. And ultimately, the funded services were not widely available until after the beginning of the spring 1987 semester.

While the community colleges in New York State are part of the SUNY system, they are funded through the counties being served. The county hiring process is extensive and requires that job vacancies be posted for a substantial period of time. Since these are county civil service positions, the hiring process cannot be hurried. Additionally, it was noted on all campuses that classroom and office space was at a premium and increased planning time would assist program personnel in acquiring needed space. While the provision of counseling services was delayed or disrupted for only a short time at each campus, the tutoring and supplemental instruction services were compromised by changes in location.

Time and money as well as the temporary nature of the grant funding prevented the investment in textbooks and supplementary resources needed for adequate provision of tutoring services. At one location, extensive resources were made available to tutors by the academic departments they worked with. At other sites, tutors requested that similar resources be purchased for them or procured through a loan arrangement. Finally, the EOP's providing supplemental instruction desired additional time to work and plan with faculty to enhance the effectiveness of collaboration and improve provision of this service.

Because funding for the increased/enhanced support services was, by nature, temporary, individual institutions did not readily provide additional support that might have eased the implementation process. Aside from resources for the tutoring component and lack of office equipment (telephones, etc.), permanent space and clerical assistance were also in short supply. Conceivably, had more planning time been allotted and a longer-term funding stream established, institutional support for such needs might have been more available. As Giacquinta (1973) notes, a successful attempt to change a school organizationally generally proceeds in three basic stages: initiation of the innovation, implementation, and incorporation as a stable part of the organizational structure. Without a clear commitment to long-term state funding of an expensive system of services that would be available to only a portion of the student body, the community colleges were cautious with regard to their degree of commitment to that program. Miles goes a step further in noting the need for institutionalization studies as a further step past implementation. He notes a commonly held notion that a "good" innovation endorsed by its users will "somehow just stay around." Certainly, the reluctance of the individual community colleges to increase their commitment to an experimental program with an uncertain funding stream would negate that notion. The assistance of the central administration in developing skill with and commitment to an innovation is seen as essential in the institutionalization of the innovation (Miles, 1983).

Planning time for future improvement in program services is essential. Notably, those institutions that had already had some institutionally supported tutoring and counseling services built in to their programs had a different view of the implementation process. Largely, these programs noted difficulties in accommodating a larger staff, and the accountability constraints of cumbersome amounts of paperwork. Conversely, the programs that did not already have some institutionally supported services found that implementation process considerably more formidable. Thus, those programs with some existing support services already had the benefit of time in the establishment process and were battling the problems of expansion; infant programs, on the other hand, did not have that advantage. The time frame for use of legislated funding did not allow lead time for planning and, ultimately, made bot the establishment and expansion processes more difficult. Huberman and Miles (1984) note that ongoing assistance and in-service were beneficial in reversing a rough start for innovative programs, but found that in the initial stages of implementation, training is less crucial than prior experience. Thus, the expanding programs were having less difficulty with implementation of the innovative programs because they had prior experience with the provision of support services on a more limited basis.

Fullan (1983), in an implementation study of "Follow Through," reminds the reader that implementation is multidimensional; it depends on planned (strategic) and unplanned (contexual) factors. The evaluation effort was commissioned and planned with this in mind. Strategic and contextual differences at each site were explored and found to have a significant impact on the implementation process and the texture of the individual programs. Time was notably both a strategic and contextual factor.

Gaps in Understanding and Conflicting Views of Ownership

One of the major trends in contemporary human services planning is the development of a coordinated system of services delivered at the local level. It is acknowledged that coordination begins with knowledge of shared concerns, functions, and data regarding the populations to be served; this is accomplished through communication and perseverance (Healy, 1983). Collaborative planning by all involved audiences, active participation in problem identification, and a closer association between and among service provider, governments, agencies, and consumers cannot happen without a communication process based on mutual desire to benefit the client and to enhance the efficiency of the system (Martinson, 1982; Baxter, 1982; Albright, Hasazi, Phelps, & Hall, 1981).

A striking feature of this evaluation was the knowledge of and commitment to disadvantaged students and their needs possessed by Office of Special Programs personnel, college administrators, EOP directors, and program staff. Administrators at the state, college, and program level indicated that a smoother working relationship has evolved over the last few years. In each case, the commitment to the disadvantaged student and active inquiry into the philosophical and practical perspectives at the other levels of administration has enhanced program implementation and functioning, and, thus, the ability to benefit the students. Certainly the input from each of the pilot sites has reduced the threats to implementation posed by a "top-down" approach (Fullan & Estabrook, 1973; Rogers and Shoemaker, 1971). However, the inevitability of a better understanding of one's own concerns and constraints at each level is certain to cause conflict when doing business among the bureaucracies.

Two conflicts were pointed out when viewing attempts at collaboration to the benefit of the student. The first is that both the Office of Special Programs and the community college claimed ownership of the EOP, as both had dedicated substantial support. The second involved the problems inherent in multisite implementation. Although a certain philosophical flexibility is desired so that each program can be maximally responsive to the local community, a degree of standardization is necessary to maintain the fiscal capacity of funded programs.

In discussing ownership consideration, college administrators referred to the level of institutional support provided to the EOP's prior to receipt of grant funding for enhanced tutoring and counseling services. They noted that the community colleges serve a large population of students that would not be eligible for admission to four-year colleges or capable of college-level work without academic assistance. The current state funding formula, based on the number of disadvantaged students served by the community college, is not adequate for meeting the costs of the remedial and developmental studies programs needed by disadvantaged students, let alone providing funding for EOP-type programs. Clearly each institution's commitment to a Full Opportunity Program is the driving force behind all programs and services to disadvantaged populations. The aid received by the community colleges cannot offset the cost of providing such services and programs. Thus, a considerable financial commitment to the EOP had been clearly demonstrated prior to receipt of grant funding for enhanced EOP support services. Furthermore, each institution indicated that the EOP and its program staff were considered an internal resource and focal unit in institutional planning and provision of services for the wider population of disadvantaged students. In light of this, the institutional determination of ownership of a valued resource is understandable.

It is also quite clear that the Office of Special Programs had proprietary concerns as well. Although the funding unit tried to allow each institution to administer its own programs, the necessity of monitoring the expenditure of grant moneys and overseeing provision of targeted services gave state-level administrators a clear leadership role. In this regard, the personnel from the Office of Special Programs maintained an active, but not excessive, presence at each community college and assisted local decision makers in clarifying policy issues so as to remain consistent with the legislated intent of the grant funding.

Undoubtedly, this feeling of ownership, and willingness to tender programmatic support, shows the program to be consistent with existing values, past experience, and the needs of the students being served. Rogers and Shoemaker (1971) indicate that such a perceived programmatic compatibility should allow adoption of the innovative program at a higher rate than would otherwise be expected. This, too, might temper the negative effects of a "top-down" approach to program implementation.

Standardization and the Need for Local Flexibility

Another issue concerning problems inherent in multisite implementation, particularly in the field of human services, indicates a need to be responsive to the clients being served. There is no doubt that the population served by each of these EOP's, while very similar in some respects, are different in others. The experimental nature of the legislative funding allowed each of the three pilot sites to develop a program that would be particularly responsive to local needs and concerns; however, the ultimate intent was the establishment of a standardized model program that could be made more widely available to community colleges across the state. Throughout the proposal, implementation, and evaluation process, the need for establishment of such a model program was highlighted. Yet, each site stressed the need to tailor support services to local needs.

This conflict was particularly evident in the institutional response to full opportunity policies. At one site, the full opportunity policy precludes distinction of EOP students within the general student body. Thus, outside of the EOP staff, there was little awareness of which students were being served by the EOP. This lack of distinction is vigorously supported by administration and faculty. Consequently, tutors hired under the grant funding were housed in academic developmental studies laboratories and were to be part of a pool of tutors available to the entire college community, without the distinction of EOP-eligibility. Similarly, program staff and students at all three sites noted the particular need and applicability of EOP-type services for a broader range of disadvantaged students and a desire to assist these students. Repeatedly, state-level staff reminded the local programs that funded services could be made available to only those EOP-qualified students in order to fulfill the programmatic commitment to economically- and educationally-qualified students. In any case, conflict exists between the need for local responsiveness and the standardization necessary to make similar services more widely available.

The conflict between the local responsiveness and need for standardization highlight the distinction between the fidelity of use view of implementation and the organizational process perspective. Fidelity of use studies involve determining the degree of implementation of an innovation in terms of extent to which actual use of the innovation corresponds to intended or planned use. A process perspective to exploring implementation differs from a fidelity approach in that it seeks to focus on the organizational changes that occur as an innovation is implemented. In a sense, the need for standardization requires a fidelity of use perspective, whereas local responsiveness would demand an organizational process perspective.

SUMMARY

. In closing, we point out that the findings of this evaluation were used to highlight formidable concerns in compensatory program implementation. It would be premature to say that there is any right way to tackle the problems or that there are any right answers to the questions that have been raised.

The program staff at both the state and local levels are seasoned professionals. They exemplify a high level of commitment to the disadvantaged student as well as a consummate knowledge of the needs of these students. These professionals have devoted a great deal of time and energy to finding right answers, and to developing and implementing increasingly responsive programs for the target population. This high level of support, input, and commitment have greatly facilitated the implementation process.

Innovative programs are rarely implemented without "start-up problems," and this was no exception. However, much of the implementation process was consistent with the framework of implementation theory. Most of the problems were anticipated at the state level and steps were taken to ease the effects of unavoidable problems. The external formative evaluation uncovered nothing that was not expected by the client. Although it is still premature to offer judgments on program components and methods that should be included in a model program, the formative evaluation has been used to ease the implementation process for similar programs at a slowly growing number of community colleges in New York State. A second-year evaluation promises to show that many of the problems uncovered in the first-year evaluation are unavoidable, but awareness of these problems can at least mitigate their efforts.

The importance of taking an ecological perspective cannot be understated. From the preceding discussion, it is evident that attention to any one of the three major implementation issues entails a consideration of the other two. The unique needs of disadvantaged students in community college settings entails adjustment of the role of the community college, which, ultimately, portends a corresponding adjustment in the larger service delivery system. Conversely, the availability of a funding mechanism at the state level makes demands on the community colleges' ability to respond to a discrete population of students. Certainly, the institutional response has an impact on the population of EOP students, and this in turn will have an impact on the entire student body. Additionally, the institutional response will change the dimensions of the larger service delivery system.

Acknowledgment of the power of change in an ecological sense will assist program planners and administrators in confronting the dichotomies we have uncovered. Notably, the conflict between current equity policies and the historical stratification within higher education will not dissolve uncontested or be resolved without some major structural changes. Additional dichotomies that must be confronted are the mandatory nature of current EOP offerings versus the philosophical urge to empower disadvantaged students; the student desire to pursue a better life versus the social and racial discrimination that prevents pursuit of this goal; the current content specialization of community college faculties versus the need for a developmental and remedial expertise among faculty; a self-contained EOP versus broader dependence on and integration with existing services; the standardization necessary for wider availability of similar support services versus the flexibility to meet the needs of the local population; and finally, the state formula funding versus local fiscal support as a basis for program ownership. Although no immediate solutions are offered, these dichotomies must be confronted before program implementation can proceed.

NOTES

This paper is based on a multi-site program evaluation conducted by the Evaluation Consortium at Albany (School of Education, the University at Albany, State University of New York). The evaluation was contracted by the State University of New York Central Administration's Office of Special Programs. The assistance and close cooperation of personnel from the Office of Special Programs, and the college administration, EOP directors, and program staff at Erie, Monroe, and Suffolk Community Colleges allowed the evaluators to conduct a fruitful assessment of the funded programs. However, this paper does not represent the position of the contractor or the participating institutions; nor does it, necessarily, imply their agreement with the presented information.

This article was coauthored; authors are listed in alphabetical order, not in order of authorship.

1. Junior colleges are explicitly preparatory for continuing education at a four-year institution.

2. Quoted in Bowles and Gintis (1976, p. 208).

3. These statistics are derived from the State University of New York Educational Opportunity Program Annual Report, which was made available to the Evaluation Consortium at Albany for the formative evaluation.

4. These words are from an orientation booklet for EOP students at one of the sites included in the formative evaluation.

5. We are indebted to Laurie Wellman and Judith Wooster for their in-depth reviews of implementation theory as it pertains to state-mandated implementation of innovative programs.

5. This is stated in an orientation booklet for EOP students at one of the sites included in the formative evaluation.

REFERENCES

Albright, L., Hasazi, S., Phelps, L.A., and Hall, M. E. 1981. Interagency collaboration in providing vocational education for handicapped individuals. *Exceptional Children,* 584–89.

Baxter, J. M. February 1982. Solving problems through cooperation. *Exceptional Children,* 400–7.

Berman, P., and Pauly, E. 1975. *Federal programs supporting educational change, volume II: Factors affecting change agent projects.* Santa Monica, Calif.: The Rand Corporation.

Bowles, S., and Gintis, H. 1976. *Schooling in capitalist America.* N.Y.: Basic Books.

Carnoy, M., and Levin, H. M. 1976. *The limits of educational reform.* N.Y.: David McKay Co.

Evaluation Consortium at Albany. 1987. A formative evaluation of three pilot community college educational opportunity programs. A technical report prepared for the State University of New York Central Administration, Office of Special Programs, Albany, N.Y.

Fullan, M. 1983. Evaluating program implementation: What can be learned from follow through. *Curriculum Inquiry* 13(2):215–27.

Fullan, M., and Estabrook, G. 1973. The process of educational change at the school level: Deriving action implications from questionnaire data. Paper presented at the Annual Meeting of the American Educational Research Association.

Fullan, M., and Pomfret, R. 1977. Research on curriculum and instruction implementation. *Review of Educational Research* 47(1):335–97.

Giacquinta, J. 1973. The process of organizational change in the schools. In *Review of research in education*, ed. F. N. Kerlinger. Itasca, Ill.: F. E. Peacock Publishers.

Healy, A. 1983. The needs of children with disabilities: A comprehensive view. Iowa City: University of Iowa Press.

Herrnstein, R. 1973. *IQ in the meritocracy*. Boston: Little, Brown & Co.

Huberman, A. M., and Miles, M. B. 1984. *Innovation up close: How school improvement works*. N.Y.: Plenum Press.

Jensen, A. 1969. How much can we boost I.Q. and scholastic achievement? *Harvard Educational Review* 39(1):1.

Lortie, D. C. 1975. *Schoolteacher: A sociological study*. Chicago: University of Chicago Press.

Martinson, M. L. February 1982. Interagency services: A new era for an old idea. *Exceptional Children*, 395–99.

Miles, M. B. 1983. Unraveling the mystery of institutionalization. *Educational Leadership*, 14–19.

Ravitch, D. 1983. *The troubled crusade: American education 1945–1980*. N.Y.: Basic Books.

Rogers, E. M., and Shoemaker, F. F. 1971. *Communication of innovations*. New York: Free Press.

Shor, I. 1987. *Critical teaching and everyday life*. Chicago: University of Chicago Press.

State University of New York Educational Opportunity Program. 1985. *Annual report 1984–85*. Albany, N.Y.: Author.

Taylor, C. A. 1985. *Effective ways to recruit and retain minority students*. Madison, Wis.: NMCC Publications.

Wellman, L. 1988. Factors relating to the implementation of the New York state curriculum for English as a second language in secondary schools. A doctoral dissertation from the State University of New York at Albany.

Wooster, J. 1987. The effects of three variables on teacher implementation of a centrally imposed curriculum. A doctoral dissertation from the State University of New York at Albany.

VII.
FUTURE RESEARCH ON INEQUALITY

THE PLIGHT OF BLACK ACADEMICIANS IN EDUCATIONAL RESEARCH AND DEVELOPMENT

Henry T. Frierson, Jr.

INTRODUCTION

The field of educational research and development is a critical area, the implications of which are important for blacks and in which significant involvement by blacks is needed. With the increasing proportion of minority enrollment in the schools, by the year 2000 minority groups will represent a majority of school enrollees in over 50 major cities. Thus, the need for more individuals in educational research and development who are sensitive to the needs of the disadvantaged is urgent.

More individuals are needed who are not only sensitive to the needs of minorities and the disadvantaged, but who are sincerely concerned with those groups' situations. Because of their experiences and backgrounds, blacks in the field of educational research and development would be particularly inclined to address needs and issues related to or affecting minorities and the disadvantaged. However, since 1975 the number and percentage of black recipients of doctorates (particularly the research doctorate, as often represented by the Ph.D. degree) in education have declined. The percentage of black doctoral recipients in education was 9.2 percent in 1975, but only 7.0 percent in 1986.[1,2] This is a foreboding trend concerning the production of black faculty in fields related to educational research and development. Indeed, the percentage of black full-time faculty in all fields was only 1.9 percent in 1985.[3] Hence, given the fact that a significant proportion of black faculty are at historically black colleges, the percentage of black faculty at major doctorate-granting research universities is quite small in all fields, including education.

Despite the fact that proportionately more blacks continue to receive doctorates in education, their percentage of 7.0 percent in 1986 of the total doctoral recipients in education was significantly below the 12.1 percent cited as the percentage of blacks in the 1980 U.S. census. Notably, in 1986, although the percentage of the black doctoral recipients in education was 51 percent of all U.S. black graduate doctoral degree awardees, the actual number, 421, pales significantly when compared to the 824 black M.D. recipients.[4,5] Indeed, the 1986 number of black M.D. recipients exceeded the total number (820) of black Ph.D. recipients. Furthermore, for blacks it appears that there is a trend toward more females attaining the Ph.D., and thus, seemingly a trend toward the feminization of the graduate doctoral degree with respect to blacks. For example, in 1986, black men represented 39 percent of the total black Ph.D. recipients. That proportion compared to 58 percent black male M.D. recipients and 60 percent white male Ph.D. recipients. The male-female proportion is thus the opposite for white 1986 Ph.D. recipients. In education, the male-female ratio for blacks is more severely exaggerated at 1:2. White women Ph.D. recipients in education also outnumber white men, but the ratio is more evenly distributed 4.5:5.5. Moreover, the proportion of white male education faculty is substantially greater than that for white women.

Although the need for more black faculty in educational research and development is critical, those who are considering careers in the field should be clearly aware of what they may face when pursuing and entering such careers. Because black faculty numbers are so small, their scholarship within their respective academic environments is often judged solely by their white colleagues. Many of those colleagues hold elitist and conservative views. Thus, some black faculty may feel constrained to compromise their research interests, and focus more on what their white colleagues may deem acceptable.

Many blacks who are currently in the field have to address the personal effects of racism, prejudice, discrimination, the lack of helpful protégé-mentor relationships at formative stages, and unsupportive job situations. Additionally, many find themselves isolated, physically and psychologically, and subsequently experience feelings of alienation. Feelings of alienation persist because these blacks perceive little professional support from their colleagues—who are generally nonblack. Furthermore, they often find that their professional interests are unrelated to those of their white peers, usually including those who have an effect on their professional advancement. Moreover, they may often receive messages, however untrue, that their work that addresses issues affecting minorities warrants little respect.

Because of unrelenting pressures to conform to the apparent values associated with mainstream educational research, black educational researchers often feel the need, consciously or unconsciously, to compromise commitments toward improving the academic status of blacks and other minorities. They may thus find themselves in academic environments that for them are intellectually and professionally stifling. Anderson,[6] for example, pointed out that although there has been a significant increase in blacks acquiring doctoral degrees in education, there has not been real improvement in their participation in educational research. In addition to obstacles faced by black doctorate holders with backgrounds in research and development, many are hired as nonresearch professionals and thus are involved in little or no research activities. Morever, the support of research by government and private foundations remains low, and seldom are sizable research grants awarded to black principal investigators.

A crucial question is, why is the visible participation of blacks in research and development relatively low? This chapter will address some of the militating factors that perpetuate this low visibility.

PREJUDICE AND DISCRIMINATION

Black faculty at predominantly white universities may experience various forms of prejudice and discrimination that can prove debilitating. This problem may be particularly evident for those who believed that upon the successful completion of their doctoral degree they would be automatically and fully accepted into the academic establishment. Such individuals eventually come to realize the fallacy of such assumptions, but for some, the psychological effects may have been quite damaging to their professional careers. Menges and Exum[7] addressed some of the problems related to negativism affecting black academicians. Menges and Exum suggested that although there is a lack of overt discrimination, black college faculty may be experiencing subtle and indirect forms of discrimination. Menges and Exum also contended that institutions have failed to ensure equity for minority faculty. They further asserted that ambiguous standards for promotion can shield both deliberate and unintentional bias.

Blacks are more likely to lack professional support from colleagues. Because of preformed perceptions associated with racism or prejudice, they often find themselves under the expectations of being able to perform only a limited range of tasks as compared to their nonblack peers. Indeed, blacks are more likely to be hired for or expected to work in special programs (e.g., minority affairs, minority student advising, etc.) in which nonminorities have little interest or view with various degrees of disdain. Furthermore, their academic credentials may be looked upon as suspect, and there is evidence that blacks in the same academic ranks as whites earn lower salaries.[8,9] Under such situations, some black faculty may be under severe pressure and believe that they must prove themselves worthy of such lofty academic status as indicated by their acquired faculty position. Moreover, some may be concerned that they are viewed merely as "affirmative action hirelings." These factors may bring on additional stress if black faculty feel that they must prove they belong. With the unsupportive environments experienced by many black academicians, such feelings may be difficult to overcome. This state of affairs may be especially problematic for young blacks, whose professional development may consequently be stifled.

Elmore and Blackburn[10] suggest that blacks in predominantly white higher education settings often pay a high psychic cost. The particular significance of Elmore and Blackburn's conclusions was that they were drawn from the perspectives of black academicians who had attained creditable professional status and who, moreover, from a professional viewpoint, had categorized themselves as generally satisfied. Thus, their conclusions were drawn from the perspective of high performing and generally satisfied black academicians. If those individuals are paying psychic costs then what costs are unsatisfied black academicians paying? There is quite probably a substantial number in the latter category.

Concerning psychic costs, black faculty who pursue academic acceptance by focusing on what could be considered mainstream research may indeed pay dearly. Usually they have to compromise or subjugate their major research interests. Those primary interests are often related to topics and issues affecting minority groups. Even though those faculty may successfully engage in mainstream research, they often remain preoccupied with questions concerning whether their work is viewed as acceptable by their white colleagues.

ISOLATION

In an academic environment, some black faculty may attempt to become assimilated into mainstream academe. Again, the psychic costs can be severe given the realization that for many, full assimilation is a difficult, if not impossible, task. Moore and Wagstaff[11] pointed out that blacks at predominantly white institutions are socially isolated from white colleagues. Possibly more important is that because of their small numbers blacks are also isolated, socially and professionally, from their black colleagues.[12] Indeed, blacks may constitute only about 1 percent of the faculty at predominantly white colleges and universities. Harvey and Scott-Jones[13] described the problems blacks confront when their numbers are small:

> When there is only one, or a very small number, of black faculty members in a given institution, the burdens of institutional and individual racism weigh heavily. The psychological safety associated with numbers is not available to persons who labor in such situations. The usual protective network of sympathetic senior fac-

ulty also does not exist. Demands on black faculty time and presence escalate. In the absence of a support group operating under the same circumstances, frustrations understandably mount. Black faculty members are subjected to the aggravating aspects of the academic milieu without enjoying some of its compensating benefits: contemplation, independence, and social and intellectual stimulation from colleagues sharing the same interests and outlook.

Unfortunately, there is the likelihood that blacks at predominantly white institutions will find little collegial collaborative opportunities. This may be related in part to the lack of interest nonblack faculty often display toward the work or research concerns of their black colleagues. Consequently, black faculty members may receive little reinforcement and support for their efforts from departmental colleagues.

Black academicians also generally find difficulty getting into the "network" to enjoy some of the professional advantages such ties allow.[14] Consequently, blacks often find themselves isolated not only in relation to their departments or institutions but from the entire academic community as well. For young black academicians, this can be psychologically and professionally devastating. Furthermore, although many black faculty at predominantly white universities suffer from isolation and a lack of collegiality, at the same time, inordinate demands are often placed on them by the need to be accessible to black students, other black faculty, the community, and by the frequent expectation to serve as minority spokespersons on many university committees.

On another point, Scott[15] argued the need for potential black academicians to attend prominent research institutions where networks can be established with prominent faculty. But he also pointed out the structural constraints that exist. Hence, attending such institutions certainly does not guarantee access to the network. In all probability, blacks who attended those institutions paid significant psychic costs for the privilege. Moreover, in all likelihood, even then they may not have enjoyed the type of protégé-mentor relationship that would fully prepare them for all the nuances associated with academia, nor were they likely afforded meaningful introductions to various key members of the network. Thus, although blacks may attend a prominent research institution, they may well be denied entry to the so-called network that could serve to rapidly advance their careers. Those situations serve to promote cynicism on the part of black faculty, which can seriously reduce productivity.

LACK OF SOLID PROTÉGÉ-MENTOR RELATIONSHIPS

In addition to not having access to the network, many black academicians have not had the advantage of having true mentors at the graduate school and professional entry phases. Consequently, those academicians have not fully participated in that informal but crucial system related to mentoring: a system that provides white males, for the most part, with support and protection during their graduate training and serves as an additional support source once they become professional academicians. Mentors often play a considerable role in career development. Long,[16] for example, reported that individuals who had mentors are more productive in their careers, and Roche[17] observed that they are promoted more quickly.

The importance of mentoring in promoting professional success has been clearly acknowledged (Levinson et al., 1978; Rawlins & Rawlins, 1983; Vaughn, 1985).[18-20] Indeed, some universities have attempted to formally institute protégé-mentor relationships between junior and senior faculty. Many black faculty, however, have not experienced the advantage of a true proégé-mentor relationship. The lack of such a relationship can severely hamper professional development.

Blackwell (1983, 1984)[21-22] reported that only one in eight black Ph.D. recipients had the benefit of a true mentor during graduate school. He further reported that while one-half of all white graduate students receive teaching assistantships, the proportion is only one-fourth for blacks. Furthermore, whereas one-third of all doctoral students receive research assistantships, only one-fifth of underrepresented minority students have received the valuable experiences so often afforded through such assistantships. Such discrepancies during the preparatory phases indicate that equal access to opportunities to professional careers in academe is far from a reality.

Blackwell (1981, 1983, 1984)[23-25] also reported that the most persistent and statistically significant predictor of enrollment and graduation of black graduate students is the presence of black faculty. This situation, of course, has Catch-22 undertones. The implications are that an increase in the presence of black faculty is critical, and this fact appears to be common knowledge, but unless barriers are removed, the current situation concerning the numbers and production of black faculty will continue or worsen.

Blacks, of course, have had advisors at the dissertation stage, but rarely have had the opportunity to form protégé-mentor relationships with individuals well established in the academic community. Naïveté is a price many pay for the lack of such relationships, and in many ways, some continue to pay the price even after being in the field for a significant period of time.

UNSUPPORTIVE JOB SITUATIONS

In actual job situations, blacks find themselves overrepresented in the lower academic ranks and are thus more subject to job loss.[26] Also, black academicians tend to be more involved in activities that usurp research time, such as teaching, advising, committee work, and community service. Research, however, is weighed heavily in tenure and promotion decisions and, as it is, blacks often find themselves at a disadvantage during tenure and promotion reviews.[27]

In addition, many black academicians have joint appointments, and although such arrangements may enhance the survival of one or more of the involved programs, it may not enhance the professional survival of the individual faculty.[28] As a consequence of joint appointments, the joint-appointed faculty often find themselves serving multiple masters. Thus, the involved faculty may be forced to manage competing and possibly conflicting demands and expectations from each department. That situation, of course, can hamper the prospects of tenure and promotion.

Furthermore, black academicians often find themselves in a "meritocracy" with an absence of clear criteria and weightings for each criterion.[29] Thus, in such situations, subjectivity that is related to attitude and personality is likely to occur.[30] Therefore, as acknowledged by Menges and Exum,[31] considerable bias, whether deliberate or not, can be shielded by ambiguous criteria and standards. Such a system can place black academicians at a significant disadvantage.

Then there is the problem of salary. As indicated earlier, blacks holding the same rank as whites often earn lower salaries and are more likely to be hired to work in special programs. Furthermore, many black academicians find that they are on soft money or are expected to generate salary support from ever-dwindling external sources. The latter becomes particularly problematic given the vagaries in the selection of funded projects. As mentioned earlier, blacks seldom find themselves ensconced in the network that would give them a greater probability of receiving large research and development grants. Grant support would more than likely enable black faculty to conduct the types of studies that would have considerable positive effects on the academic status of blacks and other minorities.

CONCLUSION

Overall, the plight of black faculty in research and development is serious, and probably more so than we realize, when the large picture is considered. The obstacles are many, and so subtle that they are difficult to address effectively. The more sophisticated forms of discrimination, the long-term effects of lack of mentors, isolation, and the continual implicit messages that black academicians are not on the same level as their white peers are but a few examples of obstacles blacks face. Under such circumstances, it is little wonder that the number of black academicians significantly involved in educational research is relatively low and that cynicism exists. Given the current state of the times, black participation is likely to remain low unless vigorous action to address the problem is undertaken.

Those black academicians involved in research and development have, however, in spite of the negative aspects of many of their experiences, received good training. But it is imperative that skills continue to be built and sharpened. This is important for a number of reasons, but three critical reasons are (1) to assist the advancement of scholarship, (2) to provide the needed and necessary support for colleagues, and (3) to play significant roles in enhancing the academic development and career status of blacks and others.

One critical and invaluable source of support for black faculty is broad networking among themselves. From such networking, they will have an available support base, which they can draw upon for a number of professional and, possibly, socioemotional needs. Given the situation of most black educational researchers, it is critical that they vigilantly seek to provide support for each other. By readily sharing collectively possessed skills and knowledge, this support can be a powerful tool to offset much of the negativism that is encountered. The need for a strong internal network is obvious. Moreover, the existence of a well-functioning and open network would be beneficial in promoting individual professional development, and related efforts to enhance the academic status of blacks.

Persistence and determination, of course, are of paramount importance. Some black academicians may receive little acknowledgment or encouragement from their administrative heads or colleagues regarding efforts to help improve the academic status of black and other minority students. Those efforts, nonetheless, are of considerable value and should be of primary concern for most of us. Thus, black academicians should be strongly encouraged to maintain and nurture the commitment to put forth their best effort in the area of improving the status of black and other minority students at all levels. For, after all, the desire to improve the status of minorities was the reason why many blacks in educational research and development chose to enter the field, and most would like to remain true to that commitment.

NOTES

1. National Research Council. 1976. *Summary report 1975: Doctorate recipients from United States universities.* (Washington, D.C.: National Academy Press.

2. National Research Council. 1987. *Summary report 1986. Doctorate recipients from United States universities.* Washington, D.C.: National Academy Press.

3. National Research Council 1986 survey, cited in the *Chronicle for Higher Education, June 22, 1988.*

4. *National Research Council. 1987. Op. cit.*

5. Association of American Medical Colleges. 1987. *Minority students in*

medical education: Facts and figures III. Washington, D.C.: Association of American Medical Colleges.

6. J. D. Anderson. 1984. *The black education professorate.* SPE Monograph Series.

7. R. J. Menges and W. H. Exum. 1983. Barriers to the Progress of women and minority faculty. *Journal of Higher Education* 54:123–44.

8. E. C. Traynham and G. Green. 1977. Affirmative action programs and salary discrimination. *Negro Educational Review* 28:36–41.

9. Department of Health, Education and Welfare, Office of Education, National Advisory Committee on Black Higher Education and Black Colleges and Universities. 1978. *Higher education equity: The crisis of appearance versus reality.* Washington, D.C.: Department of Health, Education, and Welfare.

10. C. J. Elmore and R. T. Blackburn. 1983. Black and white faculty in research universities. *Journal of Higher Education* 54:1–15.

11. W. Moore and L. Wagstaff. 1974. *Black faculty in white colleges.* San Francisco: Jossey-Bass.

12. W. Anderson, H. T. Frierson, and T. B. Lewis. 1979. Black survival in white academe. *Journal of Negro Education* 48:92–102.

13. W. B. Harvey and D. Scott-Jones. 1985. We can't find any: The elusiveness of black faculty members in American higher education. *Issues in Education* 3:68–76.

14. D. Roper. 1980. The waning of the old boy network: Placement, publishing and faculty selection. *Improving College and University Teaching* 28:12–18.

15. R. R. Scott. 1981. Black faculty productivity and interpersonal academic contacts. *Journal of Negro Education* 50:224–36.

16. J. S. Long. 1978. Productivity and academic positions in the scientific career. *American Sociological Review* 43:889–908.

17. G. R. Roche. Much ado about mentors. 1979. *Harvard Business Review* 24–27.

18. D. J. Levinson, C. L. Darrow, E. B. Klein, M. H. Levinson, and B. McKee. 1978. *The seasons of a man's life.* New York: Alfred Knopf.

19. M. D. Rawlins and L. Rawlins. 1983. Mentoring and networking for helping professionals. *Personnel and Guidance Journal* 62:116–18.

20. J. C. Vaughn. 1985. Minority students in graduate education. In *The state of graduate education,* ed. B. L. R. Smith. Washington, D.C.: Brookings Institution.

21. J. E. Blackwell. 1983. *Networking and mentoring: A study of cross-generational experiences of blacks in graduate and professional schools.* Atlanta: The Southern Educational Foundation.

22. J. E. Blackwell. October 27, 1984. Increasing access and retention of minority students in graduate and professional schools. Paper presented at

the Educational Testing Service's Invitational Conference on Educational Standards, Testing, and Access in New York.

23. J. E. Blackwell. 1981. *Mainstreaming outsiders: The production of black professionals.* Bayside, N.Y.: General Hall Publishing Co.

24. Blackwell. 1983. *Op. cit.*

25. Blackwell. 1984. *Op. cit.*

26. A. S. Wilk, ed. *The hidden professorate: Credentialism, professionalism, and the tenure crisis.* Westport, Conn.: Greenwood.

27. Menges and Exum, *op. cit.*

28. Ibid.

29. Ibid.

30. G. L. Thorne, C. S. Scott, and J. H. Beaird. 1975. Assessing faculty performance. In *Professional assessment in higher education,* ed. C. S. Scott and G. L. Thorne. Monmouth, Oreg.: Oregon State System of Higher Education.

31. Menges and Exum. 1983. *Op. cit.*

A TYPOLOGY OF DISCRIMINATION IN EDUCATION

Michael Imber

For some time, theorists have advocated egalitarianism in education, often referred to as the principle of equality of educational opportunity. Arguments for this principle come from the realm of moral philosophy, based on theories of justice, government, and the individual's relationship to the state, and from a purely practical perspective, based on the promise of benefit for all in a society with an equitable educational policy.[1] In recent years, however, a number of commentators have argued that despite widespread nominal acceptance of equality of educational opportunity, the egalitarian principle has never been adequately conceptualized.[2]

Despite this unresolved issue, educational egalitarianism has become a goal of policy makers increasingly during the past 35 years.[3] While all branches of governmnent at all levels have provided impetus for this new policy, the federal judiciary has been the most active.[4] What Justice Marshall has called the Supreme Court's "historic commitment to equality of educational opportunity"[5] began in 1954 with the Court's unanimous declaration in *Brown* v. *Board of Education* that "where the state has undertaken to provide it [education] . . . is a right which must be made available to all on equal terms."[6]

Since *Brown*, hundreds of student-plaintiffs have argued that education was not being made available to them on equal terms. Students have claimed discrimination because of race, sex, ethnicity, alienage, handicap, religion, economic status, community of residence, or language spoken, among other reasons.[7] Most of these students have advanced similar arguments. The legal basis of their claim usually has been the Fourteenth Amendment of the

United States Constitution, which guarantees to every citizen the "equal protection" of law. Simply stated, the argument is that a school district acting under color of the state has violated the equal protection clause by failing to offer a particular group of students a program commensurate with the program offered to other students.

In evaluating alleged violations of the equal protection clause, courts employ a two-tiered test.[8] Because the Supreme Court has found that education is not a fundamental right,[9] the more stringent test, strict scrutiny, applies only to cases of educational discrimination that involve a suspect classification. Thus, if one race or one ethnic group is singled out for differential treatment, courts will require the state to show that its actions are necessitated by a compelling state interest, a requirement which can almost never be met. Otherwise, differential treatment will be allowed unless a plaintiff can show that it has no rational relationship to any legitimate state goal. As a result, courts almost never accept a school district's differential treatment of racial or ethnic minorities, but they sometimes find classifications on other bases permissible.[10]

In addition to the equal protection clause, some student-plaintiffs are able to base their claim on specific federal statutes regulating the educational programs offered to specific groups by schools receiving federal funds. Most notable among these statutes are those affecting limited and non-English-speaking students, handicapped students, and female students.[11] The functions of the statutes are (1) to extend the scope of the equal protection to include nonsuspect classifications and (2) to clarify the meaning of equal protection relative to these groups.

To the extent that they perform this second function, these statutes provide courts with a standard for evaluating claims of educational discrimination against members of the statutorily designated classifications. In practice, however, when faced with claims by students that statutes entitle them to particular educational services, courts can do little more than require that school districts act in good faith to provide special services to those who qualify. In effect, federal law says that something special must be done to help students with English-language deficiencies and those with certain handicaps overcome their disadvantage, but it does not say what must be done.[12] Cases of sex-based discrimination are different, however. Here the law requires not a special program to help overcome an educational disadvantage (because no educational disadvantage exists), but rather that federally-funded school programs avoid classification by sex. Schools can meet their statutory obligations simply by treating both sexes the same.[13]

Thus, it is possible to deny equality of educational opportunity by treating a student differently from other students, but it is also possible to deny equality of educational opportunity by treating everyone the same. There are, then, at least two distinct types of discrimination in education, each based on different kinds of characteristics of the students being discriminated against. There is also a third type of educational discrimination, in which some students are provided an inferior education for reasons unconnected to any personal characteristics of the students themselves. Each of these categories of educational discrimination poses a different set of moral and legal problems.

1. *Active discrimination.* These are cases in which students are discriminated against on the basis of characteristics not intrinsically related to their educational needs, that is, when the level of quality of educational services offered to an individual is based on characteristics of the individual that are educationally irrelevant. The denial of equality of educational opportunity consists of different (inferior) treatment on the basis of, for example, race, sex, ethnicity, or social class. Ethically, this can never be justified.

Attempts to justify active discrimination sometimes are based on the argument that if factors in the larger society limit the prospects of a particular group, schools can best serve that group by offering them an education appropriate to their limited futures.[14] This argument in effect holds that a characteristic such as race, sex, or social class can be related to a person's need for education. In the days when law firms would not hire female attorneys, for example, it was sometimes argued that there was no sense admitting women to law school because they themselves would be better served by programs preparing them for jobs in fields that welcomed them. When operationalized, this sort of reasoning creates a cyclical self-fulfilling prophecy. No women are hired by law firms because none are qualified; none are allowed to become qualified because none are hired. In effect, the argument justifies educational discrimination on the basis of social discrimination. But if it means anything at all, equality of educational opportunity demands that education must allow every individual a chance to pursue any life plan that others with similar intrinsic qualifications are allowed to pursue. While it is undoubtedly true that in a racist, sexist, or classist society, race, sex, or social class can be extrinsically related to a person's need for education, these and similar characteristics can never be intrinsically related to educational needs. To base educational decisions on such characteristics abrogates equality of educational opportunity.

From a legal standpoint, however, some cases of active discrimination appear justifiable. When no suspect classification is involved and no specific statute applies, schools sometimes can argue successfully that differential treatment bears a rational relationship to a legitimate state purpose. The legitimate state purpose that is usually invoked is the promotion of an educated population. School districts have justified sex-segregated high schools for high-achieving students, for example, by arguing that students can learn more if they are not distracted by members of the opposite sex.[15] Arguments of this type should fall because they attempt to justify discrimination on the basis of a hypothesized reaction on the part of some students to a nondiscriminatory program. They are analogous to a company's attempted justification of a policy of hiring only white salesmen because clients would not buy from blacks. At the very least, the would-be discriminator should bear the burden of showing necessary *causal* connection between denial of equality of opportunity and desired educational outcomes.[16] Unless this connection is shown, claims that the best way to assure the highest level of intellectual development of the population as a whole is to provide some people with an inferior education should be rejected out of hand.

2. *Passive discrimination.* These are cases in which students are discriminated against by not being offered a specific educational program mandated by their special circumstances. The denial of equality of educational opportunity consists of failure to offer differential (compensatory) treatment, for example, to non-English-speaking or handicapped students. Unlike active-discrimination plaintiffs, who ask only to be relieved of unjustified inferior treatment, students claiming passive discrimination assert an entitlement to special treatment, often involving significantly greater than average expenditures. They argue that (1) equality of educational opportunity must be viewed not in terms of inputs but rather in terms of opportunity to benefit and (2) a person burdened by an undeserved educational disadvantage must sometimes be afforded special treatment in order to benefit from education.[17]

From both a moral and legal standpoint, passive discrimination raises more difficult issues than active discrimination. Most educational philosophers and most policy makers can agree that equality of educational opportunity demands some sort of special effort on behalf of those with certain educational disadvantages. However, the difficulty arises in trying to formulate either theoretical principles or practical policies designed to specify what sort of and how much special treatment is due in a particular case. None of the principles so far advanced have proven satisfactory. For example, it has been argued that disadvantaged students are being discriminated against unless they are afforded whatever special services they require to maximally benefit from their education.[18] This argument must fail because, first, it is unworkable as policy, since the required expenditures in some cases would exceed available resources, and second, nondisadvantaged students are not afforded the services need to *maximally* benefit from their education.[19] A somewhat different claim is that a disadvantaged individual is receiving adequate educational services if and only if the individual attains some prespecified learning criterion, for example, achievement at grade level.[20] This argument also must fail, because the technology necessary to guarantee universal attainment of all but the most trivial achievement criteria does not and probably never will exist.

Decisions concerning the sorts of educational disadvantages that implicate a right to compensation and the level of effort that is to be devoted to compensation can only be made rationally by employing some sort of cost-benefit analysis. Legislatures and other policy makers should seek to eliminate passive discrimination only to the degree that the expected benefits of the effort outweigh the costs. To this end, statutes and regulations can designate specific groups for whom special educational treatment is deemed a social good, and can specify levels of funding available for special services. For their part, courts can do no more than require that schools make a good faith effort to serve designated populations with careful attention to the procedures mandated by legislation. Unless good faith is lacking or designated procedures violated, the ultimate decision of whether a particular individual qualifies for special treatment and the specific level and types of services to be afforded should be made by professional educators.

In the final analysis, it will never be possible or even desirable to fully eliminate all passive discrimination in education. It will not be possible because, as much as we might wish otherwise, certain disadvantages will always impede the ability to benefit from education to such a degree that no amount of compensation will afford full equality of opportunity. It would not be desirable even to eliminate as much passive discrimination as technology allows because to do so would be so expensive that everyone, including the disadvantaged themselves, would be worse off for the effort.

3. *Systemic discrimination.* These are cases in which students are discriminated against as a by-product of the way an educational system is organized, not as a result of any personal characteristic. The denial of equality of educational opportunity consists of providing some students with an education inferior to that of others when there is no personal characteristic distinguishing one group from the other, or when any distinguishing characteristic is not the basis of the differential treatment. A school district's teacher transfer policy that results in an inferior instructional staff in one school is an example of systemic discrimination. State funding schemes that appropriate significantly less money per pupil for some schools districts than others are the type of systemic discrimination that has provoked the most concern.

Would-be justifiers of systemic discrimination sometimes argue that, unlike active and passive discrimination, systemic discrimination is often unintentional.[21] Policy makers have made a good faith effort to construct the best possible school system allowed by limited resources, the argument goes, and a certain amount of differential treatment has resulted. Even if true, this premise perhaps mitigates the moral culpability of those responsible for the creation of a system that discriminates, but it does not justify failure to take corrective action once systemic discrimination has been identified.

Another claimed justification for systemic discrimination is that it is not of great concern because it is easy to overcome. Any student victimized by systemic discrimination can initiate a personal remedy simply by opting out of the inferior program, for example, by moving to a different neighborhood or town.[22] This argument fails, first, because children themselves almost never have the freedom to take the action necessary to escape systemic discrimination independent of their parents and school officials; second, because economic and social conditions often severely limit a family's ability to take the steps necessary to remedy systemic discrimination; and third, because even if some students implement personal remedies, others will continue to be burdened by discrimination unless the offending system is modified.

Whatever may be said in defense of systemic discrimination, it is clear that the inferior treatment it affords is entirely undeserved. The only possible justification for undeserved inferior treatment is that the benefits of the system outweigh its defects, even for those it treats less well. Thus, it is sometimes claimed that to eliminate discrimination from an educational system would make everyone worse off. Legally, since education is not a fundamental right and since systemic discrimination usually does not involve a suspect classification, whatever contributes to the overall effectiveness of the educational system may sometimes survive the rational relationship test.[23]

This is the sort of claim that courts have sometimes accepted when state educational funding schemes are challenged: In order to eliminate differential funding for school districts, states would have to assume full control of education funding. This would inevitably vitiate local control, because regulation inevitably accompanies fiscal oversight. But local control is a traditional source of educational excellence. Conclusion: The need to maintain local control justifies the provision of an inferior education for some students.[24] This argument is weak because two of its premises are shaky. First, although it has some intuitive appeal, the notion that increased state control of educational funding inevitably leads to increased regulation has never been empirically demonstrated.[25] Second, while the American educational system traditionally has placed strong faith in local control, the supposed connection between local control and excellence has not been demonstrated either. In this regard, it is interesting to note that Japan and all the European countries whose students have regularly outperformed Americans on achievement tests in recent years have strongly centralized educational systems that admit little or no local control. Ultimately, then, the argument reduces to little more than an appeal to the way things always have been done, hardly an adequate justification for denial of equality of educational opportunity.

There is another type of local-control argument for maintaining systemic discrimination based on the oft-noted tension between the competing values of freedom and equality.[26] Like the previous argument, this one claims that the only way to eliminate systemic discrimination would be to severely limit the freedom of the people of local communities and those employed by local schools to shape their own educational programs. But, says the argument, freedom is such an important value that it justifies a certain amount of inequality. Although it is unquestionable that many sectors of American public policy tolerate a great deal of inequality in the name of freedom, this argument also fails to justify systemic discrimination. The reason is that freedom can serve as justification for inequality only if the same individuals whose right to equal treatment is vitiated also enjoy the benefits of increased freedom. But in the case of systemic discrimination, students are denied equality of educational opportunity so that *others* can have the freedom to control schools. Students in a district where teachers can transfer at will or those in a district where voters can choose the level at which they tax themselves for education are no more free to choose their educational program than students in a rigidly centralized system. They simply are subject to the decisions of those who will live close to them rather than the collective decisions of larger policy-making units. Thus, they lose the right to equality of treatment while enjoying no increase of freedom.

Although it does not justify systemic discrimination, the freedom versus equality argument does point out that in theory some systemic discrimination is acceptable. Specifically, inferior treatment arising from decisions freely made by students (or their parents in the case of those not capable of deciding for themselves) might be justified by the importance of maintaining the freedom to choose. Thus, courts will not allow a state to compel attendance at *public* school even if the state's purpose is to assure a high-quality education for all.[27] To go one step further, a family choice or voucher system of educational organization might justify widely unequal educational treatment arising from disparate choices made by students themselves. Currently, however, there is no rational basis—either morally or legally—for an educational system that provides different educational treatment to students with similar characteristics, because neither the system as a whole nor those subjected to inferior treatment benefit from it. Therefore, systemic discrimination should be eliminated to the greatest extent possible.

CONCLUSIONS AND RECOMMENDATIONS

There are three distinct categories of educational discrimination—active, passive, and systemic. Although current law is adequate to remedy cases of active discrimination based on race and ethnicity, courts sometimes have found other bases permissible. But active discrimination is never justified morally. The most unequivocal way to remedy the situation would be for state legislatures to pass statutes prohibiting the basing of an individual's educational program on any characteristic with no intrinsic bearing on the individual's need for education. Even without such statutes, courts should reject rational relationship defenses of active discrimination because the arbitrary provision of an inferior education for some individuals bears no reasonable connection to any legitimate state purpose.

Unlike active discrimination, passive discrimination is often permissible, even desirable, because it can be to everyone's benefit. Its elimination should be a goal only to the extent that the benefits of elimination outweigh the costs. In any case, the way to deal with passive discrimination is for the most part a policy matter involving professional implementation of legislatively defined priorities. Courts should avoid mandating specific courses of action in individual cases unless schools fail to serve groups designated by statute as entitled to services, or fail to follow statutory procedures. For the most part, this is what courts have been doing.

Systemic discrmination is the most insidious type, because it seems to be no one's fault. Its victims often have no distinguishing characteristics on which to base their complaints. They seem to suffer more from bad luck than from discrimination. Courts often accept systemic discrimination unless its burdens fall disproportionately on a suspect classification.[28] Even when systemic discrimination does burden a suspect classification, courts sometimes allow it, unless there is a proven intent to discriminate, in other words, unless they find that active discrimination has occurred.[29] Thus, there is currently far more systemic discrimination than can be justified in any way but by appealing to tradition, particularly in the area of school finance. Either systemic discrimination should be eliminated, or those subjected to it should receive sufficient additional benefits to counterbalance the inferior educational treatment they receive.

NOTES

1. T. I. Ribich. 1972. The case for equal educational opportunity. In *Schooling in a corporate society*, ed. M. Carnoy. New York: David McKay Co.; R. Ennis. 1976. Equality of educational opportunity. *Educational Theory* 26:3–18.

2. S. Bowles and H. Gintis. 1976. *Schooling in capitalist America*. New York: Basic Books; N.C. Burules and A. L. Sherman. 1979. Equal educational opportunity: Ideal or ideology? In *Proceedings of the philosophy of education society*, 105–14; M. Imber. 1982. Justice in education: A Rawlsian analysis. Paper presented at American Education Research Association annual meeting.

3. M. Imber and J. Namenson. 1983. Is there a right to education in America? *Educational Theory* 33:97–111. See also F. Cordasco. 1973. *The equality of educational opportunity*. Totowa, N.J.: Rowman and Littlefield.

4. K. S. Tollett. 1982. The propriety of the federal role in expanding equal educational opportunity." *Harvard Educational Review* 52:431–43.

5. *San Antonio v. Rodriguez*, 411 U.S. 1, 71 (1973, dissenting opinion).

6. 347. U.S. 483, 493 (1954).

7. Examples in each category follow.

Race: *Green v. County School Board,* 391 U.S. 430 (1968).

Sex: *Vorchheimer v. School District of Philadelphia,* 532 F.2d 880 (3d Cir., 1976), aff'd.

Ethnicity: *Morales v. Shannon,* 516 F.2d 411 (5th Cir., 1975), cert. denied.

Alienage: *Plyer v. Doe* 467 U.S. 202 (1982).

Handicap: *BOE v. Rowley,* 458 U.S. 176 (1982).

Religion: *Wisconsin v. Yoder,* 406 U.S. 205 (1972); see note 17 for a discussion of the sense in which *Yoder* is a discrimination case.

Economic status and community of resident: *Serrano v. Priest,* 487 P.2d 1241 (1971).

Language: *Lau v. Nichols,* 414 U.S. 563 (1974).

8. The two tiers are strict scrutiny and rational basis. See note 10 for a discussion of the "middle tier."

9. *San Antonio v. Rodriguez. Op. cit.*

10. See, for example, *Vorchheimer v. School District of Philadelphia,* in note 7. However, some classifications cannot even meet the rational basis test. For example, *Plyer v. Doe,* in note 7. A third standard, "substantial relationship," requiring that classification be significantly connected to an important state goal, applies in cases involving differential treatment by sex or total denial of education to an identifiable (but nonsuspect) group. Although it is sometimes called the "middle tier," substantial relationship conceptually is a more stringent form of rational relationship because there is no presumption against differential treatment. The difference is that the state now needs a good reason (instead of just any reason) to classify. Again, see *Plyer v. Doe,* in note 7.

11. Statutes affecting the education of these groups include the following: Limited English-speaking: Title VI of the Civil Rights Act of 1964, 42 U.S.C. Sec. 2000(d) (1976 & Sup. V 1981), and subsequent interpretations and implementing regulations which include "language deficiency" in the category of "national origin".

Handicapped: PL94–142 (the Education for A Handicapped Children Act, 20 U.S. C. Secs. 1400–61 [1982]).

Female students: Title IX of the Education Amendments of 1972, 20 U.S. C. Sec. 1681. (See also the Civil Rights Restoration Act of 1987, PL 100–259, 102 Stat. 28.)

12. Office of Civil Rights guidelines indicate in a very general way the sort of program to be offered to those with language deficiencies. PL 94–142 implementing regulations are even less specific.

13. See *Grove City College v. Bell,* 465 U.S. 555 (1984) and statutes cited in note 11.

14. In the past, this argument was often used to justify placing immigrant children in vocational rather than academic programs. See L. Covello, *The*

Heart is the Teacher (New York, 1958), p. 180*ff*; W. H. Dooley, *The Education of the N'er-do-well* (Cambridge, 1916). Today, although the argument is rarely made openly by educators anymore, schools continue to channel students into programs considered appropriate to their social class. See S. Bowles and H. Gintis, *Schooling in Capitalist America,* in note 2.

15. See, for example, *Vorchheimer v. School District of Philadelphia,* in note 7.

16. An empirically proven causal connection must be insisted upon, not simply the opinion of an expert that a connection exists. *Otero v. Mesa County Valley S.D.,* 408 F.Supp. 162, 164 (Co. 1975) explains the reason:

> Certainly, if the expert testimony proved anything, it provided that education theory is not an exact science, *and an expert can be found who will testify to almost anything.* Listening to these experts causes one to conclude that if psychiatrists' disagreements are to be compared to differences between educators, psychiatrists are almost of a single mind (emphasis added).

17. See *Lau v. Nichols,* in note 7. These are also a few passive discrimination cases in which plaintiffs argue that their special characteristics demand that they be given fewer educational services, specifically that they be exempted from compulsory education laws. The most well-known case is *Wisconsin v. Yoder,* in note 7, a passive discrimination case because Yoder asked for and received a different educational program because of his religion.

18. This argument was advanced in *BOE v. Rowley,* in note 7, on behalf of a deaf student who was being given some special services but not enough to do as well as she possibly could.

19. The *Rowley* court did in fact reject the argument, determining that 94–142 does not demand maximum benefit.

20. The *Rowley* decision was, unfortunately, based in part on Rowley's achievement at or above grade level. Although the decision was just, this basis serves only to cloud the issue.

21. Intentionality often plays a role in the outcome of discrimination cases. See, for example, *Lynch v. Kenston BOE,* 229 F.Supp. 740 (Ohio, 1964); *Milliken v. Bradley,* 418 U.S. 717 (1974). Generally, courts are much more likely to find impermissible segregation that results from intentional government action.

22. This is precisely what officials of the low-wealth school district attended by the plaintiff in *Serrano v. Priest,* 487 P.2d 1241 (Ca. 1971) had suggested. If he wanted to attend a better school, Serrano was free to move to Beverly Hills.

23. Whether or not a suspect classification is involved is sometimes a

major issue in these cases. See, for example, *San Antonio v. Rodriguez,* in note 5.

24. In *Rodriguez,* the need to maintain local control served as a major justification for what the court admitted was a seriously inequitable system. For a detailed critique of this argument see M. Imber and J. Namenson, "Is There a Right to Education in America?" (note 3), pp. 109–10.

25. On the issues of local versus state control of educational policy and funding, see F. Wirt and M. Kirst, *The Political Web of American Schools* (Boston: Little, Brown & Co., 1973).

26. R. M. Hare discusses the problem of balancing the competing values of freedom and equality in *Moral Thinking: Its Levels, Method and Point* (Oxford: Clarendon Press, 1981). See also R. Nozick, *Anarchy, State and Utopia* (Totowa, N.J.: Rowman and Littlefield, 1981). Nozick justifies inequality by the need to preserve freedom.

27. See *Pierce v. Society of Sisters,* 268 U.S. 510 (1925).

28. In *Larry P. v. Riles,* 793 F.2d 969 (9th Cir., 1984), the fact that using I.Q. tests resulted in disproportionate labeling of blacks as mentally retarded was sufficient to disallow the use of the tests.

29. In *Debra P. v. Turlington,* 644 F.2d 397 (5th Cir., 1981), use of competency tests as a requirement for graduation was judged acceptable even though disproportionate numbers of blacks failed, except to the extent that an inferior education afforded to blacks by a formerly segregated system had caused the disproportionate failure. In the absence of active discrimination against blacks, competency tests may be used even if the result is that a larger percentage of blacks than whites fail to graduate.